Famine in European History

D1548093

This is the first systematic study of famines in all parts of Europe from the Middle Ages until the present. In case studies ranging from Scandinavia and Italy to Ireland and Russia, leading scholars compare the characteristics, consequences and causes of famine. The famines they describe differ greatly in size, duration and context; in many cases the damage wrought by poor harvests was compounded by war. The roles of human action, malfunctioning markets and poor relief are a recurring theme. The chapters also take full account of demographic, institutional, economic, social and cultural aspects, providing a wealth of new information that is organised and analysed within a comparative framework. *Famine in European History* represents a significant new contribution to demographic history and will be of interest to all those who want to discover more about famines – truly horrific events that, for centuries, have been a recurring curse for the Europeans.

Guido Alfani is Associate Professor of Economic History at Bocconi University, Milan Italy. An economic and social historian and a historical demographer, he has published extensively on early modern Italy and Europe, specialising in the history of famines and epidemics, in economic inequality, and in social alliance systems. He is the author of *Calamities and the Economy in Renaissance Italy: The Grand Tour of the Horsemen of the Apocalypse* (2013) and is currently the Principal Investigator of the ERC-funded project SMITE, 'Social Mobility and Inequality across Italy and Europe, 1300–1800'.

Cormac Ó Gráda is Professor Emeritus of Economics at University College Dublin. He was awarded the Royal Irish Academy's gold medal for the humanities in 2009 and is currently (2017–18) President of the Economic History Association. He has published on topics ranging from the European Little Ice Age and London's last plague epidemics to the origins of the Industrial Revolution. Recent works include *Jewish Ireland in the Age of Joyce* (2006), *Famine: A Short History* (2009) and *Eating People Is Wrong, and Other Essays on Famine, Its Past, and Its Future* (2015).

Famine in European History

Edited by

Guido Alfani
Bocconi University, Milan

Cormac Ó Gráda
University College Dublin

CAMBRIDGE
UNIVERSITY PRESS

University Printing House, Cambridge CB2 8BS, United Kingdom

One Liberty Plaza, 20th Floor, New York, NY 10006, USA

477 Williamstown Road, Port Melbourne, VIC 3207, Australia

4843/24, 2nd Floor, Ansari Road, Daryaganj, Delhi – 110002, India

79 Anson Road, #06-04/06, Singapore 079906

Cambridge University Press is part of the University of Cambridge.

It furthers the University's mission by disseminating knowledge in the pursuit of education, learning and research at the highest international levels of excellence.

www.cambridge.org
Information on this title: www.cambridge.org/9781107179936
DOI: 10.1017/9781316841235

First published 2017

Printed in the United States of America by Sheridan Books, Inc.

A catalogue record for this publication is available from the British Library.

Library of Congress Cataloging-in-Publication Data
Names: Alfani, Guido, 1976– editor. | Ó Gráda, Cormac, editor.
Title: Famine in European history / edited by Guido Alfani, Università Commerciale Luigi Bocconi, Milan, Cormac Ó Gráda, University College Dublin.
Description: Cambridge, United Kingdom; New York, NY: Cambridge University Press, 2017. |
Includes bibliographical references and index.
Identifiers: LCCN 2017005107| ISBN 9781107179936 (hardback: paper) | ISBN 9781316631836 (paperback: paper)
Subjects: LCSH: Famines – Europe – History.
Classification: LCC HC240.9.F3 F35 2017 | DDC 363.8094–dc23
LC record available at https://lccn.loc.gov/2017005107

ISBN 978-1-107-17993-6 Hardback
ISBN 978-1-316-63183-6 Paperback

Contents

List of Figures		*page* vii
List of Tables		ix
List of Contributors		xi

1	Famines in Europe: An Overview	1
	GUIDO ALFANI AND CORMAC Ó GRÁDA	
2	Italy	25
	GUIDO ALFANI, LUCA MOCARELLI AND	
	DONATELLA STRANGIO	
3	Spain	48
	VICENTE PÉREZ MOREDA	
4	France	73
	GÉRARD BÉAUR AND JEAN-MICHEL CHEVET	
5	Germany, Switzerland and Austria	101
	DOMINIK COLLET AND DANIEL KRÄMER	
6	Low Countries	119
	DANIEL CURTIS, JESSICA DIJKMAN,	
	THIJS LAMBRECHT AND ERIC VANHAUTE	
7	Britain	141
	RICHARD HOYLE	
8	Ireland	166
	CORMAC Ó GRÁDA	
9	Nordic Europe	185
	MARTIN DRIBE, MATS OLSSON AND	
	PATRICK SVENSSON	

10 Eastern Europe (Russia and the USSR)   212
STEPHEN WHEATCROFT

11 The European Famines of World Wars I and II   240
STEPHEN WHEATCROFT AND CORMAC Ó GRÁDA

    Bibliography   269
    Index   311

Figures

1.1 Current European states covered by the book   *page* 5

2.1 Yearly wheat prices of the *annona* (in Roman Scudi): average buying prices and reference prices (September) compared, 1700–1798   38

2.2 Deviations from normal in wheat prices (deviations from Hodrick–Prescott trend of log values), 1480–1799   39

2.3 Italian population of the Centre-North, 1300–1800   44

3.1 Spanish provinces and regions mentioned in the text   60

3.2 Mortality in Catalonia, the Basque Country (Guipúzcoa and Biscay) and Navarre, 1780–1830   61

3.3 Annual mortality (adult deaths) in eight North-Castile provinces, 1700–1860   63

3.4 Wheat prices (reales/*fanega*) in five North-Castile grain markets, 1799/1800–1805/06   66

3.5 Monthly movement of wheat prices and mortality in Segovia, 1802–05   67

3.6 Annual mortality (total deaths) in Valencia region, 1700–1830   68

3.7 Annual deaths in New Castile, 1700–1865   68

3.8 Annual mortality (adult deaths) in Madrid, 1750–1839   70

4.1 Evolution of mortality crises in France, 1560–1790   77

4.2 The evolution of wheat prices in Paris and Toulouse, 1430–1795   80

4.3 The price of wheat in Beauvais and Châteaudun, 1600–1740   83

4.4 Births and deaths in France, 1680–1719   88

4.5 The relation between agricultural crisis and demography, 1692–95   89

4.6 Land sales in Charlieu and Albi during the crisis of 1709   92

4.7 Births and deaths in St Lambert des Levées, c. 1580–1790   99

6.1 Mortality and wheat prices in the region of Bruges, 1639–1715   138

8.1   Monthly temperature versus the mean, 1740–41   169
8.2   The price of wheat in Dublin, 1740–41   171
8.3   The ratio of potato to oats prices, 1765–1880   175
8.4   The price of wheat in Dublin and Winchester, 1739–41   178
8.5   Potato and wheat prices, 1840–50   179
9.1   The Nordic countries   186
9.2   Scandinavian consumer prices, annual deviations from
      trend (25-year moving average), logarithmic values,
      1302–1875   192
9.3   Comparison of the crude death rate according to
      official records and estimated (1751–1875)   201
9.4   Deviations from normal in rye prices in Sweden
      (logarithmic values), 1750–1875   203
10.1 Rye prices in Northern and Central Non-Black Earth
      Regions in comparison with Central Black Earth
      Region, 1707–1913   221
10.2 Crude death rate (CDR) in Russia and St Petersburg,
      1764–1913   222
10.3 Mortality in deaths per thousand in annual equivalent,
      January 1913–December 1924   228
10.4 Infant mortality per thousand births and deaths in
      population aged 1+ per thousand population, 1913–25   229
11.1 Infant mortality (per thousand births) in Germany,
      Austria and Hungary, 1900–28   249
11.2 Infant mortality in England and Wales, France and the
      Low Countries, 1900–28   250
11.3 Mortality in eastern Europe, 1909–25   251
11.4 Mortality in eastern Europe, 1938–49   259
11.5 Annualised monthly births and deaths in Leningrad per
      thousand of the population (logarithmic values), January
      1941–January 1945   260
11.6 Mortality in Moldova, January 1944–January 1950   262
11.7 Birth weight by month, 1944–46   265

Tables

1.1 Famines in Europe, 1250–1900   *page* 9

2.1 A comparison of the main famine chronologies available in the historical literature, 1470–1810   27

2.2 Identifying the main famines in central-northern Italy: communities experiencing 'crisis-level' rises in burials   30

2.3 Proportion of communities affected by a crisis (rise in burials of at least 50 per cent)   32

2.4 Compared chronologies of medieval famines, c. 1250–1470   34

2.5 Price increases during potential famines years over normal levels   40

3.1 Years of shortage and mortality in late medieval Spain   51

3.2 General mortality crises and great famines in Spain, 1500–1855   54

4.1 Two lists of French crises, 1300–1800   75

4.2 Demographic crises, production deficits and price increases in France, c. 1560–1790   78

5.1 Chronology of famines in Austria, Germany and Switzerland   117

6.1 Years of high rye prices in 11 towns in the northern Low Countries: price increase as a percentage of the 'normal' price   124

6.2 Years of high prices (as defined in Table 6.1) combined with excess mortality as a percentage above the normal level   130

6.3 Years of high rye prices in four towns in the southern Low Countries: price increase as a percentage of the 'normal' price years   135

6.4 Wheat prices on the market of Bruges and registered number of deceased owing mortmain rights in the chatellenies of Oudburg and Courtray, 1480–94   136

7.1 Comparative economic and demographic profile of years of extreme harvest failure: England, fourteenth – nineteenth centuries   148

8.1	Chronology of Irish famines	183
9.1	Famine years in the Nordic countries: indications and prices, 536–1875	194
9.2	Famine years in different counties in Sweden, 1750–1875	204
9.3	Mortality comparisons: Swedish counties, 1772–73 and 1808–09	206
9.4	Proportion of deaths by month: Swedish counties, 1772–73 and 1808–09	208
10.1	Central grain collections, in million tons, 1916/17–1922/23	227
10.2	The population of Petrograd, Moscow, Kiev and Saratov, in thousands, 1916–23	227
10.3a	Grain collections, excluding milling levy (garnts), in million tons, 1927–32	231
10.3b	Regional utilisation of collected grain, in million tons, 1927/28–1932/33	231
10.3c	Transfers of grain, in million tons (+ = received, – = exported), 1927/28–1932/33	231
10.4a	Grain collections and grain stocks, in million tons, 1939/40–1947/48	235
10.4b	Grain transportation from regions, in million tons, 1940–48	235
10.5	Moldovan grain balance, million tons and tons per head per year, 1944–47	238
11.1	Grain production in the United Kingdom and Germany relative to 1914, 1913–19	245
11.2	Grain production in the United Kingdom and Germany relative to 1939, 1873–1945	253
11.3	Grain balance in Moldova, in million tons, millions of population and tons per head per year, 1945–47	261

Contributors

GUIDO ALFANI Bocconi University, Milan, Italy

GÉRARD BÉAUR CNRS/EHESS, Paris, France

DOMINIK COLLET Heidelberg University, Heidelberg, Germany

JEAN-MICHEL CHEVET INRA, Paris, France

DANIEL CURTIS Leiden University, Leiden, Netherlands

JESSICA DIJKMAN Utrecht University, Utrecht, Netherlands

MARTIN DRIBE Lund University, Lund, Sweden

RICHARD HOYLE University of Reading, Reading, United Kingdom

DANIEL KRÄMER Oeschger Centre for Climate Change Research, Bern, Switzerland

THIJS LAMBRECHT Ghent University, Ghent, Belgium

LUCA MOCARELLI Bicocca University, Milan, Italy

VICENTE PÉREZ MOREDA Complutense University, Madrid, Spain

CORMAC Ó GRÁDA University College, Dublin, Ireland

MATS OLSSON Lund University, Lund, Sweden

DONATELLA STRANGIO Sapienza University, Rome, Italy

PATRICK SVENSSON Lund University, Lund, Sweden

ERIC VANHAUTE Ghent University, Ghent, Belgium

STEPHEN WHEATCROFT Melbourne University, Melbourne, Australia

1 Famines in Europe: An Overview

Guido Alfani and Cormac Ó Gráda

In a memorable passage in his *Essay on the Principle of Population* (1798) Thomas Malthus claimed that 'in every State in Europe, since we have first had accounts of it, millions and millions of human existences have been repressed' by the struggle to maintain food supplies in line with population. This was his principle of population at work. Yet, he added, 'perhaps in some of these States, an absolute famine has never been known' (Malthus 1798: ch. 7). If Malthus's second claim were true, then there would be no basis for this book. But, in fact, it would be truer to say that in no country in Europe 'an absolute famine has never been known'.

It is a widely held belief among historians, economic historians and historical demographers alike that situations of severe food scarcity were quite commonplace in medieval and early modern Europe (though some countries – such as England – are usually considered to have been able to 'escape' from famine much earlier than others). Slicher van Bath (1977: 60), for example, famously argued that in pre-industrial Europe harvests were poor in one year out of four. By itself, one bad harvest was not usually enough to cause concern, never mind lead to a famine, yet quite clearly this estimate suggests that, for past European populations, severe food shortages were a recurrent, and a relatively common, phenomenon. It is somewhat surprising, then, that so little has been done until now towards establishing a comprehensive comparison of the experience of hunger and famine across different parts of the European continent. Researchers have focused instead on either limited areas (a single country at most) or on specific events, of which very few have been the object of truly wide-ranging studies. The exceptions are episodes such as the so-called Great Famine of 1315–17, the Great Winter of 1708–09, the mortality peak of the early 1740s, the 'Year without a Summer' of 1816, and the 1840s, when the potato failed.

A distinctive characteristic of this book is that it has been planned from the very beginning with a comparative perspective in mind. Each contributor has been asked to cover very large European regions, and to attempt a reconstruction of the chronology of the main events as a key part of his or her discussion of the characteristics, the consequences and the causes of famine. The significant variability often found within each region receives due attention, but we also made a conscious attempt at making it possible to identify the truly major, supra-regional or even 'continental' famines. An overview of such famines will be provided below, as well as a brief description of the methods used to ensure the maximum possible comparability across chapters.

Before doing that, though, we should clarify a fundamental aspect: what was a famine – or, to use Malthus's definition, what was an 'absolute famine'? A few years before the publication of the *Essay on the Principle of Population*, such a fundamental protagonist of the European Enlightenment as Adam Smith distinguished between 'famine' and simple 'dearth' or scarcity of food. Only under specific circumstances did dearth develop into a famine. In fact, according to Smith famines in Europe had never arisen 'from any other cause but the violence of government attempting, by improper means, to remedy the inconveniences of dearth' (Smith 1976 [1776]: 526). As we will see, Smith's views about the causes of famine are in fact contentious – but the distinction between 'normal' dearth and 'exceptional' famine is something that has become common currency in the social sciences, though not always on the grounds of a clear definition of the two phenomena.

In this book, we focus on situations of severe food scarcity only – i.e. on famines. Throughout the chapters, we use a common definition of famine, which is also, to the best of our knowledge, the most recent one: '[F]amine refers to a shortage of food or purchasing power that leads directly to excess mortality from starvation or hunger-induced diseases' (Ó Gráda 2009: 4). We have chosen this definition, first, because it provides a clear view of what we should look for in terms of famine outcomes (famine is defined as a *killing* event) and as such considerably eases our comparative effort (see below) and, second, because it provides a synthesis of two different views on the causes of famines, which can be seen either as man-made events or as 'natural' events. This is an important topic, which for a period was highly debated and risked transforming scientific discussion into a clash between contrasting ideologies. Although we will not provide a full reconstruction of such debate here, it is important to at least recapitulate the main points.

According to Malthus, famine was 'the last, the most dreadful resource of *nature*' (Malthus 1798: ch. 7, emphasis added), and as such it contributed periodically to solve the demographic unbalance generated by the tendency of population to grow at a rate quicker than any possible improvement in the *production* of food resources. As we have seen, however, for Smith famine in Europe was instead a man-made tragedy – a point also made, more recently and most famously, by the economist Sen. In his classic *Poverty and Famines: An Essay on Entitlement and Deprivation* (1981) Sen proposes what has become known as the 'entitlements approach' to famine, which 'shifts the attention from the simple availability of food resources in a given territory to the "right" of the local population to have access to them' (Alfani 2013a: 47). According to Sen, human action can produce a situation of famine even when there is sufficient food to feed the entire population. In other words, famines result from the inefficient (or unfair) *distribution* of food, and not from a deficit in production or food availability. Sen modelled his original interpretation on the Great Bengal Famine of 1942–44, but his framework soon gained much wider currency and remains highly influential (e.g. Tilly 1983; Fogel 1992; Desai 1993). The ensuing debate saw the clash between promoters of the entitlement approach and staunch new-Malthusians. The debate also had its political side, since it called into question the behaviour of ex-colonial powers, and also pitted support for free markets against a stance more favourable to public intervention.

In this book we have tried to avoid ideological traps (at least those we were aware of). In particular, we are convinced of the fact that two common views of famine – either that they are man-made catastrophes or, instead, that they are the result of inadequate production – should not be seen as conflicting but as complementary. This is because the actual characteristics of historical famines were very varied and different causal factors seem to have prevailed in different places and epochs. Recent comparative works have suggested that, in areas such as Italy, at least the most serious famines of the early modern period were associated with a number of consecutive years of poor harvests (Alfani 2010; 2013a: 47), and more generally it has been argued that, while Smith may have misinterpreted the nature of seventeenth- and eighteenth-century famines, he would have been closer to the mark regarding those of the twentieth century (Ó Gráda 2009: 13). In addition, the regional reconstructions proposed by this book go a long way towards re-establishing inadequate production as the main (but not the only) driver of famine in the medieval and early modern period. However, they also analyse distribution: both in the sense of considering the ways in which grain markets operated and developed in time, and of showing how public institutions influenced (for the better, as it seems, more often than for the worse) the actual availability of foodstuffs to different components of the society. Generally speaking, they demonstrate that, although many famines were in fact triggered by inadequate production, the final outcomes (the actual characteristics of each famine) were *never* the pure result of 'natural' processes but were always mediated by human agency and by institutions (private and public), which could go a long way towards making specific episodes more or less catastrophic. A brief overview of the causes of famines in different areas will be provided later. Now something more should be said about the areas we have covered, and the methods we have used to compare the timing and the intensity of famines across them.

1   Book Structure and Methodology

We have aimed to cover the whole of Europe as thoroughly as possible and practicable, with a good balance between north and south, and between west and east. The core of the book consists of nine regional chapters, all of which for the sake of simplicity refer to current political boundaries. This has some consequences also in terms of intra-region variability, as, for example, while Chapters 3 and 4 – on France and Spain, respectively – relate to countries that had unified by the sixteenth century, Chapter 2 – dedicated to Italy – covers a large number of pre-unification states that managed to stay independent until the second half of the nineteenth century, a fact that affected aspects such as famine relief and the functioning of markets within the region. Some chapters cover more than a single contemporary state. This is the case for Chapter 6, on the Low Countries (Belgium and the Netherlands); for Chapter 5, on a broad central European area that encompasses present-day Austria, Germany and Switzerland; for Chapter 9, on northern Europe, which groups together all the countries once belonging to the Kingdom of Denmark (Denmark, Finland, Iceland, Norway and Sweden); and for Chapter 10, on eastern Europe, which covers some of the countries once part of the USSR (in particular, Russia and Ukraine). Finally, the chapters on Britain and on Ireland (Chapters 7 and 8) consider the geographic boundaries of the respective islands. Figure 1.1 describes the areas covered by each chapter.

Moreover, in order to be as comprehensive as possible, we have striven to cover the whole period from the late Middle Ages to when famine ended in each area. Obviously, the ability to account properly for the Middle Ages depended greatly on the availability of earlier studies as well as of good documentation, a circumstance that places southern Europe, plus Britain and the Low Countries, in a clearly favoured position. In fact, the chapters on Italy and Britain can conduct a more or less systematic analysis of famines from c. 1250, and those on France, Spain and the Low Countries from soon thereafter (c. 1300). For other regions this can be done only from later, sometimes considerably later, periods – but all chapters try to provide at least a general picture of the earlier times, using

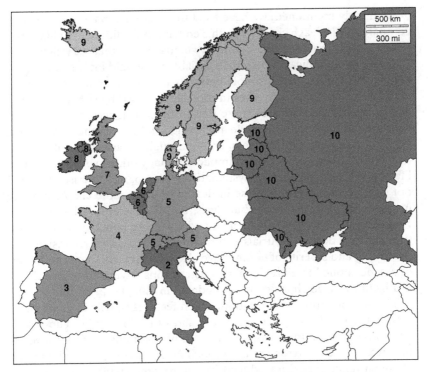

Figure 1.1 Current European states covered by the book

Note: The chapter numbers are in bold.

what information was available. In some instances, this allowed us to include very interesting episodes indeed – such as the AD 536–37 famine described in the chapter on the Nordic countries, an episode so dramatic that, according to some recent reconstructions, it had long-lasting consequences for the religious beliefs and the attitudes of survivors and their descendants, de facto fostering the beginning of the 'Viking Age'.

All regional chapters, with the exception of Chapter 10, which includes the Russian and Ukrainian famines of 1917–22, 1931–33 and 1941–47, end at some point during the nineteenth century, because during the twentieth there were no famines in Europe, apart from those induced by war. Those famines, though, had some distinctive characteristics and a cross-regional character. For these reasons, we decided to add an additional chapter that focuses specifically on famines occurring during World Wars I and II or in their immediate wake – which, for the vast majority of the European population, were the last episodes of extreme and lethal food scarcity.

As already mentioned, we have tried to ensure the maximum possible comparability of each chapter. To this end, not only did we use Ó Gráda's definition of famine as the common standard, but that very definition also gave us an indication of which variable we should invoke in order to distinguish famines from simple episodes of dearth, as well as to measure famine intensity: increases in mortality, caused by either starvation or hunger-induced diseases (note that in most instances it is very difficult, if not altogether impossible, to distinguish between the two). In this book, famines are killing events, and, although we are aware of the fact that famines also had a marked impact on many other aspects of human life, we are not considering systematically demographic crises that did not cause a significant increase in deaths (though some chapters partly integrate these in the general analysis: see, for example, Chapter 4, on France). This is why, in all chapters and whenever possible, we relied on time series of deaths or burials as fundamental sources for reconstructing the timing and severity of famines. We also defined a common methodology to be applied to all regional reconstructions relying on time series of deaths/burials, which is described in detail in Chapter 2, on Italy.

The second kind of information, which features heavily in many chapters, is time series of prices of wheat and other foodstuffs. These have always been a common basis for the study of famines across Europe – they were the cornerstone of the French *histoire sérielle* and of the notion of 'subsistence crises' introduced by Labrousse (1944) and refined by Meuvret (1946), and they have since featured, at least to some degree, in all or almost all accounts of famine; see, for example, the seminal work on central Europe by Abel (1974), or the very recent book by Ó Gráda (2015a). Some additional information about the importance of the French Annales historical school in the early developments of modern famine historiography is provided in Chapter 4. Time series of prices have the double advantage of often being available before series on deaths/burials, and of allowing the historian to take account of larger sub-regional areas ('markets') than the parish or community level at which burials were usually recorded. On the other hand, they do not allow, either in principle or in practice, the detailed coverage of the territory that time series of burials make possible, and, secondly, they do not give a direct indication of our marker of real famines: mortality increase. The sensitivity of excess mortality to increases in the price of cereals varied considerably over time and across space (Weir 1984; Solar 2007; Kelly and Ó Gráda 2014b). As a consequence, we combined information on prices with that on deaths/burials whenever possible, and in general this book is less reliant upon inferences based on price data than is often the case. As for the use of time series of burials, we applied insofar as possible a similar methodology across chapters, focusing on as simple an indicator as the evaluation of how many times the peak prices increased over the pre-crisis level, sometimes coupled with more refined techniques such as the analysis of the residuals of Hodrick–Prescott filters (see Chapters 2 and 9).

Sometimes neither time series of deaths/burials nor grain prices were available. This was usually the case for the earlier periods covered by each chapter. In this situation, we based our reconstructions on comparisons of the findings in published case studies (as many as available) produced by specialists in the history of famines or of food provisioning – something we will refer to as the 'expert method'. If and when we found universal or at least very broad agreement that a specific famine occurred in case studies related to different areas/communities, we made a reasonable hypothesis that the event fitted our definition and included it in the regional reconstructions. Vice versa, we tended to reject episodes on which distinct case studies disagreed.

Taken together, this eclectic combination of information and methodology was used to reconstruct a chronology of the famines affecting each area. In some instances, these were very wide, and even pan-European events – as discussed in the overview that follows.

2   The Main European Famines, c. 1250 to the Present

The distinctive history of famines in Europe owes much to European economic exceptionalism. At the beginning of the period covered in this book, Europe may already have had an edge on the rest of the world in terms of economic development, though some might claim that the most developed regions of China or the Islamic world at the time were more developed (Pomeranz 2005; Goody 2006). The hard data required to corroborate such claims are lacking. By c. 1800, however, thanks to the much-debated 'great divergence', living standards in Europe were already considerably higher than anywhere else apart from the European 'outpost' of North America. By c. 1800, too, the economies of north-western Europe had forged ahead of those of southern and eastern Europe (Broadberry and Gupta 2006; Clark 2007; Allen et al. 2011). By then Europe was the most commercialised, urbanised and industrialised part of the globe. The living standards of the masses in most places, while pitiful by our standards, were considerably above barebones subsistence. This increased their power to resist famine. Broadly speaking, rising incomes were accompanied by reduced vulnerability to famine, and, as the chapters that follow make plain, the most developed parts of the continent (i.e. the Netherlands and England) were the first to become famine-free, or almost so.

The research conducted by the authors of this book on different parts of the continent allows us to propose the first truly comparative chronology of European famines in the historical long run, as well as to provide, if not an absolute ranking of the different episodes in terms of severity (a task that would probably be doomed to fail, given the heterogeneity of the information currently available for different areas and periods), at least some indication about which the worst famines of all were, as well as which famines seem to have been somewhat overrated by earlier historiography. To this end, a synopsis is provided in Table 1.1, in which we list only the famines reported by at least two regional chapters.

To some degree, the reporting of famines for a specific area reflects the local availability of primary and secondary sources. In particular, the apparent scarcity of famines in eastern Europe does not reflect a condition of better food security but the relative scarcity of information usable for this area. As a consequence, the significance of this comparative synopsis can be fully understood only if it is coupled with the detailed reconstructions proposed by each regional chapter.

However, the comparative information we collected allows us to identify quite clearly some general trends. First of all, regarding the occurrence and the intensity of famines over time, we find a clustering of fairly severe events in the half-century or so preceding the Black Death epidemic of 1347–51. This is consistent with the view that demographic pressures were placing a non-negligible stress on the European population before the Black Death – especially, as it seems from the reporting of particularly frequent famines, in the south of the continent. On the other hand, the worst famine of the period, in 1315–17, affected central and northern Europe more severely, and, although Spain did not escape, Italy did.

The Black Death, which, according to the most recent estimates may have killed up to three-fifths of Europe's population (Benedictow 2004), was followed by a century and a half when large-scale famines were relatively few in Europe. This point is corroborated by some of the regional chapters, such as those on Italy, on Britain and on Nordic Europe. There seems to have been only one major famine in the fifteenth century (that of 1437–38, affecting central European countries as well as Britain), and, although we find some signals that the situation was changing in the first part of the sixteenth century, it is only from about 1550 on that the frequency of famines begins to increase very quickly – culminating with the terrible famines of the 1590s.

It is the seventeenth century, though, that clearly stands out as the period during which food security across the continent became a truly

Table 1.1 *Famines in Europe, 1250–1900*

Europe	Italy	Spain	France	Germany, Switzerland, Austria	Low Countries	Britain	Ireland	Nordic Europe	Russia, Ukraine
1256–58	1256–58	1255–62				1256–58			
1302–03	1302–03	1299–1304							
1315–17		1313–17	1315–17	1315–18	1315–17	1315–17	1315–17	1315–17	
1328–30	1328–30	1327–28					1330–31		
1339–40	1339–40	1339–41	1347				1339		
1346–47	1346–47	1346–48							
1374–75	1374–75	1374–76							
1437–38			1438	1437–40	1437–38	1437–38			
1521–23					1521–22		1523	1520–23	
1530	1527–30			1530–31					
1556–57		1557			1556–57	1555–57		1556	1556–57
1569–74	1569–72		1573	1569–74	1572–73			1571–74	1567–70
1585–87	1586–87		1585–87		1585–87	1585–87	1586–89		
1590–98	1590–93	1591–95	1593, 1598	1594–98		1594–98		1590–97	
1600–03	1600–01						1600–03	1600–03	1600–03
1620–23	1618–22			1620–23		1622–23		1621–24	
1625–31	1628–29	1630–31		1625–30	1625–26	1629–31		1628–30	
1647–52	1648–49	1647–52		1651–52	1648–52		1641–52	1648–52	
1659–62		1659–62	1661		1661–62				

Table 1.1 (*cont.*)

Europe	Italy	Spain	France	Germany, Switzerland, Austria	Low Countries	Britain	Ireland	Nordic Europe	Russia, Ukraine
1675–76			1676		1674–76			1675–77	
1678–79	1678–79	1678–85							
1693–97	1693–95	1694–95	1693–94	1691–95	1692–94			1696–98	1695–97
1698–1700		1699		1698–1701	1698–99			1699–1700	
1708–11	1708–09	1709–11	1709–10	1709–12	1708–10			1709–11	
1719			1719					1719	
1728–30						1727–30		1728–30	
1740–43	1743–45	1741–42		1739–41	1740–41	1741–42	1740–41	1740–43	
1763–65	1764–67	1763–65						1763–64	
1771–72				1770–72				1771–73	
1787–89			1788–89	1787–90				1786–87	
1794–95				1793–95	1794–95				
1803–05		1803–04		1805					
1816–17	1817			1815–17	1816–17		1816–18		
1845–50				1845–48	1845–50		1845–52		
1866–68								1866–68	1866–68

Notes: In the first column ('Europe'), famine duration has been derived by retaining only years for which famine was reported in at least two regions. In the other columns, duration has been evaluated on the basis of the evidence available for each region (see the relevant chapters for additional details). In the first column, the major European famines of the entire period are marked in bold.

critical issue. In southern Europe this is apparent from looking at Italy and Spain, but Portugal (not covered by our regional chapters) also seems to have suffered much, enduring widespread famines, usually coupled with typhus epidemics, in 1593–1600, 1616–23, 1630–32, 1647–52, 1657–63, 1675–78 and 1693–97 (Ferreira Rodrigues 2008: 178–85, 229; 2009: 652). The southern and part of the central regions of Europe possibly suffered more than the northern ones, but the real outliers seem to have been southern England (though not northern England and Scotland: see Chapter 7), which was free of major famine from the late 1590s on, and the northern Low Countries (Dutch Republic), where apparently no major famine occurred after that of 1556–57. During the early modern period, though, the southern Low Countries performed much more poorly (see Chapter 6). The advantage that at least part of northern Europe seems to have developed over the centre and south of the continent went hand in hand with fundamental changes in the international grain trade: from the 1590s the Baltic replaced the Black Sea (made difficult to access by the Ottoman Empire) as a key provider of grain to densely populated areas of Mediterranean Europe, such as Italy (Studer 2015). The Italian merchant republics (in particular, the Genoese) were responsible for opening most of the new international trade routes, but they were quickly taken over by Dutch and English merchants (Alfani 2013a: 71–2; and Chapter 6 here).

An important feature of this book is that it places the eighteenth century in a new perspective. Although some of the most notorious famines of this period covered all or almost all the continent (as in 1708–11), food crises seem, generally speaking, to have been on a smaller scale than in earlier times. The same is true for the nineteenth century, though in this case the outlier status of the so-called Great Famine of 1845–50 was already well known (and, moreover, that famine struck only a relatively small and well-defined part of the continent: see below). Another non-obvious outcome of our comparison is that, from the second half of the eighteenth century (a more precise threshold might be the last general 'southern' famine, in 1763–65), the relative advantage of the North seems to disappear and the situation even shows a tendency to invert, with central-northern regions experiencing more frequent famines compared to the central-southern ones. Britain is, again, the exception. Southern England had experienced its last major famine in the 1590s and northern England in the 1620s, whereas in Scotland the 'Ill Years' of the 1690s were lethal, but the 'great' Highland famine of 1846–48 was minuscule by comparison (Devine 1988; Cullen 2010).

The reasons behind this inversion would be worthy of further study. Only for Italy, and in particular for its northern part, has the crucial role played by the expansion of maize been underlined (Alfani 2013c), and Chapter 2 in this book shows that even the poorest northern Italian regions were well insured by their reliance on this poor but highly productive and resistant crop imported from the New World (compare Chen and Kung 2016). Interestingly, it was extreme reliance upon another high-yield American crop, the potato, that was the root of the worst European famine of the nineteenth century, that of 1845–50 (Ó Gráda, Paping and Vanhaute 2007). The famine, triggered by a fungal disease (*phytophthera infestans*) that entered Europe (seemingly from Belgium) in 1845, assumed truly catastrophic proportions in Ireland, where it caused about 1 million deaths (Ó Gráda 2009: 93). The famine in Ireland was also truly exceptional in its ability to trigger long-range mass emigration (see Chapter 8), causing Ireland to lose at least another million inhabitants. The second worst-affected west European region was the Low Countries, as both the Netherlands and Belgium were heavily reliant on the potato (Chapter 6). Further east, parts of Galicia suffered severely (Stauter-Halsted 2001: 26). The crisis was felt in parts of Germany, too, but here its demographic consequences were modest (Chapter 5).

Generally speaking, the so-called 'potato blight' is surely responsible for at least part of the aforementioned north–south inversion – but it by no means explains in full the complex relationship between economic development and susceptibility to famines in late eighteenth- and nineteenth-century Europe (especially considering that the roots of the inversion are seemingly to be found in the pre-blight period). For example, in the German-speaking part of Europe, some key proto-industrial areas proved the most susceptible to famine, seemingly due to their reliance upon food imports and, consequently, to their higher vulnerability to swings in bread prices (Chapter 5) while, in the Netherlands, increasing vulnerability to famine from the late eighteenth century can also be connected to a steady decline in poor relief expenditure from the late eighteenth century (Chapter 6). See Section 3 for a general discussion of the role played by public institutions in avoiding or containing famines.

During the twentieth century Europe was mostly famine-free. The exception was eastern Europe, and particularly parts of what became the Soviet Union in 1917. Here, extensive famines occurred during World War I and the revolutionary period that followed (particularly in the years 1917–22), as well as in 1931–33 – a string of events (detailed in Chapter 10) that have sometimes been labelled 'socialist famines' (Ó Gráda 2009: 235–6) but whose interpretation is debated (see Section 3). The last famines affecting the Soviet Union began in 1941 and were again triggered by war. But the geographic reach of the famines of World War II and its aftermath was far wider than the Soviet Union. They affected places as different as the high-income western Netherlands in 1944–45, Nazi-occupied Greece in 1941–44 and the new Soviet fiefdom of Moldova, where the crisis reduced some to cannibalism in 1946–47. Consequently, the period 1942–47 corresponds to the last truly European famine (until the present at least), albeit of a very specific kind (Ó Gráda 2015a). As highlighted in Chapter 11, an important and distinctive feature of these final famines is that what caused most people to die during them was not the infectious diseases that had been responsible for most famine mortality before the twentieth century but starvation dystrophy and pneumonia. The citizens of Amsterdam, Warsaw and Leningrad knew how to protect themselves against typhus and other famine fevers but they had no defence against the lack of calories.

We will provide some additional insights into the characteristics and the causative factors of different famines in Section 3. Before doing this, though, it is worth singling out and briefly detailing the events that seem to have been the most general and severe European famines of the last 800 years: those occurring in 1315–17, 1590–98 and 1693–97.

- 1315–17. Usually labelled the 'Great Famine', this was almost certainly the worst food crisis of the late Middle Ages. Triggered by intense rain and low temperatures during the summer of 1315 (Jordan 1996; Ó Gráda 2009: 15; and Chapter 9 in this book), it caused huge human losses in the worst-affected areas. In the southern Low Countries, for example, it caused a decline of about 10 per cent of the urban population, and there is evidence that rural areas were affected at least as badly (Chapter 6). In England, the harvest failure was worsened by aggressive Scottish raids and by an almost concomitant cattle plague (Chapter 7). Of all the regions covered by this book, only Italy was spared. And, although documentation is sparse, it would seem that Poland (not covered by our regional chapters) and the coastal Baltic region did not escape either (Hybel and Poulsen 2007: 66; Aberth 2013: 28). While in general central and northern Europe seems to have been most severely affected, in Spain too this developed into a severe and widespread famine (Chapter 3). This implies a significant revision of the boundaries indicated by earlier literature, which (correctly) ran westwards along the Alps into France, but excluded southern France as well as the Iberian Peninsula (Jordan 1996: 8).[1]

---

[1] Southern France, like Italy but unlike Spain, seems to have been spared the 1315–17 famine: see, for example, Laurénaudie (1952) for the Languedoc region.

- 1590–98. The occurrence of a 'European crisis of the 1590s' is a fact well established by the literature (Clark 1985), though it is not entirely clear to what degree this was a unitary phenomenon or a succession of events covering southern and northern parts of the continent in different periods and possibly associated with a critical phase of the so-called Little Ice Age (see Section 3). Our regional reconstructions clearly show that the crisis periods overlap in many areas, so here we will treat this as a single episode, though it probably affected southern Europe more severely in its initial phase (1590–93) and the centre and the north in the subsequent phase (1594–98). In Italy the situation was particularly dire, as this was 'the worst famine since the Black Death at least. Its consequences were not purely demographic, but are better understood as a "system shock" affecting demographic, social and economic structures' (Alfani 2011: 44) – an evaluation that the new data presented in Chapter 2 confirm and generalise to the whole of the Italian Peninsula. These years do not feature in William Wilde's famous table of Irish famines (though severe famine followed in 1600–02), but England certainly did not escape (Crawford 1989b: 9; Ó Gráda 2015b) and, as a matter of fact, 1594–98 are the last famine years recorded in southern England (Chapter 7). Of the regions covered in this study, only Ireland, Russia/Ukraine and the Low Countries seem to have been spared. The fact that the Low Countries were spared goes hand in hand with the large-scale restructuring of European grain trade routes, both maritime (see above and Chapter 6) and through central Europe (Chapter 5), triggered by the famine itself. After the famine, the grain produced by the Baltic area acquired an unprecedented significance for the food security of the whole continent.
- 1693–97. Of all the major European famines, this seems to have been the one that has attracted the least attention. An exception is France, where *les années de la misère* ('the years of dire poverty') have been highlighted as the final crisis of the long reign of Louis XIV (Lachiver 1991). The famine was particularly severe in France, as in 1693–94 about 1.5 million people died, many of them killed by typhus (see Chapter 4). In Italy, the new findings presented in Chapter 2 suggest that this food crisis, though overlooked in most of the literature, was second only to that of 1590–93, and about on a par with the other great seventeenth-century famine in 1648–49. The famine seems to have been particularly severe in northern Italy, where a crisis-level increase in deaths is found in 72 per cent of the communities considered (though increases in wheat prices were less dramatic than in earlier events). In central and southern Italy, as well as in Spain, the crisis was less acute. In Spain, as in France, much of the mortality seems to have

been caused by typhus epidemics (Chapter 3). In Germany the years 1691–93 had devastating consequences, with intense rain and cold destroying up to a half of the harvest and causing a famine on a scale that would never be reached again (Chapter 5). But possibly the worst affected of all were certain regions of northern Europe, as the famine that occurred in 1696–97 seems to have killed 25 to 33 per cent of the population of Finland, while in some areas of Sweden mortality rates in the range of 90 to 160 per thousand have been reported (Chapter 9; and Lappalainen 2014). The crisis was equally severe in other areas of the eastern Baltic then under Swedish control; in particular, about one-fifth of the populations of Estonia and Livonia seem to have perished during the famine (Chapter 10). The famine also wreaked havoc in Scotland (Cullen 2010; and Chapter 7). Of all the regions covered in this study, only Ireland and England seem to have been spared.

Although other severe famines straddled large swathes of Europe, none could be safely placed on the same scale as the three aforementioned 'super-famines'. These include some well-known and much-researched eighteenth- and nineteenth-century famines. One such is the *grand hiver* ('Great Winter') of 1708–09, which seems to have been popularised and promoted mostly by early studies in the history of climate (Lamb 1982; Le Roy Ladurie 1983). This was truly a Europe-wide event, but one that did not generate, generally speaking, a rise in mortality comparable to what had been relatively common up until 10 to 15 years beforehand. The exceptions were France, where about 600,000 people died, and Spain – but, in these instances, the famine was aggravated by war (see Chapters 3 and 4). Other well-known events include the so-called Great Frost of 1740–43, which had terrible consequences in certain limited areas of northern Europe such as Ireland (Chapter 8), but elsewhere was at most a medium-sized event (Post 1985); the famines of the early 1770s, which were devastating in the Czech lands, in parts of Germany and in Nordic Europe (Pfister and Brázdil 2006; and Chapters 5 and 9), and which in France led to the reversal of trade liberalisation measures introduced in the 1760s; and the 'Year without a Summer' of 1816, when food shortages resulted from the alterations to temperatures and meteorology caused by the eruption of the volcano Tambora a year earlier (Post 1977; Luterbacher and Pfister 2015; Chapter 3 below). This last episode has recently, and possibly too emphatically, been dubbed 'the eruption that changed the world' (Wood 2014); in reality, at least in Europe and from the standpoint of food scarcity, its consequences were of only secondary importance. Finally, we should remember the worst of all the nineteenth-century famines: the 'potato famine' of 1845–50, which we have already outlined above (also see Ó Gráda, Paping and Vanhaute 2007; and Curran, Kuciuk and Newby 2015). This famine, though hugely important in Ireland and Europe's costliest in terms of lives lost since the 1690s, was restricted to a fairly limited part of the continent, and – in the broader perspective offered by this book – hardly qualifies for inclusion in a shortlist of the main European famines of all times.

3   What's in a Famine? Some Reflections on the Nature and the Causes of Severe Food Scarcity

Famines are extremely complex events. Their occurrence and characteristics are shaped by a large range of factors. As a consequence, in many instances the same event can be understood in deeply different ways. At the beginning of this introduction, we briefly recalled the centuries-long controversy between those who see famines as the result of 'nature' (a shortfall in production) and those who tend to identify their roots in human agency and shifts in purchasing power due to inefficient distribution (entitlements). This juxtaposition is an oversimplification, however, and one that cannot be resolved in a satisfactory way in a synthetic account such as this, not least because, ultimately, an attempt at explaining any single famine must take into account the specific context in which it occurred. Consequently, we are relying upon the individual chapters to provide a more detailed discussion of the varied characteristics and causes of specific famines. Here, we will limit ourselves to briefly recall some important aspects, and to point out which chapters discuss them in greater detail.

As already mentioned in Section 2, the collective research conducted by the authors of this book suggests that periods of particularly frequent and intense famines were also characterised by high population density and by pressure on available resources, particularly land. A consolidated historical tradition, which we basically confirm, suggests that this was the case with the decades prior to the Black Death, but a similar point can be made, for example, for Italy during the late sixteenth and late seventeenth centuries (Chapter 2) or for Ireland in the eighteenth and nineteenth centuries (Chapter 8). Demographic pressure on available resources is definitely an important factor in establishing the conditions in which a severe famine can occur – but it is unable, per se, to trigger it. In the European historical experience, in most instances this role was played by meteorological conditions particularly unfavourable to fundamental crops – usually intense rain during the spring, highly harmful to wheat and other crops (either by means of direct damage to the plants, or by favouring the spread of crop diseases, such as the 'wheat rust' that played an important role in the famine of the 1590s, at least in southern Europe: Alfani [2013a: 54–5]). As all historical European societies had necessarily developed a degree of resilience against crop failures – through reliance on food reserves (both private and public), temporary migration or credit, for example – it took a recurrence of such unfavourable meteorological conditions two or more years in a row for a famine to develop. Naturally, the severity of the crisis increased with the number of subsequent back-to-back harvest failures (see, for example, Ó Gráda 2009: 31–2). All the regional chapters of this book report heavy rain in the spring or summer (as in 1315–17, 1346–47, 1590–98, 1693–97 and 1708–11) and, sometimes, truly exceptional cold weather (as in 1708–11 again, or in 1740–41) as the trigger of a famine. Drought, too, could be the cause of significant problems, at least in southern European areas such as Italy or Spain (see Chapters 2 and 3).

Moreover, the occurrence of such extreme meteorological events does not seem to be entirely random, and it has been suggested that it is linked to changes in more long-term climatic trends. Phases of inversion of the cycle – from cooling to warming, or vice versa – seem to be correlated with an increase in the frequency of meteorological and climatic anomalies. This point has been made, for example, for northern Europe in the late Middle Ages (Campbell 2010a; 2010b); for Italy in the early modern period (Camuffo and Enzi 1992; Alfani 2010; and Chapter 2 in this book); and for the entire continent in the seventeenth century (Parker 2013). More generally, the occurrence of famines in Europe has often been framed in the theoretical framework of the so-called Little Ice Age: a relatively cool period, characterised by declining temperatures from the early fourteenth century, a bottom level touched during the late sixteenth century and lasting through the seventeenth, and finally a warming period starting in the eighteenth century and completed only during the nineteenth (the exact timing of the different phases is debated: about this and the Little Ice Age in general, see, for example, Bradley and Jones [1992]; Fagan [2000]; and Luterbacher et al. [2012]). Many of the regional chapters included in this book recall in one way or another the Little Ice Age theory. This is the case with Chapter 5, dedicated to Austria, Germany and Switzerland, which makes explicit possible links between climate change and the occurrence of famine. For example, the so-called Spörer Minimum in sunspot activity might be responsible for the string of bad harvests resulting in the main European famine of the fifteenth century (1437–38), while the Maunder Minimum could be associated with the terrible late seventeenth-century famines, in 1693–97 and 1698–1700. Finally, a more favourable weather system developing after the end of the Little Ice Age might contribute to explaining the disappearance of famine in Europe from the second half of the nineteenth century. Although the Little Ice Age framework is quite popular among historians of famine, it should be noticed that it is also a contentious one. Some paleo-climatologists argue that the cooling of the Northern Hemisphere was very modest (see, for example, Crowley and Lowery 2000) and, very recently, it has been suggested that the Little Ice Age is basically a statistical artefact without any real historical significance (Kelly and Ó Gráda 2013; 2014a). However, rejecting the Little Ice Age hypothesis does not mean rejecting the (empirically very strong) association between extreme meteorological/climatic events and the occurrence of famines. It simply requires altering the theoretical framework in which the occurrence of such events is placed.

To conclude this synthetic analysis of the relationship between famine and climate, we should mention at least two additional aspects. First, major volcanic eruptions, insofar as they can be identified, led to marked declines in temperatures as well as dramatic changes to weather patterns in subsequent years. One such case is the eruption of Laki in southern Iceland in 1783, which led to the catastrophic Icelandic famine of 1784–85 and smaller famines further afield (Vasey 1991; Oman et al. 2006). Another is the 1815 eruption of Tambora in (present-day) Indonesia, which led to the famine of 1816–17 (see Section 2 as well as Chapter 5). Second, Campbell (2010a) has analysed the empirical association between climatic instability, famines and major outbreaks in detail for the mid-fourteenth century. In fact, the Black Death was preceded by frequent famines, as may easily be seen from Table 1.1, as well as by a Europe-wide panzootic in 1316–21. As argued in Chapter 2, the same association can be found for the 1629–31 plague, which was exceptionally severe in southern Europe, approaching, in some areas at least, the intensity of the Black Death (Alfani 2013b). It might well be that, in these instances, meteorological and climatic instability favoured the spread of both famine and plague – but we may also wonder about the possible causative link between famine and plague. On the one hand, we know very well that malnutrition can favour the spread of diseases such as typhus or dysentery, but the causal link from famine to plague is much more contentious, as in fact it calls into question the complex issue of the identification of the pathogen of the disease (see, for example, Cohn 2002: 31–3). On the other hand, many scholars have underlined the fact that plague can 'cause' famines, as it leads to the isolation of entire communities, disrupts the trade of foodstuffs and compromises rural activities (Pérez Moreda 2010b; Alfani 2013a: 45–6; and Chapters 2 and 3 in this book). Finally, it should be recalled that perturbations in the biological environment can lead to famines by means not only of human or cattle diseases but also of crop diseases, usually caused by fungi and consequently favoured by particularly wet seasons – as in the aforementioned case of wheat rust in the 1590s, the potato blight of 1845–50, discussed in Section 2, or ergotism affecting rye (Cavaciocchi 2010; Alfani 2013a : 54–5).

The possible impact of plague on the trade in grain and other foodstuffs, or on the local availability of food in quarantined communities, is only an example of a more general issue: the role played by institutions, both private and public. Let us begin with private institutions, and particularly markets. Many chapters underline the fact that well-integrated markets are a fundamental factor of protection against famines, and that improvements in market integration, both at the national and international level, may help explain why certain areas were able to become almost famine-free earlier than others (particularly so in the case of the northern Low Countries and of southern England: Chapters 6 and 7), and why from the eighteenth century on food security seems to be steadily improving across the continent (see, for example, Chapters 5 and 9). Famines themselves could act as promoters of new trade routes, favouring integration of the international grain market, as was the case in the 1590s, when Mediterranean countries started importing grain from the Baltic as a replacement for imports from the Black Sea (see Section 2). As this move became necessary due to the hostility of the Ottoman Empire, the episode is also a good example of how human action could cause, or contribute to causing, famines by disrupting trades and markets (see below for the relationship between famine and war). Human action harmful to food markets took the shape not only of open war or other forms of 'aggressive diplomacy' but sometimes also of bad legislation, such as the Corn Laws that kept the price of bread artificially high in the United Kingdom during the first half of the nineteenth century; it was the failure of the potato and the prospect of catastrophic famine in Ireland that eased their repeal in 1846.

Public institutions, too, are crucial in understanding the context in which famines occurred (Walter 1989). On the one hand, public institutions were an important factor in the resilience against famines across Europe, especially in pre-industrial times. In central and southern Europe, cities hosted food-provisioning institutions, whose origins are to be found in the Roman system of the *annona* (Reinhardt 1991; Marin and Virlouvet 2003). These aimed at securing access to foodstuffs for the urban population, ensuring that the local food market functioned effectively, maintaining public reserves of grains and monitoring private reserves (Alfani 2013a: 70–8). Food reserves were also maintained in rural villages, as in the case of the Spanish *propios* or 'commons', which played a crucial role in moderating the demographic consequences of severe harvest failures (Chapter 3). A more detailed description of food-provisioning institutions is offered in Chapter 2 and elsewhere (see too Persson 1999). Here, it will suffice to underline that their development from the late Middle Ages and into the early modern period seems to be another response of European societies to food problems; in the case of Italy, for example, many of these institutions were established at the time of the great famines of the early fourteenth century, and were strengthened during the sixteenth century when food security again became an issue. In Germany, similar institutions developed during the famines of the 1430s, taking as a model the Italian system (Chapter 5). In the northern Low Countries (Dutch Republic), it was the development of a system of formal and decentralised poor relief that helps explain the progressive disappearance of famines from as early as the mid-sixteenth century (while a decline in this kind of social spending could contribute to explain the re-emergence of famine in this area from the late eighteenth century: see van Bavel and Rijpma [2016]; and Chapter 6). Even in a much later period, organised public relief, mostly managed by the United States, played a key role in preventing widespread famine across most of western and central Europe in the aftermath of World Wars I and II (Chapter 11).

A point worth stressing is that the occurrence of famines triggered the development of *both* private and public institutions. The relative importance of the two is notoriously contentious, and as a matter of fact both the functioning of private markets and the development of public control over foodstuffs have also been counted among the possible *causes* of famines. Certainly, ordinary Europeans often saw unfettered food markets as a possible source of hoarding and speculation (see, for example, Chapters 2 and 4). On the other hand, a voluminous 'pro-market' literature, of which, as will be remembered, Smith was one of the initiators, has argued that public interference in the functioning of markets made matters worse and, indeed, might convert simple dearth into famine (Persson 1999: 1–22; Ó Gráda 2015a: 92–7). In this perspective, institutions such as the *annone* could have been detrimental to the development of better food security, as they hindered market integration. Corruption, too, constrained the benefits of public action. In truth, the European experience as a whole prevents us from taking a strong position on whether private or public institutions were more important in preventing famines or in moderating their consequences. In fact, any answer to such a question would need to be placed into context: each famine had different characteristics, as is shown by our regional chapters. However, it is also quite clear that, taken as a whole, the research presented in this book offers a fairly positive view of the role played by public institutions for food provisioning in societies as socially stratified as those of early modern Europe – without denying that, at least in some specific settings, such as that of England (Chapter 7), early choices made in favour of the market versus public stocks of grain could have worked very well, improving considerably food security (though, even in England, the last countrywide famine, in the 1590s, led to the reintroduction of legislation against enclosures, which a large part of the population considered the culprit in terms of production failures and high foodstuff prices). Equally clear is the fact that, from the late Middle Ages on, famines were *always* also the result of the failure of the institutions that were expected to make food available – be they markets, public food-provisioning authorities or even rationing authorities during wartime.

Among 'man-made' famines, war-related events occupy a special position. Like epidemics, wars disrupted trade and the circulation of food across the land. Additionally, the presence of armies could cause considerable damage to the harvest and could deprive the local population of their food reserves by means of confiscation, pillage or theft. Finally, armies could actively attempt to starve local populations, for example (but not only) during sieges, in order to weaken their willingness and their ability to resist (Ó Gráda 2009: 228–31; Alfani 2013a: 32–4, 43–6). According to Malthus (1798), causation could also be reversed, as populations experiencing a scarcity of food and other resources could be induced to try and conquer them from others. Gaining control over food-producing areas seems to have been one of the reasons for the Swedish attempts at expansion southward during the seventeenth and early eighteenth centuries (see Chapter 10). Most of the literature on famine tends to stress the causal link from war to famine, however, and not vice versa. This book is not an exception. The link is most direct in the case of sieges; the siege famines of Siena (1554–55), Leiden (1573–74), Augsburg (1634–35) and Leningrad (1941–44) are classic examples. More generally, episodes of the Italian Wars of 1494–1559 are closely associated with the famines of 1502–05 and 1527–29 in Italy, the Thirty Years War (1618–48) was a major source of food insecurity across central Europe, and the War of the League of Augsburg (1689–97) deepened the famine of 1693–94 in the southern Low Countries. The War of the Spanish Succession (1701–14), one of the major conflicts of the eighteenth century, considerably aggravated the famine of 1708–11 in France, Spain and the southern Low Countries. The Napoleonic Wars of 1803–15 also created food problems in many areas, and had particularly dire consequences in Spain and, to a lesser extent, parts of Portugal.

By and large, war seems to have increased over time its ability to bring famine to the European continent – an empirical finding that is entirely consistent with what we know about the increase in the size of armies and, more generally, in the scope of war through the early modern period. However, before the twentieth century war was never able per se to cause a famine on the continental scale. This changed in the twentieth century. While World War I and the subsequent Russian revolutionary wars were a cause of famine in eastern Europe only, World War II was the direct cause of the last Europe-wide famine, affecting places as far apart as Amsterdam and St Petersburg, or Greece and Moldova, and causing the deaths of millions of people (see Chapter 11).

As mentioned above, the famine that devastated parts of the Russian Empire from 1917 was an important cause of political unrest – and, in fact, it was the failure of the rationing system in Petrograd, in February, that led to the demonstrations that triggered the Revolution (see Chapter 10). More than a century before that, a food crisis in 1789 may have helped trigger the French Revolution – an hypothesis originally proposed by Labrousse (1944), though it has been much nuanced by subsequent research (also see in Chapter 4). Similarly, the famines and high food prices of 1846–48 may have played a role in the revolutionary events of 1848, which affected many European countries, though the precise link is a much-debated one (Berger and Spoerer 2001; also Chapter 5). The Portuguese 'Revolution of the Minho' (1846) has been linked to the failure of the potato in that part of the country, where it was an important element in subaltern diets. The combination of floods and drought that led to a major famine in Anatolia in 1873–74 led to tax increases elsewhere in the Ottoman Empire, which sparked off the 'Great Eastern Crisis' of 1875–78 in the Balkans (Zürcher 2004: 71–2). However, the revolutionary response in Ireland, which suffered most in the 1840s, was muted, whereas in France, where there was no famine, the events of 1848 had an enduring impact (Chevet and Ó Gráda 2007; Vivier 2007). While famines could sometimes lead to large-scale political unrest, at local level they were always capable of producing a revolt against bakers, grain merchants, moneylenders or the authorities. Part of the activism of food-provisioning institutions was due to the fact that they had to prove they were doing all they could to keep the community supplied. Revolt, in fact, was never against the famine per se – as Europeans, at least up until the eighteenth century, knew that bad harvests and food shortages were a real possibility and considered them as a fact of life – but against perceived injustice, in the form of frowned-on practices such as hoarding and speculation or of inaction on the part of the public authorities (see Thompson 1971; Guenzi 1995; Eiríksson 1997; Bohstedt 2010; and the discussion in Chapter 2). Food riots and revolts are reported by most chapters of this book and have to be considered one of the normal consequences of famines.

Not only were famines capable of causing political unrest, both at the national and at the local level; it is also claimed that political motivations lay behind certain famines. The Great Irish Famine of 1845–50 is still sometimes seen as the product of deliberate policy on the part of politicians in London, just as a voluminous literature has presented the famines ravaging Ukraine in 1931–33 and Moldova in 1946–47 as deliberately engineered for political reasons by the Soviet authorities (see, for example, Conquest 1986). In the case of Ireland, this view was once influential in nationalist rhetoric, but the verdict of modern scholarship is much more nuanced (e.g. Gray 2007; MacSuibhne 2013). This does not mean that the authorities were blameless or that they could have done nothing to reduce the appalling mortality of those years. In the case of Ukraine, most recent literature has tempered this interpretation, suggesting instead that, although Stalin and the Soviet government did indeed take decisions that exacerbated the consequences of poor harvests caused by adverse weather – for example, insisting on the planned procurements, which resulted in the requisition of even the following season's seed – the crises were not intentional but, rather, the consequence of poor judgement (see, for example, Davies and Wheatcroft 2004; Ó Gráda 2009: 235–9). In his contribution to this book (Chapter 10), too, Wheatcroft embraces the revisionist camp, showing besides that the area affected by the famine spread far beyond the borders of Ukraine, covering the northern Caucasus and the lower Volga regions. The interpretation of potentially 'political' famines always tends to relate to current politics, however, so there is reason to suspect that the causes of the great Ukrainian famine of the 1930s will continue to be much debated in the next few years.

Until now we have focused on the causes of famines. Much might be added about their consequences, which were complex and multifaceted, at both the micro and macro levels. We have mentioned some of them. Clearly, the short-run demographic consequences of famines were not limited to increases in mortality but also involved declines in marriages and births, as well as a surge in temporary and final migrations. In general, it did not take population growth long to restore the losses caused by famine (Watkins and Menken 1985); the obvious exception here is Ireland after the 1840s. The short-run socio-economic consequences of famines were not limited to social and political instability culminating in food riots – or, sometimes, even in revolutions – but included aspects such as religious change or the impoverishment of ample strata of the population. They could trigger processes of agrarian innovation, possibly leading to better and more intensive ways of farming (and maybe to improvements in food security) – but the actual long-run consequences of famines are usually hard to predict, as they depend heavily on the pre-existing social and economic structures as well as on the occurrence (or not) of quick demographic recovery after the crisis. It would be impossible to detail all these aspects in this introduction, so we must leave to our hungry readers the task of delving more deeply, searching the regional chapters for different perspectives on one of the most terrible, and also most fascinating, topics in European history: famine.

2   Italy

Guido Alfani, Luca Mocarelli and Donatella Strangio

The main objective of this chapter is to construct a reliable general chronology of Italian famines, building upon earlier attempts but also taking into account the results of recent research, as well as conducting systematic new tests on previously unavailable databases. Such tests allow us both to confirm widespread ideas about the significance of some specific events and to challenge the received wisdom about some others (especially for the eighteenth century). Additionally, we are attempting for the first time to integrate studies of famines in specific epochs into a very long-run picture: approximately from 1250 up until 1810. Although tracing and measuring the occurrence of famines over time is our main aim, we also provide some information about their demographic and socio-economic consequences and about the role played by institutions charged with managing food provisioning. We conclude with a synthetic discussion of causality, developing an analysis of a whole range of factors potentially involved in originating a famine, including population dynamics, climate change, war and pestilence, institutional failures, the conditions of food production and distribution and changes in crops and in agrarian technologies.

1   Reconstructing a Chronology of Italian Famines

Two partial chronologies of famines affecting Italy in the late medieval and early modern period exist. They rely on different methods for identifying the main events. The older chronology is Del Panta and Livi Bacci's classic reconstruction of Italian mortality crises, 1600–1850, which also

We thank Massimo Livi Bacci, Cormac Ó Gráda, Paolo Malanima and Giuliano Pinto, participants at the workshop 'Famines in Europe' (Bocconi University, Milan, Italy, May 2014) and at the conference session 'Famine in Europe: Long-Run Approaches' (European Society of Historical Demography Conference, Alghero, Italy, September 2014) for their many helpful comments on an early draft of this chapter. We are also grateful to Lorenzo Del Panta for having provided us with Tuscan time series of burials, and to Alessio Fornasin for having provided us with the Udine wheat prices series.

includes a (partial) classification of the crises distinguishing epidemics (for example, of plague or typhus), famines and others. A more recent attempt is Alfani's reconstruction of famines in northern Italy, 1470–1700, which uses an 'expert' method – i.e. one reliant upon a number of case studies produced by scholars specialised in the history of famines or food provisioning to identify the main events. One of the explicit objectives of this method is 'to solve, at least in part, the problem of differentiating "famine" from simple "dearth"' (Alfani 2015).

These pre-existing chronologies are summarised and compared in Table 2.1. Our aim is to produce a general chronology of Italian famines that integrates, updates and verifies them and, additionally, expands them in time (covering the whole period from about 1250 until today) and space (covering the whole of the Italian Peninsula). To this end, we will employ a variety of methods, to make full use of the information and of the sources available for different epochs and areas.

Ó Gráda's definition of famines offers a clear identification of what should be considered the main marker for the occurrence of a 'famine': excess mortality – i.e. an increase in mortality over the 'normal' level, caused by either starvation or hunger-induced diseases, such as typhus. A simple dearth might cause hunger but does not kill people, while a proper famine is a killing event – and, as such, it requires an acute and prolonged period of hunger, as the human body can resist being seriously deprived of food for very long periods (Livi Bacci 2000), or at least it has to be debilitating enough for a sufficiently large part of the population to favour the spread of disease. The link between famine and disease is a particularly complex one and has been developed in detail elsewhere (Alfani 2013a: 43–6), including with specific reference to the Italian case. Here it will suffice to note that, to begin with, what we are interested in is the outcome of famine in terms of deaths, and not so much how those deaths were 'produced', which should be considered simply as part of the description of specific events, or as an element to explore in order to provide causal explanations for the occurrence of such events (some examples will be provided below).

Del Panta and Livi Bacci's method, then, which focuses on mortality trends to identify periods of crisis, seems to be very well suited to our aims and offers a number of advantages. First of all, to be applied it requires only time series of deaths (burials): a kind of information that is fairly abundant across Europe from the early modern period, as parish records of burials exist quite systematically from the early seventeenth century. The Roman Catholic Church made them mandatory for all parishes with the *Rituale Romanum*, introduced in 1614 (Alfani, Dalla Zuanna and Rosina 2009), and similar sources exist for most Protestant

Table 2.1 *A comparison of the main famine chronologies available in the historical literature, 1470–1810*

Del Panta and Livi Bacci	Alfani
	1472–1474
	1476
	1482–1484
	1493
	1502–1505
	1518–1520
	1527–1529
	1533–1534
	1539–1540
	1544–1545
	1550–1552
	1558–1560
	1569–1572
	1586–1587
	1590–1593
	1600–1601
1607–1608	1608
1622	1618–1622
1629	1628–1632
1648–1649*	1648–1649
1672	
1678–1679	1678–1679
	1693–1695
1709	
1716	
1724	
1764	
1767	
1801	

Notes: * Del Panta and Livi Bacci attribute this crisis to typhus (see discussion in the following).
Sources: Elaboration from Del Panta and Livi Bacci (1977) and from Alfani (2015). The first part of Alfani's chronology, covering 1470–1627, was first published (including greater detail, as well as a comparison with plague chronology) in Alfani (2013a: 176–7).

areas from about the same period. However, parish books of burials are rare before 1600 and almost non-existent before 1550, even in an area particularly rich in this kind of documentation such as Italy. Before 1600 other sources exist, the city books of the dead, that have characteristics similar to the parish books of burials and are sometimes available since the fifteenth century. However, these can be found for the main urban settlements only, and, consequently, any method relying upon time series of deaths or burials could not be applied systematically before the middle of the sixteenth century.

Del Panta and Livi Bacci define a mortality crisis as a short-term perturbation of mortality that reduces the dimension of the generations so much that they are unable to reproduce themselves entirely even making full use of their potential for recovery. A mortality crisis, then, happens when one generation is prevented from giving birth to another at least equal in size, even when the rise in fertility and nuptiality that always follows a peak of deaths is taken into account. A 50 per cent rise in deaths is enough to prevent the generation born in the year of the crisis from fully reproducing. This would be a 'small' crisis. A 300 per cent rise in deaths could not be counterbalanced by the recovery potential of all the generations under the age of 15 at the moment of the crisis. This would be a 'major' crisis. Key to the application of this process is the measurement of 'normal' mortality – i.e. the number of deaths compared to which a peak level can be defined as a crisis (if it exceeds by 50 per cent or more than 'normal') or not. Del Panta and Livi Bacci suggest calculating the normal level of deaths by recurring to an 11-term moving average, centred on the year under consideration and excluding the two higher and the two lower terms (Del Panta and Livi Bacci 1977: 409–10). While this method is indeed able to identify short-term perturbations in mortality levels that might have to be ascribed to a real crisis, its practical application presents some difficulties, especially in the presence of time series with frequent gaps (as is usually the case with the older time periods, especially in rural communities) or in the aftermath of severe mortality crises able to alter for many years the normal death levels (such as the 1630 plague, which in northern Italy killed about one-third of the overall population).

Consequently, a variant of the original method, as introduced by Alfani in his study of the 1630 plague (Alfani 2013b), has been used. The difference lies in the definition of the normal level of deaths, which is taken as the five-term average, maximum and minimum values excluded, covering from the sixth to the second year preceding the first crisis year (the year immediately preceding the crisis is omitted, to avoid pre-peak disturbances in the deaths level). Crisis mortality is taken as the maximum yearly mortality to be found in the whole crisis period, and is then compared to the normal level. The method is particularly well suited for identifying the communities affected by a *known* possible crisis – which is exactly our case, as we can make use of pre-existing chronologies to test the extent of given famine-induced crises. The interpretation of the outcome, in terms of the ability of generations to fully reproduce, does not change compared to the original model.

As can easily be seen from Table 2.1, for the period during which they overlap (the seventeenth century) the two earlier chronologies match very well – especially if one considers that the 1672 famine reported by Del Panta and Livi Bacci affected, according to their estimates, only southern Italy (not covered by Alfani) and the 1600–01 famine reported by Alfani was a relatively minor event, seemingly affecting only Emilia and southern Lombardy. The only relevant discrepancy lies with the 1693–95 event, reported by Alfani only. 1693 is in fact mentioned as a crisis year by Del Panta and Livi Bacci, but without any indication of its causes (save for Milan, where they connect it to smallpox: Del Panta and Livi Bacci [1977]: 418), though more recent literature clearly connects it to dearth or famine (Bellettini 1987: 68–71; Alfani 2010: 40). Some discussion is also needed for the famine of the late 1620s and early 1630s. In fact, this period is much more closely associated with the plague epidemic (the worst since the Black Death in the fourteenth century) that started in late 1629, covered almost all of the North in 1630, and in 1630–31 also affected Tuscany. Given the magnitude of this epidemic, and considering that plague cannot be considered a famine-induced disease (Alfani 2013a: 45–6), it would be very difficult to distinguish the specific impact of famine, which was at most a minor contributor to the overall mortality. Consequently, in the following analyses the occurrence of famine will be tested for 1628–29 only and particular care will be used in interpreting the results.

2   Famines in Central and Northern Italy

Earlier chronologies (Table 2.1) provide us with a number of possible famines whose actual severity we can test, at the local and supra-local levels, by applying the method described in the previous section. In order to do this, we used the largest existing database of Italian time series of burials, first used by Alfani for his study of sixteenth-century general demographic trends and of seventeenth-century plagues (Alfani 2013a; 2013b) and further expanded to cover the whole of the eighteenth century and beyond, and to include part of central Italy (Tuscany and Umbria). This database, which is by far the largest of its kind existing for Italy, comprising 210 distinct communities, allowed us to shape our study of famines chronology as a natural experiment: are the hypotheses found in the literature about the occurrence of famine-related mortality crises in specific years confirmed by our database and methodology, and what can we say

Table 2.2 *Identifying the main famines in central-northern Italy: communities experiencing 'crisis-level' rises in burials*

	Percentage with crisis	No crisis (n.)	50–99% rise in burials (n.)	100–299% rise in burials (n.)	300% at least rise in burials (n.)
1569–72	50.0	5	5	0	0
1586–87	24.0	19	6	0	0
1590–93	78.8	7	9	7	10
1600–01	30.6	34	7	8	0
1607–08	39.8	56	16	20	1
1618–22	52.5	56	26	33	3
1628–29	47.7	69	23	32	8
1648–49	72.5	44	33	64	19
1678–79	53.8	86	55	41	4
1693–95	65.4	64	60	55	6
1708–09	45.6	87	44	28	1
1716	21.4	121	28	5	0
1724	12.2	137	17	2	0
1764–67	42.1	88	36	24	4
1801	32.5	56	19	6	2

Notes: While the North is covered systematically, of the central Italian regions only Tuscany and Umbria are included in the database.
Source: Database Alfani.

about the intensity and the territorial coverage of specific events? (Note that, in their original study, Del Panta and Livi Bacci used only 15 time series of deaths, of which just eight were for the North, three for Tuscany and four for the rest of Italy, all – with one exception – referring to cities.)

Due to the extreme scarcity of information about burials preceding the second half of the sixteenth century, the analysis covers the period from the 1569–72 famine only. The number of communities available at different periods is highly variable, from just 10 at the time of the 1569–72 crisis up to a maximum of 186 for the 1678–79 crisis. Table 2.2 summarises the results obtained for central-northern Italy as a whole, distinguishing between 'small' crises (with an increase of deaths of 50 to 99 per cent over the normal), 'medium' ones (increases in the 100 to 299 per cent range) and 'major' crises (with a fourfold increase in the level of deaths and more). For the reasons discussed above, crisis year 1672 has not been included in the analysis. Additionally, crisis years 1764 and 1767 have been merged and the whole period 1764–67 has been tested, as, according to Finzi (1986: 356), 1766, which followed a long period of drought, might have been the year when the crisis peaked.

The data presented in Table 2.2 indicate quite clearly that the most severe crisis was that of 1590–93, confirming that this was 'the worst famine ever faced by Northern Italy during the Late Medieval or Early Modern period' (Alfani 2011: 19). In fact, not only did almost 80 per cent of all the communities considered show the signs of a crisis, but in 10 cases (30.3 per cent) the crisis can be labelled a 'major' one, with deaths increasing by 300 percent or more over the normal (in a single year: also notice that this was a particularly long-lasting famine). The second worst episodes seem to be that of 1648–49, when 72.5 per cent of all the communities considered experienced a mortality crisis and, what is more, in 11.9 per cent of them (19) it was large, and 1693–95, when a crisis is found in over 65 per cent of the communities (71.8 per cent if we exclude the mildly affected central regions from the calculations). One could wonder, though, if this outcome is the result of a sampling bias – for example, in the case of a localised crisis in regions over-represented in the database. To keep this potential issue in check, as well as to give a picture of the territorial coverage of each famine, in Table 2.3 the occurrence of crises has been measured on a region-per-region basis (an exception being made for the 1569–72 episode, due to the small sample size).

The data presented in Table 2.3 confirm the conclusion reached about the particular severity of the famines of 1590–93, 1648–49 and 1693–95. In the case of the first two, the only regions where fewer than half the communities were affected was Piedmont; for the 1590–93 famines at least, this can be explained with the relative ease with which alpine and pre-alpine communities weathered the crisis (Alfani 2007; 2013a). However, this apparent advantage of north-western Italy seems to disappear from the second half of the seventeenth century, an interesting finding that calls into question the issue of causality (see the discussion in the following sections). From the 1670s the situation was usually inverted, with north-eastern Italy showing greater resilience to famine compared to the north-western part of the peninsula. In 1707–08, though, Veneto seems to be affected a bit more severely than Piedmont (though much less than Lombardy). This particular crisis, which is associated with the famous 'Great Winter' that caused widespread famine across Europe, is striking for appearing to be much less momentous than is held by a sizeable literature (Salmelli 1986: 27–41; Bellettini 1987: 97), with just one community out of 160 experiencing a great crisis. Admittedly, however, this was possibly the worst famine occurring in the eighteenth (and nineteenth) century – though the 1764–67 crisis seems to have been of a comparable scale, as also demonstrated by the analysis of changes in food prices in Section 3, and in fact a marked

Table 2.3 *Proportion of communities affected by a crisis (rise in burials of at least 50 per cent)*

	Piedmont	Liguria	Lombardy	Emilia-Romagna	Veneto	Tuscany
1586–87	0.0	33.3	37.5	16.7		
1590–93	40.0	**100.0**	**80.0**	**100.0**		
1600–01	9.1	22.2	44.4	**50.0**		
1607–08	33.3	46.2	36.4	42.1	36.4	41.7
1618–22	25.0	**61.1**	20.0	**62.1**	46.2	**74.1**
1628–29	47.4	25.0	**56.3**	48.3	**80.0**	44.8
1648–49	38.1	**76.0**	**71.4**	**74.4**	**56.3**	**94.7**
1678–79	**71.8**	**69.6**	**50.0**	45.5	33.3	46.5
1693–95	**73.0**	**61.9**	**77.3**	**78.3**	**56.3**	44.2
1708–09	42.9	**66.7**	30.0	37.8	**50.0**	**55.8**
1716	12.5	16.7	35.0	16.2	18.8	27.9
1724	15.2	14.3	0.0	18.4	12.5	9.5
1764–67	26.5	**66.7**	11.1	**52.6**	6.3	**69.8**
1801	46.7		0.0	44.8		11.8

Notes: Regions with at least half the communities affected are in bold. Piedmont includes Aosta Valley, Veneto includes Trentino Alto Adige and Friuli Venezia Giulia, and Tuscany includes Umbria.
Source: Database Alfani.

difference between the pre- and post-1700 famines can be noticed and needs to be underlined.

We could recur to regional-level data to elaborate a kind of index of the overall severity of the famines affecting central-northern Italy, which also takes into account territorial coverage. If we single out the episodes in which at least 50 per cent of the communities of at least three regions experienced a crisis, we discover that the three worst famines all fall into this category, plus what was possibly the fourth worst, in 1678–79, as well as the 1618–22, 1708–09 and 1764–67 events (the period 1628–29 is borderline, though we can presume that at least in some communities – in Piedmont, Lombardy and Veneto in particular – the mortality crisis that occurred in 1629 was due to an early outbreak of the 1629–31 plague). Instead, considering territorial coverage, total intensity expressed as the overall proportion of communities affected, and the occurrence of great (local) crises, the 1586–87, 1600–01, 1607–08, 1716, 1724 and 1801 famines appear to be less important events. These findings improve significantly our knowledge of the Italian famines, first because they allow a better appreciation of the importance of the late seventeenth-century events and especially that of 1693–95, overlooked in much of the literature. Second, they put into the right perspective the eighteenth-century famines (1801 included), which on the contrary had been magnified by a specialist literature influenced by accounts of 'European' crises, such as that on the Great Frost of 1708–09 (Lamb 1982; Le Roy Ladurie 1983; Lachiver 1991). Third, our analysis of the occurrence per region and over time of famines has much to offer for a proper discussion of causality (see Section 4).

As already mentioned, it is not possible to recur systematically to time series of burials to check for the occurrence of famines preceding that of 1569–72. However, the fact that Alfani's chronology for the late sixteenth and seventeenth centuries has been largely confirmed by the extensive tests we conducted suggests that, by and large, it should be valid also for the late fifteenth and early sixteenth centuries. Furthermore, Alfani tested the relative importance of sixteenth-century famines by making use of a source much more widely available, for this period, than burial records: the parish books of baptisms, made mandatory for all Catholic parishes by the Council of Trent in 1563, but often available for much earlier (it is a well-known fact that baptisms/births are very responsive to situations of acute scarcity of food: Cattini 1983; Bellettini 1987; Alfani 2007). Regarding the second half of the sixteenth century, such sources confirm the pre-eminent place occupied by the famine of 1590–93 (Alfani 2013a: 56–61). More interestingly, regarding the earlier period, of the eight crises recorded in Table 2.1 that occurred between 1500 and 1560, two can be singled out as the most severe: 1502–05 (a period when plague was also ravaging Italy: Alfani 2013a: 88–9) and 1527–29, 'a general crisis in northern Italy, involving the central and eastern part of the Po Valley, …and sparing only western Piedmont and Liguria' (Alfani 2013a: 56). To these we should probably add the 1539–40 crisis, when high increases in wheat prices were common throughout Italy (see Section 3).

For earlier periods not even baptismal records are available. Consequently, we can rely solely on the 'expert' method, looking for concordance in partial and local chronologies. In Table 2.4 we charted the longest and most complete we could find, overall covering the whole period from about 1250 up until 1470 (when Alfani's chronology in Table 2.1 begins). The chronologies cover the cities of Pistoia (Herlihy 1967) and Florence (Pinto 1978; de La Roncière 2011) in Tuscany as well as Lombardy (Savy 2011). The more general account provided by Corradi (1973 [1865–94]), based on chronicles and other documentation, is also included.

The chronologies we collected suggest that in late medieval Italy, as elsewhere in Europe (Campbell 2010a), the period characterised by the

Table 2.4 *Compared chronologies of medieval famines, c. 1250–1470*

Pistoia	Florence	Lombardy	Corradi
			1256–58
			1271–72
	1275–77	1276–77	1276–77
	1285–86	1286	1286
	1302–03		1302–03
1313		1311–12	
1328–29	1328–30		1326–30
1339–40	1339–41		1339–40
1346–47	1346–47		1346–47
	1352		1352–53
	1369–70		1368
1375	1375		1374–75
			1384–85
1389			
1393			
1410			1410–12
			1458

Notes: The chronology published for Lombardy covers the period 1270–1330 and includes events of different kinds; we considered only those for which human mortality was reported. The chronology published for Pistoia covers the period 1313–1458 and includes both years of 'scarcity' and of 'famine'; only the latter have been included in the table. Regarding the information provided by Corradi, although he also refers to local famines we included in the list only those episodes that involved the whole of Italy or at least a large area. For Florence, we reconstructed a chronology combining the works of Pinto and de La Roncière, which together cover the period 1250–1375.
Sources: Herlihy (1967: 105) for Pistoia; Pinto (1978; 2012) and de La Roncière (2011) for Florence; Savy (2011) for Lombardy; Corradi (1973 [1865–94]) for other areas.

worst and most frequent famines was that immediately preceding the Black Death. In the first half of the fourteenth century we find four major famines: 1302–03; 1328–30; 1339–40; and 1346–47. As well as the earlier famine of 1275–77, these seem to have been large-scale events, covering the whole of Italy or at least most of it, as also confirmed by the most updated general account of the Italian population of the late Middle Ages currently available (Pinto 1996: 45–6). Instead, Italy seems to have been largely spared by the so-called Great European Famine of 1315–22, triggered by unfavourable weather and further exacerbated by the concomitant cattle panzootic of 1316–25 (Campbell 2010a). It has been hypothesised that, during this crisis, starving England was provisioned with Italian grain, though the evidence for this is limited and caution is needed (Jordan 1996: 173–4). However, the advantage of the Italian Peninsula was short-lived, as '[t]he famine of 1328–30 had for Italy the same significance as the one which has been given, for Europe, to the great crisis of 1315–17' (Pinto 1996: 46, our translation). This episode contends with the 1346–47 one for the position as the worst famine of the fourteenth century. Triggered by intense rain since autumn 1345, the 1346–47 famine covered a large European area, particularly the south of the continent. In Florence, for example, city authorities distributed 94,000 certificates allowing the collection of bread from public bakeries: one certificate per head, in a city of 85,000 to 90,000 inhabitants, indicating that the whole of the urban population, as well as many rural dwellers, had to recur to public help (Pinto 2012: 70). To a degree, however, the actual demographic impact of this famine pales compared to the human losses caused by the Black Death, which entered Italy in late 1347 and by the end of the following year had spread to almost all of the peninsula, causing the loss of between 30 and 60 per cent of the entire Italian population (Del Panta 1980; Benedictow 2004; Alfani and Melegaro 2010). In the century or so following the Black Death, famines become relatively rare, and they seem to have been of inferior magnitude compared to those of the early fourteenth century as well as to those of the early modern period – though it should also be noticed that these episodes are clearly under-researched compared to the preceding and following ones.

3 Famines in the Kingdom of Naples and in the Papal States (Latium)

For the southern regions, which during the late medieval and early modern periods were all comprised in the Kingdom of Naples, as well as for part of central Italy and in particular for the region of Latium, which constituted the heart of the Papal States, very few time series of burials of good quality are available, so that we cannot proceed in the same way as for the North and the Tuscan–Umbrian area (in the following, we will indicate these two parts of Italy as Centre-South and Centre-North, respectively). Consequently, we rely on qualitative information and on the specialised literature to construct a famine chronology comparable to that described in the earlier section. An analysis of time series of food prices (of wheat in particular) will be used as an additional tool to both check whether the main events affected the whole of the peninsula, and to deepen our general account of Italian famines. Finally, some information will be provided about the Italian food-provisioning authorities.

Regarding the Middle Ages, the discussion in the earlier section also applies to the Centre-South, and, in particular, the main famines we listed for the pre-Black-Death period involved the whole of the peninsula. For Latium, we found confirmation of this in Palermo's (1990; 1997) works on the city of Rome and the *annona*. Consequently, here we will not develop the matter further, focusing instead on the early modern period. A first aspect to be mentioned is that the literature on famines and food security in central-southern Italian regions relies upon even more disparate sources than those available for the Centre-North. Additionally, the two states that covered almost the whole of this large area were characterised by a complex and fragmented territory.

In the Papal States, fragmentation made each province a separate and distinct entity, with its own customs obstructing inter-state trade, its own currency and systems of measurements, which considerably complicated exchanges (Caravale and Caracciolo 1978: 525–36). The Kingdom of Naples was less fragmented, though composed of two separate kingdoms – Naples and Sicily – that, while politically united under the same sovereign, had distinct and deeply different administrations. Particularly relevant for our analysis is the fact that the southern Italian area was divided into many markets, often isolated one from the other due to the lack of adequate land routes – and, consequently, it was a frequent occurrence that food prices differed sharply on different markets of the Kingdom. However, the existence of regional markets and prices did not prevent, during the main famines, grain prices from increasing sharply even in the theoretically most favoured areas. In fact, in these areas hoarding activities, usually very profitable, counteracted the (local) benefices deriving from the existence of natural barriers and the ensuing territorial fragmentation.

In the Centre-South, the first severe famines of the sixteenth century are closely related to warfare, as they occurred during the Italian Wars (1494–1559), triggered by the decision of the French king, Charles VIII, to try and enforce his claim on the Kingdom of Naples. As in the Centre-North, the main crises occurred in 1502–05 and 1527–29 (Alfani 2013a). In the second period famine was exacerbated in Naples by the siege suffered in 1528 at the hands of the French troops led by Lautrec, and in Rome by the sack inflicted by the Landsknechts in 1527 (Alfani and Rizzo 2013: 19–20; Alfani 2013a: 55). Also during the second half of the sixteenth century, as well as in the seventeenth, it seems that the chronology of the main events matches quite closely that already described for the Centre-North. We have some confirmation of this in the dynamics followed by grain prices, as well as – for the seventeenth century – in Del Panta and Livi Bacci's (1977) early work, which included an analysis of time series of burials in three of the main cities of the Kingdom of Naples: Bari, Palermo and Naples itself. Although, for the South, the

picture provided by Del Panta and Livi Bacci is very sketchy, the worst
famine of the late sixteenth and seventeenth centuries is clearly the 1590–
93 one. In this period the only other crisis involving all three cities is the
1648–49 one, while in other instances Palermo (the capital city of the
island of Sicily, a traditionally wheat-exporting area) seems to have been
spared the consequences of severe hunger; this was particularly the case
for the 1607–08 and 1618–22 crises. Of the main events identified for
the Centre-North, the 1678–79 and 1693–95 famines did not affect any
of the three cities; however, both Bari and Palermo (as well as Catania
and the rest of Sicily: Fazio 1993; Bulgarelli Lukacs 2009) were affected
by the previously mentioned 1672 famine, which possibly involved only
the southernmost areas of the Italian Peninsula.

For the eighteenth century a much more sizeable literature is available,
and, in particular, the works by Strangio (1998; 1999), Revel (1972;
1975; 1982) and Reinhardt (1991) on the Papal States and by Alifano
(1996), Coniglio (1940), Orlandi (1996) and Malanima (2013) for the
Kingdom of Naples. In the Papal States, on the grounds of the records of
the *annona* and other sources, the main crises (which were essentially due
to a scarcity of wheat) occurred in 1708, 1721, 1728, 1743–45, 1748–49,
1764–67 (the worst of all), 1779–80 and 1797 (Strangio 1998). Revel
proposes a slightly different chronology of wheat production crises: 1719,
1724, 1744, 1747 and, finally, the whole period 1769–1779 – the 'grand
cycle de crise' (Revel 1982: 229). To clarify the matter, Figure 2.1 represents the prices paid by the Roman *annona* to provision wheat, as well as
the reference prices that it fixed yearly (usually in September).

Of course, not all these peaks in grain prices are indicative of a real famine (see below for a discussion of the shortcomings of grain prices series
as famine markers in the pre-industrial period). 1764–67 and 1779–80
seem to have particular significance, however, as they were characterised
both by sharp increases in the prices of wheat and by the activities of
the Monte Nuovo Abbondanza delle Comunità, a temporary institution
that was aimed at easing, at the local level, the situations of greater scarcity (Strangio 1999; 2013). For the Kingdom of Naples, according to
the available literature, food crises occurred in 1723, 1759–64, 1764–66,
1780–81, 1790–91 and 1802. Of these, 1764 seems to have been the
most severe (Malanima 2013: 346), as in the Papal States. For the kingdom, significant food crises have been reported for the nineteenth century, too (particularly in 1817, 1854 and 1858: Malanima [2013]: 348).

As can be seen, there are significant analogies between the partial
chronologies proposed for Latium/Papal States and for the Kingdom of
Naples, as well as for the Centre-North. In order to better distinguish
between secondary events and major crises (proper 'famines' covering

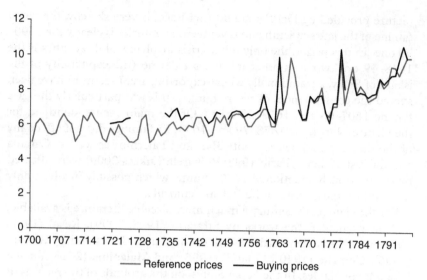

Figure 2.1 Yearly wheat prices of the *annona* (in Roman *scudi*): average buying prices and reference prices (September) compared, 1700–1797

Sources: Archivio di Stato di Roma (ASR), *Presidenza Annona e Grascia* bb. 2212–2249; ASR, Bandi, b. 460; Nicolai (1803: 155); Revel (1972: 255).

a large part of Italy), in Table 2.5 we recur to some of the best and longest time series of wheat prices available, also trying to ensure territorial representativeness across the North, Centre and South of the Italian Peninsula. All prices are average yearly prices on urban markets, and, overall, our time series cover three centuries (about 1500 to 1800). To identify the occurrence of a crisis, we took the peak yearly price found in a crisis period and compared it to 'normal' prices, defined as the seventerm average, max and min values excluded, covering from the eighth to the second year preceding the first crisis year (a procedure similar to that applied earlier to time series of burials). We tested all the main crisis years identified in the earlier section for the Centre-North, plus 1672, 1743–45 and 1779–81. In Table 2.5, cities are arranged along a North–South axis. As an additional check, for the most complete time series we also analysed the deviations of wheat prices from the Hodrick–Prescott smoothed trend (log price, with a smoothing parameter of 6.25). The results are shown in Figure 2.2.

Time series of prices largely confirm the list of major events identified in our systematic analysis of the Centre-North, and allow us to infer that they have much wider general significance. On the contrary, 1672

(a)

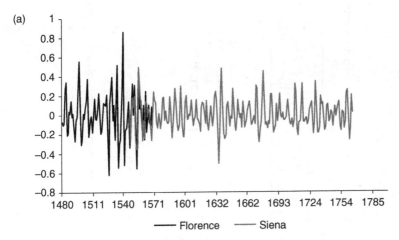

——— Florence ——— Siena

(b)

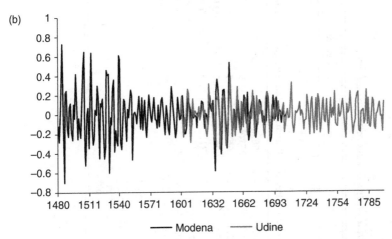

——— Modena ——— Udine

Figure 2.2 Deviations from normal in wheat prices (deviations from Hodrick–Prescott trend of log values), 1480–1799

(a)

Central Italy

(b)

Northern Italy

does not seem to be a year of widespread famine (confirming our earlier hypothesis that the crisis was confined to the southernmost part of Italy), and the same is true for the extra dates tested for the eighteenth century. If we focus on those events that were associated with a doubling

Table 2.5 *Price increases during potential famines years over normal levels*

Years	North					Centre					South		
	Udine	Bassano	Pavia	Modena	Pesaro	Florence	Sansepolcro	Siena	Rome (buying p.)	Rome (fixed p.)	Naples	Bari	Catania
1502–05			62.1	**163.5**		58.5	**202.9**						
1527–29	**175.2**		**221.0**	**301.1**		**271.4**	167.7						
1539–40	77.4		**119.6**	71.5		66.5						**122.4**	38.7
1590–93	82.8	**114.0**	**120.6**	**175.9**		96.8	**123.7**	90.9			59.5	**114.5**	59.3
1618–22	31.0	54.4	32.1	55.4		21.4	92.6	67.8			31.0	46.2	13.1
1648–49	**143.6**	**167.0**	**118.8**	**222.9**				**118.8**			**240.7**	**242.2**	
1672	–2.4	11.2	9.8	27.7				38.9			3.2		
1678–79	27.3	31.0		39.5				**118.8**			37.5		
1693–95	56.3	71.8	63.3	94.1				79.3					
1708–09	34.0	34.6			20.3			68.7		16.2	61.3		
1743–45	9.5	–26.7			39.1				–1.7	9.8	10.5		
1764–67	60.0	43.2			64.3			63.2	63.3	56.3	63.0		
1779–81	–7.9	–3.8			6.6				40.8	34.5	–1.1		

Note: Increases of 100 per cent or more are in bold.
Sources: Databases Alfani and Strangio.

at least of the average yearly price of wheat (in bold in Table 2.5), we find widespread sharp increases in wheat prices in 1527–29, 1539–40, 1590–93 and 1648–49. Obviously, yearly averages hide much wider intra-year oscillations; for example, the fourfold increase in wheat prices found in Modena during the 1527–29 famine, the almost threefold increase found in the same city in 1590–93 and the increase by three and a half times found in Naples and Bari in 1648–49 should be considered indicative of a really extreme condition of perturbation of grain markets and of entirely compromised access to food. Time series of prices also confirm that eighteenth-century famines were on a much smaller scale compared to those of the preceding two centuries. The largest increases are recorded for the 1764–67 crisis, which, from this perspective, seems to have been worse than the 1708–09 one. Interestingly, on the basis of wheat prices alone, the 1693–95 famine would have to be defined as a medium-sized event. In addition, deviations from the trend suggest that events were more extreme in the sixteenth century and in the first half of the seventeenth compared to later periods. However, it must be noted that time series of prices present some limitations as markers of famine intensity.

First of all, given our definition of famine, food prices are quite an indirect source for considering the final outcome of a crisis: excess mortality. From this point of view, the burial records used for the Centre-North are obviously much better sources. Price increases, in fact, though positively correlated with mortality increases, are a perfect reflection of neither mortality nor – and more importantly – the actual availability of food, as, 'in the case of extreme famines…, food prices fail to fully reflect the gravity of the situation. At a certain point during the crisis, the price paid for wheat and other cereals on the urban markets is no longer an index of the real possibility of finding food in the cities. To put it bluntly, there is a price, but there is no wheat. For the authorities, then, the problem becomes that of finding resources which are to be rationed and distributed to the starving population, mostly freely (practically nobody can afford to pay, and anyway there is no food being sold on the market)' (Alfani 2011: 28). In the Italian case, then, the significance of food prices can be understood only by also taking into account the activities of the public food-provisioning authorities.

Since antiquity, feeding the large cities of the Mediterranean required the establishment of institutions responsible for provisioning. The city of Rome, capital of the Roman Empire, was a pioneer in this, as its needs were far too large to be met solely with the produce of the surrounding countryside. However, over time similar problems led to similar solutions, as recent comparative studies have clearly shown (Marin and Virlouvet

2003). In Italy, from the Middle Ages urban provisioning institutions looked to the surrounding area, the *contado*, as the first, and usually the main, source of provisions. Asserting their right to a primacy based on ancient medieval traditions, the *annone* aimed to establish a monopoly over 'their' rural areas and to control as far as possible the actual flows of all basic foodstuffs (not only wheat and other grain) entering and leaving the territory (Guenzi 1995; Strangio 1998). The *annone* also published the *calmiere*, a list of reference prices calculated periodically on the basis of prices actually determined, on the urban market, by the meeting of supply and demand. Famine years were the exception, as in those instances the *calmiere* prices had to take into account the resources the poorest had at their disposal (De Maddalena 1949). Another typical function of the food-provisioning institutions was the control and management (direct and indirect) of primary food supplies (Corritore 2007; Alfani 2013a: 73–5).

The development of this complex system of food-provisioning institutions is closely tied to famine chronology, as we know that often the roots of the late medieval and early modern *annone* go back to the great famines of the early fourteenth century. By the fifteenth century the main characteristics of the system were already established; this is, for example, the case for Rome (Palermo 1990: 163). However, it was during the sixteenth century that the control traditionally exercised by the cities on the countryside evolved into more complex forms of organisation, with the final aim of monitoring (and, if need be, regulating) food availability throughout the territory of the state. This happened, for example, in Florence, Milan, Rome (Delumeau 1957–59; Pult Quaglia 1982; Falchi, Pasturi and Sinisi 1995; Palermo and Strangio 1997; Parziale 2009). Even though in many places the new trends were fully developed only in the seventeenth century, often it was the great famine of 1590–93 that provided the necessary stimulus to complete the process of reform, as was the case in Bologna (Guenzi 1978). Although the *annone* were, generally speaking, the main institutions charged with ensuring food security, in times of severe food shortages the intervention of the public could involve other important parts of the administration, up to the highest levels – sovereigns or ruling bodies (Alfani 2015). In this regard, one aspect that needs to be underlined is that the authorities had to demonstrate that they were active and vigilant in order to maintain order and avoid revolts. It is a well-known fact that during famines the crime rate and the general propensity for violence increased dramatically (and city authorities were well aware of this), but as a rule the cause of bread riots was not only hunger – which was, basically, considered a fact of life, like the unreliability of harvests (Guenzi 1995: 292) – but also the suspicion of injustice. If it was thought that bread was available but that somebody was hoarding or removing it from the market, or that what bread was available was being unfairly distributed to the advantage of the privileged classes, and that the provisioning institutions and the authorities were not trying to prevent such abuses, then people rebelled in search of justice as well as of food (Thompson 1971; Kaplan 1976; Guenzi 1979; 1995). We have many examples of such revolts during the main famines, as in 1590–93 (Alfani 2013a: 75) and 1648–49 (Guenzi 1979). Violence was not limited to the cities, however, as armed bands roamed the countryside looking for food, further worsening the situation of rural communities, where, during the most severe crises, the traditional ties of solidarity risked collapsing entirely (Alfani 2011; 2013a: 65–70). A more detailed analysis of the functioning and the development across Italy of the food-provisioning authorities during the sixteenth and early seventeenth centuries is provided elsewhere (Alfani 2013a: 70–5).

4   Explaining Famines: Demographic, Environmental, Agrarian and Institutional Factors

Earlier, we reconstructed a reliable famine chronology covering the whole period from about 1250 to the nineteenth century. Now the time has come to provide a synthetic, overall comment about the factors explaining the occurrence of famines – a question notoriously difficult to answer, not least considering how different episodes seem to call for different explanations. However, if we focus on the worst famines of the whole period – i.e. those that seemingly affected all or almost all of Italy, producing a significant increase in mortality – we find that most of them happened at times of high population pressure on the available resources. In Figure 2.3, the current estimates of the population in the Centre-North are represented (by and large, the trend for the whole of Italy would not differ much). As can be seen in the figure, twice during the period (in the early fourteenth century as well as in the late sixteenth/early seventeenth centuries) Italy's population rebounded from a level that corresponds to the maximum carrying capacity, which the peninsula had proved unable to overcome since Roman times (Alfani 2013c). Only during the seventeenth century, and for the first time in history, was that level (corresponding to about 14 to 15 million people in the whole of Italy: Lo Cascio and Malanima 2005) finally exceeded.

The main famines of the late thirteenth century and the fourteenth (1275–77, 1302–03, 1328–30, 1339–40 and 1346–47) happened in a period of acute pressure on the available resources. The same is true for the worst famine of the early modern period, in 1590–93, as well

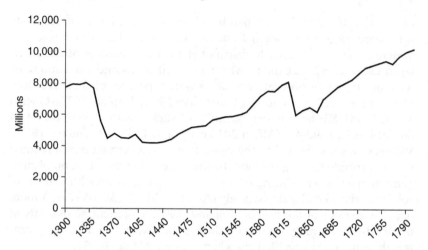

Figure 2.3 Italian population of the Centre-North, 1300–1800

Sources: Database kindly provided by Paolo Malanima, with small corrections around years 1630 and 1656–57 to take into account recent revisions of plague mortality in the seventeenth century (Alfani 2013b).

as for the 1618–22 and 1628–29 ones. Three other general famines occurred when the recovery from the great plagues of the seventeenth century (in 1630 in the Centre-North, minus Liguria; in 1656–57 in the Centre-South, plus Liguria) was completed or on its way to completion: 1678–79, 1693–95 and 1708–09. High pressure on food resources is not sufficient per se to explain the occurrence of a famine, however. No matter how fragile an equilibrium is, something is needed to break it. As a rule in the aforementioned cases, the crisis was triggered by crop failures – usually, back-to-back failures covering two years or more – caused by bad weather, particularly of the kind unfavourable to wheat. For the northern European famines of the early fourteenth century (though the argument can be generalised to the southern European ones), it has been suggested that several episodes of intense cold, as well as incessant rain in the spring, have to be associated with changes in the trend of average temperatures: from cooling to warming (Campbell 2010a; 2010b). Something similar has been suggested for the late sixteenth century and early seventeenth, when the so-called Little Ice Age reached its bottom level (Alfani 2010). It should be underlined that the key factor here was not so much exceptionally low temperatures (as wheat can survive intense cold fairly well) but heavy rain during the spring: exactly the kind of climatic instability that in Italy is empirically associated with an inversion of the temperature trend, from cooling to warming or vice versa (Camuffo and Enzi 1992). This was surely the case, for example, with the great 1590–93 famine (Alfani 2011; 2013a: 56–7). It seems, however, that from the second half of the seventeenth century, when a phase of global warming started, another kind of meteorological anomaly – drought – was ever more frequently reported as the 'cause' of food shortages or famines. This would be particularly the case from the mid-eighteenth century onwards (Alfani 2010: 40–1). Another aspect worth mentioning is that the worst plagues of the whole period, the Black Death of 1347–49 and the 1629–30 epidemic, also seem to have occurred in periods of climatic instability. Concerning the Black Death, Campbell (2010a) suggests that climatic instability may have favoured the spread of the disease (as well as of the panzootic that occurred some decades earlier). If this is the case, possibly malnutrition did not contribute significantly to the spread of the plague – a causative link that is in fact contentious (Alfani 2013a: 45–6) – but bad weather 'caused' both famine and plague, so that we would have an additional reason to consider the periods 1346–49 and 1628–31 as marked by long crises, whose characteristics and nature changed during the crisis itself but are referable as a whole to specific causative factors. This is a complex issue, though, which would be worthy of further research.

Apart from the connections between famine and plague, those between famine and war are also worthy of being mentioned. In fact, the two major famines of the first half of the sixteenth century, in 1502–05 and 1527–29, seem to be closely connected to the Italian Wars, when French, Spanish and Imperial troops, in varying alliances with the Italian states, fought for pre-eminence over the peninsula. As a matter of fact, during this exceptionally long conflict the vicissitudes of war weld together many different episodes: general famines, as in the aforementioned periods; local food crises; and simple situations of dearth. Plague and other infectious diseases further complicate the picture (Alfani 2013a: 56–7). What should be stressed here is the ability of human actions both to 'create' famines locally, as in the case of sieges, even in normal years (though, in the medieval and early modern periods, this ability was exerted upon limited areas only) and, more importantly, to worsen the conditions for the production and distribution of food in years of suboptimal crops, allowing a shortage that could have been manageable in other circumstances to develop into a full famine. For example, the food crisis that occurred in Milan in the years 1799–1801, when wheat prices reached their highest value for the period 1700–1860, was due mainly to grain requisitions in order to feed the French army (Mocarelli 2012).

This point is obviously connected to the role played by food-provisioning institutions such as the *annone*, which we briefly described in

Section 3. In the late medieval and early modern periods it has been suggested that famines were not simply crop failures but have to be understood also as institutional failures, given that those who were charged with keeping the population (or the urban dwellers at least) sufficiently provisioned failed their objective. Obviously, this issue relates to the general debate about whether public or private institutions were better suited to ensuring adequate provisioning. In addition, in the Italian case, advocates of inefficient distribution – possibly exacerbated by the misguided activities of the *annone* – as the main cause of pre-industrial famines are not lacking (Palermo 1990; Epstein 2001), though those underlying production problems and providing a more positive interpretation of the work of the food-provisioning authorities seem to be prevalent. What is more, a detailed recent analysis of the main early modern famines (Alfani 2015) has made the point that, in the worst instances, and particularly during crises covering vast territories and having a marked 'supranational' character, private actors or 'market forces' had neither the strength nor the incentives to provide solutions to the problem. In 1590–93, for example, the Republic of Genoa managed to be the first Italian state to re-establish a situation of acceptable provisioning (even reaping a nice profit from reselling foodstuffs to other states), but it could do so only thanks to the intervention of the highest ruling body (the senate) side by side with the *Magistrato dell'Abbondanza*, the local food-provisioning authority. These public institutions provided the financial means, the diplomatic and political clout and even the ships to open entirely new trade routes to import grain from the Baltic – and, in doing so, contributed to changing for good the structure of grain commerce in the wider European area (Alfani 2015). The relative successes of the Italian food-provisioning authorities in the sixteenth century should not hide the fact, however, that, in general, the literature seems to be quite less favourable to the actions of the *annone* in the eighteenth century (Reinhardt 1991; Strangio 1999).

Of all the main famines we have identified, only the 1648–49 and 1764–67 ones have not been already mentioned and need some additional comment. For 1648–49, we know from Del Panta and Livi Bacci (1977) that famine mortality was further increased by widespread epidemics of typhus, which is a typically famine-related disease. Regarding 1764–67, we know that drought affected the Italian countryside for several years in succession (Finzi 1986: 356). If we consider that, in this period, population density in the Italian Peninsula was steadily increasing to unprecedented levels, we might imagine that population pressure was again playing an important role. However, for the eighteenth century, the occurrence of (relatively mild, in our long-run perspective) famines is less interesting than the fact that the ancient maximum carrying capacity had been exceeded, and that, as will be remembered from Section 2, north-eastern Italy seems to be the front-runner of improved food security. It is probable, in fact, that both processes have the same cause: the spread of maize, whose key importance in allowing Italy to escape the 'Malthusian' barrier that had constrained it for so long has recently been underlined (Alfani 2010; 2013c). More generally, maize seems to have contributed very significantly to improving Italian food security, not only because it led to a substantial increase in calories per hectare but also because it prospered in meteorological conditions adverse to wheat, so that Italian farmers, especially in the Centre-North, started to cultivate this new crop imported from the Americas as a kind of insurance against the failure of wheat (Finzi 2009). This process had been under way since the early seventeenth century (even earlier in some areas: Alfani 2012), and can be described as a 'Boserupian'[1] process of agrarian innovation put in place by a population feeling a growing pressure on the resources available (Alfani 2007; 2013a; 2013c). In north-eastern Italy (Veneto) the spread of maize was particularly intense, a fact that is usually considered a sign of the progressive decline into relative poverty and underdevelopment of the area, also due to the spread of the pellagra disease, a form of severe avitaminosis that can result from a diet excessively reliant upon maize. (Something similar happened in the State of Milan, where maize production more than doubled in the second half of the eighteenth century and where the first complaints about the presence of pellagra date to the first half of the same century: Mocarelli [2015: 42–45].) Apparently, pellagra was the price that Veneto had to pay for the exceptionally good food security it acquired during the eighteenth century. This is a paradoxical conclusion, which allows us to stress one last time the complexity of events such as famines, whose boundaries are never as clear-cut as first imagined, and whose causes and implications can be deeply different from one instance to another – though, for exactly the same reasons, these dramatic events represent one of the most fascinating topics for historical research.

---

[1] According to Boserup (1965; 1981), demographic pressure itself promotes technological micro-innovations to traditional practices in agriculture and permits a slow increase in total population by starting a chain reaction.

3   Spain

Vicente Pérez Moreda

The Spanish literature on agrarian crises, famines and starvation is plentiful and has a long history. It has made great strides in recent decades in the study of mortality crises of the modern period – from the sixteenth to the nineteenth centuries – and especially in the analysis of the link between dearths or famines and short-term fluctuations in the price of cereals at the local, provincial and regional level. The coverage of these works is quite uneven, however, in terms of chronology (with some periods, especially the eighteenth and early nineteenth centuries, better studied than others) and space (since the great environmental and economic diversity of Spanish regions, the peculiar historical evolution and uneven nature of the documentary sources in many of them and the autonomous functioning of markets require that they be studied separately). Thus, the information available for an attempt to provide a general summary for the whole of Spain is diverse and unbalanced. In this chapter I will review what the classical literature and recent regional research have to tell us. I first summarise the scope of the major food and mortality crises on the mainland in the late medieval period (c. 1300 to 1500), then discuss, in more detail, famines in early modern and modern times (from the sixteenth to the mid-nineteenth centuries).

1   Late Medieval Period (1300–1500)

Reliable information – descriptive, rarely quantitative and very basic – on years of scarcity begins to become available from the late thirteenth century. It is most abundant, or at least better known, for the northern part of the Iberian Peninsula. There is little detailed information on famines or food crises in the kingdom of Navarre before 1300, though 1260 and 1283–84 are listed as crisis years (Berthe 1984: 199–206).

I sincerely thank the editors, Cormac Ó Gráda and Guido Alfani, as well as Rafael Dobado-Muñiz for their help in translating this chapter. The financial support provided by the research projects CSO2011-29970 and HAR2012-33810 must also be acknowledged.

More detailed sources for the first half of the fourteenth century highlight shortages in 1313 ('very serious' in the jurisdiction of Sangüesa and severe in Pamplona), 1314–15, 1328, 1333 (a very bad year in many parts of the peninsula) and 1337 (Berthe 1984: 206–20; 1991: 32–4). Shortly afterwards, the famine of 1347, recorded with the same horror as the plague epidemic that followed it, marked the beginning of a notorious period of *fambre et grant mortaldat*. The neighbouring kingdom of Aragon, like Navarre, endured a food crisis in 1283–85, though it did not match the severity of the famines of the fourteenth century. Among the latter, that of 1313–14 ('dear' and hard years), which was also shared by Navarre and Valencia (drought and *sterilitas* affected both kingdoms), and the truly catastrophic 1333–35 period are highlighted (Rubio Vela 1982; Laliena Corbera 2011: 286–92). In Aragon the last recurrence of famine in the first half of the fourteenth century also seems to have coincided with the arrival of the Black Death in 1347–48 (Laliena Corbera 2011: 295).

The chronology of epidemics and famines in Catalonia in the last two centuries of the Middle Ages is well established. During the fourteenth century there were grain shortages of varying severity in 1300–04, 1309–11, 1315–17, 1322–27, 1333–36, 1339–41, 1346–48, 1374–76 and 1382–85. In addition, there were milder and more local crises in 1400, 1406 and 1426–29; then, 'from 1462 on shortages and famines reappeared, though more as a consequence of the Catalan Civil War than adverse weather shocks' (Riera Melis 2009: 256, 267, my translation).

The early years of the fourteenth century were difficult not only in Catalonia. Judging by the Chronicle of Fernando IV, 1301 was also a dramatic year in the territories of Castile, and perhaps more generally, since it was claimed, albeit with undoubted exaggeration, that 'starvation killed a quarter of mankind' (Valdeón 1984: 1052, my translation). Regarding 1302, Villalba says that 'at this time' Spain suffered a massive harvest shortfall because of a drought 'and there was much hunger and death' (Villalba 1803: I, 38, my translation).

Between 1309 and 1311 adverse weather struck Catalonia, Castile and various parts of central and western Mediterranean again. However, this did not result in food crises of the severity recorded soon afterwards in Catalonia or the neighbouring kingdoms of Aragon, Navarre and other peninsular territories, such as Castile and Valencia. The first general famine of the fourteenth century was that of 1315–17, on the heels of famines in Aragon, Navarre, Castile and areas of northern France in the immediately preceding years (Valdeón 1969: 13; Laliena Corbera 2011: 289). The famine of 1333 to 1336/7 was also general, and certainly the first of the great famines of the century in the peninsula; it was preceded by difficulties in the supply of wheat in northern Castile between 1331 and 1333 (Valdeón 1984: 1051) and by rising prices in 1332. In Catalonia 1333 became known as 'the first bad year' (Rubio Vela 1982). From 1346 on another cycle of agricultural difficulties, exacerbated by poor harvests and famine in 1347, also extended to many areas of Spanish territory and forced wheat imports up to the spring of 1348, which raises the possibility that the transmission of the Black Death to the peninsula was facilitated by the intensification of maritime traffic. The severe drought and shortage of 1374, followed by another poor harvest in 1375, caused another severe famine, comparable in intensity to that of 1333, and leading in Catalonia to talk of the *any de la fam*. Thereafter the food problems facing the principality grew milder and less frequent, or better managed, but they were still present in the early fifteenth century or as a factor during the Rebellion of the Remensas, which began in Catalonia in 1462 (Riera Melis 2009: 257–66).

In the Kingdom of Valencia, as in the whole peninsula during the fourteenth century, the worst famines coincided with three that were also recorded as severe in territories already mentioned: 1333, which was 'the first evil year' in Catalonia; 1347, known in Valencia as 'the year of the great famine', was also mentioned in other regions, such as Navarre, and, more generally, was considered the immediate antecedent of the great epidemic of the following years (Valdeón 1984: 1052; Ladero Quesada 2014: 47–8); and 1374, cited by contemporaries in the Valencian country as the year of the second great famine: '*En l'any MCCCLXXIIII fonch l'any de la segona fam, la qual fonch general quasi per tot lo món*' ('The year MCCCLXXIIII was the year of the second famine, which was of general, almost worldwide scope') (Furió Diego 2010: 42–3; 2011, my translation). Finally, the dates listed for Andalusia in Table 3.1 correspond rather well to Seville and its hinterland, which is representative of the situation in the region, as brought together in the work of Collantes de Terán (1977: 431–40). The dates referring in this table to conditions in Spain as a whole are at least documented for the territories of the Crown of Castile. They are cited as general famines in Villalba's work, and, indeed, all coincide with the great crises of this nature affecting other regions of the peninsula around the same time.

2   Early Modern Times (c. 1500–1800)

The transition from the fifteenth century to the sixteenth corresponds to the reign of the Catholic Monarchs (1474–1516). The chronology of epidemics, dearths and famines occurring in that period is fairly well known, thanks to the detailed narrative made possible by chroniclers (Gómez

Table 3.1 *Years of shortage and mortality in late medieval Spain*

Navarre	Aragon	Catalonia	Valencia	Andalusia	Castile	Spain
1260					**1255–62**	
1283–84	1283–85					
		1300–04			**1299–1301**	**1301–02**
		1309–11		1311		
1313–15	**1313–14**	**1315–17**				1314–17
1328		1322–27				
1333–37	**1333–35**	**1333–36**	**1333**		**1331–34**	**1333**
		1339–41		1343		
1347	**1347–48**	**1346–48**	**1347–48**		**1344–48**	**1347–48**
		1374–76	1374	1374–75		1374
		1382–85				
		1400				
		1406		1413		
		1426–29		1435		
				1462		

Notes: The main events are in bold.
Sources: Berthe (1984) and Laliena Corbera (2011) for Navarre; Laliena Corbera (2011) for Aragon; Riera Melis (2009) for Catalonia; Collantes de Terán (1977) for Andalusia (Seville); Valdeón (1984) and Reglero (2011) for Castile; Villalba (1803), Furió Diego (2010; 2011) and Valdeón (1984) for Valencia and Spain.

Mampaso 1975), a reconstructed series of annual prices (Hamilton 1934) and the food supply policies that have been analysed by modern historians (Ibarra Rodríguez 1944). The reign began with drought, crop failures and famine in northern Castile (Tierra de Campos) and the southern plateau (New Castile, Murcia, Andalusia) in 1475–77, which spread to Extremadura and Andalusia in 1478. In 1479 there were reports of 'excessive rainfall' and wheat shortages in Castile. The next decade was also marked by heavy rainfalls, causing severe flooding in Castile and Andalusia in late 1485, with the destruction of livestock, silos, dams and mills, and resultant increases in the cost of wheat and flour (Villalba 1803: I, 66). Again, between October 1488 and March 1489 torrential rains caused crop losses and a severe famine in the south of Castile and Aragon.

The real famine period dates from 1502, however, and lasted until the great plague year of 1507. In 1502 famine led to the imposition of price control on wheat, and the following year, 1503, on flour. Excessive rains caused crop failures again in 1504–05, and the following two years, 1506 and 1507, were characterised by prolonged drought (*'las secas de*

los años DVI e DVII: Gómez Moreno and de Mata Carriazo 1962: 484).
Hamilton's series suggests that the price of wheat in New Castile rose
by 96 per cent above the already high average of the previous five years
(Vilar 1969: 87). The description of the famine of 1506 left by one of the
great chroniclers of the time, the parish priest of Los Palacios (Seville),
Andrés Bernáldez, is famous:

> There was a gigantic famine all this year…in all these provinces and many others
> in Castile; the countryside and the villages were emptied of people, and leaving
> behind their homes men and women went from one place to the next, with their
> children on their shoulders, by road, in search of bread, and holding other chil-
> dren by the hand, starving, asking help from those who had some for God's sake,
> which was very painful to see. And many died of starvation…
>   (Gómez Moreno and de Mata Carriazo 1962: 516 ff., my translation)

Price controls were abolished in October 1506, blamed for being one of
the reasons for scarcity, the withdrawal of stocks, the abandonment of
cultivation and the lack of cereal imports '*por el baxo prescio*' (due to low
prices) and the impossibility of selling bread at market prices. Imports
of wheat from abroad followed (from Flanders, Brittany, north Africa,
Sicily and Greece), and prices fell – but very soon, in early 1507, plague
also arrived. In these two years, according to Alonso de Santa Cruz
(1927 [1552]), 'half the population of Spain perished from famine and
pestilence', while the curate of Los Palacios says that 'in most communities, cities and towns, on average half died, in some places more, and in
others those who died outnumbered those who remained by two to one'
(Gómez Moreno and de Mata Carriazo 1962: 518; Gómez Mampaso
1975: 637, my translation).

During the rest of the sixteenth century reports of famine extending across the peninsula were uncommon. Villalba – whose famous
work consists of a chronicle, incomplete but still quite detailed, of the
epidemics endured by the Iberian Peninsula up to 1800, sometimes
including concrete references to the worst years of hunger and famine –
cites few for the sixteenth century: he mentions only 'the great hunger
which [Seville] endured' in 1508, as a result of a plague of locusts –
and undoubtedly the final effect of the grave crisis of preceding years
and particularly the plague of 1507 (Villalba 1803: I, 81; Collantes de
Terán 1977: 439); the high price of wheat and the hunger that 'the poor
people' endured in the kingdom of Aragon in 1533 (Villalba 1803: I,
91); and 'the great shortage of bread due to the poor harvest of August
1598', which struck the city of Segovia the following year, at the height
of the great end-of-century plague (Villalba 1803: I, 128). There is mention too of the first known outbreak of typhus – the 'spotted fever' – in

Spain in 1557 (Villalba 1803: I, 99), coinciding with the dearth mentioned for several parts of the interior at this time. In this same year the Segovian chronicler Diego de Colmenares locates 'universal hunger in the whole of Spain', due to a rainy winter 'which drowned the fruit and crops' of 1557 (Colmenares 1969 [1637]: II, 247–8; Pérez Moreda 1980: 250–1). One might also mention the successive subsistence crises endured by some regions, such as Andalusia in 1521–22 (Collantes de Terán 1977: 440; Carmona 2000: 243), and more generally, in addition to the dearth linked to deaths from typhus in 1557 and following years, that of the early 1590s, between 1591 and 1595; little known or studied, it affected several parts of the Castilian interior, and undoubtedly also Andalusia and other regions, to judge from Hamilton's price data (Pérez Moreda 1980: 254–6; 1998). In the city of Barcelona, moreover, 1503, 1584 and 1592 were also years of dearth – coinciding on some of these dates with scarcities elsewhere in Spain – but without significant repercussions on mortality, and only those of 1528 and 1530 can be declared genuine famines with clear impacts on mortality (Betrán 1996: 101–3).

The sixteenth century ended with the extremely serious plague outbreak of 1596–99, which lasted in some areas till 1602 and which several witnesses, such as the above-cited Colmenares and Villalba, linked to a subsistence crisis and genuine famine that coincided with or preceded the epidemic; several contemporaries and some historians today support this interpretation. However, other scholars argue that the famine may have followed the plague due to the social and economic paralysis this latter occasioned (Pérez Moreda 1980: 266–81; 2010b; Lázaro Ruiz and Gurría García, 1989: 40, 55; Lázaro Ruiz, 1994: 54–7). From the beginning of the seventeenth century on we have good continuous series of local burials (of all burials or, in the worst of cases, those of adults, excluding children – *párvulos*), which permits the more precise construction of a chronology of major mortality crises, based on statistical methods similar to those employed by Del Panta and Livi Bacci (1977).[1]

In Table 3.2 I include, in addition to references by other authors to years of excess mortality and famine in the sixteenth century (the 'expert method'), crisis years of overall mortality detected in a sample of some 60 small towns in the Spanish interior (Castile, Aragon and Extremadura) between 1600 and 1855. The dates and periods of the greatest mortality crises are indicated in the first column and the three most intense in every century are highlighted in bold. The second column contains the

[1] An 11-term moving average centred on the year under consideration was used, excluding the two lower and the two higher terms as well as the central year. This specific method has been developed in the context of a broader research project on mortality in Spain hosted by the Universidad Complutense, Madrid.

Table 3.2 *General mortality crises and great famines in Spain, 1500–1855**

Mortality crises, inland Spain**	Famine mortality, mainland Spain**
1506–07	1506–07
1521–22 (Andalusia)	
1557	1557 (with typhus)
1591–95	1591–95
1599–1600	
1605–07	
1615–16	
1631	1630–31
1647–52	1647–52
1659–62	1659–62
1684	1678–85
1694–99	1694–95, 1699
1706–10	1709–11
1730	
1741–42	1741–42
1748–49	1748–49
1762–65	1763–65
1780–82	
1786–87	
1798–99	1798–99
1803–04	1803–04
1809	
1812	1812
1834	
1855	

Notes: * In the first column the three most intense mortality crises in each century are high-lighted in bold. ** Here 'inland' refers to the Spanish interior whereas 'mainland' refers to peninsular Spain without the islands.
Sources: Pérez Moreda (1980: 109, 117), Villalba (1803) and this chapter.

dates of excess mortality that can be attributed to shortage and hunger – i.e. general famines in Spanish history – that were detected in this sample of inland Spain but can also be extended across the entire Spanish peninsular territory. There are five in the seventeenth century and the same number in the eighteenth.

After the catastrophe at the end of the sixteenth century the next major famine was that of 1630–31, which the evidence of high prices and a poor harvest in 1630, as well as tithe data, reveal to have been a serious crisis in the central territories and other regions. However, this had nothing to do with the Italian and Catalonian plague (Pérez Moreda 1980:

298–300, 309–10). The same applies to the period from 1647 to 1652, years of the last great plague outbreak in the Spanish Mediterranean (Catalonia, Valencia, Andalusia), but of the worst grain harvests and the highest grain prices of the century in the interior of the peninsula and in Andalusia. Adverse weather conditions and crop losses were at the origin of the next food crisis, that of 1659–62 – years in which there is no news whatsoever of epidemics of any kind (Pérez Moreda 1980: 302–3, 310–11). And, although a number of diseases with epidemic potential (most likely typhus, but possibly the plague, in some regions of the Mediterranean coast) punished the Spanish population in the years leading up to the serious crisis of 1684, agrarian problems were again the root cause of that crisis, linked to difficulties that appeared as early as 1678 taking on a dramatic character by 1684, with people reduced to consuming 'barley, grass and acorns, as if they were animals', and recorded deaths from starvation (Domínguez Ortiz 1969: 202–3). The last food crisis of the seventeenth century may be decomposed into two phases: that of 1694–95, which saw poor harvests and probably typhus in the interior of the peninsula and in Catalonia (Nadal i Oller and Giralt 1960: 44); and that of 1699, another typical famine that caused the prices of bread and oil to rise, and led the people of Madrid to riot in late April 1699. This was one of the first such riots to be recorded in the kingdom's capital, and it had replicas of less political significance in cities such as Valladolid and Medina del Campo (Egido López 1980; Gutiérrez Alonso 1989: 251–3). It is worth noting that this chronology of major subsistence crises, which refers mainly to the interior of the peninsula, is very similar to that for other regions such as Catalonia and Valencia. Apart from the coincidence of the Catalan crises in 1629–30 and 1694–95, in the case of Barcelona large famine-related mortality crises may be detected in 1614 and on all other seventeenth-century dates for which we observed food crises in the Castilian interior: 1651, 1660 and 1684 (Betrán 1996: 103). The chronology of major mortalities in the Valencia region from the seventeenth century to the nineteenth also tallies with the general outline for the peninsula (Bernat i Martí and Badenes Martín 1988: 547–8).

The eighteenth century began with the War of the Spanish Succession and, in the final stages of that war, the terrible crisis of 1709–11. This was a typical subsistence crisis in terms of origins and symptoms, and it was preceded by poor harvests between 1704 and the fateful year of 1709 (Anes 1970a: 155). The failure of successive harvests, uninterrupted rains in 1708 and in the spring of 1709, and the *grand hiver* of 1708–09 greatly increased prices and caused a dramatic situation in all Spanish regions, from Andalusia and Murcia in the south to Galicia, the Asturias and the Basque Country in the north, and embracing regions of cereal monoculture in the Castilian interior, such as Valladolid. Wheat prices rose by 86 per cent in New Castile in 1706, and again by 40 to 50 per cent between 1709 and 1711. The famous author who produced these data sums up the situation of those years perfectly:

> The upheaval was due largely to the occurrence in 1708–09 of one of the most frigid winters that Europe has ever experienced. The cold wave in December–January damaged vineyards, killed young animals, froze growing grain, and irreparably injured fruit and nut trees. The effects of the cold weather were extremely severe in Old Castile–Leon, the most northerly region included in this study. Both animals and crops suffered also in New Castile, but in semi-tropical Andalusia the abnormal cold proved even more devastating.
>
> (Hamilton 1969: 143, appendix 1, B)

These were, indeed, years of acute generalised poverty and 'terrible hunger in practically all of Spain': a plague of locusts in 1708 (Pérez Moreda 1980: 361), urban riots by the starving population of Santiago de Compostela in Galicia in 1709, eyewitness accounts in the same year of 'ten or twelve people dropping dead on the street every day from starvation' in Seville (Domínguez Ortiz 1976: 29–32, my translation), bread rationing in Valladolid and elsewhere in 1710. Moreover, the crisis was spread by war, which does not square with Kamen's thesis that it was exclusively meteorological and agricultural in origin, with significant epidemical outbreaks of which typhus was undoubtedly the most important (Kamen 1974: 393). Villalba describes 'an epidemic emerging out of war with the [new] century' and 'a malignant spotted disease [that was] the effect of wars, famine...that created such havoc throughout most of the kingdom of Spain between 1709 and 1711' (Villalba 1803: II, 93, 96–7, my translation).

The Spanish mortality crises of the 1740s were not among the gravest of the century, and only in some local or regional cases might they qualify as true food crises linked to famine and starvation. They are better seen as crises of a mixed character, notable for their link, particularly in 1741–42, with the severe weather that affected other regions of northwest Europe at the time (Dickson 1997; Post 1985; Engler et al. 2013; Ó Gráda in this book). Beginning in 1738–39 the medical literature of the period recorded news of a 'catarrhal epidemic' in various places in Andalusia, extending north to Extremadura and Aragon by 1747–48, in the form of a 'malignant catarrhal fever' or 'pleuritic-epidemial pain'. It is also said that the 'crop failures, poor fruit yields, famine, hunger and misery, led to the spread of epidemic diseases' (Villalba 1803: II, 120–8). In several provinces of the northern half of the country – Old Castile, Cantabria and Biscay – there were also steep increases in the wheat prices in 1740–42, resulting from poor crops in the region, as evidenced by the annual series of agricultural production (proxied by the ecclesiastical tithe on cereals) in the province of Segovia in 1740 and 1741. In Segovia and in Biscay in 1741, and in Burgos in 1741–42, famine was accompanied or followed by a significant excess adult mortality, and the same happened again in 1748–49 in the neighbouring provinces of Ávila, Zamora, Guadalajara and Palencia. Thus, the mortality crises of this decade arose mainly in the northern plateau, the same region where – along with the coastal northern provinces, Biscay and Cantabria – famine and excess mortality were more of a problem in 1741–42 and also, to a lesser extent and on the basis of weaker evidence, in 1748–49. It seems, therefore, that the crisis of the early 1740s probably originated, as elsewhere in western Europe, with a climatic shock that was particularly harsh, not surprisingly, in the northern regions of the country, with a resultant fall in output and sharp famine. These climatic and agricultural accidents favoured the development of pulmonary diseases affecting mainly the adult population, and spread across the peninsula during the remainder of the period, as during the minor mortality crisis of 1748–49, which was characterised by the same symptoms (Llopis Agelán, Pérez Moreda and Sebastián Amarilla 2015).

The next mortality crisis, that of 1763–65, was one of the most extensive and most serious of the century (similar to that of 1709–11), and clearly related to the successive agrarian crises beginning at the start of the decade, and to the scarcity of wheat and the main staple commodities – soap, olive oil and charcoal (Hamilton 1969: 155–9, and appendix I, C; Llopis Agelán et al. 2007). In fact, it was this famine that provoked riots that resonated in Madrid and other cities in the spring of 1766, on which there is a wide and well-known literature. The riots were a reaction not only to the high price of bread and of these other articles but also to the liberalisation of internal trade that had been enacted in July 1765 (Hamilton 1969: 193–5). Price controls on cereals, which had been established at the beginning of the first great famine of modern times – in 1502 – were abolished in imitation of French reforms in the previous two years under the physiocrat-influenced Turgot. However, as happened later in France, the price rises caused by recurrent crop failures were attributed not to meteorological accidents but to the actions of hoarders, who were benefiting from the new measures of commercial freedom. In April and May 1766, when the price of bread and other staples reached a peak, rioting against the Marquis de Esquilache, the king's favourite minister, broke out in Madrid, followed by popular uprisings in other provinces, comprising the most notable series of food riots of the final period of the Spanish *ancien régime* (Vilar 1972; Rodríguez 1973; Anes 1974).

After this major crisis agricultural prices began a climb, which lasted till the end of the eighteenth century, though with sharp fluctuations, and led to major crises in the late eighteenth and early nineteenth centuries. Neither monetary inflation nor the vagaries and indecisiveness in implementing a policy of trade liberalisation in cereals explain such price fluctuations, which were due instead to the succession of bad harvests aggravated by wars in the period extending from the last decade of the eighteenth century to 1814 (Anes 1970a: 221, 346). In this situation, food supplies also faced the growing demands of a population increasing at a continuous, though slow rate of around 0.43 per cent per year during the eighteenth century (Livi Bacci 1968: 90). In this period there were mortality crises in 1780–82, 1786–87 and 1798–99, but only the latter can be classified as a subsistence crisis. That of 1780–82 contained a high component of infant and child mortality (perhaps due to smallpox), while mortality in 1786–87 was mainly due to a severe malaria epidemic affecting much of the interior, especially New Castile (the southern sub-plateau). It is true that some parts of the country recorded subsistence-related mortality in 1780, and that the widespread and severe epidemic of 1785–87 that exacted the highest mortality toll in 1786 was accompanied by the abandonment of fields, rising prices and hunger, but this was more the effect than the cause of the significant morbidity due to malaria: up to 26 per cent of the entire population of the 12 most affected provinces, nearly 1 million in total, contracted malaria in that year (Pérez Moreda 1984; 2010b: 208). It is also worth remembering that soon afterwards, in 1789, many parts of the country recorded another serious shortage of wheat and a widespread subsistence crisis. However, although attention to needy populations presented serious problems for the authorities, and even led to unrest and riots in cities such as Madrid and Barcelona, it did not result in high mortality, and it may be said that the crisis 'was not exceptional' (Castells 1970; Anes 1970a: 431). Public action by the central government, administered by municipal authorities through granaries (see below) and the localities' own reserves (the *propios* or 'commons'), definitely helped to dampen the demographic impact of these famines, which were very serious indeed (Hamilton 1969: appendix I, C; Pérez Moreda 1985: 18; Llopis Alegán et al. 2007).

The mortality crisis of 1798 to 1799 qualifies as a famine as defined in this book. Again there was a major shortage in New Castile in those years, and in Old Castile in 1797–98. But scarcity and mortality then and during the entire final decade of the eighteenth century were more serious in the northern regions of the Basque Country, Navarre and

Catalonia, areas affected by the war against the French Convention since 1793. The channels through which famine spread and its particular intensity, which in these regions and in inland Spain was the most severe for several centuries, compel us to devote special attention to the period stretching from the late eighteenth century to the Napoleonic era (1800–14).

3   The Great Mortality Crises of the French Wars (1793–1814)

For the eighteenth and nineteenth centuries, parish registers of many Spanish regions provide enough data to define the scale of mortality as subsistence crisis or famine. Today a wide sample of annual series of locations in many provinces and regions is available, some of which span an even longer period, back to 1600 or at some point in the seventeenth century. But burial records in those early days are often irregular and discontinuous, and may not include all infant and child deaths – i.e. children aged under seven or 10 to 11 years, depending on the region. So the data shown in this section almost always relate to adult mortality from 1700 on.

The curves shown in the following figures describe the annual number of adult deaths (unless the contrary is noted) in each province/region (the map in Figure 3.1 shows the location of each). They are based on annual series of deaths from 410 localities, most of which (295) refer to provinces in the interior – i.e. the two Castiles. They cover New Castile (26 local series: Reher 1991), Burgos (68), Zamora (39), Palencia (23), Ávila (38), Segovia (22), Soria (21), Guadalajara (29), Ciudad Real (14) and Albacete (14).[2] I have added the number of adult deaths in the city of Madrid for the period 1750–1839 (Carbajo Isla 1987: 316–24), as well as that from a sample of 27 parishes in the province of La Rioja (Lázaro Ruiz and Gurría García 1989: 154). The rest (115) refer to the peripheral regions of Cantabria (20), the Basque Country (27 in Guipúzcoa and 12 in Biscay), Navarre (19), Valencia (24) and Catalonia (13), the latter collected by Nadal i Oller (1991) for 1780–1820 only. These provincial or regional series allow us to identify the major mortality crises and famines in many of these Spanish territories, and to prepare a new chronology of mortality crises for some of them that, in general, confirms that presented above. We must focus our attention, however,

---

[2] Most of these series have been recently collected by a team of researchers at the Universidad Complutense led by Enrique Llopis (see Grupo Complutense de Historia Económica Moderna 2013; Llopis and Abarca 2014; Llopis Agelán, Pérez Moreda and Sebastián Amarilla 2015).

Figure 3.1 Spanish provinces and regions mentioned in the text

on the late eighteenth and early nineteenth centuries, when, during the Revolutionary Wars and those of the Napoleonic era (1793–1814), Spain suffered the biggest mortality crises and famines in all its modern and contemporary history.

3.1   The Crises of the War against Revolutionary France (1793–95)

The first great mortality crises occurred during the years 1793–95 in regions bordering France – the Basque Country, Navarre and Catalonia – due to the War against the National Convention, which resulted in extreme scarcity and the spread of typhus transmitted by French troops from the end of 1793 (García-Sanz Marcotegui and Zabalza Cruchaga 1983; García-Sanz Marcotegui 1985: 355–63; Arizcun Cela 1988: 147–53; Nadal i Oller 1991). As may be seen from Figure 3.2, the worst year of all was 1794 in Catalonia and Navarre, and 1795 in Guipúzcoa and Biscay (Basque Country). Undoubtedly, the severity of these crises was exceeded in some of these provinces a few years later: marginally so in Biscay in 1812–13, and easily by the crisis of 1809 in Catalonia. In some regions

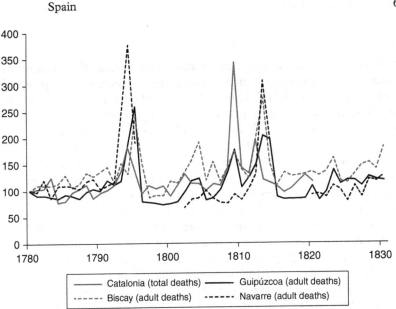

Figure 3.2 Mortality in Catalonia, the Basque Country (Guipúzcoa and Biscay) and Navarre, 1780–1830

Note: Index numbers (base: 1775–85 = 100).

of the north, namely the Basque Country and Navarre, the disasters of the Spanish War of Independence (the 'Peninsular War') – dearth, famine and extremely high mortality – extended to the final years of the conflict, 1813–14, which is when the final victory of the Anglo-Spanish forces led to the retreat of Napoleon (Arizcun Cela 1988: 154; Piquero 1991: 159; Fraser 2006: 745–7; Pérez Moreda 2010a: 313, 327). The demographic repercussions of these great mortalities of the late eighteenth and early nineteenth centuries were reflected in the 'missing' or decimated generations evident in the rest of the nineteenth century, as Nadal i Oller demonstrated some time ago for the Catalan case (Nadal i Oller 1991: 41–3).

Even without taking the high mortality recorded in those northern provinces bordering on France in 1793–95, the Napoleonic period as a whole (1800–14) witnessed an overall population loss of almost 1 million (800,000 is the low estimate) in Spain (Pérez Moreda 2010a: 308–11). Most of these losses occurred in the pre-war years: about 500,000 losses compared to a number between 215,000 and 375,000 for the war period from 1808 to 1814 (Fraser 2006: 758–9, 813–21). This high mortality, anticipating the sufferings of the War of Independence, occurred mainly during the grave crisis of 1803–05. This crisis deserves special attention.

3.2   The Great Mortality of 1804

Among the factors at play during this crisis period, the catastrophic series of successive crop failures in many areas of the country in the early nineteenth century is well known. From the beginning of the new century, harvests were poor in many areas, with particularly serious deficits in 1800–01, 1803–04 and 1811–12. Wheat prices, rising continuously from early 1802 on, rose sharply in 1803–04 in the two Castiles, León and Extremadura, and also at this date or in the following year, 1804–05, in Andalusia; but data from various Catalan or Galician towns reveal that coastal areas escaped this crisis (Anes 1970a: 432; a detailed description of the problems caused by climate accidents, crops failures and rising prices in 1804 in various regions of the country is given on pp. 402–22).

As might be expected in such disastrous agricultural conditions, social protests against high prices and against the export of grain destined to supply the needs of Madrid were not long in coming. These included the riot organised by women from the outskirts of Segovia in March 1802, others in Madrid, Toledo and La Mancha in following years and disturbances at several points of sale in Madrid itself (Espadas Burgos 1968: 601; García-Sanz 1977: 188–9). These were popular riots similar to the *entraves* linked to the French flour wars of pre-revolutionary France (Tilly 1972; 1985: 142; Bouton 1993: 213–49).

The demographic effects of the crisis became apparent during 1804 in large areas of the peninsula, as the famine reached catastrophic proportions and a series of plagues and epidemics of various kinds raised mortality rates to levels not seen for a long time. From 1803 an epidemic of malaria, similar to the one that had struck the Mediterranean region and New Castile and Andalusia some 20 years previously, spread to many regions (Pérez Moreda 1984: 336–9). This time the malaria epidemic was more widespread, triggering alarms even in regions of the northern plateau. In 1803 Almagro, Ciudad Real and 54 other communities in the archdiocese of Toledo were affected, and they continued to suffer in 1804, just as did Guadalajara and Cuenca. The disease then affected many areas of Old Castile, reaching the extreme north of the region, the provinces of Palencia, Burgos and León, La Rioja and even Asturias. All these northern regions of Castile and the Cantabrian coast, from where most of the provincial series of adult mortality in Figure 3.3 are derived, were so affected by the epidemic that it was stated that 'all of Castile is being depopulated'. Malaria was accompanied in the summer and autumn of 1804 by dysentery or typhoid in the interior, while yellow fever returned to punish urban populations in Andalusia – Seville, Cadiz, Jerez and the south-east – as it would again in some of these populations,

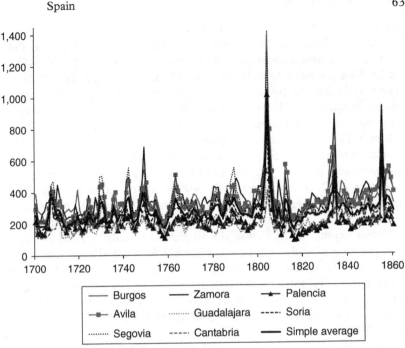

Figure 3.3 Annual mortality (adult deaths) in eight North-Castile provinces, 1700–1860

such as Cadiz, in 1810 and 1813 (Pérez Serrano 1992: 301, 432–3). The true roots of the demographic crisis were complex, with contemporaries pointing to 'bad food and poor harvests of wheat and other grains' as among its causes, and, with the high degree of absenteeism caused by the same epidemic, it was common to see 'abandoned crops in the fields, with no manpower left to reap them' (Pérez Moreda 1980: 382–3). An additional cause of this crisis that has not been sufficiently disclosed – a new invasion of locusts – was probably induced by the meteorological mishaps of those years. These were already detected around 1799 near Madrid, and spread thereafter to many places, causing most damage in 1803 and 1804 in many parts of central Spain, with serious economic damage to the peasantry of the region (Blanco García 1987: 67–74).

The crisis of 1803–05 resulted in appalling mortality rates in many parts of Spain, higher than in any previous or subsequent periods (the last two mortality crises seen in Figure 3.3 are due to cholera epidemics in 1834 and 1855, respectively). Some 11 per cent of the population of the city of Cuenca and of several villages in the province perished in 1803–04, and 13 per cent of a significant rural sample in Segovia in 1804

(García-Sanz 1977: 88; Reher 1980: 176). Rates similar to the latter are found for a large sample of localities in the provinces of the northern half of the peninsula represented in Figure 3.3, and also in 27 localities of La Rioja, a neighbouring province (Lázaro Ruiz and Gurría García 1989: 193). But the Bishop of León, another province of northern Spain, stated in August 1804 that his diocese in the previous three years had lost 'a third of the population, and some villages have been deserted' (Pérez Moreda 1980: 390). The demographic impact of the crisis was similar, if not even more dramatic, in the major urban centres. In Madrid, despite the measures taken to mitigate the effects of the famine – bread made of potatoes, the 'economic soups' devised in central Europe by the eccentric Count Rumford (Benjamin Thompson) and health checks on the fraudulent sale of certain herbs 'harmful to public health' – the number of adult deaths (11,307) was almost three times the annual average of the previous decade (see below, Figure 3.8). In addition, the number of inmates in asylums and hospitals catering for the indigent and marginal population from the hinterland or villages nearby reached unprecedented levels, surpassed in some cases only by the crisis of 1812, which was even harsher on the population of Madrid (Demerson 1969; Carbajo Isla 1987: 370).

The causes of the crisis of 1803–05 were similar to those of all the major famines of earlier times: severe weather and back-to-back harvest shortfalls in 1800–01, 1801–02 and 1803–04, serious shortages and rising grain prices in other countries making imports difficult and more expensive, and war with Britain, which hindered maritime traffic in the Atlantic. The crisis was complicated and seriously aggravated by infestations of locusts, malaria epidemics in the central and northern half of the interior and yellow fever in the south, and probably typhus and dysentery in other regions. Such a combination of factors helps explain the severity and high mortality of the famine of 1804. But other social and political factors and the incompetent management of urban food supplies – all man-made factors – also played a role in the exceptional gravity of this crisis. Warehouses and rural grain stores (the *pósitos*), which had operated in previous centuries as a system for regulating the supply of cereals and protecting the peasantry against the risks of price fluctuations, had just been dismantled by the Royal Treasury's disastrous policy of confiscating their funds a few years earlier.[3] On the other hand, the domestic market

---

[3] The *pósitos* were municipal grain depots that functioned as rural credit banks for the peasantry. They accumulated stocks of cereal bought at low prices in good times, and lent grain (at an interest rate of about 4.2 per cent) to be sown by the farmers, or for their livelihood in hunger years (at a lower rate of 3 per cent). In the second half of the eighteenth century the total number of *pósitos* exceeded 8,000, located throughout Spain,

was strangled by the reaction of the peasantry and local authorities, who refused in multiple locations during 1802–04 to lend their means of transport to haul crops destined especially for Madrid. These popular uprisings (responding to the classical typology of *entraves*) isolated urban and rural populations and further contributed to exorbitant increases in the price of wheat and other cereals (see Figures 3.4 and 3.5). The similar – indeed, almost identical – trajectory of prices in various points of the same region – Old Castile – should not be interpreted as evidence of market integration but as evidence that all were affected by the same shortages. It is likewise when we look at the evolution of wheat prices in different markets in southern Castile (New Castile) – Toledo, Talavera, Ocaña and Madrid – in the same 1800–06 period (Fernández Hidalgo and García Ruipérez 1989: 248–351). Moreover, there was a significant increase in avoidance of the tithe, implying an even sharper decline in marketable surpluses.

Given the magnitude of the crisis, the authorities tried to alleviate it with a battery of measures, some traditional, and effective in the short term, some more innovative or entirely novel, but that proved only palliative. Among the former, the policy of free trade in cereals was abandoned and price controls reintroduced, first in the Madrid region in September 1803, and later, in May 1804, on a more flexible basis at provincial level; attempts were made at importing food from abroad after a close-to-normal harvest in neighbouring countries in 1804; and some bishops and institutions, such as the Sociedades Económicas de Amigos del País (Patriots' Economic Societies), sought to encourage ecclesiastical or private charity in various ways. Among the new measures to fight the crisis, the rent that tenants owed landowners was lowered at the end of 1803

---

though there were few of them in the coastal Mediterranean or Cantabrian provinces, where imports of cereals were used to mitigate the risk of famine in bad crop years. In 1773 the country's 8,090 *pósitos* kept reserves of 7.3 million *fanegas* of wheat and flour and more than 43 million *reales* in cash funds, all of which amounted to about 54.2 *reales* per capita; that is the equivalent of somewhat more than one *fanega*, enough to enable a man to eat almost a kilogram of bread daily for more than two months. The wars and the financial collapse of the Treasury at the end of the century placed this institution, so important for the maintenance of the agriculture and the defence of the peasants against the sharp fluctuations in harvests and grain prices, under severe pressure. The *pósitos* were harassed, between 1798 and 1801 and in the following years, with extra taxes and forced loans to the Royal Exchequer (14 million reales in 1798, a further 48 million – equivalent to 20 per cent of their funds both in cereals and cash – in 1799, another 'temporary subsidy' in 1800, etc.), which were never repaid. At the same time the interest rate of the loans to the peasants rose by one percentage point (to 5.2 and 4 per cent). Thus, at the beginning of the nineteenth century, on the eve of the great famines of those years, the *pósitos* were unable to fulfil their function of relief and 'self-defence of the commoners', because their funds had been greatly diminished due to the demands of the state and the inability of many farmers to repay the grains and money previously borrowed (Anes 1968; 1970c: 71–94).

Figure 3.4 Wheat prices (reales/*fanega*) in five North-Castile grain markets, 1799/1800–1805/06

by between a fifth and a third; and municipalities were allowed to retain 20 per cent of the tithe in order to secure consumption and seed for the succeeding harvest. Also around that time local boards of health were ordered to fight malaria by cleaning up lagoons and backwaters, and to introduce new public health measures such as constructing new cemeteries. And, as a means of mitigating the effects of agricultural unemployment and reducing vagrancy and migration, an ambitious public works programme encompassing road repairs, the construction or arrangement of bridges and fountains, the paving of streets (to give employment to the destitute) and the rebuilding of town halls was implemented. This was managed and financed by municipalities through the ploughing, lease or sale of forests and communal lands. This entailed an expansionary or counter-cyclical fiscal policy that would apply in other European countries from 1816 to 1817 and in Sweden in the 1820s and 1830s (Llopis Agelán and Sánchez Salazar 2014).

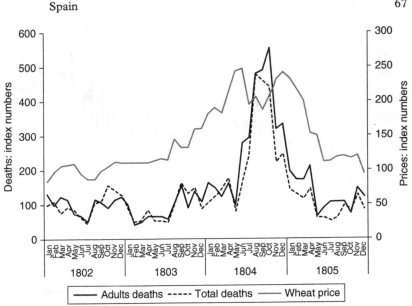

Figure 3.5 Monthly movement of wheat prices and mortality in Segovia, 1802–05

Note: Index numbers (base: average January–December 1802 = 100).

3.3 War, Famine and Mortality during the Spanish War of Independence (1808–14)

We have already seen that 1809 brought the major crisis of the War of Independence (the 'Peninsular War') in Catalonia. Some other provinces of the Mediterranean littoral, such as Valencia and Castellón, were also affected by the military crises of the final years of the war: it can be seen from Figure 3.6 that the highest mortality was recorded, as in Catalonia, in 1809, but note also the mortality, at a slightly lower level, in 1812–13 (Bernat i Martí and Badenes Martín 1988: 555–6; Fraser 2006: 715; Pérez Moreda, 2010a: 313–14).

In New Castile, south of Madrid, the main crisis of these years was in 1803–05, but in some other provinces of this region, such as Ciudad Real and Albacete, the mortality was higher in 1809 (Figure 3.7).

As noted above, 1812 was the last major crisis of the Napoleonic period, as the war spread its disasters to the northern regions, and even more intensely in 1813–14 to the border provinces of Guipúzcoa and Navarre (see above, Figure 3.2). In some other regions of the peninsula, too, 1812 was the worst of the war years. The harvest of 1811 was again very poor,

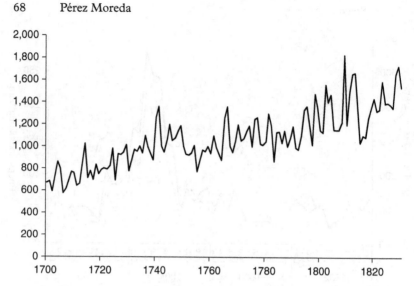

Figure 3.6 Annual mortality (total deaths) in Valencia region, 1700–1830

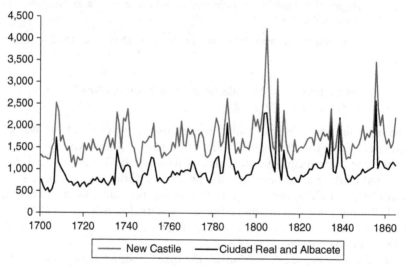

Figure 3.7 Annual deaths in New Castile, 1700–1865

but other factors directly related to war – labour absenteeism, the conceal-
ment from or requisition of supplies by large armies – had to act as drivers
of the crisis. In any case, the famine was spectacular, forcing the price of
cereal to multiply fourfold or fivefold in a few months, from the summer

of 1811 to the spring of 1812. The consequences were terrible for the inhabitants of Madrid, flooded with its own and immigrant beggars: from the end of 1811 over 11,000 poor had to be assisted by public and private institutions, but this could not prevent attacks on bakeries and a complete breakdown in civic norms nor the cruel progression of diseases and famine-related mortality (Espadas Burgos 1972: 384; Fraser 2006: 697–705). The price of wheat rose by 150 per cent between January and June (Anes 1970b: 252). In the absence of the usual staples, maize, barley and vetch (*almortas*, i.e. *lathyrus sativus*) were used as alternatives, and especially bread made from potato flour, as well as ingenious substitutes such as 'onion sandwiches with vetch flour, chestnuts and acorns' (Espadas Burgos 1968: 611–13). A significant number of Goya's famous 'Disasters of War' engravings – 18 out of 82 – refer precisely to the famine that struck the city of Madrid in 1812. One of them is entitled 'Thanks to the vetch' ('*Gracias a la almorta*') (Espadas Burgos 1968: 615; Fraser 2006: 703–4).

The estimated number of deaths proposed by the Count of Toreno – 20,000 deaths in a population of fewer than 170,000 inhabitants, between September 1811, 'when the famine began', and July 1812 (Queipo de Llano y Ruiz de Saravia 1839: 101–2) – is frequently cited. This is probably no exaggeration, because the recorded number of adult deaths in the city's parishes in 1812 (8,129) was almost four times the figure for the previous year and 135 per cent higher than in 1804 (3,462). If deaths in city hospitals, for which records are lacking, increased as much relative to 1804 as they did in the parishes, that would yield a figure as high as 26,000 adult deaths in 1811–12, and this does not include infant and child mortality (Carbajo Isla 1987: 99–100). This calculation underpins the estimate of total adult deaths in Figure 3.8. The depictions by contemporary authors of trucks collecting corpses in the streets in the mornings are confirmed by other sources, such as the testimony of the French vice-consul in the capital, in July 1812: 'Not a day passes when the police don't remove the corpses of individuals who have died of starvation from the streets' (Anes 1970b: 253, my translation). Little surprise, then, that 1812 is remembered in Madrid as 'the year of famine', the most disastrous ever known in the history of the capital. Never in the previous two centuries did the city suffer such mortality, nor as low a number of marriages as those in 1812 and 1813; nor had the low recorded number of baptisms in 1813 been matched since 1606, when the court had been temporarily transferred to Valladolid.

4   Final Remarks and Conclusions

Having survived the hard times of the War of Independence, Spain never again experienced major famines, nor even significant increases

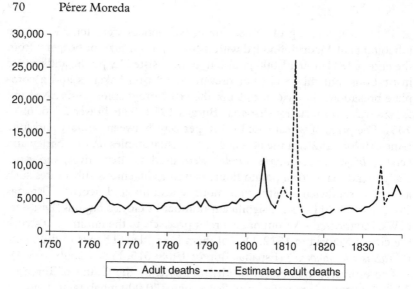

Figure 3.8 Annual mortality (adult deaths) in Madrid, 1750–1839

in mortality in years or periods of high food prices, which, moreover, have been carefully analysed for the remainder of the nineteenth century (Sánchez-Albornoz 1968; Peña Sánchez and Sánchez-Albornoz 1983; Díaz Marín 2003; 2006). The sharp mortality peaks seen in many local or provincial series during the middle decades of this century usually originated in successive epidemics of cholera. And even those that might be classified as 'food crises' (1847, 1857, 1868), which brought severe shortages to some inland regions, qualify as dearths rather than famines. Those described as such had little impact on aggregate mortality, and caused only slight simultaneous declines in marriage and fertility (Sánchez-Albornoz 1968: 40, 133). However, at local or regional level, especially in regions of cereal monoculture such as Old Castile, they caused considerable unrest, accompanied by major riots and disorders, proving their significance in some provinces, but they may not be comparable to crises typical of the 'old regime' (Sánchez-Albornoz 1968: 107–8; Moreno Lázaro 2009).

As far as the main causes of famines are concerned, all the literature – from medieval times to the nineteenth century – stresses the importance of meteorological uncertainty: prolonged dry periods or continuous rainfall (*lluvias torrenciales*) were responsible for the destruction of crops and subsequent famine, a traditional explanation on which the 'classic' subsistence crisis model of Labrousse, Meuvret and Goubert was based. Catastrophic years preceded by torrential rains (rainstorms, floods) and overflowing rivers (*fluminis inundationes, tempestatis*) are frequently cited, such as those that gave rise to the famine of 1305 in Navarre (Laliena Corbera 2011: 288), the great floods of 1435 and 1462 in Seville (Collantes de Terán 1977: 436–7) or the uninterrupted rains of 1708–09 accompanying the Great Winter.

Equally pernicious were prolonged droughts, which prevented normal sowing or resulted in very poor harvests, such as those of 1301 and 1302, or the *sterilitas* of 1313–14 in Navarre and Valencia, and others that are at the origin of the great famine of late medieval Castile (Valdeón 1984: 1053). Successive years of rain and subsequent drought were also very common, and particularly serious, as in 1374–75 in Seville, or in 1504–05, when copious rainfall was followed by the notorious drought of 1506 and 1507, especially in Andalusia, which gave rise to the terrible famines of that date and 1508. Great floods destroyed crops and damaged not only agricultural infrastructure (roads, bridges, mills, warehouses, etc.) but also the housing of farm animals and farm labour; and, when they were followed by long periods of drought, they gave rise to sudden environmental changes and the emergence of stagnant water and cesspools – ideal habitats for mosquitos and the spread of malaria, and, possibly, other pests and diseases that were no less serious to human and animal populations. Weather-induced environmental changes were also to blame for periodic locust plagues, often cited as one of the main reasons for total crop failure and famine, whether it be in the late Middle Ages (1355–56) or later (1508) in Andalusia (Collantes de Terán 1977: 432, 439), and in more recent times, such as in 1708 and especially in 1803–04.

One of the factors linked to many famines is, inevitably, war. Medieval and more recent chronicles are full of allusions to the misery and horrors endured by affected populations not only in times of war but whenever the temporary occupation, accommodation or transit of troops arose. Although in the early eighteenth century the entire country, as elsewhere in western Europe, suffered extremely adverse climate shocks, we have seen from Villalba that there could be no doubt that the disaster of 1709–11 was mainly the product of war and hunger, after years of continuous massive troop movements that surely, on this occasion (as on many others), led to the spread of typhus and other epidemics.

The mortality crises during the wars against France and the War of Independence, in particular, offer the clearest examples of the importance of the military factor as cause or catalyst of major famines. During the War against the French Convention, which took place in the Basque/Navarre provinces and in Catalonia between 1793 and 1795, war and dearth led to the spread of typhus, which was the cause given for most of the recorded excess mortality. During the War of Independence (1808–14) it was the 'disasters of war', above all fevers and famine, rather than military actions or sieges affecting the local population that led to the major death tolls of 1809 and 1812–14. The war led to dearth and famine directly through the requisition of animals and provisions, the paralysis of agrarian activity, the destruction of crops and grain warehouses and the spread of epidemics, which in turn prevented trade and provoked the breakdown of all ordinary economic activity. And, indirectly, the war (including warfare abroad) forced tax increases, weakening the ability of the population and institutions (such as the public granaries or *pósitos*) to cope with crisis, or ruled out public action such as the importation of food or provision of public relief. All these factors combined, as we have seen, to produce the grave crisis of 1804.

Finally, another important determinant of dearth and famine must not be forgotten: epidemics. This statement deserves particular attention. It may seem paradoxical, in that the intuitive causal link most often mentioned by contemporaries was the opposite: hunger leads to or facilitates the spread of plague or epidemic diseases. There is ample evidence, however, of an inverse relationship: epidemics and, above all, plague made supplying affected populations, often isolated by quarantine and sanitary cordons, very difficult; they caused the flight of the wealthy and the ruling classes, leading to the neglect of medical services and public and private charity directed at the rest of the population; and the same morbidity and mortality paralysed agricultural and commercial activity (Brumont 1988; Lázaro Ruiz and Gurría García 1989: 40–55; Lázaro Ruiz 1994: 54–7). Documenting this link between epidemic and famine is even easier in the case of the most serious outbreaks of malaria, such as those affecting Spain in 1786–87 and 1803–04 (Pérez Moreda 1984; 2010b). In the history of famine and major European mortality crises there is ample documentary evidence of causal relationships between epidemic and dearth or famine, and this calls for careful case-by-case analysis of the timing (monthly, for example) of increases in prices and mortality: a reverse causal link to that usually assumed may well be found (Pérez Moreda 2010b).

4   France

Gérard Béaur and Jean-Michel Chevet

During the years known in France as *les 30 Glorieuses* (1945–75) no issue captivated French rural historians like that of famines. Of course, it had long been known from chronologies, documents and witness accounts, and also from well-known historical studies, that Europeans had been subject to many severe subsistence crises, and had frequently suffered from hunger (Abel 1935). Even so, nowhere else did these calamities attract so many researchers, eager to track even the mildest shift in population trends or grain prices. The infatuation was such that a conviction grew that France alone experienced such dramas, and, moreover, that famines were like mad cows, in that if one didn't search for them, one risked not finding them. This frenzy produced a double result: a literature so enormous that it is virtually impossible to survey, and an overuse of this way of addressing the problem. French historians sidelined the issue of crises when rural history began to decline in the 1980s – unless rural history itself was a victim of the overdose of those graphs of population and prices. They did so just as foreign historians began to address the question, discovering or rediscovering the notion of 'subsistence crises'.

What explains this passion, which contrasted so starkly with British historians' focus on the agricultural revolution? To be sure, British studies of ancient demography and grain price fluctuations were not lacking, and French scholars did produce some solid studies of French agriculture. Nonetheless, the fact remains that, while British historiography yielded many studies of high quality on advances in agriculture, the dominant focus of French historiography was on subsistence crises. This distortion led to two conflicting and durable historical myths: the misery and retardation of 'French agriculture' (to the extent that this concept makes sense at the outset) and the glory and dynamism of British agriculture. Today little remains of what were stark representations, but they continue to irrigate a significant share of specialist and, particularly, non-specialist historiographies.

But why this fervour on the French side of the Channel? One answer is that, in the wake of a war marked by hardship, there was a vivid memory of privations endured by populations. Moreover, there was above all access to innumerable sources inviting analysis, especially parish registers and prices extracted from *mercuriales* (market price listings). And then there was the sheer ability of the great pessimistic historians of the 1950s and 1960s, and pure chance. When Goubert arrived in Beauvais soon after World War II and stepped into the archives, then in a state of indescribable disorder, the first accessible series of registers he came across, purely at random, related to the apocalyptic year of 1694. The experience had an enduring influence on Meuvret's perspective. Following the examples set by their illustrious predecessors, Henry and Goubert, historians plunged into the litanies of burials, baptisms and marriages that punctuated these documents; they revelled in the price series extracted from *mercuriales* in the wake of Labrousse and followed the traces of Meuvret to locate, describe and explain the price increases that leapt on their graph paper (Labrousse 1933; Meuvret 1946). Grenier's (1985) list of time series of demographic data for the modern era included 123 items. When *Annales de Démographie Historique* undertook a count of works on population trends in 1980, they reached a total of 550 (Le Mée 1980) and today the total exceeds 2,000! When Grenier turned to series describing grain and bread prices, he listed no fewer than 273, though many of the underlying data remained unpublished. Most of the time the results were reported in graphs, deemed more reader-friendly than arid tables. In sum, we have a lot of information about subsistence crises, which reveals much about their chronology, their duration and their consequences. These have given rise to a variety of interpretations (Béaur et al. 2011).

1   Identifying Famines

1.1   Chronicles and Climatic Indicators

The preoccupation with famines was not entirely new. For a long time historians and economists had addressed the question, both by using the same sources in a less than systematic way and by identifying from contemporary or near-contemporary chronologies moments when food supplies were threatened to a greater or lesser extent. In this way over a century ago Levasseur (1893: 111–34) extracted a list of the main shocks from classical sources.

From a different perspective, it was reasonable to link periods of cold weather or excessive humidity to famine. Working from climatic variations enabled Le Roy Ladurie (2006) to enumerate in a plausible way episodes that could have led to famine. In matching the two lists, one can for the first time propose a chronology of remarkable harvest events

Table 4.1 *Two lists of French crises, 1300–1800*

Levasseur	Le Roy Ladurie
1304 great dearth	
1310 dearth	
1315–17 severe famine	**1315**
1330–34 high prices	1330?
1344 high prices	
1349 famine	1348? 1351?
1360 big famine	1360
	1369–71
	1374–75
1390 high prices	
	1407–08
1410 high prices	
1414–15 high prices	
1418–19 mortality and extreme dearth, 1420–21 famine, dearth	**1420**
1421–24 dearth	
1429–31 awful famine	**1431–32**
1437–39 big famine then big dearth	**1438**
	1455–57
1480–81 bad harvest	**1481–82**
1515 big famine	
1521–22 big famine, then near-general famine	1521–22
1526–1528 big famine, mortality, 1531–32 high mortality, famine	1527–32
1544 et 1547 high prices	**1545**
	1556
1561 harsh winter	**1562**
1565–67 dearth	**1565–66**
	1573–74
1586–87 severe dearth	**1586–87**
1590 high prices	
	1596–97
	1608
	1625–27
1631 severe dearth	1630–31
	1642
1648–51 high prices, misery…	**1648–50 and 1651–52**
1658 and 1660 bad harvest and no harvest, 1662 cruel famine	**1661**
1668 very severe winter	
1693–94 extreme dearth	**1693–94**
1700–02 poor harvests	
1709–10 frost, no wheat, high prices, mortality	**1709**
	1712–13
1723 and 1725–26 bad harvests, high prices	1725
1738–39 bad harvests and 1740–41 famine	1738–40
1748 bad harvest	
1752–53 bad harvest	
1759 high prices	
1766–73 high prices	1768–70
1774–75 bad harvest and high prices	1775

Note: Famines identified by Le Roy Ladurie are in bold.
Sources: Dupâquier (1988).

in French population history, with their *chertés* (high prices), mortalities and major harvest deficits.

There would seem to be general agreement on the affected periods, with some insignificant divergences but also some differences regarding the severity of some events. These differences stem from two concurrent phenomena. First, the concept of 'famine' covers a range of experiences. Do 'big' and 'terrible' dearths amount to a famine? What is meant by 'high prices' and by 'poor' or 'very poor' harvests? Where does one place the cursor? Levasseur remarked that, in compiling various documents, he counted 151 dearths in the 10 centuries between 987 (the beginning of Hugues Capet's reign) and 1891. That seems like a lot, particularly when one considers that there would have been 48 years of famine out of 73 in the eleventh century, 20 in the twelfth century and 10 to 16 in each of the following centuries. It is difficult to believe that our ancestors were on the verge of starvation more than one year in two at the beginning of the millennium before last, and still so threatened in one year in five in an era of economic and demographic expansion. Contemporaries had a strong tendency to emphasise every disorder they discovered and to qualify as a famine every difficulty in food supply. Can one trust the distinctions they drew? In any case, it is probably far-fetched to talk of the 'return of hunger' in the fourteenth century, as it was stated at the time. There were famines before 1315–22 and many more thereafter.

Levasseur's study of these data suggested a second limitation. The frequency of the events recorded is so great that we can presume that certain texts do not refer solely to general famines, but include local events affecting just the community or the area where the chronicler lived. In reality, it is important to distinguish between localised famines, which, along with the ambiguity regarding dearth/famine, largely explain the discrepancies between the two columns in the table, and generalised famines, about which there is broad agreement.

In addition to these qualitative data, certain quantitative indicators are also available. Some, referring to mortality, are direct; the others, referring to price increases, are indirect.

1.2   Mortality and Prices

Mortality seems the more appropriate measure, since it clearly captures famine as defined in this book. Unfortunately, it is not so easy to identify it, never mind interpret it. Although some registers of burials survive from the sixteenth century, and increasingly continuous series for burials, marriages and births from the seventeenth century on, our data are terribly

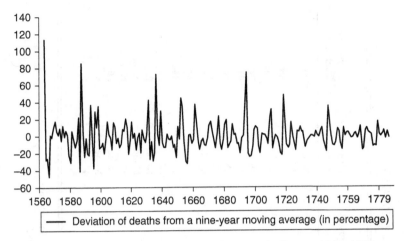

Figure 4.1 Evolution of mortality crises in France 1560–1790

fragmentary before then. In theory, before 1539, with the Ordonnance de Villers-Cotterêts, reliable demographic data are at a premium. The lack of data risks the distorting effect of exaggerating the importance of crises in the modern era relative to those of the medieval era.

Armed with parish registers, in the 1950s, French demographers began to reconstitute the population from the sixteenth century on. Annual series of marriages, births and burials for the whole country were estimated on the basis of a representative sample of parishes. With these, we can produce a graph of deaths for the country as a whole and detect the outliers.

A first look at Figure 4.1 reveals the presence of some major deviations from trend. Thus, for example, the crisis of 1563 is characterised by an increase of 113 per cent in burials – and note that the use of the calendar year, rather than the harvest year, is likely to reduce the size of the deviation. The increase over trend exceeded 40 per cent on seven occasions (see Figure 4.1 and Table 4.2); and we rediscover more or less the major catastrophes signalled by contemporaries or identified through climatic shocks. Much smaller deviations of 20 to 40 per cent come next. Moreover, negative fluctuations were fewer than positive fluctuations, and only two of those exceeded 40 per cent. The outcome implies – and this is important for judging the impact of crises on population size – that the number of deaths had a tendency to fall for a year, and sometimes more, after a crisis. Crises also decreased in intensity over time, before virtually disappearing after the Big Winter of 1709.

Table 4.2 *Demographic crises, production deficits and price increases in France, c. 1560–1790*

	Excess mortality	Deficits in baptisms	Deficits in production south	Deficits in production north	High prices Paris	High prices Arles	High prices Toulouse
1573	113	11	50	No data	65	None	58
1587	85	25	20	20	37	13	37
1694	74	None	No data	None	89	3	53
1636	72	None	9	None	1	21	11
1718	48	None	19	32	None	50	62
1652	44	2	4	No data	55	1	41
1631	42	13	23	None	45	28	88
1661	37	None	None	No data	33	None	7
1593	37	9	33	No data	None	52	45
1598	35	14	54	37	17	36	52
1653	35	14	None	No data	55	12	84
1747	35	3	None	None	None	22	22
1710	31	23	None	None	32	22	22
1639	29	7	No data	25	None	None	None
1596	29	6	80	No data	12	8	None
1693	27	26	None	None	53	None	26
1676	23	None	None	No data	None	None	5
1585	22	None	47	None	None	4	8
1709	22	3	No data	No data	108	58	61

Notes: Production deficits and price increases are calculated as deviations from a seven-year moving average.
Sources: Dupâquier (1988); Baehrel (1961); Morineau (1970a); Baulant (1968); Goy (1968; 1982).

Crises aside, the graph reveals a decline over time in year-to-year fluctuations of burials. Thus, during the 1600–1790 period, the deviations from the moving average fluctuated between plus and minus 20 per cent, but in the eighteenth century this variability was reduced to half that. The variability of burials has a funnel-like shape.

Even so, we cannot be sure that all these mortality peaks were caused by hunger and not, for example, by the spread of diseases. We address this question by examining grain prices to detect food availability decline and the famous *crises de subsistances*.

Without continuous *mercuriales*, economic fluctuations cannot be reconstructed in a plausible and evocative manner. From the sixteenth century on there is an embarrassment of choices. True, the results may be distorted by the monetary machinations of the monarchy before 1726 (though with some periods of respite before then, particularly in the second half of the seventeenth century), but these shortcomings would affect our results only over the long run and not during the short run that marks a 'crisis'. By contrast, data are rare before the sixteenth century.

Data on the price of wheat in Douai in northern France and in Albi in the south have survived (Mestayer 1963). They reveal several crises in the fourteenth and fifteenth centuries. In Albi in 1315 the price of wheat was four times as high as in 1312 and about double that of 1313, and similarly in Douai. Another crisis erupted in 1342–43, less severe than that of 1315 because the price of wheat remained much lower. By contrast, these two *mercuriales* reveal no crisis on the eve of the Black Death. It was only in 1359 and 1361 that mortality rose significantly again at the doubling of prices. Thereafter, the Albi *mercuriale* did not take off again until after 1420, while that of Douai remained stable except in 1439 and 1440.

The trend in the number of burial pits dug offers a second index for the late medieval period. It identifies episodes of high excess mortality occurring c. 1370–1470, in particular the main ones occurring in 1419, 1431 and 1438. There were three more, less intense, crises in the second half of the century, in 1454, 1468 and 1470 (Biraben 1977; Neveux 1980). All these mortality crises are linked to a significant rise in grain prices, though strict proportionality is lacking. Mild variations in prices have little impact on the number of burials, since increases in the numbers of burial pits are not systematically linked to price increases, as in 1413 and 1414 and in 1454. The rise in prices therefore had to be significant for there to be a famine.

Let us identify subsistence crises by tracking price movements. Figure 4.2 describes those of wheat prices in Paris between 1430 and 1789 and in Toulouse between 1486 and 1795. Let us set aside trends

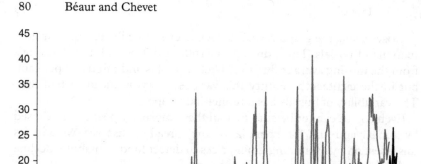

Figure 4.2 The evolution of wheat prices in Paris and Toulouse, 1430–1795

Sources: Baulant (1968) and Frêche (1974).

to focus on the erratic movement of the two series between 1486 and 1560. One identifies six crises when the deviation from a moving trend exceeded two-fifths and 20 when the deviation exceeded one-fifth, totalling 28 per cent of the years in this period. In Toulouse the number of crises was almost identical. But there is little point in dwelling on this period, since we lack information on its demographics. For the succeeding period (1560–1785) we can identify 14 crises when the deviation exceeded two-fifths and 42 when it exceeded one-fifth, or 18 per cent of the years in this period. In Toulouse the number of crises was again roughly the same as in Paris. These crises, for the most part, coincided, though this is sometimes difficult to confirm because the price series are not strictly comparable: one, that for Paris, refers in part to calendar years. That suggests that the severity of crises was significantly greater in Paris than in Toulouse. Moreover, practically all these high price events coincided with excess mortality (compare Table 4.2). This was not always the case: in Paris in 1741, for example, the price of wheat rose by 92 per cent but there is no discernible impact on mortality. But that is because we have only a mortality series that covers the whole country, whereas, in order to capture regional crises, we would require series for each region.

1.3   Famines versus Epidemics

A problem that arises is whether these dearths really coincided with mortality. If we accept that famines were mainly due to shortfalls in production, we need to know which crises corresponded to a lack of available food and, of course, whether this was correlated with an increase in prices. Unfortunately, data that throw light on this are very rare. For output, we have two series, one each for the north and south of France (Baehrel 1961; Goy 1968; 1982; Morineau 1970a; Neveux 1980), and for prices we have relied on three series dating back to the late sixteenth century. The results are shown in Table 4.2 in the knowledge that shifts in the series are possible because deaths and prices are calculated by calendar years, not crop years.

All mortality deviations of over 20 per cent above the moving average are reported in this table. The lack of data expressed in harvest years has led to some adjustments. The data in the table are not easy to interpret. While the origins of some crises (1587, 1694 and 1709, for example) lie without doubt in a cereal deficit leading to an increase in prices, this does not rule out the influence of epidemics. Even so, this deficit does not always lead to a drop in births (as in 1719 or 1709, for example). Moreover, the demographic crises of 1636 and 1652 were not due to a production deficit or a price rise but were the result of the plague, which still raged in the seventeenth century. But it could sometimes happen, as in 1653, that famine followed the disorganisation of production provoked by plague in the preceding year, and an ensuing sharp rise in prices. Of the 19 demographic crises listed, six, or about one in three, occur at the end of the sixteenth century and, more precisely, during the Wars of Religion. Nine occurred during the seventeenth century, of which two coincided with the end of the Fronde. But, of these nine crises, a few are epidemics or the plague, and not famines: 1636, for example. Finally, four are listed for the beginning of the eighteenth century (there might be fewer if one had data on burials for calendar years); should these be classed as *disettes* (dearths) rather than famines proper?

These considerations prompt two fundamental points. First, not all excess mortality was due to famine. An epidemic outbreak could produce a mortality peak in the absence of any major shortfall in food availability. Some, indeed, have argued that people died only of diseases. There is reliable evidence, however, that during the Ancien Régime people succumbed to starvation during the most severe crises. Numerous mentions by clergy in the parish registers testify to it. It is impossible to deny individual deaths from starvation, as the work of Lachiver has made plain. The question is, rather, how many of these individuals died of starvation and did hunger alone cause their deaths? In certain cases, there is no room for doubt, but it is not always so. 'Morts de faim et de misère,' it is written (Lachiver 1991: 158). One might make the case that deaths from starvation were not as common as claimed in the past. Yet, contrary to what some historians feign to believe, Meuvret and other specialists on subsistence crises never claimed that famines alone were responsible for all instances of excess mortality. Most resulted from the conjunction of famine itself and its secondary effects in the form of illnesses striking people whose bodies had been weakened by malnutrition. Mortality is therefore a revealing measure of famine, albeit an imperfect one, complicated by external factors.

Second, there were certainly several crises whose geographic reach was very wide. They include those of 1661 (la crise de l'Avénement), 1693–94 and 1709 (Goubert 1967; Lachiver 1991), and there were others too. In the majority of cases, however, famines were local, whatever the domino effects were of high prices one market on the next. This is why there were considerable spatial differences in the sensitivity to crises, which, in themselves, varied from one episode to another. Unfortunately, the regional analysis of crises is not possible before 1670, because the data are lacking before this date, and we stop the analysis in 1739 because after that date the severity of crises is much attenuated and it becomes difficult to consider them as real famines.

During the crisis of 1676, mortality was severest in the north and east of France. It also struck the south and east to a lesser extent, but the Paris region and the centre escaped unscathed. This crisis, so variable across regions, also caused a striking reduction in baptisms. The lack of harvest year data makes studying the two great famines of 1693–94 and 1709–10 rather complicated. In the case of the first, this is because the crisis struck some regions in 1693 and others in the following year, although, if mortality in both years is considered, it seems clear that the whole country was affected, with the exception of the east and west and to a lesser extent the south-east. This outcome may reflect purchases of grain on the international market. The subsistence crisis caused by the *grand hiver* of 1709 takes on a more national aspect than its predecessor because only the south-west was not affected by the crisis. In that region, the data imply a reduction in mortality relative to the moving average. As for baptisms, they declined everywhere except in the west. In some regions, the deviation from the moving average exceeded 40 per cent. The crisis of 1719 affected only the Parisian region, the centre and the south-west. A group of lower mortality regions in the east and west is apparent, whereas the north, the south and the south-west escaped the crisis (compare Table 4.1).

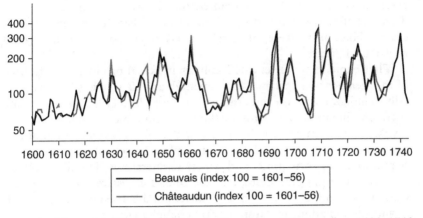

Figure 4.3 The price of wheat in Beauvais and Châteaudun, 1600–1740
Sources: Goubert (1960).

2 Accounting for Famines

2.1 The Weather

Libera nos domine a peste, fame et bello. The ancient prayer clearly defines famine as one of the calamities that regularly afflicted pre-industrial societies. The point of departure generally was a poor harvest that reduced in a drastic fashion the quantity of available grain in an era when cereals were the staple food and when the production of *bleds* (corn) was far from generating considerable surpluses. Scarce grain then rose sharply in price and rapidly beyond the reach of the poorest (Goubert 1960).

Thus, no sooner was the shortfall revealed, even before the crop was harvested, than the price of corn began to rise and dearth threatened. Usually, however, a single harvest deficit was generally not enough to produce a real famine: 1709 is an exception. That required a series of poor harvests, the famous *séquences* highlighted by Morineau (1970a). The rise in wheat prices could become, in effect, vertiginous and make bread inaccessible to the poor, and eventually to a growing number of consumers. Among the hundreds of graphs produced by French historians, let us look at that for Beauvais and Châteaudun between 1600 and 1740 in order to see the size of these cereal peaks (Goubert 1960: II, 88–9). This is reproduced as Figure 4.3.

Given seed requirements and taxes in kind, food availability fluctuated much more than gross output. According to King's law,[1] moreover,

---

[1] Gregory King's law estimates how much a deficiency in the supply of grain raises the price of grain.

prices fluctuated much more than output. Thus, any crop shortfall had dramatic effects, magnified by a kind of multiplier that accentuated its gravity. High prices were intricately linked to harvest deficits and could provoke a famine.

What explains these repeated failures in cereal production? The role of the weather was certainly fundamental, and its role has been repeatedly highlighted in the literature. Grenier's data (1996) show a link between climate and dearths in the short run, and Georgelin (1982), invoking agronomic research, highlights the role of rainfall and temperatures in some key seasons. Three factors played a key role: the rainfall, in September and springtime, and winter temperatures. The die could be cast by late spring, therefore, and the role of excessive rain or drought during the summer was less important. A good harvest required the following combination: an autumn warm enough to conserve seeds and wet enough to permit their sowing – but not too wet to delay or limit ploughing and to cause seeds to rot; a winter with no more than 100 to 200 mm of rain, and a dry cold, if possible, with a snow that protects seeds from freezing, but without abrupt or sharp falls in temperatures and without late frost; an early spring with sunshine to support plant growth, and then rain in April/May, but not enough to promote the growth of weeds that prevent grain from maturing; summer heat, but not to the extent that it resulted in shrivelled grains and promoted fungal diseases; and light summer rains after fertilisation (around 20 June), and no heatwave or hailstones like those that destroyed harvests on 13 July 1788.

2.2   Speculation

Populations threatened by famine always blamed hoarders and speculators – farmers and merchants who were accused of retaining stocks in order to sell at a higher price later, or of moving to more profitable markets and thereby forcing up prices. Those at risk were virtually incapable of recognising that harvests could be inadequate. Some historians, echoing such sentiments, insist on the potential of speculation to cause famines. In support, they invoke evidence that farmers often began to release stocks as soon as there were signs of a good harvest, so that they had sold them off before the new harvest drove prices down. This explains the emphasis placed (following Labrousse) on the pre-harvest *soudure* when reserves were exhausted and the new wheat not yet ready for delivery, particularly when the harvest promised to be in deficit (Labrousse 1933: 158ff.).

Even so, it has not been convincingly proved that farmers speculated on a rise in prices and kept back grain to make this happen, nor that they were systematic gainers in the case of bad harvests. The fall in saleable surpluses could be compensated for by a rise in prices, but that was far from being always the case. In addition, storing grain in the hope of rising prices was risky, knowing that old grain was worth less than new and that the calculation could be negated by shifting market conditions or a better than expected harvest. One really had to be a risk-taker to expose oneself to such calculations. In the medium term, there was no significant difference between the quarterly price of corn and nothing to gain from seeking to profit from the effects of scarcity (Béaur 2007).

2.3 Fiscal Exactions and Depredations

Fiscal dues are deemed an important trigger of famine. By depriving rural areas of part of their output, the system of exactions through rents, seigneurial dues and tithes played a major part in the process that led to grain shortages. In this regard, from the Middle Ages on the growth of towns and urban markets increased the strain on supplies and helps explain the persistence of famines despite advances in agricultural production. It is clear that the effects of these exactions were even more catastrophic when harvests were mediocre.

In addition, the link between wars, famines and epidemics is long familiar. At the end of the nineteenth century there was a tendency to view catastrophes as the product of war. Since then the discussion of their impact has been more nuanced, partly because the size of the armed forces present were usually quite small but mostly because regions unaffected by war also suffered from crises (Lorcin 1981; Gauvard 2005).

In fact, it was not so much war itself as the presence of the military that had devastating effects on the countryside. Not only did soldiers or looters rampage all around them but they caused an insecurity that discouraged farmers from cropping land too exposed to danger. Like the wandering bands that caused havoc during the Hundred Years War, mercenaries involved in the religious wars of the late sixteenth century contributed largely to the outbreak of famine during the terrible 1590s. Such was also the case during the Fronde (1648–52), when royal and rebel troops criss-crossed the devastated countryside (Jacquart 1974). No wonder that communities everywhere were prepared to pay dearly to keep troops at bay. One might argue that the creation of barracks and the transfer of war to foreign territories caused some relaxation in the impact of some famines, just as the medieval crusades undoubtedly relieved populations from a turbulent knighthood, and Duguesclin's Spanish expedition in 1366 was a means of removing bands of armed thugs.

Finally, there is the issue of commercialisation and markets. Probably too much has been made in past of the local character of the grain trade. It was largely so, but interregional and even international flows also played a part, and the growth of urban populations meant that non-producers accounted for an increasing share of consumption (Bourin, Drendel and Menant 2011: 16–24). More and more people relied on markets for food and were increasingly vulnerable to price movements and production transfers (Bourin, Drendel and Menant 2011). Instead of being dependent on the vagaries of production, their subsistence became subject to the unpredictable and sometimes excessive vagaries of the market. The threat of famine led to panic on markets and a reluctance to allow grain flow to deficit areas at times when local authorities or the state did not prohibit exports. This led to speculative practices, waiting or the drying up of the grain supply in some areas, in favour of others where sales were more remunerative. In this way a high price in one region could influence others and thereby degenerate into widespread famine.

Even when this did not happen, information about prices was 'telegraphed' from market to market. The simple prospect of sales being more profitable on one market than another prompted an alignment of prices without adverse side effects. Today some French historians, influenced by Sen's analysis of famine, take a more nuanced view of how markets function during famines, and consider famines as much 'a crisis of distribution as of production' (Sen 1981; Tilly 1983; Bourin, Drendel and Menant 2011: 16–24). Yet, while practices linked to markets and transfers probably exacerbated subsistence crises and their selective social effects, they did not create those crises. Without a shortfall in production, there was no speculation, no hoarding, no panic and no wasteful exactions.

3   Analysing Famines

In order to understand the importance of these crises, we must remember not only that the French diet was based mainly on cereals but also that the majority of the population, including its rural component, were purchasers of bread. No sooner did the price of wheat start to rise than a large proportion of the peasantry and rural dwellers could no longer afford to buy the grain needed to feed their families. The examples given by Goubert for Beauvais show that, when the bread price doubled, quadrupled or worse, misery was inescapable. The problem was made worse by competition on the labour market as the demand for labour fell. As the wages of farm labourers declined, industrial unemployment dried up other sources of income. The only solution was recourse to inferior grains – rye, in particular – or substitute foods such as the potato. Such consumption shifts had a knock-on effect on the price of such items.

The shortage of food weakened the resistance of undernourished organisms and rendered them particularly vulnerable to disease. The poorest resorted first to substitute foods such as bran bread, unusable seed, bark, grasses, nettles, ferns, roots, cabbage, stems, nutshells, etc. In desperation they also consumed contaminated products such as carrion, the flesh of horses, dogs and other dead animals. How far did this go? How many resorted to cannibalism as a final resort? There is some documentary evidence for cannibalism, at least during the great medieval famines, but it is rather rare. Lachiver (1991: 168; compare Ó Gráda 2015a) cites the case of a 15-month-old infant whose corpse had been exhumed and partly consumed by his family, but proof is lacking apart from some vague contemporary allusions.

Unhealthy and unfamiliar foods evidently led to disease, and death could have intervened before starvation struck. These starving individuals succumbed, having shed up to 30 to 40 per cent of their weight, and lost their muscles, as their innards and their hearts gave up the struggle. Such emaciation was sometimes masked by oedema, but always accompanied by lethargy, weakness, low blood glucose, hypothermia, excess cholesterol and anaemia. Starving, prostrate, diarrhoeaic, the poor lay down and became incapable of eating. They were carried off by pneumonia, tuberculosis or tetanus, or, more typically, by typhus, typhoid or dysentery (Lachiver 1991).

The spread of disease was encouraged by the erratic displacements of population attracted by the mirage of food availability in urban areas. True, that is where the grain due in fiscal exactions was held, as well as grain bought up by merchants in the hope of selling it at a higher price, or held in warehouses (Meuvret 1977). The disinherited masses migrated in all directions: towards cities suspected of holding reserves, from one region to another more likely to be better supplied, following the paths of rumour, or else moving from the city to the countryside, either because they had been pushed out or in order to flee from epidemics or unrest.

These episodes had dramatic demographic consequences. In the short run mortality surged, while at the same time conceptions and marriages plummeted. Marriages were put off, even if waves of remarriages could mitigate or correct this movement. Couples tended to limit births, for a range of reasons: amenorrhoea (Le Roy Ladurie 1969), a reduction in libido or a reluctance to procreate in the context of severe economic depression (Deyon 1967). The graphs of births, particularly when lagged by nine months, validated this inverse relationship between mortality

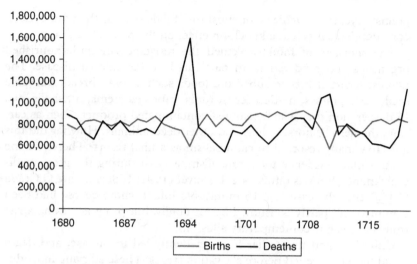

Figure 4.4 Births and deaths in France, 1680–1719

Sources: Lachiver (1991).

and fertility when food is very scarce. Figure 4.4 describes the pattern for France as a whole (Lachiver 1991: 480).

The number of deaths could soar relative to the norm. The crisis of 1693–94, often analysed by historians as one of the worst but also the best documented, can serve as a model. In Breteuil in the Beauvaisis, as in Meulan (or in Amiens or Rouen), the same scenario is repeated. When the price of grain quadrupled or more at the peak of the crisis, the number of burials exceeded all records, quintupling at the height of summer, before the prospect of a better harvest offered respite to body and soul (Goubert 1960: 56). Then, by a new inversion, mortality collapsed with the removal of the weakest, marriages soared to compensate for those ended by death and delayed births led to an increase in the number of births despite the disappearance of many adults of reproductive age. Data bearing on these classic demographic responses are plentiful (e.g. Deyon 1967; Bardet 1983).

The effect of this crisis was all the more severe because it happened in the middle of a war and in the wake of a decade of bountiful harvests (the 1680s were the years of *gros épis*: big ears of corn), which had the effect of depressing prices and may have discouraged cultivation. According to the lawmaker and proto-economist Boisguilbert (1646–1714), peasant production responded to dearth and high grain prices, a response that could lead in turn to overproduction and depressed prices when meteorological conditions improved. Low prices in turn might discourage

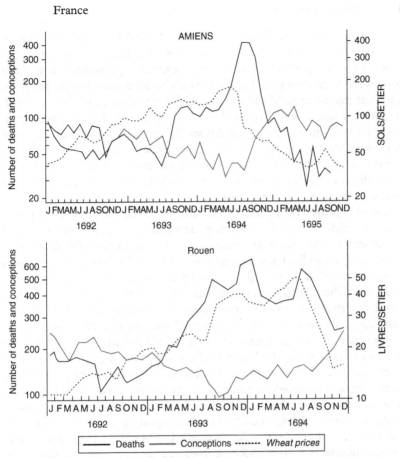

Figure 4.5 The relation between agricultural crisis and demography, 1692–95

Sources: Deyon (1967: 498); Bardet (1983: 187, documents [wheat prices in Pontoise]).

productive investment and, with a lag, reduce production. Such a reaction could prove costly in the event of a poor harvest, and made the agricultural economy vulnerable to the slightest meteorological shock. The overall effect was erratic oscillations between crises of under- and over-production. As Perrot (1984: 544) has put it, '[L]ike earthquakes in a fragile zone, these crises are both probable and unpredictable.'

To make matters worse, the crisis confirmed that the memory of the famine that had occurred three decades earlier, which linked to Louis XIV's ascent to the throne in 1661, had faded, and with it the reactions required in such circumstances. Fifteen years later France barely escaped an even worse disaster during the Grand Hiver of 1709, which also coincided with a major war. All crops were ruined; if the crisis led to only 600,000 deaths that was because everything possible was planted from early April onwards. That meant above all barley, which, sown on land that had been fertilised for wheat and was clear of weeds, and with predatory animals and insects destroyed by the cold, and favoured in the end by optimal climatic conditions for crop growth, produced what was called 'the barley miracle'. For a year barley was practically the only cereal consumed, but at least there was food: evidence that English solutions, already experimented with in the Middle Ages, were not unknown on the Continent (Lachiver 1991).

Not all regions were affected simultaneously. The arable plains, reputed to be the richest but also the most dependent on the production and consumption of wheat, were undoubtedly the most vulnerable. Without a substitute food to fall back on, and relieved of all their corn by merchants hoping to resell it at a profit on the Paris market, the grain-producing areas languished. Some regions appear much less vulnerable because they were less dependent on grain as a staple. This was the case of the Breton west, the south-east and the south-west. Thus, the crisis of 1693–94 was very severe in the north, centre and south of the country, but absent in the east and in Brittany and relatively light in the other regions. Others were more exposed, such as those in mountainous areas, chronically dependent on migration. Traditionally, mountain populations relied on lowland areas in order to make ends meet, but the decline in employment in their usual catchment areas discouraged them from migrating. Thus, the highlands had more mouths to feed on less income. In mitigation, these people had a more diverse diet than those in the large grain-growing regions, and were removed from the routes that spread famine-related diseases. As a result, they sometimes escaped more lightly, but that was not so during the last crises of the reign of Louis XIV.

The poorest were worst affected, but the crisis climbed the social pyramid as the price of grain rose. Purchasers relied increasingly on the market by the end of winter – or earlier, depending on the gravity of the crisis – as their reserves dried up. Day labourers were the first to be affected, even if their wages were partly paid in kind, as well as sharecroppers and smallholders. Even in ordinary times their output was barely enough for their own use; in a crisis, the cycle of indebtedness to the landowner or noble in the nearest town began. Freeing oneself of debt in the years that followed was not easy, especially if another crop failure was looming on the horizon before the debt was repaid, even if we must admit that credit also played a more positive role than generally recognised and that the poor would have been even worse off without it

(Ó Gráda 2009: 79–81). Of course, in this process, household composition was a crucial feature. Families with several young children were most at risk because their income/expenditure balance was most precarious.

Mortality was age-selective. Although infant and child mortality were very high, adults were proportionately the worst affected, which disturbed the balance between age groups. Their excess mortality had lasting effects. It reduced the supply of labour available to both agriculture and manufacturing, and the reduction in the number of couples of reproductive age had immediate and more long-term impacts on fertility (Bardet 1983: 356).

As the price of bread rose, the weakest lost ground and were condemned to misery, begging and vagrancy. The number of migrants multiplied, particularly if the crisis was severe. Wandering skeletons lined the roads. Lachiver refers to 2 to 3 million men and women forced to leave their homes in search of food in 1694. They perished of exhaustion or cold along the roads and in ditches, or else died in hospitals, as child abandonment became rife (Gascon and Latta 1963). This mass of epidemic-prone migrants infected others in turn, even among groups not short of food, and this spread of disease resulted in massive mortality in urban areas, even among affluent families.

Squeezed between rising expenses and declining incomes, small farmers, cottiers and labourers were hit hardest. They cut back consumption and borrowed if they could, selling their land or their homes if necessary. The case of Maintenon demonstrates how crises related to the grape harvest or wine forced small-scale wine producers into the land market (Béaur 1984). Although the dearths of the late eighteenth century were small compared to those that had preceded them, many were still forced to sacrifice some properties. During the major crises it was much worse, and this was the fate of smallholders of the Beauvaisis and the Hurepoix during the seventeenth century (Goubert 1960; Jacquart 1974). Sales of land multiplied in Albi, as in Charlieu, in 1709 (see Figure 4.6) (Floutard 1972; Dontenwill 1973). Vulnerable, marginal families joined those who were habitual vagrants in the countryside.

4   Interpreting Famines: Malthusian Illusions

Two competing theories have been invoked to explain secular population trends in the Western world between the Middle Ages and the late eighteenth century. According to the first, population pressure led to the innovations of the late seventeenth century. There is no need to make further reference to it here, because it concerns only the end of this period, and famines had disappeared by then. According to the

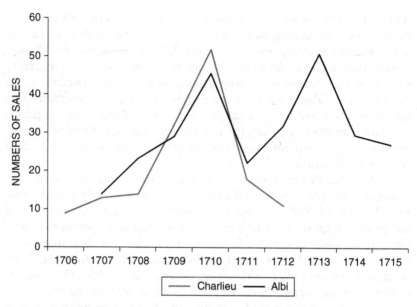

Figure 4.6 Land sales in Charlieu and Albi during the crisis of 1709

Notes: The figures for Albi have been divided by 10 to make them comparable with Charlieu.

Sources: Floutard (1972) and Dontenwill (1973).

second, Malthusian, theory, population would several times hit the ceiling imposed by a static technology. Rebuffed like Sisyphus at the peak of each Malthusian cycle, population would again resume its climb to the ceiling. This 'French' socio-biological version of Malthusianism (Le Roy Ladurie 1974; Dupâquier 1989) contrasts with an 'English' version according to which, at the approach of the ceiling, certain checks such as a falling birth rate and reduced nuptiality intervened in order to stabilise the situation. While the biological influence on the health and growth of populations cannot be denied, it appears to us, as we shall try to show, that making it the main or only regulator of population is going too far.

The Black-Death-related crisis of 1348 was not at all a famine like that of 1315–16, which was due to a serious shortfall in production. Even so, the famine of 1348 deserves our attention because of the sense that it was a 'creeping' crisis brought on by rural overpopulation before the Black Death. This overpopulation weakened resistance and made people vulnerable to diseases, including the plague (Le Roy Ladurie 1978). But this is not the only interpretation available.

For some researchers, plague does not depend on nutritional status (Biraben 1975). This seems irrefutable, since it attacked well-fed bishops as well as the poor (Biraben 1977). Plague, like wars, has been proposed as a Malthusian positive check, but this is not obvious, since, according to the latest estimates, population on the eve of the Black Death was below the level reached in the eighteenth century, while agricultural progress in the following centuries made it possible to feed more mouths. Finally, note too that the famine of 1315–16, the product of an extreme climatic shock, did not bring population growth to a halt. In certain regions such as Upper Normandy, for example, population growth resumed in the wake of the famine (Le Roy Ladurie 1978). The demographic impact of both the Black Death and the 1315–16 famine highlight the sensitivity of population to the environment.

Prices offer an indication of the state of the crops on the eve of the Black Death but not of the true extent of the deficit. Thus, in Douai prices hardly rose between 1342 and 1343 (data are lacking for 1340–41), then fell back in 1344 and remained static until 1351, which saw a new peak in prices after the plague had already reduced population. The *mercuriale* reveals a peak in 1343, but it was tiny compared to that of 1315–17 (Mestayer 1963). Prices could also be the product of monetary manipulation, which was frequent in this period (D'Haenens 1959). In Albi, where prices before the Black Death were only one-quarter of their 1315 level, it was a similar story (Levasseur 1893). In the Lyon region, wills offer an indirect measure of the harshness of the crisis. Between 1300 and 1510 an annual average of 20 wills were recorded. During the crisis years of 1343, 1348, 1361, 1392 and 1482 they leapt in number to 92, 376, 206, 91 and 89, respectively. Again, though, plague rather than famine was responsible for most of this implied mortality (Lorcin 1981). In the Bordelais, floods caused a food shortage in 1347. One might infer that this facilitated the spread of disease (Boutruche 1963). But note again that this involved a meteorological accident, not the malnutrition of the population at large. In Paris, indeed, the plague struck a population that did not seem to be suffering from chronic malnutrition. There was no alert and food supplies were not lacking (Fourquin 1964).

The kind of long series of grain production and prices required for a proper test of the Malthusian model are very scarce for this period. One source for the north of France contains output and yield data for the property of the Notre-Dame-des-Prés in Douai between 1330 and 1380. It implies a big reduction in output in the 1330s, a decade of crisis. However, production and yields are stable from 1342. The years before the Black Death were not crisis years, unlike those that followed (Fossier and Fossier 1955). Fourquin (1964) reached the same conclusion for the Parisian region. Thus, the greatest fluctuation in France's population resulted from a fortuitous element, the Black Death, and not to a famine sometimes linked to it.

How big an impact did famines have on France's population? Let us focus on 1693–94, a major famine, with this question in mind. There is no lack of documentation for claims that a proliferation of peasants died of starvation during the great famines of the Sun King's reign. In *Les années des misère* (1991), Lachiver highlights the extent of the demographic crises towards the end of Louis XIV's reign. He reckons the annual death toll in the preceding decade (1683–92) to have been about 780,000 deaths. In 1693 and 1694 the number of deaths were around 1,236,400 and 1,600,400, respectively. This implies an excess mortality of 876,800 over those two years (Lachiver 1991: 480). To these 1.3 million deaths must be added a deficit of about 0.4 million births, producing a demographic deficit of 1.7 million in two years. The 1693–94 famine's death toll of 1.3 million made it as murderous in relative terms as World War I, and it achieved its toll in half the time. But within a decade much of this loss had been made good by a combination of reduced mortality (since famine had hastened the deaths of some of the elderly and most vulnerable) and increased births (Chevet 1984; Lachiver 1991: 480).

Subsistence crisis obviously could upset demographic trends. Nonetheless, their effects were not long-lasting. During the decade following the catastrophe of 1693–94 annual deaths averaged only 590,000, or 110,000 fewer than before the crisis, while the number of births rose. Famines could put a brake on population growth, but there can be no doubt that it was the excess of births over deaths that dominated population trends. Thus, despite repeated famines, according to the estimates of the Institut national d'études démographiques, population remained more or less stable at about 20 million – that is, at approximately the same level as the pre-Black-Death maximum.

The subsistence crisis of 1693–94 suggests certain hypotheses regarding the link between famines and epidemics. Thus, the poor 1693 harvest is usually believed to have caused the deaths. However, typhus was responsible for much of the excess mortality in the autumn and spring of 1693–94 (Le Roy Ladurie 2007), as indicated by the increase in adult mortality. Typhus often accompanies famine, but it is not a nutrition-sensitive disease. Moreover, this reduction in the population should have reduced the pressure on the demand for food as early as March 1694, when an increase in mortality fell into place. One wonders if the excess mortality due to epidemics did not impact on market prices. In the Paris region, where food availability fell by 30 per cent, prices rose by 80 per cent relative to the average of the previous three years. The implications for the entitlements of those dependent on the markets are grim, but for others only epidemics posed a threat. Such would seem to have been the case for the ladies of Saint-Cyr during the winter of 1709 (Bruegel et al. 2013). This suggests that each famine must be analysed using as many sources as possible: production, prices and information about epidemics.

5   Fighting Famines

Appeals to heaven were common in seeking an end to famines. In Chartres in 1681 a procession following a statue of the Virgin to the abbey of Josephat sought to eradicate the scourge. In Paris the shrine of Sainte-Geneviève was carried through the streets. But the intervention of saints could not replace the role of policy.

5.1   Coping and Substituting

In order to survive, the peasants abandoned non-essential items and turned to substitute foods. Wheat was replaced by less prized substitutes such as buckwheat, rye and chestnuts. Potatoes replaced corn, cereals replaced meat and dairy products. In the extreme distress that followed the *grand hiver* of 1709, peasants switched to barley and escaped the worst, retracing paths taken long before. In the same way, the safety valve of buckwheat in the west of France helps explain why Brittany escaped relatively lightly during the great famines of the seventeenth century (Nassiet 1998). The spread of this high-yielding crop, whose ecology was sufficiently different from wheat, helped mitigate famines, though it did not make them disappear altogether, just as the expansion of maize cultivation in the south-west contributed to their gradual elimination (Frêche 1974). In the poor regions of the Massif Central the chestnut fulfilled this role, except in 1709 when 'the tree of bread' froze (Molinier 1985).

The potato, to which some have attributed a very important role, did not appear until the very end of the seventeenth century, and then uniquely in periods of destitution. Significantly, perhaps, the first reference to a trade in the root dates from 1694, in the middle of a severe famine (Molinier 1985). Incapable of being converted to flour and for a long time limited in culinary potential, the potato remained a food lacking in taste, quite apart from the cultural resistance of those who were determined to restrict it to animal fodder. That said, one cannot be sure of its role. Did this drift towards other foods reflect the extreme distress of populations forced to sacrifice quality for quantity in order to survive? Was this the sign of an accelerating impoverishment and dietary degradation of past populations, as claimed by Morineau (1970b)?

5.2   The Attitude of the Authorities

When confronted with the threat of famine, towns and cities sought to procure wheat at any price and to feed the needy. They paid for the distribution of bread by imposing a special tax on the wealthy. They also sought to build up stocks, but, in the case of serious shortages, they were typically left no choice but to borrow heavily in order to acquire supplies, which led to persistent fiscal imbalance. This is one of the reasons – though there were others, such as billeting soldiers and financing their departure – for the high indebtedness of urban communities at the end of the reign of Louis XIV. Conversely, municipal authorities sought to keep out destitute migrants, as they were new mouths to feed and likely to cause disturbances. Rescuing them or giving them alms were forbidden, and attempts were made to return them to their parish of origin, including the use of coercive means, ranging from imprisonment and flogging to shackles or the galleys. The ill were consigned to charity hospitals.

The policy of royal governments, like that of cities, was to protect urban consumers for fear of violent unrest and to regulate the market in order to ensure supplies for urban areas. This was to avoid the troubles that might arise from supply shortfalls and speculation. Every effort was made to extract the maximum from rural areas up to the point of leaving them with little. Thus, in 1694, the survival of Paris was ensured at the expense of producing regions such as the Beauce and Île-de-France, which, already in deficit, suffered a terrible famine; efforts were also made to move wheat from areas in relative surplus to those more heavily in deficit. The barges and the wagons charged with this task were the target of people who saw food reserves leaving and feared, in turn, being hit by hunger. In the eighteenth century local administrators (*intendants*) were equally reluctant to relinquish their grain for the benefit of other provinces. Such transfers fed many 'emotions' because the masses were constantly on guard against those *affameurs* (literally, 'starvers') who were bent on availing themselves of more attractive prices elsewhere, even at the risk of leaving their own regions at risk.

It is unlikely, however, that these grain merchants maximised their gains. In fact, they were administratively and 'morally' constrained to supply the market in a more or less regular way.[2] Their appetite for speculation earned them the wrath of the authorities and the disapproval,

---

[2] By 'moral economy', we mean the pressure exercised by consumers to ensure that the market is supplied with provisions, born of the conviction that the wealthy were morally bound to supply corn to the poor.

to use a mild term, of the less well off in rural areas. The example of the Chartier family in Île-de-France shows clearly the annoyances associated with attempting to make the most of the circumstances. Fines and discredit were heaped on François Chartier, who had tried to sell at the maximum during the 1740 crisis (Moriceau and Postel-Vinay 1992). The constraints of the 'moral economy' severely limited the freedom to trade in grain. That is why, surprisingly perhaps, a wealthy and prudent farmer such as Chartier regularly delivered bag after bag to the market, indifferent to the profitable opportunities open to him – quite different from the caricature of a speculator who exploited the lean months of the year.

The conviction that traders were hatching a conspiracy that might lead to famine regularly mobilised crowds, which prevented convoys of grain from leaving for other areas, seized grain stored by ecclesiastical institutions or big farmers, looted markets or, more frequently 'taxed' grain at a price deemed fair (Kaplan 1982). During the eighteenth century (with the 'Flour Wars' in 1775 and 1789) and again in the nineteenth century, such protests, both peasant and urban, remained endemic and were more or less severely repressed.

In the France of Louis XIV a cascade of regulations strictly controlled the trade and sale of wheat. Such regulations extended much older measures taken by the monarchy in the sixteenth century (Buat 2010). A close eye was kept on markets to curb speculative manoeuvres by producers and, especially, by traders; off-market negotiations were prohibited, there was a ban on bringing unsold grain home, strict rules were defined for ordinary consumers, bakers and merchants. The state taxed bread, and stored grain in order to curb rising prices (Miller 1999). In some cities (e.g. Lille, Lyon) granaries (*greniers d'abondance*) were set up at the initiative of stewards or councillors to stem dearths (Cerisier 2004). This intrusion had paradoxical effects. There is no denying that it did reduce the impact of speculation to some extent, but it also fuelled rumours that the government was trying to starve the people by hoarding food and the resultant persistent rise in prices. It thus broke the implicit contract that linked the king as provider to his people and gave rise to the myth of the 'famine conspiracy' (*complot de famine*).

The authorities kept a close eye on fluctuations in production. During crises they took steps to ensure that urban areas were provided for, took inventories of food availability, required merchants to declare their stocks, visited granaries and requisitioned surpluses, forced traders to supply markets, prohibited the purchase of unripe grain, punished speculators, reacted to the price recorded by *mercuriale* and controlled increases in the price of bread – at the expense of bakers. Penalties were severe;

generally, the galleys. The monarch forbade grain exports and removed prohibitions on imports. He sought to encourage grain imports through the Mediterranean and present-day Ukraine or through the Baltic from the plains of Russia and Poland. The problem was twofold: cumbersome transport networks, which meant that the grains often arrived too late; and the need for convoys in wartime, which led to further delays. In times of conflict, it relied on Jean Bart and other privateers to seize some Dutch ships transporting grain. Smuggling was another way of getting corn. Of course, neighbouring states also banned the export of grain during famines. This presented strong incentives to those who could evade border surveillance to supply grain to deficit border provinces (Cerisier 2004): 'Des mesures d'urgence dont l'efficacité fut mitigée mais qui atténuèrent autant que faire se pouvait l'impact des crises de subsistances' ('The effectiveness of such emergency measures was uneven but they did ease the impact of food crises').

6   Conclusion: an End to Famines

After 1709 there were still periods of tension regarding food supplies, but nothing comparable to what had been experienced previously. Apart from a few difficult episodes, such as the regional crises of 1740–41 or 1747 or that of 1768–70, these were a far cry from the catastrophes of the era of the Sun King. 'Dearths' erupted here and there in 1749–50, 1753–55 and 1757–58, and again in 1776, 1785 and 1789 (Béaur 2000), probably following harvest shortfalls that were out of proportion to the ensuing price increases.

The great famines of the seventeenth century had disappeared, however. When classic demographic patterns reappeared they were in a much-attenuated form (Weir 1984; 1989; Chevet 1993). That is why historians have taken to referring to these crises as 'latent', as distinct from the 'lethal' crises of previous decades. Goubert's famous graph describing Saint-Lambert-des-Levées in the Val-de-Loire (see Figure 4.7) shows these 'towers' of death and their slow but steady reduction in the eighteenth century (Goubert 1960: II, 48–9). Even in the nineteenth century, and, indeed, right up to the final crisis of 1853–57, there were occasional failures of the productive system. But one can hardly speak of famine. Neither the crisis of 1817 nor that of 1848 would have shaken the July Monarchy, nor did they lead to any excess mortality (Chevet and Ó Gráda 2004; 2007).

What, then, explains this unexpected disappearance of famine in the eighteenth century? How did France escape from the grain 'trap'? Any answer should free itself of the notion that this transition was sharp and

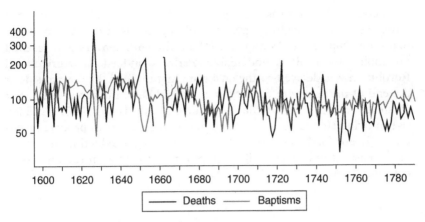

Figure 4.7 Births and deaths in St Lambert des Levées, c. 1580–1790
Source: Goubert (1960: tab. 2, 48–9, fig. 17).

involved a rapid shift from an old to a new economic regime. What part did climate change and the end of the famous Little Ice Age play, so much part of the historiography but now subject to challenge? How important was public policy that exerted an ever tighter control on the flow of goods? What of technological progress, which eased the difficulties facing consumers by improving the storage and the transport of grain? What role did increases in production, more regular harvests and more efficient markets also probably play in the disappearance of famine?

Let us conclude with some hypotheses. It is possible that improved inventory management helped to counter deficits in bad years. In some regions, the cultivation of new crops such as potatoes, buckwheat and maize helped to mitigate famines and food shortages (Morineau 1970a; Frêche 1974; Nassier 1998), particularly in the nineteenth century (Chevet and Ó Gráda 2004). Given that these crops were restricted to certain regions and tended (especially potatoes) to become available late in the season, they were no insurance against all famines, particularly in the eighteenth and early nineteenth centuries and in the Paris Basin. It seems too that the year-to-year variation in crop yields decreased (Neveux and Tits-Dieuaide 1979; compare Campbell and Ó Gráda 2011). Chevet (1984) suggests that shifting cultivation methods, by permitting the soil to store water when rainfall was plentiful (retention capacity) and release it when required, and by allowing the soil to store mineral nutrients, were responsible for this improvement, which offered an important buffer against climatic variation. Taken together, these two complementary elements contributed to the attenuation of oscillations in yields.

Of course, it is not easy to say which of these explanations mattered more. The role agricultural progress played in sustaining a population that grew from 22 to 28 million in the eighteenth century and reached 40 million by 1900 is undeniable. Perhaps, indeed, an Agricultural Revolution was delayed by the civil wars that ravaged the countryside at the end of the sixteenth century and the middle of the seventeenth. For whatever reason, a major change occurred towards 1715–20: a sudden rise in living standards and consumption, as reflected in probate inventories (Béaur forthcoming); and, simultaneously, a reduction in poverty or, at least, of indigence – signs that France was then in the process of entering a new era.

5 Germany, Switzerland and Austria

Dominik Collet and Daniel Krämer

Famines affected Austria, Germany and Switzerland for centuries. For a long time they constituted 'normal exceptions' to the daily life of their population. Episodes of *Teuerung* (dearth) and *Hungersnot* (famine/starvation) marked disastrous but regular intervals well until the nineteenth century. Several large-scale famines had such severe effects that they continued to frame collective memory and individual action long after their demographic impact had faded. Their hold on the public imagination and policy has prompted some historians to characterise these societies as *Mangel-* or *Knappheitsgesellschaften* (societies of want, scarcity societies) (Szöllösi-Janze 1997; Odenwälder 2008).

The historical centre of Europe was extremely diverse. Its political and natural environments both varied substantially. The region encompassed vastly different ecotypes and agrarian systems as well as polities ranging from the Swiss canton to the Holy Roman Empire. However, this heterogeneity was bounded by a well-established and strikingly uniform 'canon' of famine policy and a shared repertoire of coping strategies. Famines did not stop at political or natural borders. As the most serious events were initiated by cross-regional weather anomalies, they affected all German-speaking areas simultaneously. The repeated exposition to these shocks resulted in a shared political, economic and cultural response.

The historiography in this field remains highly fragmented due to political and disciplinary boundaries. Abel's initial overview (1974) has been supplemented by a range of case studies. Most of them focus on public policy during famines. Very few include more recent concepts (vulnerability approach, historical climatology, environmental history) or research informal practices of subsistence, the gendered economies of survival and the cultural consequences of famines. We will therefore begin with a walk-through, identifying and outlining major famine events spanning the period from the Great Famine of 1315–17 up to the last major crisis in 1845–48. In a second step we distil some general trends of famines in the area and discuss their causes as well as responses and adaptations to them.

1   Tracing Famines

This chapter focuses on severe, cross-regional famines in the area of modern-day Switzerland, Germany and Austria. In historical Europe this corresponds roughly to the territories occupied by German states within the borders of the *Deutscher Bund* of 1815, the Swiss federation and the Habsburg Empire excluding Alsace-Lorraine, Hungary, Bohemia and Moravia. For this region a typical 'famine year' can be described (Pfister and Brázdil 2006: 120; Reith 2011: 14).[1] It would usually involve adverse weather conditions, often aggravated by societal stress. Famines resulting exclusively from war or economic turbulence played a secondary and often more localised role. The biophysical drivers invariably included cold and rain: severe winter with late frosts and persistent rain during the growing season and harvest were particularly damaging.[2] Of these, it was the excessive rainfall that hit the grain-based agrarian systems of the region hardest. The resulting reduction of available food was aggravated by the asymmetrical distribution of food entitlements. In the highly stratified societies of central Europe biophysical and social drivers of famine went hand in hand.

The areas most affected by famine were those without access to the cheap transport offered by rivers and coasts. Rural regions were often hit harder than towns, which had easier access to credit, though city states and small territories often fell victim to disastrous blockades by neighbours. In the later period proto-industrial areas became disproportionally vulnerable as high bread prices were accompanied by economic stagnation, offsetting the benefit of additional monetary income. As a result, the Ore Mountains, the Eichsfeld, the inner Swiss cantons and some Austrian upland areas remained vulnerable for most of the time.

Due to the buffers provided by grain storage and transport or by grain substitutes, a single bad year was usually not enough to threaten the regional food systems. Famine conditions usually occurred only during back-to-back harvest failures or long-term perturbations. When adverse conditions persisted for more than one harvest year, the weak precautionary systems in place were prone to collapse. Famine cycles usually ended with the first good harvest. However, political inaction, economic

---

[1] The striking uniformity of the famine cycles with their demo-economic framing inspired Abel to adapt Labrousse's models of a *crise de type ancien* and a *crise larvée* to the German-speaking regions of Europe (Abel 1974). Both terms remain in use but are often loosely applied (Pfister 2007a: 98). The concepts have also been criticised and extended because they marginalised important cultural and climatic factors (Mauelshagen 2010).

[2] In a marked diversion from the south-Alpine and Iberian climate systems, droughts play a minor role for central Europe: see Pfister (2005).

turbulence and the ensuing epidemics could prolong excess mortality for some time.

The sources available to trace these historic catastrophes are varied and often patchy. Demographic data for the many territories of central Europe are not available in the same density and quality as for England or France. Parish registers of baptisms and burials start only in the seventeenth century and vary widely in scope and quality. As a result, most population studies focus on the proto-statistical area (post-1740) and are often biased towards larger territories and geared towards aggregated long-term trends.[3] These gaps are partly compensated for by the progress of historical climatology. The detailed reconstruction of past climates and weather for the German-speaking regions in recent years helps to trace one of the main drivers of historical famines (Pfister 1999a; Strömmer 2003; Glaser 2008; Jäger 2010).[4] However, not all palaeoclimatological studies based on proxy data offer a resolution high enough to identify bad harvests. As a result, the patchy demographic and climatological record has to be supplemented by historical source material ranging from administrative and economic documents to eye-witness accounts and material culture. It is particularly rich and broad for this area and forms the backbone of many local studies.[5]

Price data, while locally available, are only partly reliable. Official prices often did not represent market prices. They frequently omitted peaks and ignored non-market transactions. Additionally, authorities often intervened in prices and markets (Piuz and Zumkeller 1985; Gerhard and Engel 2006). Differences in market integration further complicate comparisons between prices in landlocked Swiss regions with the German lowlands or in towns down the Danube or the Rhine (Studer 2008). As a result, (grain based) consumer price indices (CPIs) are available only for towns in the Swiss Plateau for the years 1501 to 2006 and need to be treated with caution (Studer and Schuppli 2008).

2 Early Famine Events (1315–1570)

The earliest substantiated records of famines date from Carolingian times (Jörg 2010). For the years 805–06, 1005–06, 1043–46, 1099–1101, 1144–46, 1150–51, 1195–98, 1217–18 and 1225–27 multiple and independent accounts of severe, cross-regional food shortage exist

---

[3] See Pfister and Fertig (2010) for an overview of demographic data on historical Germany and an assessment of challenges and biases.

[4] Historical weather data for the area are available at www.tambora.org and www.euroclimhist.unibe.ch.

[5] For an edition of regional sources on famine and dearth in the area, see Pallach (1986).

(Curschmann 1900).[6] The early chronicles and capitularies that list these events often lack the detail necessary to trace the scope, severity and causes of the events. But they do illustrate the *longue durée* of many later famine policies. The sources list the proclamation of export bans, price caps and fast days as well as the collection and distribution of alms to discourage migration. Although little is known about the implementation of these instructions, they highlight the famine policy as an early keystone of legitimate rule. They also offer insights into how these famines were interpreted: the plurality of provisions is based on the concept of an 'economy of sins' that tied religious, social and natural interpretations together.

With more sources available, the famine of 1315–17 is the first that can be identified with certainty as an event affecting all German-speaking regions – and, indeed, much of Europe (Jordan 1996). Contemporary texts invariably point to sustained wet and cold weather as the initial driver that caused widespread food shortage accompanied by epidemics and epizootics. Although its severity is clear, more detailed exploration has been limited by the absence of serial records comparable to the English manorial accounts used by Kershaw (1973) and the highly fragmented historical record.

For the famine of the 1430s the documentation is somewhat broader, due to the interim rise of the cities. During this period a decade of cold and wet conditions, triggered by the Spörer Minimum in sunspot activity, initiated a long series of bad harvests. The weather anomaly hit most of Europe, but in Germany it coincided with political tension between the booming cities and sovereigns. By 1437 epidemics appeared that devastated urban as well as rural areas. Although precise vital data are not available, the sources give a clear indication that famine conditions prevailed from 1437 to 1440 in large parts of the German-speaking territories (Jörg 2008). In the city environment the full 'canon' of famine policy was now put in place: attempts to control the import and export, the price and the sale of grain as well as regulations on the movement of people and their moral and religious behaviour. Many aspects mirror the *annona* system developed in Italy a century earlier, with much effort directed to the construction of public granaries (Collet 2010). Brandenberger (2004: 365–408) and Jörg (2008: 386–95) also stress the role of famine policy as a catalyst for the intensification of administrative activities in general. The welfare policies paved the way for the appropriation of competences by city

---

[6] For lists of regional shortages and famines, see Curschmann (1900), Abel (1974) and Militzer (1998).

authorities in many related fields. In the central European context, this entanglement of food policy with the process of governmentalisation marks a momentous development that later spread from the cities to the territorial states (Kaplan 1976).

The major famines of the 1570s and the 1590s were initiated by similar weather patterns. Cold winters, late frosts and strong, untimely rains caused multi-annual harvest failures. They are frequently framed in the context of the Little Ice Age (Behringer, Lehmann and Pfister 2005). Some historians have attempted to explore the 'cultural consequences' of these famines, focusing on their impact on public life and religion. The shortages have been linked to a rise in millennialism and religious fervour (Lehmann 1981; Pfister 2005). The most prominent (and contended) connection has been the attempt to link these famines to contemporary witch-hunts. Accusations of witchcraft often circled around the defendants' supposed ability to provoke unfavourable weather and induce harvest failures. The correlation of climate anomalies and a peak in witch-hunts found by Behringer (1995) highlights the use of witch trials to provide scapegoats – a conjunction he relates to the political turmoil and the religious division of the time, which threatened traditional explanations of food shortages.[7]

3   Famines in the Seventeenth and Eighteenth Centuries

During the Thirty Years War (1618–48) severe food shortages affected much of central Europe. The repeated experience of hunger colours most narratives of these catastrophic times. The constant interplay of war, weather and epidemics opens up the panorama of historical food crises. At the same time this entanglement complicates attempts to discern individual episodes of famine and their causes. The severe shortages of 1620–23 are often attributed to the strategic debasement of currencies (*Kipper und Wipper*) as well as violent conflicts, the closure of borders and trade routes and aggressive requisitioning by the competing forces. They are probably the best example of a 'man-made' or 'green famine' on a large scale, with minor biophysical stress. However, in 1625 and 1627–30 (and again in 1651–52) it was exceptionally bad harvests that initiated famine conditions in the German territories and parts of Austria, which in turn prepared the ground for epidemic diseases. During the 1630s episodes of famine remained frequent but more local, often tied to military occupations and the sieges of major cities (Roeck 1987: 216). Most contemporaries blamed the catastrophic consequences with regional

---

[7] For the nexus between climate and witch-hunts, see also Pfister (2007b).

population losses of 30 to 50 per cent on man-made interventions, such as sieges and marauding mercenaries. Their interpretations are in clear opposition to modern research, which stresses a marked decline in overall weather conditions instead (Parker 2013).

After some calmer years the 1690s brought another string of bad harvests and subsistence crises. These occurred on a European scale (Lachiver 1991; Cullen 2010) and are often associated with the Maunder Minimum of sunspot activity. Severe bouts of rain and cold reduced harvests by up to 50 per cent in the years 1691–93 and again in 1698–1701. In the stratified societies of the time this translated into a trebling of food prices, with consequences so disastrous for the poor that famine conditions prevailed in wide areas. Research has so far focused on the Swiss Plateau (Mattmüller 1987) and Saxony, which was hit particularly hard (Militzer 1998; Bräuer 2002).

In comparison, the crises of 1708–09 and 1740 seem to have caused less devastation in German-speaking Europe. This might be attributed to the reduced impact of epidemic diseases and warfare (compared with France in 1709) or the fact that the associated weather anomalies brought acute, extremely cold winters rather than persistent rainfall during summer and harvest (Post 1990; Monahan 1993; Glaser 2008). Both crises did lead to famine conditions among the poor in many areas, however, and desperate struggles for food and relief. The 'Great Winter' of 1708–09 is also notable for a well-documented episode of early long-distance migration, which saw thousands of (pseudo-) Protestant refugees stranded in London and living in tent cities awaiting their transfer to America (Otterness 2004; Schulte Beerbühl 2004). Such a break with traditional patterns of predominantly local and temporary migration was uncommon. Up to the mid-eighteenth century most societal responses and policy measures stayed within the framework established centuries ago: intense but often unsuccessful market regulation, the scapegoating of minorities, the promotion of prayer, penitence and alms-giving alongside the varied strategies of the informal economy of survival. A marked break with the old regime of 'facing famine' occurred only towards the end of the eighteenth century, starting with the famine of 1770–72.

The famine of 1770–72 marks the last subsistence crisis that was felt universally across all the German-speaking lands as well as most neighbouring countries. It is also the first event in which an independent secular understanding of famine asserts itself. As a result, the crisis became a catalyst for changes in education, economics, welfare and medicine. Due to the proliferation of sources during the Enlightenment, the 1770–72 famine is the first in this area for which reliable vital data are available on a larger scale.[8] There is also rich documentation on weather patterns, as well as on the reactions and actions of the affected population, particularly in the numerous volumes of *Teuerungsliteratur* (dearth literature) that appeared during the famine (Soden 1828).

The crisis was triggered by severe back-to-back harvest failures. It originated in heavy, persistent rains that affected an area stretching from France to Poland and from Scandinavia to Switzerland (Pfister and Brázdil 2006).[9] The long duration and the large area affected quickly overwhelmed the temporal and interregional buffer strategies of food storage and transport. Moving and storing grain was limited further by the wet conditions at harvest time and the persistent flooding of the major river systems. Malnutrition and increased migration soon encouraged the spread of epidemic diseases. Combined with a substantial decrease in conceptions and marriages, this all resulted in a marked reduction of the population. In Saxony alone an estimated 60,000 people died due to famine and its related diseases. In combination with 36,000 deferred births, this led to a population loss of 6 per cent (Blaschke 1967: 127). Bavaria and Prussia seem to have suffered losses on a similar scale, of around 5 to 7 per cent (Kluge 1987; Rankl 2005). In the Ore Mountains and neighbouring Bohemia, where a military survey took place, some 200,000 or 10 per cent of the inhabitants had either perished or fled by 1772 (Brázdil et al. 2001). Some areas in western Germany fared better, particularly those with good transport links, access to credit and less exposure to regional epidemics.[10] However, many local parish registers across Austria and Germany reported a quadrupling of deaths and few if any marriages.[11] Excess mortality was high but probably less pronounced in Switzerland, where the emigration of up to 10 per cent of local inhabitants may have accounted for much of the decline in

---

[8] Several states initiated their statistical series in response to the famine: see Rankl (2005: 779) for Bavaria, Uebele, Grünebaum and Kopsidis (2013) for Saxony, and Pfister and Fertig (2010) more generally. For an edited early survey on Austria and Bohemia in 1770–71, see Hochedlinger and Tanter (2005). For Switzerland, several local studies ('Mattmüller Schule') and the database BERNHIST (www.bernhist.ch) are available. Due to serious gaps and biases, national estimates remain difficult.

[9] As synchronous weather anomalies (and famines) occurred in India and Central America, a common climatic trigger has been conjectured but not yet identified (Collet 2014b).

[10] Zimmermann (1994) suggests a *crise larvée* for Württemberg. Schlöder (2014) observes similar muted conditions in the cities of the Rhineland. The demographic studies of Post (1990) and Gehrmann (2000: 108) suggest that epidemics rather than economic variables account for these geographical disparities. The assumption that Prussia escaped the crises through the prowess of its leader, Frederick the Great, has been questioned as a borrusophile myth: see Collet (2014a).

[11] See Hruschka (1940), Abel (1974: 252–54) and Priewer, Göbler and Priewer (2002). Rankl (2005) reports a doubling of deaths all across Bavaria.

population (Mattmüller 1982). In the German and Austrian territories migration was similarly widespread. Next to the crowds of people looking for temporary relief in cities thousands more chose to emigrate permanently. Many went to Hungary via the Danube. Some travelled with permits as part of the second *Schwabenzug* (Swabian trek). Many more migrated informally and often illegally.[12] The demographic impact was substantial. For much of the population, burials replaced baptisms in their daily lives.[13]

During the 1770–72 event we can trace profound changes in the way famines were perceived. Religious, social and physical interpretations that had previously coexisted were increasingly conceptualised in opposition to each other (Collet 2014b). Whether people understood famine as a *punishment* by an angry god, as the vicious result of human *profiteering* or as a consequence of real *scarcity* caused by adverse weather had profound impacts on their coping strategies. During the 1770s vocal advocates of social and natural interpretations used the crisis to promote and implement changes. Physiocrats urged the restoration of a 'natural' flow of goods by removing market regulations. Even though their free-trade experiments failed, they used the disaster to establish themselves as a professional body, preparing the ground for major changes in economic thought, such as the development of *Nationalökonomie* or classical economics (Zimmermann 1987; Graber 2010). Physicians used the famine to press for a public health system and initiated a widespread medicalisation of the crisis, relabelling the starving people as sick rather than poor (Rankl 2005: 772). Other reformers understood famine primarily as a social challenge. They advocated changes in education and welfare in order to turn starving children into productive citizens. By circulating dedicated *Hungerzeitschriften* (famine papers) they raised funds for schools and poorhouses that gradually replaced traditional forms of outdoor relief and alms-giving. As a result, the famine became a trigger for a more comprehensive school system (Collet 2015). In Switzerland Pestalozzi founded his first reform school at the height of the famine. Saxony proclaimed compulsory education laws in 1772, the same year that Bavaria dissolved the Jesuit order in the context of the reform of its public school system (Rankl 2005: 775; Jahn 2010: 269–75).

---

[12] See Rankl (2005: 771) for Bavaria, Pfrenzinger (1941) for Franconia, Schmahl (2001) for Hessia and Kurmainz and Hippel (1984) for Württemberg. On the peak of emigration to Hungary during the famine, see the many studies by Hacker in the *Südostdeutsches Archiv*.

[13] For tentative regional estimates, see Vasold (2008) and Pfister and Fertig (2010). Based on incomplete aggregations, Post (1990) lists 160,000 excess deaths and a reduction of births by 80,000, while Le Roy Ladurie (2006: 71) reports a reduction of Germany's total population by between 2.5 and 4.5 per cent.

The new interpretation of famine also opened pathways for the interaction of subjects and sovereigns. In many places rulers and their people entered into 'empowering interactions' (Collet 2014b), circumventing established channels of communication at the expense of third parties – often the Church or local administration. In the extremely disaggregated German territories this could initiate a streamlining of governmental structures. Practices of collusion at the expense of distant others are clearly visible during the First Partition of Poland at the height of the famine (Collet 2014a). They also motivated the rise of anti-Semitic 'Grain Jew' imagery in central Europe during this period. By targeting supposed racketeers and grain hoarders in carefully staged food riots they sought to activate entitlements and assume new participatory rights (Gailus 2001). The 1770s famine thus marks a *trading zone* in which the competition of religious and secular famine interpretations increasingly became a catalyst for change.[14]

4   An End to Famines: 1816 and the Hungry Forties

The 'Year without a Summer' in 1816 became a turning point for famines in central Europe. Its harvest failures still initiated a large-scale subsistence crisis, motivated fierce debates and left a deep impression in cultural memory. The actual number of casualties was considerably lower than in similar previous events, however. In contrast to most of the earlier famines, the trigger for the crisis is known: the eruption of Mt. Tambora in Indonesia in April 1815 exceeded most volcanic eruptions of the last 7,000 years in magnitude and influenced the global climate. In western-central Europe it caused persistent rainfall and a plummeting of temperatures that ruined regional wine and grain harvests (Auchmann et al. 2012; Brönnimann and Krämer 2016). However, the 'last great subsistence crisis in the Western world' (Post 1977) was also triggered by socio-economic stressors: the previous Napoleonic Wars had caused economic and political upheaval and left behind thousands of demobilised soldiers. Innovations such as mechanised looms had put pressure on local economies. The fallout from the Congress of Vienna (1814–15) tied up the administrative resources of states such as Prussia, the Kingdom of Bavaria, the Kingdom of Württemberg and Switzerland. When prices rose rapidly in 1816 economic and political resilience in central Europe was weak (Krämer 2015).

[14] Paradoxically, in public memory the famine is associated with the supposed proliferation of Germany's national crop – the potato. In spite of the many well-meaning treatises, however, there is little indication that it went into large-scale cultivation before the nineteenth century, as it was ill-suited to the demands of the established agro-social system (Teuteberg and Wiegelmann 1986).

Relief was impeded further by flooding. Major rivers such as the Rhine became unnavigable, delaying grain transports (Weber 2005). In 1817 prices rose throughout the German-speaking lands, particularly in inland areas (Post 1977; Weber 2005). The demographic consequences were moderate, however: in Prussia population growth decreased only slightly, and in Bavaria the demographic impact was short-lived (Sieglerschmidt 1992; Müller 1998). Mortality exceeded fertility only in Württemberg, but even in the southern states emigration was more important for the loss of population than excess mortality. In the first seven months of 1817 alone more than 30,000 people left their homes, overwhelming the established system of emigration to the United States (Moltmann 1989; Bade 2000; Grabbe 2001).[15]

Famine conditions occurred only in the eastern parts of Switzerland. They hit the densely populated proto-industrialised regions rather than the western grain-growing districts.[16] The distribution mirrored the degree of market integration as well as the dependence on grain imports: weavers and cotton spinners were affected by decreasing nominal wages, tariff barriers and structural changes in textile production. At the same time the integrated economic zone around Lake Constance collapsed. To prevent rioting, Württemberg, Baden and Bavaria embargoed grain exports, cutting eastern Switzerland off from its breadbaskets and leaving the area exposed to famine (Krämer 2015).

Such actions fell in line with the established 'canon' of famine policy. Similar grain embargoes came into force throughout much of central Europe (Medick 1985; Bass 1991).[17] However, the rise of free-trade ideas among the ruling elite led to numerous conflicts, frequent policy changes and much local variation. In Württemberg the successor to King Frederick I triumphantly reinstated state interventions. In Baden and Bavaria the sovereigns staged themselves as protectionist 'father-kings' to secure their power in turbulent times (Medick 1985). In Switzerland the western cantons pursued a more active grain policy drawing on the 'canon' of famine policy than their less experienced and well off eastern counterparts.

In spite of this staged benevolence, the state was not the most important protector and provider of the poor. After the Napoleonic secularisation

---

[15] In Switzerland, emigration cannot be quantified. However, Ritzmann-Blickenstorfer (1997: 489) assumes an 'exodus of the poorest of the poorest'.

[16] A similar east–west pattern can be traced in the Swiss famines of the 1690s and the 1770s. During the eighteenth century mountainous regions were generally less vulnerable than the crop-growing regions in the Swiss Plateau or the cattle-breeding and cheese-producing areas in the Swiss Prealps and inner alpine zones (Netting 1981; Ostrom 1990).

[17] In Prussia, proto-industrialised areas were also more vulnerable than grain-exporting regions or areas with a subsistence economy: see Bass (1991).

of many religious institutions, charities and benevolent societies played an increasingly important part. They established soup kitchens and subsidised the cost of bread to alleviate the greatest poverty. Although most initiatives were only temporary, the understanding of hunger changed gradually. Starvation was no longer seen as a sign of a moral failure or, more generally, the fault of the hungry. Instead, the plight of the weavers and spinners everywhere raised the awareness of structural economic causes, paving the way for an institutionalised public welfare in the coming decades that eventually superseded Christian *caritas*.

Older interpretations of famine continued to evolve, however. In many areas the crisis of 1816–17 initiated a marked resurgence of religious feeling. Pilgrimages that had been discouraged by the Church for decades flourished again in Bavaria, now in a new, popular guise. In the pietistic communities of Württemberg private prayer circles thrived (Gestrich 2003). Many fell for a new breed of spiritualists, with the visionary mystic Thomas Pöschl and the doomsayer Juliane von Krüdener commanding large audiences of well-educated followers in Austria, Switzerland and southern Germany (Sommer 2013).

The famine of 1816–17 therefore marks a transition period from a moral to a market economy. This transfer increased the vulnerability for parts of the population. High levels of market integration did not necessarily protect from shocks. They could just as easily become a liability and increase exposure, particularly for the proto-industrialised regions, with vulnerabilities shifting across regions and time during the crisis (Krämer 2015).

After 1816–17 the potato became more important as a subsistence food, particularly on marginal land (Bass 2007; Schanbacher 2015). When it failed in 1845 due to the potato blight and a bad grain harvest ensued in 1846, the last episode of mass hunger in central Europe began (Salzmann 1978; Bass 2007; Schanbacher 2015). In fact, dependence on the potato seemingly played a key role in making large areas of nineteenth-century central and northern Europe somewhat more susceptible to famines compared to some southern European countries (see the introduction to this book, Chapter 1, for a general discussion of this point). However, in central Europe the crisis of 1845–48 is most frequently associated not with mass starvation but with political struggle. The link to the revolutionary events of 1848 is still a matter of debate (Berger and Spoerer 2001; Schanbacher 2015).

Although prices rose sharply and birth rates declined, the overall demographic consequences were moderate. In Prussia around 40,000 hunger-related deaths were registered, in the Kingdom of Hanover the crisis was less severe and in the Canton of Bern in Switzerland the increasing mortality was limited to poor districts (Pfister 1990; Bass 2007; Schanbacher 2015).[18] In Prussia the risk of being undernourished depended on the diversification of income sources and crops as well as trade relations. The purchasing power of cities or states could reverse commodity flows. As a result, the enhanced transport capacities, accelerated grain trade and improved market integration could alleviate shortfalls for some, while increasing the vulnerability of grain-exporting regions (Hecht 2012: 137–8). By this time it was structural poverty rather than production shortfalls that can be identified as the most important factor (Bass 2007). A regional gradient also existed in Bern. The disparities were significant in the crop-growing district between wealthy farmers and the landless, and they have entered cultural memory.[19]

As a result the 'Hungry Forties' became the setting for bitter and often violent political struggle. In Switzerland food imports and the establishment of soup kitchens by the ruling elites levelled inequalities to a certain degree and largely prevented disorder, mass starvation and mass migration (Salzmann 1978; Pfister 1990).[20] Similar attempts can be traced in Austria, but only after food riots had broken out in Bohemia and Vienna (Schanbacher 2015: 49). In the western provinces of Austria, as well as in Baden, Württemberg and Bavaria, grain tariffs were still a part of the 'canon' of famine policy (Mahlerwein 2007). The more reluctant northern states of Germany experienced a disproportional share of riots and protests. Saxony, then a Prussian province, recorded 20 major riots in spring 1847, with a focus on smaller towns and their artisans rather than the industrialised areas. They later fed into the larger struggle of 1848, which shifted the focus from food entitlements to political participation in general (Hecht 2003; 2012).

Why famines in central Europe came to an end in the second half of the nineteenth century is still a matter of debate. The list of possible reasons is long: agricultural innovation, improved market integration and transport systems, increased political participation and better welfare systems, advances in hygiene and combating epidemic disease, positive trade balances with the non-European world and a more benign weather system

---

[18] Consequences were not extreme compared to Ireland. However, the population seems to have suffered more than in Flanders, Denmark or Sweden: see Bass (2007). In the district of Osnabrück, Lower Saxony, 1847 was the only year with a birth deficit between 1815 and 1860: see Schanbacher (2012: 122–4).

[19] Jeremias Gotthelf described the striking disparities in his novels. For the crisis in the years 1845–47, see *Käthi, die Grossmutter*.

[20] In Switzerland, the potato blight was followed by the Sonderbund War in 1847 and a series of bad harvests in the early 1850s. Together with an economic depression, these were the trigger for the mass migration to the United States in these years. See Ritzmann-Blickenstorfer (1997: 556–69) and Pfister (1999b: 62).

after the end of the 'Little Ice Age' have all been put forward. Whatever their relative weight might have been, the sheer scope of these suggestions reflects the sweeping hold the experience of famine had on all aspects of life in historical central Europe.

5 Facing Famine

For much of the time the famines in historical Austria, Germany and Switzerland followed stable patterns of action and reaction. Most of the crises, and particularly the severe ones, developed initially in response to an external biophysical trigger. Man-made 'green famines' were rare. However, the societal set-up, the (in)action of administrations, the agricultural system and the weaknesses of buffer strategies had a substantial influence on the outcome of harvest shortfalls. In many cases vulnerability to famine was built into the system of food storage, distribution and entitlement. The unwillingness or inability to maintain larger granaries or to organise effective interregional exchange and a more flexible agronomic polyculture reflect societal choices. They mirrored the internal inequalities of the central European 'Society of Estates'. Its social arrangements shaped a food system that locked the area in the 'prison' of its specific grain culture (Landsteiner 2000).[21]

Another clear pattern is the strong link of famine events with epidemics. Disease, not physical emaciation, constituted the main killer during a famine. Its presence often transformed a mere shortage into a full-blown famine. Retrospective diagnosis of disease is fraught with difficulties: pathogens change, historical descriptions are vague, illness is often experienced differently in the past and research on historical epidemiology is limited (Pfister 2007a: 99). The main diseases seem to have been fevers and infections of the digestive system. They are often identified as *Faul-* or *Fleckfieber* (typhus) and *Ruhr* (dysentery).[22] As they have a low etiological link with nutritional status and weather conditions they seem to have spread through increased migration and social disorder (Hecker 1839; Post 1990). Climate, demographic pressure, disease and the policy choices of historical grain societies provided the setting for famines in central Europe.

This socio-natural framing encouraged the development of a remarkably widespread and resilient canon of famine policy across

---

[21] For the path dependencies of Europe's grain-centred societies that used its staple crop not just for nourishment but also as a source of wealth and the pillar of tax regimes, see Landsteiner (2005) and Graber (2010: 206 f.).

[22] Earlier famines often saw outbreaks of St Anthony's fire (*Mutterkorn*), a fungus contamination. Later events often coincided with cholera. Reasons for the high incidence of plague and smallpox during famine events are still debated.

the German-speaking areas of Europe. It provided a carefully graded series of actions that could be escalated or retracted in tune with the development of the crises. The measures started with the encouragement of moral behaviour and stretched via (symbolic) market regulation and prayer days to the closure of borders, the forceful confiscation of food stocks, long-distance imports and the execution of trespassers and hoarders (Huhn 1987).

However, even within these 'built environments' (Oliver-Smith 2004), with their traditions, canons and limitations, the responses of the people are characterised by their plurality. Side by side with better-documented market exchanges, people made use of an informal economy. This *Schattenökomomie* or *économie d'aléatoire* included bartering, pawning, gleaning, smuggling, poaching and petty crime.[23] Some people lobbied secular and religious authorities to secure help, evoking the principle of *Hausnothdurft* or *Auskommen* (household subsistence). Others called in favours from neighbours and family, sold non-essential assets, switched to subsistence foods and increased their use of woodlands and commons. Women occasionally used their reduced access to food within household and society as an argument to claim relief (Ulbrich 1993). For some, migration provided another, surprisingly flexible option. Their movements were not limited to permanent, long-distance point-to-point migration. When lasting emigration did occur, the famine usually provided only the catalyst for a process that was already established. More often the threat of permanent migration was used as a tool to acquire help (Bräuer 2002: 228, 235; Hochedlinger and Tanter 2005). Instead, migration was often local, temporary and limited to parts of the household (Jäger 2010: 183f, 196). People frequently shifted to towns or transportation hubs, where relief and entitlements could be activated and medical help was available. Their itineraries illustrate the gaps that existed between the political map of central Europe and the economic or personal geography – gaps that opened up spaces for negotiation (Collet 2011).

In some cases this plurality of social responses led to the exploration of new solutions and initiated adaptations and lasting change. Famines served as catalysts that accelerated ongoing processes of transformation. The 1590s crisis established new trade routes in central Europe (Landsteiner 2005). Famines were also instrumental to the development of *Gute Policey*, legislation aimed at public order through 'good rule'. As a result, shortages sped up processes of governmentalisation in the cities

---

[23] On this hard-to-trace shadow economy, see Buchner and Hoffmann-Rehnitz (2011). For a case study on pawning and trading second-hand goods in Vienna, with a link to the 1770–72 famine, see Stöger (2012). On smuggling, see Collet (2011).

(Roeck 1987; Jörg 2008). Later on they legitimised the expansion of the territorial state (Collet 2014b). Famines also initiated changes to welfare and relief. In many areas they encouraged the general trend towards regulation, proliferation and tighter control of welfare institutions (Jütte 2005). In the late eighteenth century the new, increasingly secular interpretations of famine encouraged even more widespread changes, concerning economic thought, political participation, agriculture, science and education.

Compared to the rest of Europe, Austria, Germany and Switzerland experienced a frequency and magnitude of famine similar to their neighbours. The crises ended somewhat sooner than in Scandinavia but lasted longer than in the trading nations of England and the Netherlands. Many major events were experienced in parallel with bordering territories. Synchronicity is particularly high with France and the North and less obvious with Italy or the Iberian Peninsula.

Research on the social responses to famine has often emphasised differences between central Europe and France or England. This is particularly evident in the discussion of three fields: riots, regulation and relief. The supposed absence of food riots in central Europe (Löwe 1986; Schmidt 1991) has recently been called into question, however (Odenwälder 2008). Mob actions, blockades, price fixings or incidences of *taxation populaire* seem to have been as popular in the Holy Roman Empire and very similar in style to 'riotous' actions in France or England. The scholarly impression of a pacified central Europe is probably due to the more dispersed archival documentation of protests rather than the existence of a 'moral economy from above' that dulled citizens into 'passive obedience' (Medick 1985). Only Switzerland, with its small prosperous polities and traditions of limited political participation, remained relatively peaceful. Similarly, the assumption of more intense market and food regulation in Austria, Germany and Switzerland is at least partly the result of a flood of decrees during crises. Case studies illustrate that compliance was often extremely low (Collet 2011). Many proclamations must be read as symbolic gestures by rulers attempting to portray themselves as concerned and benevolent. The supposed gap between a tightly regulated Empire and England or the Netherlands becomes even less obvious when we consider that many 'free-trade nations' regularly resorted to regulation during food scarcities. It seems that, in times of famine, the otherwise different economic regimes became rather more alike.

Differences prevailed in the set-up of welfare. Relief did not achieve the same coherence that it did in more centralised France or England. Many different agents, from churches to cities and charities, remained involved (Jütte 2005). As no formal poor law set the rules for basic provisioning, people resorted to ad hoc negotiation to safeguard the commitment of authorities to relief. It is probably this piecemeal and localised approach to welfare that is most characteristic of central Europe, with its competing and heterogeneous polities. It was this logic of securing inclusion in the fragmented welfare systems via the exclusion of socially or geographically distant others that encouraged the area's peculiar choice of scapegoats: nowhere else in Europe was the 'Grain Jew' metaphor, with its anti-Semitic embodiment of hoarders, more popular.

6   Famines: Biophysical, Ecological and Social Environments

The populations of historical Austria, Germany and Switzerland suffered severe cross-regional famines until the mid-nineteenth century. Several of these did not just have a demographic effect but carried significant cultural consequences as well. From the designation of potatoes as *Angstknötchen* (fear-knobs) to the setting of popular fairy tales such as *Hänsel and Gretel*, food shortages were deeply embedded in public consciousness. Their devastation inspired intense debates on collective identity, the causes and culprits of the crises and suitable measures of relief and prevention.

All the major events are characterised by the entanglement of natural and man-made impacts. They developed out of the confluence of weather anomalies, usually involving heavy, untimely rains and internal socio-economic vulnerabilities. The fragile precautions in place in the area were regularly overcome by the combination of back-to-back harvest failures with political conflict, economic turmoil, the asymmetrical distribution of entitlements to food, demographic pressure and the agro-social limitations inherent in the *built environments* of its grain societies.

The repeated exposure to famine triggered the development of a long-lived canon of famine policy. It was adopted and accepted across the heterogeneous German-speaking territories, even though the area lacked the central power of France or England. In many respects the canon actually filled the void left by the weak central institutions of the Empire or the Swiss Confederacy and proved instrumental for the development of more local forms of governance. Its origins can be traced back to Carolingian times. The chosen measures reflected the long-lived coexistence of religious, social and natural interpretations. They could involve moral, spiritual and economic action. Their resilience reflects the importance of food provision for legitimate rule during the *ancien*

Table 5.1 *Chronology of famines in Austria, Germany and Switzerland*

Year(s)	Area	Commentary
1315–17	AU, CH, GER	'Great European Famine'
1437–40	CH, GER	
1516–18	CH, GER	
1530–31	AU, CH	
1569–74	AU, CH, GER	Peak in witch-hunts, crop failures, plague
1594–98	AU, GER	
1620–23	GER	'Kipper und Wipper'
1625–30	AU, GER, (CH)	Second peak in witch-hunts, crop failures, plague
1635–36	AU, CH, GER,	Famine and plague during the Thirty Years War
1651–52	GER, (CH)	Economic depression or epidemic, no price peak in Switzerland
1691–95	AU, CH, GER	Only 'real' famine in seventeenth-century Switzerland
1698–1701	AU, CH, GER	
1709–12	AU, GER	'Großer Winter', emigration of German palatines
1724–25	GER	
1739–41	AU, GER	'Große Kälte'
1755–58	GER	Crop failures, Seven Years War
1770–72	AU, CH, GER	Famine in central and northern Europe, heavy rains and inundations, epidemics and epizootics
1787–90	GER	Dearth but no famine
1793–95	CH	Extreme price hikes due to war, but no large-scale famine
1815–17	CH, GER	Eruption of Mt. Tambora in 1815, consequent 'Year without a Summer' in 1816, last outbreaks of famine in the area
1845–48	AU, GER, CH	Potato failure, bad harvests, political struggle, severe dearth locally

Notes: As calendar years differ from the agricultural cycle, broader dates have been given when in doubt. Years in bold indicate particularly severe events.
Sources: Blaschke (1967), Abel (1974), Pfister (1984), Mattmüller (1987), Militzer (1998), Strömmer (2003), Glaser (2008), Studer and Schuppli (2008), Jäger (2010), Reith (2011) and Kurmann (2011).

régime. The precise application of this broad canon of policies provided space for agency and negotiation between the different actors involved. In fact, it frequently became a framework for empowering interactions between sovereigns and subjects that encouraged forms of 'state-building by catastrophe'. Many political, economic and religious groups used this regulatory body as a tool to pursue their own interests and to 'socialise' extreme climate events. Their actions highlight the plurality of human responses to famine and external stressors.

As a result, famines in this area can serve as a probe to study the hidden fault lines of its historical societies. These socio-natural disasters do not just constitute extraordinary events. They provide a mirror for deeper social conflicts and illustrate the hierarchy of values within the stratified *Ständegesellschaft* (society of estates) of central Europe. Their ties to witch-hunts and anti-Semitic imagery, for example, reflect the religious and economic debates of their time. Famines also focused contemporary debates on the role of the sovereign. They highlight the accretion of governmental powers and reveal the existence and persistence of an embedded economy in the heart of Europe. As a result, they must be understood as crucial, socio-natural events. Amid all the suffering and hardship, they highlight the historical plurality of human–environment interactions and their relevance for crucial societal transformations.

6   Low Countries

Daniel Curtis, Jessica Dijkman, Thijs Lambrecht and Eric Vanhaute

Episodes of dearth and famine can be discerned in documents from the Low Countries from as early as the late Carolingian period. As with other parts of Europe at this time, though, we rely ultimately on the perception and opinion of contemporary chroniclers, making it difficult to say anything quantifiable or comparative. For example, one seventeenth-century humanist writer compiled a number of medieval chronicles detailing *twere zeit* ('hard times') in Frisia from as early as 851, and then intermittently disrupting the eleventh century in 1006, 1051, 1062 and 1069 (Sax 1986 [1636]: 145). Medieval chroniclers further noted serious periods of dearth in the twelfth century; one in 1146–47 connected with *carestia* ('dearth') and a 'darkening of the skies', suggestive of abnormal climatic conditions, while another in 1191 apparently was noted for its wide geographical impact (De Ram 1861: II, bk. 14, no. 2; Kuys 1983: nos. 220, 251). Chronicles from ecclesiastical institutions are our main evidence for harvest failures and dearth in the thirteenth century too: abbot Menko of the monastery of Wittewierum remarked in Groningen in 1250 that city officials had imported grain from unknown 'other lands' to compensate for scarcity (Jansen and Janse 1991: 380–1).

Quantifiable data appear from the fourteenth century onwards in the Low Countries, and then with increasing frequency in the transition into the early modern period. However, it is clear that research into the interaction between food availability and mortality in the late medieval and early modern period is still a task fraught with source limitations and methodological difficulties. Moreover, the region of the Low Countries, roughly comprising the modern countries of the Netherlands and Belgium (and Luxembourg), underwent profound political transformations. Up to the sixteenth century the region was referred to as the Burgundian Netherlands or the Seventeen Provinces. After the political secession of the autonomous Dutch Republic in 1581 in the north, the Southern Netherlands remained under the political control of the Spanish and Austrian courts. The north and the south were temporarily reunited

119

between 1815 and 1830 as the United Kingdom of the Netherlands, to be divided thereafter in two autonomous countries. Data on prices are available from the fourteenth century, though in greater amounts for the south than the north. From the fifteenth century onwards, however, both the north and the south are well served with excellent price series for different grains and other agricultural products.

More problems exist with the reconstruction of mortality rates. The northern Low Countries have notoriously scarce sources for reconstructing demographic trends in the medieval period, especially for the countryside (exceptions are De Boer 1978; Van Schaïk 1987), though the situation is slightly better with regard to the south (see the survey in Thoen 1995). Nonetheless, while some towns have burial records starting in the second half of the sixteenth century, for many villages the systematic registration of burials only really begins in the early stages of the seventeenth century. Significant time series for mortalities for the countryside, therefore, can be done only from the seventeenth and eighteenth centuries. Before the period of systematic burial registration, historians are forced to use indirect measures for rising mortalities, such as numbers of probate inventories recorded by city and village magistrates and the revenues from post-mortem taxes raised by lords (Thoen 1988). As with other parts of Europe, one methodological difficulty is distinguishing between mortality rises caused by subsistence crises and poor access to food, and mortality rises caused by diseases such as plague and dysentery. Given that plague outbreaks repeatedly occurred from 1349 to 1670, often in the same places again (Noordegraaf and Valk 1988; Rommes 1990), it is inevitable to have some overlapping plague years and harvest failures. These problems are further exacerbated by the fact that it is now well known that medieval and early modern populations did not necessarily die directly from starvation, but from diseases and illnesses caused by the knock-on effects of sustained exposure to poor nutrition.

1   The Great Famine, 1315–17

The first abundant wealth of information we have on severe famine in the Low Countries comes from the period 1315–17 (or even 1315–22) with the 'Great Famine' – labelled 'great' on account of its longevity and scale (Jordan 1996: 7). Partially, at least, this was connected to the terrible and prolonged abnormal weather conditions in the North Sea area, including large amounts of rain and wind. Although, as with earlier episodes of famine, we are reliant on contemporary commentary, we also have quantifiable information in the reporting of prices and the fates and fortunes of ecclesiastical institutions – particularly from the south. Scholarly tradition has tended to suggest that the southern Low Countries were particularly hard hit by the early fourteenth-century famine, with the scale of human suffering at some of the highest levels seen across Europe (Jordan 1996). In contrast, an impression has also been created that the north got off 'relatively lightly' from the terrible crisis period, though probably this is to some extent a function of the relative inequality in the distribution of quantifiable sources. Indeed, the premier book and synthesis on the subject, by Jordan (1996), cites barely any material from the area roughly comprising the present-day Netherlands.

Demographic evidence for the famine is patchy in both north and south. It has been calculated that just under 10 per cent of farms were abandoned after the famine hit in the easternmost region of Twente in Overijssel (Slicher van Bath 1970: 97), while in rural coastal Flanders it has been said that settlements lost anything from 10 to 30 per cent of their populations on the basis of archaeological evidence for shrinkage and desertion (Verhaege 1984: 152–6). In such extreme weather conditions, however, depopulation of coastal regions was probably as much related to the effects of flooding as it was to harvest failure (Soens 2009). It is possible that there were regional variations in the demographic impact of the 1315–17 famine, but the evidence is so fragmentary and unevenly distributed that no real patterns can be confirmed. Larger population contractions seem to have occurred in the cities and towns of the southernmost parts of the Low Countries, such as the 10 per cent decline cited for Ypres (Carpentier 1962: 1076), compared to Flemish cities further north such as Bruges, with a figure of less than 5 per cent cited (Blockmans et al. 1980: 56). Going even further north, Utrecht was said to have had 'no noticeable population decline', though this is only from contemporary observations (Struick 1981). Yet the fragmentary and anecdotal information pieced together from other views of contemporaries at least instructs us not to underestimate the demographic impact of the 1315–17 harvest failures in the northern Low Countries. In some references wage labourers were employed to pick up the corpses of the dead from the public highways for mass burial (Curschmann 1900), while chroniclers from Egmond Abbey frequently testified to the paupers and beggars left roaming country lanes without food (Aberth 2013: 24). Certainly, the 1315–17 famine enhanced the likelihood of the spread of life-threatening contagious diseases: see the high numbers of deaths in conditions of close contact in the confined monastery of Rijnsburg near Leiden during the period (Ladan 2012: 19).

Information for the northern Low Countries on agricultural prices is quite rare for the period around the Great Famine; time series for grain are not available until the late fourteenth century (Dijkman 2011: 288). One chronicle from 1316 did mention that prices for wheat, rye and barley had more than doubled in parts of the central Dutch river area of Gelderland (Meister 1901: 51), while further along the Rhine a 'Great Death' was mentioned for the region of Xanten in the same year (Weiler 1935: no. 462). More references can be found for the southern Low Countries at this time, though still not enough for full time series. Prices in 1315 and 1316 were recorded everywhere as highly volatile – particularly in Antwerp and Liege (Prims 1933: 140; Van Werveke 1959: 10; Nicholas 1992: 207). In Louvain prices for grain tripled between November 1315 and the summer of 1316 (though caution needs to be heeded with comparing prices for different times of the year) (Lucas 1930: 353–4). Some prices cited by chroniclers, such as 17-fold increases, were probably exaggerations, particularly from clerics looking to secure special dispensations for their ecclesiastical institutions; many monasteries found the years 1315 to 1317 to be a period of severe crisis, culminating in the alienation of landed estates. Evidence recently compiled from Saint John's Hospital in Bruges shows how, in the years after 1317, the relative expenditure on grains (in relation to dairy products, meat and beverages) was suddenly reduced (Dehaeck 2004), while the actual cost per hectolitre of grain increased substantially by a factor of around 2.5 (Thoen and Soens 2010: fig. 4, 495). And, while price rises may not have been on the scale suggested by contemporary commentators, scarcity was such that some urban governments resorted to long-distance imports of grain, often from the Mediterranean (Van Werveke 1959: 469, 474, 485). It must be noted too that incessantly poor weather conditions in the late 1310s leading to harvest failures in the Low Countries also had repercussions other than for the cultivation of grains. Wet soils led to murrains and sheep plagues, hitting pastoral economies. Accounts from the southerly rural regions of Luxembourg provide good evidence for declining flocks and herds across this period, while elsewhere the rise in prices for grains was matched by equivalent increases in other products such as salt – a necessary component of dairy production (Jordan 1996: 63).

Overall, based on the compilation of fragmentary source material for the Great Famine of 1315–17 in the Low Countries, it seems that the southern areas were harshly afflicted, while the paucity of sources means that it is impossible to come to a strong conclusion on the fortunes of the north. Probably there were regional divergences in its severity, impact and consequences; after all, the medieval Low Countries are known to have exhibited very sharp differences between regions close together on the basis of agricultural organisation, tenure, socio-political freedoms

and population density (Van Bavel 2010). The fragmentary and anecdotal nature of the evidence remains the biggest obstacle to teasing out
regional differences. One thing that may be significant, nonetheless, is
that, while the 1315–17 harvest failures in other places, such as central
and south-east England and northern France, occurred simultaneously
with conditions of widespread rural impoverishment as a result of the
extreme fragmentation of peasant landholdings and strong pressures on
increasingly restricted common resources (Fossier 1968; Schofield 1997;
Bailey 1998), in many regions of the Low Countries, such as Holland
and Groningen, these 'Malthusian ceilings' had not been reached, cour-
tesy of late paths towards land occupation and colonisation (Curtis and
Campopiano 2014). That, at least, may point to a more favourable demographic, socio-political and institutional context for some regions of the
Low Countries to escape the worst of the 1315–17 crisis (see the favourable situation presented in Van Bavel and Van Zanden [2004]), though it
is certainly a matter needing further systematic research.

2   The Northern Low Countries, Fifteenth
to Nineteenth Centuries

Existing literature suggests that the northern Low Countries managed
to escape from hunger from the late sixteenth century due to the central
position of Amsterdam in the European grain trade, ensuring a steady
supply of cheap wheat and rye (Faber 1976; Noordegraaf 1980; 1985b).
In this section, this claim is scrutinised in an analysis of a range of price
series from various parts of the northern Low Countries. Admittedly,
grain prices in themselves are not the best indicator of famines, but an
analysis of high grain price peaks provides a starting point: it renders a
list of years in which famine risk was high. Other indicators can then nar-
row this list down further.

An analysis of grain price spikes between the early fifteenth century
and the middle of the nineteenth in 11 towns across the northern Low
Countries shows the years during which this staple food was unusually
expensive. Rye was the most common bread grain in the northern Low
Countries from the fifteenth century onwards. Its prices usually show
more and sharper spikes than wheat prices, as in times of dearth demand
shifted to the cheaper grains. Table 6.1 lists the episodes in which rye
prices in any of the towns under investigation were at least double the
'normal' rate.

An assessment of the impact of grain price peaks must take into
account the development of purchasing power in the long run. As in
other parts of Europe, real wages in the northern Low Countries rose in

Table 6.1 *Years of high rye prices in 11 towns in the northern Low Countries: price increase as a percentage of the 'normal' price*

	West and middle			North		East			South			Welfare ratio
	Amsterdam	Leiden	Utrecht	Groningen	Coevorden	Kampen	Arnhem	Nijmegen	Maastricht	Breda	Roermond	
1427			59%						110%			1.03
1438–39			142%						192%			1.25
1457			118%						83%			1.77
1482–83			256%						12%			0.98
1491–92			154%						306%			1.16
1517			44%						138%			1.25
1522			126%						124%			1.11
1556–57			116%				168%		301%	127%		0.66
1565–66			67%				99%	127%	54%	75%		0.91
1572–73			122%				122%		116%	139%		0.79
1586–87			19%				30%	29%	83%	121%		1.23
1622–23	71%		59%				94%	98%	65%	122%		1.23
1626	28%	25%	28%				16%	24%	171%	53%	68%	1.16
1630	81%	58%	66%				109%	74%	24%	61%	26%	0.88
1649–51	77%	101%	66%	92%			87%	82%	58%	74%	105%	1.02
1661–62	95%	126%	114%	157%	211%		124%	121%	155%	117%	119%	1.00
1675–76	91%	110%	60%	78%	110%	71%	72%	94%	182%	83%	142%	1.19
1692–94	85%	63%	78%	88%	141%	83%	92%	128%	109%	110%	119%	1.24

1698–99	101%	103%		94%	137%	168%	134%	164%	104%	130%	154%	1.03
1709–10	141%	158%	198%	228%	170%	181%	143%	121%	194%	145%	1.12
1724	–5%	–23%	34%	61%	45%	58%	49%	15%	74%	102%	1.56
1740–41	73%	83%	76%	78%	114%	113%	140%	110%	134%	158%	121%	1.16
1771	68%	50%	63%	87%	100%	96%	93%	89%	90%	71%	1.15
1795	103%	104%	84%	63%	85%	97%	113%	264%	183%	110%	0.98
1800	66%	63%	120%	86%	82%	74%	91%	26%	100%	8%	1.12
1816–17	66%	49%	56%	49%	62%	94%	129%	83%	131%	0.87
1855	66%	86%	86%	67%	71%	85%	81%	103%	0.84

Notes: The 'normal' price level is defined as the average price in the ninth to second years before the crisis, leaving out the highest and the lowest values. Increases of more than 100 per cent above the normal level are printed in bold. For episodes of dearth covering more than one year, the figures in the table are the prices in the most expensive year for each town. The welfare ratios are those of the year in which the ratio was lowest.

Sources: Posthumus (1964: I, 573–6) for Amsterdam; Posthumus (1964: II, tab. 233) for Leiden; Posthumus (1964, II, tabs. 21a, 152–3) for Utrecht; Tijms (2000: tab. 6) for Groningen; Tijms (1977: II, 28–32) for Coevorden; Tijms (1977: I, 313–14) for Kampen; Tijms (1977: I, 136–44) for Arnhem; Tijms (1977: II, 313–24) for Nijmegen; Tijms (1977: II, 37–40, 47–9, 55–9) for Maastricht; Tijms (1977: I, 164–9) for Breda; and Tijms (1989: 112–63) for Roermond. Welfare ratios were constructed from R. Allen, datafile 'Labourers', available at www.nuffield.ox.ac.uk/People/sites/Allen/SitePages/Biography.aspx (corrected for the years 1544–95) and J. L. van Zanden, datafile 'Reconstruction of national accounts of Holland, 1348–1514', available at www.cgeh.nl/reconstruction-national-accounts-holland-1500-1800-0.

the fifteenth century but declined sharply in the sixteenth century, due to rapidly rising price levels. In contrast to most other parts of Europe (the southern Low Countries and England excepted), this was followed around 1580 by a recovery owing to the catching up of nominal wages, which continued in the seventeenth and early eighteenth centuries. After 1750 a gradual decline of real wages set in, which lasted until the middle of the nineteenth century (Allen 2001; Van Zanden 2009). These long-term trends determined how close to the edge the most vulnerable groups in society lived. A method that allows for comparisons with other European countries is provided by the welfare ratios introduced by Allen: wages expressed as the number of family 'subsistence baskets' the daily wage of an unskilled urban construction labourer would buy. In addition to price peaks, Table 6.1 gives the welfare ratios during these peaks for the northern Low Countries.

The highest price peaks, with increases of 250 per cent or more over the normal level, are found in the late fifteenth century (1482–83 and 1491–92) and the middle of the sixteenth century (1556–57). Spikes were not quite as high between the late sixteenth and late eighteenth centuries, but they were by no means absent. The years 1661–62, 1698–99, 1709–10 and to a lesser extent also 1740–41 stand out as years of widespread and significant price increases. At least in the south of the country, the price spike of 1795 was as extreme as those of the sixteenth century. This was a year marked by bad weather but it was also the year of the French occupation of the northern Low Countries: wartime destruction and disruption of trade were probably at least partly to blame for rising prices. The year 1816–17 witnessed another, more moderate rye price spike, which appears to have been the last one of significance. Although between 1845 and 1847 rye prices rose, they did not double, while in 1855 the only town where this happened – but only just – was Roermond.

Analysis of the welfare ratios partly confirms these findings, but also provides an additional perspective. It suggests that, from a long-term perspective, the worst episodes of dearth were those in the third quarter of the sixteenth century. At this point in time standards of living were so low that even a relatively modest price rise, let alone one as sharp as in 1556–57, could cause serious trouble. In the fifteenth century, and again in the seventeenth and early eighteenth, wages were higher, so price surges, even if they were as impressive as in 1482–83 or in 1709–10, were less likely to push people over the edge. Only at the end of the eighteenth and in the early nineteenth century did welfare ratios of unskilled labourers repeatedly drop below the level required to feed and house a family again, even though they did not return to sixteenth-century levels.

Regional differences within the northern Low Countries were considerable. In general, in the towns in the west and middle, and also in the northern town of Groningen, price peaks appear to have become less prominent and less frequent after the fifteenth century. The most notable exception is the year 1709–10, when prices all over the Dutch Republic, including the west and middle, rose dramatically. At the opposite end of the scale were the towns in the south – Maastricht, Roermond and Breda – where high price peaks remained a fact of life throughout the early modern period. Coevorden, in the north-east, and the eastern towns of Kampen, Arnhem and Nijmegen took an 'in between' position. One likely explanation for these regional differences is location. Inland towns faced higher transport costs than towns in coastal regions, and especially in years of dearth they may have had difficulty ensuring the steady supply of grain.

Price analysis provides a starting point, but by no means gives conclusive evidence for the occurrence of famines. Ideally, mortality figures are needed to measure the impact of the shock. For the medieval period and most of the sixteenth century no mortality rates are available. However, contextual evidence suggests that the three highest fifteenth-century price peaks, those of 1437–38, 1482–83 and 1491–92, must all be assessed as serious crises. The years 1437 and 1438 were marked by famines in many parts of northern and western Europe (Jörg 2008). The sources speak of food riots, starvation and disease. Government reactions betray alarm and despair. For the first time, as far as we know, towns did not just issue restrictions on the export of grains or on the quantities to be bought and sold at the local market but also started buying and storing grain themselves. They also organised inspections of private grain supplies (Unger 1916: 464–5; Van Schaïk 1978: 225–7, 236–7). The crisis of 1437–39, moreover, witnessed the first serious interventions of the 'national' authorities in food provisioning. In Holland, the Burgundian government attempted to maximise prices and even tried to put the entire grain trade in the hands of a small number of grain merchants. (Dijkman 2011: 297–8). The crises of 1482–83 and 1491–92 bear similar characteristics. In 1483 a chronicler reported that many died for want of food. The *Enqueste* of 1494, a report on the financial and economic state of the towns in Holland, frequently refers to extreme impoverishment, up to the point at which people sold their land in order to buy food (Noordegraaf 1985b: 30, 33). Dearth policies first introduced in 1437–38 were reapplied on a larger scale than before (Van Schaïk 1978: 247).

For the sixteenth century it seems safe to conclude that, because of the decline of real wages, all price spikes in the first three quarters of the century gave rise to serious trouble. By the late sixteenth century export prohibitions, urban grain storage, grain inspections and other measures to combat dearth had become standard procedures in virtually every town (Unger 1916: 473–9). The years 1556 and 1557 were the worst. Towns desperately tried to acquire grain supplies but frequently failed to do so. Merchants from the southern Low Countries who had bought grain in Amsterdam were no longer allowed to ship it home; some grain shipments already on their way to the south were arrested. People in Delft were reportedly eating the refuse of the town's breweries (Friis 1953: 202–6). Although there were also widespread problems in the years 1565 and 1566, marking the beginning of the Dutch Revolt (Kuttner 1949: esp. 228), and in 1572 and 1573, when sieges, the stationing of troops and pillaging in the countryside wrought havoc (e.g. Nijmegen: Offermans 1972: 122), the situation was probably not as catastrophic as it had been in 1556–57 (Friis 1953: 210–3). The earliest mortality figures we have – fragmentary burial series from the second half of the sixteenth century – lend some support to this impression. The number of burials in the main churches of Gouda and Alkmaar, for instance, peaked in 1557, but for the 'hunger year' 1565–66 no significant increase can be discerned (Goudriaan and Ibelings 2002: 43–5). Problems in the 1580s and 1590s appear to have been mainly local in nature. Reports of food riots, raised mortality and starvation for 1586 and 1587, for instance, are all from the south and east of the country, where fighting and plundering caused destruction and disturbance of trade (Noordegraaf 1985a: 74–7).

The possibility of a relation between mortality peaks in the eighteenth and early nineteenth centuries and food shortages has been the subject of some discussion. Faber's claim that the late eighteenth century witnessed a return of hunger-related mortality (Faber 1976) has been contested by a series of authors, who, in their studies of living standards in a single town or region, were unable to establish firm connections between mortality rates and high food prices (Mentink and Van der Woude 1965; 't Hart 1983; Noordam 1986). When information from various towns and regions is combined, however, a somewhat different picture emerges. The best sources for this purpose are studies for towns or regions in the west and middle of the Dutch Republic in the early modern period: Rotterdam, Amsterdam, Alkmaar, Edam and Utrecht. For each dearth episode rendered by the grain price analysis average mortality per year has been calculated. Table 6.2 summarises the results, expressing the average number of burials during the crisis years as a percentage of the 'normal' level.

Up until the early eighteenth century price spikes appear to have left but few marks on mortality figures. Only in the years 1649 to 1651 was the number of burials above normal in more than one town at the same time, but even then the increase was modest. Signs that the tide was turning became increasingly clear through the eighteenth century. In Rotterdam and Amsterdam all years of high prices from 1740 onwards were marked by raised mortality, though never by more than 50 per cent. The same is true for Utrecht in the late eighteenth and early nineteenth centuries. In the middle of the nineteenth century the potato crisis left its mark in the form of substantially raised mortality figures in four of the five towns under examination.

Drawing firm conclusions based on such limited data is difficult. Even within the western part of the country there were probably regional differences, for in the small towns in North Holland (Alkmaar and Edam) nothing of note appears before 1780, when the early modern burial series unfortunately stop. In addition, some years of high prices in the eighteenth century were marked by epidemics, creating confusion over the actual causes of raised mortality. Some of these epidemics apparently bore no relation to food shortages, but at least for 1771 and 1795 the spread of infection due to malnutrition has been suggested as one of the causes of raised mortality (Gerritsma 1981: 386–7; Jansen and De Meere 1982: 197–8). Finally, information on mortality in the north, east and south of the Dutch Republic is even scarcer than for the west and middle. For the time being, the only conclusion that can safely be drawn is that there is no reason to believe that the impact of price peaks on mortality in the east of the Dutch Republic was substantially greater than in the west. In short, the notion that the Dutch Republic was not at all affected by hunger-related death appears to be not quite true – at least, not for the eighteenth century. By combining mortality data from various locations the beginnings of a pattern can be shown. It suggests that conditions worsened in the course of the eighteenth century and confirms Faber's suspicion that at the end of that century, and the beginning of the next, hunger did take a death toll.

In a way, the northern Low Countries' last brush with hunger-induced mortality is an outlier to what has been discussed previously, because, in contrast to the harvest failures of previous centuries, the crisis of 1845–50 was connected to the failure of a different crop – the potato. By 1845 the Netherlands, like other northern European countries (see the chapters on Germany and Ireland in this book), was heavily reliant on potato cultivation. As a consequence, the potato blight immediately led to an increase of poverty and to raised mortality figures. In 1847 – the worst year – mortality in the Netherlands as a whole was 32 per cent above normal, but in the coastal clay regions figures were higher: in the province of Groningen, for instance, excess mortality was 43 per cent and in

Table 6.2 *Years of high prices (as defined in Table 6.1) combined with excess mortality as a percentage above the normal level*

	Rotterdam	Amsterdam	Utrecht	Alkmaar	Edam (19th century: Edam-Volendam)
1649–51	23%		7%		
1661–62	–4%		4%		–2%
1675–76	5%				–49%
1692–94	–3%				38%
1698–99	12%				–46%
1709–10	8%	10%		–6%	–8%
1740 ·	6%	21%		–15%	–15%
1771	5%	1%		–11%	–5%
1795	24%	16%	48%		
1800	25%	37%	24%		
1817	25%		20%		
1845–47*	15%	51%	50%	96%	49%
1855	9%	26%	13%	–25%	26%

Notes: The 'normal' level has been calculated from the annual data in the same way as for grain prices: as the average number of burials in the ninth to second years before the crisis, excluding the highest and the lowest values.
* The years of the potato famine are not included in Table 6.1, but have been added here because these years were clearly marked by raised mortality.
Sources: Early modern period: Mentink and Van der Woude (1965: 124–9) for Rotterdam; Diederiks (1982: 16) for Amsterdam; Van der Woude (1972: 635–9) for Alkmaar and Edam: and Rommes (1991: 119–20) and 't Hart (1983: 242–3) for Utrecht. All figures for 1845–47 and 1855 are derived from the Hofstee dataset (up until 1850) and the *Historisch-ecologische databank* (HED) assembled by H. Knippenberg (after 1850). We thank the Nederlands Interdisciplinair Demografisch Instituut (NIDI) for providing us with these data.

North Holland it even reached 51 per cent (Paping and Tassenaar 2007: 176). The mortality figures in Table 6.2 for Amsterdam, Utrecht, Edam and, in particular, Alkmaar confirm this impression. Of course, it is inevitable that societies more dependent on the production of the potato felt the sting of its failure more than those with diversified agricultural portfolios. More significant were the extreme disparities between rich and poor. In Groningen, for instance, the mass of (quasi-)proletarianised wage labourers was hit much harder than the 'gentleman farmers' of the coastal polders (Curtis 2014). The potato was, first and foremost, a subsistence foodstuff for auto-consumption, grown by labourers cultivating microplots intensively (Roessingh 1976); it was not a particularly marketable product. The reality of the potato disease was then crushing for these labourers, who were forced to purchase other food products at prices that were invariably outstripping wages (given their nominal decline) (Paping 2004). Changes and malfunctions in the distribution of poor relief exacerbated the situation – leading to a failure of 'collective insurance' (Paping 1995: 289–90). As stated earlier, grain price increases in the mid-nineteenth century were not extreme. The severity of the crisis was instead down to the fact that a much larger proportion of the rural population of the northern Low Countries was now exposed to the vicissitudes of the market. It seems, then, that in the late eighteenth and nineteenth centuries the northern Low Countries were, overall, more susceptible to famine than some southern European countries (see the introduction to this book, Chapter 1, for a general discussion). The fact remains, however, that before the potato crisis significant hunger-related excess mortality had been absent: Table 6.2 suggests that, until then, it had not exceeded the 50 per cent level. Which factors allowed the northern Low Countries to escape from severe famine from as early as the late sixteenth century (a truly remarkable achievement if seen in the broader European perspective, as shown by several of the contributions to this book)? Was the central role of Amsterdam in the international grain trade indeed the decisive factor? It is certainly true that the northern Low Countries, from an early stage onwards, depended on grain imports. Since at least the early fifteenth century the most populous western part of the northern Low Countries, Holland, was unable to feed its population due to subsidence of the region's extensive peat soils. Agriculture had shifted to dairy farming, the products of which were marketed in the nearby towns and also in Flanders, the German Rhineland and England. Moreover, in addition to farm work, the inhabitants of the countryside usually engaged in various non-agrarian activities, such as peat digging, shipping and the construction of dykes and canals. At the same time, urbanisation increased rapidly: as early as 1500 45 per cent of the inhabitants of Holland lived in towns (Van Bavel and Van Zanden 2004).

This transformation was accompanied by the increasing importation of bread grains. Until the last quarter of the fifteenth century these grains mainly came from the Seine region in France and, to a lesser extent, the eastern parts of the Low Countries and the adjacent German lands. The role of Baltic grains grew during the two food crises of the late fifteenth century under the influence of disturbed political relations with France. It gained further importance in the second quarter of the sixteenth century, when profit margins on the French grain trade diminished. The shift of the grain trade to the north stimulated the development of Amsterdam as an important grain trade centre, at first mainly for the northern Low Countries, but from the 1530s or 1540s onwards increasingly also for other parts of Europe (Van Tielhof 1995). The crisis of the 1590s also consolidated and extended trade connections with the Mediterranean (Noordegraaf 1985a: 78; Alfani 2013a: 71–2). From the late sixteenth century until at least the middle of the seventeenth century the Amsterdam staple market supplied much of Europe with Baltic grains. The east and south of the Dutch Republic were never as dependent on grain imports as the west, but the easy availability of import grains did keep them from developing their own sizeable market-oriented grain production (De Vries and Van der Woude 1997: 207).

When, between 1650 and 1730, new regions of production emerged and consumption patterns changed, Baltic grain exports declined and Amsterdam lost its dominant position in the European grain trade. Only in times of dearth, as in 1740, did Amsterdam temporarily resume its earlier role as Europe's grain staple. The city at first continued to supply markets within the Dutch Republic with grain, but this too changed when in the course of the eighteenth century internal grain production grew and the traditional dependence of the country on grain imports decreased (De Vries and Van der Woude 1997: 414–19).

The rise of the Baltic grain trade in the course of the sixteenth century is in keeping with the decrease of grain price spikes after the middle of that century. It is also in keeping with the finding that the second half of the sixteenth century certainly knew great hardship and dearth, but probably no large-scale famines after 1556–57. Likewise, the decline of the Baltic grain trade in the late seventeenth and early eighteenth centuries heralds the return of hunger-related mortality. The fact that, in the eighteenth century, all years of high prices were marked by raised mortality in Amsterdam, Rotterdam and Utrecht supports the impression that, instead of an abrupt transition, this was a gradual process.

In both the seventeenth and the eighteenth centuries, however, grain prices in the northern Low Countries on the whole do not seem to have been lower or more stable than in other parts of Europe. This does not necessarily imply that Amsterdam's international grain trade had no effect on price levels and price fluctuations. It may also be taken as a sign that this trade benefited towns all over western and southern Europe – or, at least, towns with easy access to sea routes – as much as the northern Low Countries themselves. However, it does follow that the absence of famines from the northern Low Countries at a time when other areas of Europe still struggled with them cannot be explained from the grain trade alone; other factors must also have contributed. One of these factors has already been discussed: the development of purchasing power. This was affected by grain prices, but also by prices of other products and, more importantly, by nominal wage levels. Earlier we saw that low wages in the sixteenth century increased the impact of even moderate price peaks. Recurring price spikes in the seventeenth and early eighteenth centuries were not as damaging, simply because wage levels were much higher than they had been, and also much higher than they were in most other parts of Europe. Wage levels also go a long way in explaining the recurrence of hunger-related mortality in the late eighteenth and early nineteenth centuries, even if the situation was not as bleak as 200 years earlier.

A second explanatory factor can be found in the presence of a well-developed system of formal poor relief. Charity in the Dutch Republic was decentralised, organised by local communities and local churches (Heerma van Voss and Van Leeuwen 2012). For the purpose of relief during food crises, the most important institutions were the public poor tables and the diaconates of the churches, which provided 'outdoor relief': assistance through the distribution of bread, other basic necessities such as cloth, and frequently also small amounts of cash. These institutions could be found everywhere: not just in the towns but also in many villages. Recent research has shown that, between the middle of the sixteenth century and the middle of the eighteenth, the percentage of gross domestic product spent on relief in the republic as a whole may have tripled; around 1760 it sufficed to cover the needs of almost a tenth of the population. In the late eighteenth century a decline set in; by 1820 spending on relief had fallen to late medieval levels (Van Bavel and Rijpma 2016). The disappearance of famines from the northern Low Countries from the middle of the sixteenth century coincided with the rise in social spending, and the return of hunger-related mortality with its decline. This does not provide conclusive proof that the two are connected; this requires more detailed research, especially on the way in which the poor tables reacted to rising food prices. It does suggest, however, that other factors than simply the Amsterdam grain trade contributed to the disappearance of severe famines from the northern Low Countries.

3   The Southern Low Countries, Fifteenth to Nineteenth Centuries

Famine history in the southern Low Countries from the late fifteenth to the late eighteenth centuries shows a clear link between food crises and warfare. Periods of high food prices and high mortality coincided in many cases with periods of intense warfare. During the early modern period many European political conflicts were settled military in the territory of the southern Low Countries. This had important consequences that might account for the somewhat higher occurrence of famine compared to the northern Netherlands. Although the southern Low Countries have been characterised by advanced agriculture with relatively high yield ratios since the Middle Ages, domestic production was frequently insufficient to feed the rising population. From the late Middle Ages onwards grain was imported from neighbouring regions (for example, northern France) and the Baltic states. It has been estimated that domestic production of grain in the southern Low Countries covered only three-quarters of the needs in the 1560s (Van der Wee 1966: 284). It was only in the middle of the eighteenth century that the southern Low Countries became (temporarily) independent from foreign grain imports (Vandenbroeke 1975). High levels of urbanisation and heavy reliance on imports made this region particularly vulnerable to famine during periods of warfare. Military movements disrupted both interregional and international trade. Wars also made it more costly and risky to trade foodstuffs. From the early sixteenth century onwards urban and rural magistrates started collecting information on the availability of grain during years of high prices in order to organise redistribution and international sales. When the threat of a food shortage was real, central, regional and local governments organised censuses to take stock of the available foodstuffs. These censuses informed the government in a detailed manner how much food was available, which regions had surpluses and how much grain had to be imported (Wyffels 1985: 113–20; Scholliers 1960: 57–8). However, regional differences in grain prices during the early modern period suggest that the redistribution of food during periods of harvest failure or shortfall coinciding with warfare encountered many difficulties. Next to the disruption of trade, the wars placed additional burdens on the population and the communities in terms of food availability. Villages and cities were forced to supply food, fodder, horses and carts to passing armies in addition to paying wartime taxes. Armies literally lived off the land and consumed much of the food stock (Gutmann 1980: chs. 2–3). Probably, fewer famines might have occurred if the reduction in food availability had not coincided with war, though we can only speculate about that. From this perspective, the resilience of the economic structures of the southern Low Countries communities and their ability to cope with food shortages remain somewhat obscured. This region had without doubt the institutions to cope with famine, but they could never fully function during periods of warfare. War disrupted their operation, thereby turning food shortages into real famines.

As emphasised before, the link between high food prices, famine and excess mortality is very difficult to establish and is often non-existent.

Table 6.3 *Years of high rye prices in four towns in the southern Low Countries: price increase as a percentage of the 'normal' price years*

	Rye				Wheat
	Ghent	Bruges	Antwerp	Brussels	Bruges
1408		100%	50%		71%
1437–38		168%	113%	86%	152%
1456		105%	104%	96%	78%
1481–82		138%	172%	147%	118%
1491–92		93%	131%	117%	101%
1502			110%		81%
1521	115%		170%		58%
1531–32	107%		93%		39%
1556–67	203%		160%		148%
1584–86	278%		394%		
1595	141%		102%		66%
1608	131%				32%
1661	106%				
1675	123%				31%
1709	219%				218%
1740	115%				120%
1795	111%				111%
1802	106%				
1817	110%				

Notes: See Table 6.1 for definition of 'normal' price years.
Sources: Chiefly www.sfu.ca/~djacks/index.html; Jacks (2004); www.iisg.nl/hpw for Bruges in the fourteenth and fifteenth centuries; and Tits-Dieuaide (1975: 273–5) for Brussels in the fifteenth century.

In the fifteenth century the early 1480s stand out as a famine-stricken period. Between 1480 and 1483 harvests failed as a result of climatic conditions, exacerbated by civil war in Flanders between 1483 and 1492. On the Bruges market grain prices more than doubled between 1480 and 1482. In many Flemish regions there was a peak in the number of deaths, measured by the number of post-mortem taxes. In the region of Bruges the number of recorded post-mortem inventories more than doubled in 1483 compared to the preceding years (Dombrecht 2014: 82). A similar parallel between prices and the registration of mortmain receipts shows up in data for other Flemish regions. The rise in grain prices in 1482–83 coincides with a rise in the number of recorded deaths. The relationship between prices in 1490–92 and mortality is less clear. It seems that mortality in these regions preceded the rise in grain prices.

Table 6.4 *Wheat prices on the market of Bruges and registered number of deceased owing mortmain rights in the chatellenies of Oudburg and Courtray, 1480–94*

Year	Wheat price (gr. Flemish per *hoet*)	Mortmain receipts in chatellenie of Oudburg	Mortmain receipts in chatellenie of Courtray
1480	72	19	14
1481	84	69	2
1482	140	21	33
1483	156	80	27
1484	59	42	18
1485	50	59	26
1486	72	26	
1487	91		6
1488	90	24	31
1489	88	366	16
1490	104		5
1491	160		4
1492	103	76	12
1493	79		11
1494	48		8

Sources: Verhulst (1965: 35) for wheat prices; Boudia (2000) for mortmain rights: 174 (Oudburg), 207 (Courtray).

Research for the sixteenth century has identified 1521–22, 1556–57 and 1585–86 as years of exceptional dearth in Antwerp (Scholliers 1960: 12). A comparison with indirect data on mortality from the registration of post-mortem inventories shows no upsurge of deaths in 1520–21, contrary to the crisis years 1556 and 1557. In 1557 and 1558 the aldermen of the village of Pamele recorded two and a half and four times more post-mortem inventories than in the years before, suggesting a positive relationship between prices and mortality during the grain crisis of 1556–57 (Thoen 1988: II, 1142–5). The effects of the dearth years of 1585–86 on mortality are more difficult to gauge, as this period was characterised by massive emigration as a result of the Eighty Years War.

Between 1660 and 1750 food shortages were a recurrent feature in the southern Netherlands. Most harvest failures were triggered by climatic factors, in combination with the almost endemic warfare that characterised the late seventeenth and early eighteenth centuries. These decades were especially harsh, but only in 1709 did grain prices more than double.

The frequency of famines increased in the seventeenth century, especially after 1650. The seventeenth century has been characterised by historians as a century of catastrophic mortality. The research by Bruneel on mortality in the duchy of Brabant indicates periods of food shortages and rising mortality rates in 1625–26, 1648–51, 1661–62, 1674–76 and 1692–94. Years of high prices also included 1630–31, 1639–40, 1696–98 and 1708–09, but without significant impact on mortality. Bruneel has advanced the hypothesis that the latter selection of years of dearth did not result in catastrophic mortality because the weakest elements of the population had already perished in earlier years of scarcity and famine (Bruneel 1977: 577–98). The chronology of Bruneel fits with other research on the relationship between high food prices and mortality. For example, in the western part of Flanders excess mortality as a result of food prices occurred in 1651–52, 1661–62, 1692–93 and 1708–09 (Dalle 1963: 165–76). Other regions experienced crisis mortality too during these periods, though the relationship with food prices has not been researched systematically (Ruwet 1954: 451–76).

With the exceptions of 1693–94, 1698 and 1709, few of these harvest crises have been studied in detail. These harvest failures can be related to catastrophic climate conditions, in particular heavy rainfall (the 1690s) and a cold winter (1709). The famine of 1693–94 occurred in the middle of the War of the League of Augsburg (1689–97). The regions bordering France suffered most from these military campaigns. The famine of 1698 was triggered by the end of the military activities in the southern Low Countries. Emigration caused labour shortages and much of the land remained uncultivated. The combination with heavy rainfalls resulted in a harvest crisis and subsequent excess mortality (De Visscher 1978). The dearth in 1709 was instigated by a cold winter in a period when the southern Low Countries were engaged in the War of the Spanish Succession (1702–13). In the years preceding 1709 the cities and villages had been the victim of massive requisitions. These requisitions not only reduced the food stock but also deprived the rural population of their farm stocks and working capital (Van Osta 1969). The complex relation between food prices and mortality in the seventeenth and early eighteenth century is illustrated in Figure 6.1. There seems to be hardly any direct relation between grain prices and mortality, though we must keep in mind that these data cover only a very small region. High prices in 1652 had no effect on mortality. High wheat prices in 1693 were followed by a sharp rise in deaths in 1694, but a similar spike in food prices in 1709–10 resulted in a mortality peak only in 1711, when prices had normalised again.

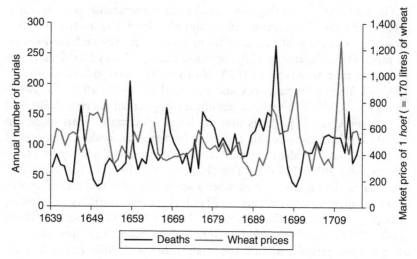

Figure 6.1 Mortality and wheat prices in the region of Bruges, 1639–1715

Notes: Mortality estimated as annual numbers of burials in four parishes north and south of Bruges. Wheat prices as recorded on the market of Bruges.

Sources: Brusselle (1997: II, 1–2, 6–7, 11–12) (parishes of Jabbeke, Stalhille and Varsenare) and Mus (1984: 166–8) (parish of Aarsele) for burials, and Verhulst (1965) for wheat prices.

After 1750 large-scale food shortages became increasingly rare. Traditionally this has been seen as the result of both substantial rises in agricultural production and more efficient government action on and monitoring of food supplies. We are able to compare village-based data for the province of West Flanders, a region with high mortality risks. Only 1740 (a 30 per cent increase), 1741 (75 per cent up), 1794 (85 per cent up) and 1847 (42 per cent up) stand out in this respect.[1] 1740–41 is sometimes viewed as the last great food and mortality crisis of *ancien régime* Europe (Vanhaute and Lambrecht 2011). Low harvests in 1739 and the exceptionally long winter of 1739–40 (*le long hiver*) severely reduced per capita food supply (Vandenbroeke 1975: 76–236). When stocks were exhausted in late April/early May and the prospects of an

[1] Surplus mortality, based on data from the province of West Flanders: rises in crude mortality rates, compared to the three-year average prior to the crisis. For the eighteenth century, the data come from 23 villages; for the nineteenth, they are from the total province. Sources: Sentrie (2007) and LOKSTAT, the historical database for local statistics of Ghent University (www.lokstat.ugent.be).

early and abundant harvest had dwindled, prices started to rise. Probably incited by panic as well as a severe distortion of supply and demand, 1740 prices peaked at 25 to 30 per cent above the already high levels of 1739. From 1736 to 1740 the purchasing power of labourers declined by about 60 per cent. The demographic effects of the crisis of 1740 are less straightforward. Reconstructing mortality figures, 1740 does not stand out. Mortality was particularly high in 1741, when food prices started to drop. According to contemporary observations, increased mortality during this period was the result of typhus, typhoid fever and 'relapsing fevers'.

The late eighteenth century marked a short return to the *ancien régime* pattern when, in 1794–95, a combination of war and harvest failure resulted in high mortality rates. During the first half of the nineteenth century the southern Netherlands experienced food shortages in 1816–17 and in 1845–47. This was the last food crisis with a clear impact on mortality rates. The direct cause of the mid-nineteenth-century subsistence crisis was the failure of potato harvests in the years 1845 to 1850 (Vanhaute 2007). The potato blight destroyed 87 per cent of 1845 harvests, and in Flanders, the epicentre of the potato disease, losses amounted to 95 per cent of the crop. Over the following years harvests were also poor, because fewer potato seedlings were planted and yields remained low. Between 1846 and 1850 barely a third of the 'normal' potato harvest was gathered in Flanders. The food situation became very precarious in late 1846 and the first half of 1847 due to poor bread grain harvests. Bad weather conditions in 1846 caused the rye harvest (by far the most important bread grain) to decrease by more than a half, though the losses for wheat and maslin were smaller (each 10 per cent).

Calculated in grain equivalents, the combined loss of bread grain and potato harvests in 1846 was 66 per cent. As a result, there were only 125 litres of grain equivalents (bread grains and potatoes) available per head, compared to 375 litres in previous years. Because all harvests were affected (half the bean and pea harvests were lost too), the threat of famine loomed in 1846–47. Prices peaked in the spring of 1847, after the partial failure of grain harvests. Potatoes were sold at 3.5 times the 1844 level. Rye cost 2.4 times as much as in 1844 and wheat cost twice as much. Rice was three times as expensive while peas and beans were 1.8 times as expensive as in 1844. A crisis in the rural flax industry coincided with the subsistence crisis of 1845–47. Compared to the reference years of 1841 to 1845, Belgium recorded in 1847 a surplus mortality of some 23,000 (a 30 per cent increase), adding up in the three-year period 1846 to 1848 to 44,000 (15 per cent up). The number of births decreased by 47,000 during the same years (–12 per cent), and there were 17 per cent fewer marriages. High mortality in 1846–47 was limited to the geographical area of Inner Flanders, with excess mortality of 40 per cent and averages of up to 47 to 53 per thousand in 1847. Most deaths were a consequence of nutrition-related diseases such as dysentery and typhus.

1740 and 1845–47 were the last severe food crises in the southern Low Countries, but they did not turn into sharp famines (very little is known about the food crisis of 1794–95 due to the complete disruption of public authorities and public records). The main explanation is that the peasant economy and village society maintained sufficient resilience to absorb the main shocks of these crises. However, the way this happened shifted greatly between 1750 and 1850, due to structural changes in the rural economy. Until the early nineteenth century severe cracks in the food system were mostly met by internal and often informal village relations. Village externalities became much more prominent in the nineteenth century. In the 1840s – contrary to the infamous Irish example – a severe Flemish famine could be avoided because of the survival of the small but mixed and productive peasant farms, and because of the swift and sometimes anticipatory actions of the local and supra-local institutions. The elites resorted to the institutional initiatives of aid, employment and repression more than ever before, backed by an active state apparatus, in both a legal and a financial sense.

7   Britain

Richard Hoyle

Famine is an extreme human condition and one that will, mercifully, be outside the experience of most readers. Except in wartime, continental Europe has escaped famines for over 100 years. Indeed, the European revolution in agriculture in the twentieth century has resulted in too much rather than too little food. The proportion of household income spent on food has persistently diminished. Seasonal shortages and price rises have mostly disappeared. There is still hunger in Western society, especially among the unemployed, but obesity has replaced malnutrition as the Western problem. For the most part we are sanguine that the food we want will be available for us to purchase when we want it. There could be no such certainty in the past, when the price of staple foodstuffs – bread, for one – varied from year to year and season to season, when we have to assume that seasonal hunger – even in good years – was the reality of life for many people and when, just occasionally, crops could fail, leaving whole populations with little or no access to food. On the eve of World War I, in much of Europe, famine was something that, even if people hadn't experienced it for themselves, was a part of the collective memory: it was conceivably something that could happen again.

England was probably the first European country in which the possibility of famine became unthinkable. Scotland suffered famines in the eighteenth century when the English merely had to tighten their belts, while Ireland, most notoriously, continued to suffer famines resulting from the failure of the potato harvest. Unlike Ireland, there was no collective memory of famine in England. Laslett asked rhetorically whether there had ever been any famine in England in his 1965 book *The World We Have Lost*; his question was answered definitively in the affirmative by Appleby in 1978. It would now be conceded that England did suffer famines through to at least the mid-seventeenth century, but the English escape from famine came early, though as late as 1800–01 food shortage brought real distress, even if its impact was not demographically marked. Given the early escape from famine, it is perhaps a paradox that the history of famine in England can be traced from an earlier date and in greater detail than perhaps anywhere else in Europe.

1   Approaches and Sources

Famine is susceptible to both quantitative and qualitative approaches. England has good qualitative data on prices and yields from the mid-thirteenth century onwards. This has encouraged a number of attempts over the years to identify high-price years, but high prices cannot immediately be taken as indicating famine conditions. (The earlier work of Hoskins and Harrison is conveniently summarised in a table in Outhwaite [1991]: 17–21. Dyer [1989]: 262–3 provides a table of 'bad harvests, 1208–1530'.) The price data are continuous, though, whereas the yield data peter out in the early to mid-fifteenth century as landowners progressively withdrew from demesne farming. On the other hand, England (but not Wales) has first-rate and continuous demographic data from the mid-sixteenth century, compiled by Wrigley and Schofield (1981). Data on deaths, derived mostly from the deaths of landowners or men and women leaving wills, can be taken back into the late thirteenth century. It is easy enough from these data to identify sudden upward movements in the number of deaths, less easy to determine the underpinning cause of the crisis. The seasonality of heightened death may contain clues. Plague, as has often been observed, has an autumn profile. Finally, though, any antithesis between famine and disease is a false one. It is recognised from modern famines that it is disease rather than starvation that kills, and that malnourished people may be more prone to disease, especially if they were also on the move and seeking food in poor weather conditions. What is much more compelling as the means to diagnose famine is the coincidence of high mortality and high prices, and perhaps also low yields, where such data are available. Famine is also associated with a decline in the number of people marrying and the number of births to those already married: inevitably, the trough of the latter follows the peak of mortality by some months.

The problem with price data is that they can identify periods of high prices ('dearth') but cannot tell us whether these years saw famine – that is premature deaths caused ultimately, if not directly, by food shortage, or difficulty accessing food – as opposed to simple hunger. Mortality data may demonstrate famine, but they will not show hunger. People may well be hungry and malnourished, even though the death rate is not conspicuously higher.

It is the qualitative data that demonstrate the existence of famine beyond all doubt. Extreme shortage of food was so exceptional (as well as traumatic) that medieval chroniclers noted it, together some-times with the aberrant weather that provoked famine and with com-ments on the social dislocation that famine caused. From the early fourteenth century, evidence for famine (or, perhaps more correctly, evidence of fear of imminent famine) can also be seen in the actions of government, whether the closing of ports to keep domestic produc-tion at home and the search for grain abroad, or attempts to manage local markets and the suppression of alehouses, malting and brewing to reserve grain for bread. Famine might also be referred to in private records, in letters and diaries.

What I might suggest, then, is that the price and yield data have a predic-tive quality that can be confirmed by the mortality data, but it is often the witness of people who live through the famine that proves its presence. This approach is not without its problems, though. One of them is that the price data are largely derived from London and the home counties of southern England. This is a notable problem when grain markets were far from inte-grated and the costs of interregional transport (except by sea) were high. In general, the data are poorer for the north of England and worse still for Wales. There are few systematic price data for Scotland before the mid- and late sixteenth century, after which we have the series of county 'fiars', prices determined by county juries that allowed rents and payments in kind to be turned into a current money value (Gibson and Smout 1995). It might be added that Irish quantitative sources are worse still. One may, therefore, deduce two rules of thumb and say that the further west and north one goes in the British Isles, the greater the danger of famine, but, equally, the later continuous data start and the more reliant the historian of famine is on chronicle evidence, comments in letters reporting on local conditions and the behaviour of local and national government.

We need to insist that famine is essentially regional in its impact. A famine in the north-west of the country might be only a dearth in East Anglia, and vice versa. We can see evidence for this in the interregional flows of grain that develop in high-price years. So the town of Shrewsbury was attempting to buy grain in Ipswich in 1585 and Norfolk corn in London in 1597 (Hoyle 2016). The Fells of Swarthmore in Lancashire over the Sands were part of a party that chartered ships to take grain to Bristol in 1674 and Cornwall in 1677, sailings that make sense only if the Fells had market intelligence of high prices in the West Country in those years (Holt 2013: 48–52). The full force of a regional famine cannot be caught by a price index based largely on sources drawn from Oxford, Cambridge and London.

If we see harvest shortfalls as being largely caused by extreme weather, it may be useful to think of a core area with severe crop loss, with a surrounding area of diminished crops and heightened prices, and beyond that a peripheral area of near-normal production but heightened prices as produce drained into the deficient area. In the core area there might well be heightened mortality, but one might also expect people to leave this area to seek charity or work in better-provided areas. In surrounding areas one might expect to find high prices, hunger, rising levels of employment, references to itinerants on the road and disturbances as people impeded the movement of grain. Alehouses might well be suppressed and markets regulated by justices. Marriages might well be deferred. In more distant areas, life might be little touched by the crisis. There might be a heightening of prices, the management of markets and an increase in the number of vagrants and travellers, and in the petty criminality that they brought as they stole to live.

For these reasons, famine is not susceptible to treatment as a national phenomenon, and national data (or what purport to be national data) may not catch its full enormity. Some sense of this can be gained at the regional analysis of parish register data published by Wrigley and Schofield in 1981 (this is capable of expansion to generate a fine-grained atlas of crisis: remarkably, this is still to be done). In 1586–88 the crisis seems to have been concentrated in the north-west of England, a few Midland parishes and some parishes in the West Country. In April 1586 a boat on the river Severn below Gloucester was stopped by a crowd, who unloaded and took its cargo of malt. In the following weeks other crowds tried to impede the passage of grain- or malt-bearing boats down the Severn. There is compelling evidence of the gravity of the situation in Gloucestershire at that time with a report from the justices of the peace (JPs) investigating the seizure of grain that local people were reduced to living off oats, docks and nettle roots (Sharp 1980: 15). Prices may have been high but the cause of distress was a local collapse of employment. Nonetheless, there is no sign of crisis mortality in this district this year or over the south of England generally.

This geographical pattern fits for four famine episodes, 1585–87, 1594–99, 1622–23 and 1647–49, when famine was felt most keenly in north-west England, to a lesser degree in the West Country and probably in Wales (about which little work has been done). (1647–49 shows weakly in the demographic data: for the case for famine conditions, see Hindle 2008.) Certainly, there are graphic reports of famine in north-west Wales in 1622–23 (Wynn of Gwydir Papers nos. 1060, 1064, 1075, 1078, 1085, 1160). This localisation of famine led Wrigley and Schofield (1981: 677–88) to speculate that two Englands had appeared, one pastoral and remote, and the other engaged in arable farming but with a high degree of occupational specialization reflected in a relatively dense network of small towns. While access to grain, together with ease of transport and the well-developed communications in the south-east made the area much less vulnerable to harvest failures, its greater economic integration facilitated the spread of disease.

This idea was later recast in terms of entitlements and the collapse of markets (Walter and Schofield 1989: 32). The problem that the north-west faced, it was suggested, was that it was a specialist producer of cattle and cloth for southern markets, and that it imported grain out of those markets for its own sustenance. In a year of crisis its export trade dried up, and it was therefore unable to enter into the market for grain. There may be some truth in this, but more recent work has shown the gravity of the agricultural crisis in Lancashire in 1622–23 (Hoyle 2010). An account that explains the appearance of famine within the bounds of one of the three British countries will simply not serve: how are we to explain the contemporaneous problems in Scotland and Ireland? It is entirely possible that demand failure exacerbated an already bad situation, but did not create it.

We also have years that seem not to have created any problems in the north-west and the west of Britain generally. The complaints of shortage in 1483 were said to come from Essex, Suffolk and Norfolk and not generally (Horrox and Hammond 1980: 100–1). From Edward Hall's more or less contemporary account, the adverse weather of the winter and spring of 1526–27, which led to harvest failure in 1527, seems to have been most marked in the south of England. Famine in the city of London was avoided by the import of considerable quantities of Baltic grain (Hall 1809 [1548]: 721, 736). The same analysis could be applied to other years, but let us skip forward to the autobiography of Leonard Stout, the Lancaster merchant (1665–1752). He brought a merchant's eyes to the economy, and he was careful to discuss years when the weather, and agricultural fortunes, of southern England were quite distinct from those of the north but still impacted on it. So, in 1727, there was plenty of corn in Lancashire, but in the south and east of England it was 'scarce and dear' and this drew the corn out of Lancashire, raising prices. In 1719 there was drought in the south and so the trade in cattle stopped, there being no water in the south to keep cattle alive, but it was a good year for corn (Marshall 1967: 179, 201).

A final caveat may be mentioned here. A single year of high prices does not necessarily imply famine. It may imply social dislocation, unemployment and hunger, but it may not have any significant demographic impact. Campbell and Ó Gráda (2011) have demonstrated that it is *two* successive years of high prices that produce famine – in the second year. It is not hard to speculate why this should be. A single year of shortage could be overcome by drawing on stocks of grain, by using savings to procure grain from a distance, even by living off body fat. A second year of the same might not be so supportable.

In explaining the incidence of famine, this chapter maintains the primacy of environmental considerations over distributionalist factors. It also suggests that, over time, with the increased sophistication of famine management and relief, steps to manage or redistribute foodstuffs, as well as enlarging the supply by the purchase of distant stocks, became increasingly important in mitigating or alleviating famine. That is to say that the same order of shortfall in food supply might have quite different consequences in 1300 from 1800 because the management of the crisis would be quite different at the later date.

Given that the data are quite different in character and quality, it seems only reasonable to consider the English data first before turning to the Scots data, and finally looking at the English data, so far as it is possible, in a British and Irish context.

2   The Statistical Identification of English Famine Years

There is evidence for famine in England from before the beginning of the continuous data series (Britnell 2004: esp. 287; Keene 2011: 45–6). Using a variety of chronicle sources, famine has been identified in 793, 975–76, 1005–06, the mid-1040s, 1087, 1111, 1124–26 (which are also known as very hard years in the Flemish towns) and 1193–98. There were extremely high prices in the first years of the thirteenth century. Of 1124 Symeon of Durham reported that the bodies of the dead lay unburied in both town and countryside. There was a prolonged episode of famine in 1256–58 following on abnormal weather conditions, which produced a succession of poor harvests (for what follows, see Keene 2011). The harvest of 1256 was poor; 1257 was worse, but the first months of 1258 were extremely cold and the grain failed to grow in the counties on which London depended for corn. In London there was an awareness that the following harvest was likely to be deficient. As the city was flooded by refugees from the countryside, steps were taken to deal with the bodies that began to be found in the streets, doorways and wherever people could find shelter. Civic initiatives were taken to dig mass graves for the dead, one of which has been excavated. The worst of the famine may have been alleviated with the arrival of corn from Germany procured by the king's brother, Richard of Cornwall; but the harvest of 1258 was a washout and famine returned in 1259, when it seems likely that one of the mass graves started in 1258 was reopened. It seems possible that the famine of these years should be treated as being equivalent in scale to the much better known famine of 1315–17; certainly, the reported price of grain in London was close to that of April 1316. The figures of 15,000 and 20,000 dead in London given by the chronicles need not be taken as exact, but they are intended to impress upon readers that something truly awful took place in these years.

Campbell has already pulled together the available data on yields, prices and real wages and the Wrigley and Schofield vital statistics for England. From this he has selected the ten worst famine events in English history: his table (taken from Campbell 2009) is reproduced in Table 7.1 with his kind permission.

I have already mentioned Campbell and Ó Gráda's contention that it is only two successive years of high prices that have a severe demographic effect and that it is runs of years that are especially dangerous. So, in 1555 the grain price was 130 per cent over the 25-year average and in 1556 160 per cent over the average (and real wages at 75 per cent of the average), but these are still years that saw strong population growth (of 1 per cent per annum). It was in the third year of high prices, 1557, that we see a reversal in population growth, which continues in the following two years even after grain prices have fallen to below-average levels. One would not like to make too much out of the crisis of the 1550s because it was – notoriously – a mixed crisis, with famine ebbing into an outbreak of influenza. But something similar can be seen in the 1590s: prices were high in 1595 and 1596 yet population continued to rise, but in the third year of high prices there was negative growth. The same pattern – of population loss being deferred for a year or two after the advent of high prices – can be seen elsewhere. By the time of the high prices of 1800 and 1801, famine was enough to slow population growth but no longer to reverse it. Years of high prices therefore have to be distinguished from years of famine. A single year of high prices – when government and local authorities might well activate the machinery of dearth management – might pass without observable demographic consequences at the national level, though it might bring considerable distress locally. But there is also the paradox mentioned earlier: the more successful relief is, then the lower the mortality rate, to the point at which one might doubt that there was ever a famine, or a likelihood of one.

Of the crises identified by Campbell's methodology, that of 1315–17 is recognised as being a general north European crisis, which bit hard in the towns of the Low Countries as well as in northern Ireland and in Lowland Scotland. The dislocation of harvest failure was worsened by aggressive

Table 7.1 *Comparative economic and demographic profile of years of extreme harvest failure: England, fourteenth–nineteenth centuries*

	Percentage of 25-year moving average				Real wage indexed on 1451–75	Percentage of 25-year moving average			Crude rate of natural increase per thousand
Year	Grain yield	Tithe receipt	Grain price	Real wage		Crude death rate	Crude birth rate	Crude marriage rate	
1313	106	109	74	116	51				
1314	114	87	83	107	47				
1315	57	81	122	94	41				
1316	35	80	230	62	27				
1317	84	64	222	65	28				
1318	111	128	107	89	39				
1319	107	NI	63	113	49				
1347	110	116	122	73	40				
1348	117	117	127	68	38				
1349	51	84	79	89	49				
1350	43	65	103	109	60				
1351	64	75	142	115	63				
1352	94	82	171	94	52				
1353	95	84	130	108	60				
1436	90	104	90	104	99				
1437	56	91	92	104	98				
1438	71	47	147	83	79				
1439	108	100	229	68	65				
1440	150	116	107	82	78				
1441	99	120	65	117	111				
1442	61	106	67	118	113				
1479	115	105	105	95	90				
1480	159	99	97	97	92				
1481	NI	88	101	92	87				
1482	78	84	142	78	73				
1483	80	NI	189	85	81				
1484	94	101	131	85	82				
1485	51	105	91	109	104				
1554			89	102	62	73	92	59	11.2
1555			130	91	55	86	100	86	10.1
1556			160	75	45	82	98	69	10.8
1557			170	75	45	144	76	67	−15.1
1558			79	107	65	185	87	101	−22.8
1559			82	92	57	165	76	106	−20.1
1560			83	107	66	111	97	133	2.9
1594			82	104	54	84	108	107	14.8
1595			128	89	46	85	100	95	11.8
1596			145	87	44	97	92	91	6.3

Table 7.1 (*cont.*)

	Percentage of 25-year moving average				Real wage indexed on 1451–75	Percentage of 25-year moving average			Crude rate of natural increase per thousand
Year	Grain yield	Tithe receipt	Grain price	Real wage		Crude death rate	Crude birth rate	Crude marriage rate	
1597			194	70	**35**	**133**	**88**	**79**	**–4.1**
1598			147	82	**40**	**105**	**89**	**97**	**2.7**
1599			86	87	43	90	110	104	13.4
1600			96	101	49	84	103	102	12.8
1620			69	110	47	88	110	106	12.7
1621			66	112	48	83	108	100	13.2
1622			107	**94**	**40**	**83**	**101**	**81**	**11.0**
1623			117	**95**	**41**	**120**	**87**	**75**	**–2.3**
1624			99	96	41	108	93	95	2.2
1625			100	101	43	164	100	89	–9.6
1626			110	101	43	98	94	98	4.7
1725			114	92	54	84	100	99	7.8
1726			112	90	53	91	103	105	6.7
1727			107	**96**	**57**	**117**	**102**	**93**	**–1.2**
1728			135	**85**	**51**	**130**	**86**	**92**	**–10.8**
1729			125	**85**	**50**	**145**	**87**	**96**	**–15.4**
1730			94	**100**	**60**	**116**	**94**	**122**	**–4.7**
1731			85	104	62	108	108	126	2.3
1738			94	108	67	90	104	96	7.8
1739			91	107	67	90	106	99	8.3
1740			126	89	56	103	100	94	2.6
1741			144	84	**53**	**118**	**92**	**84**	**–3.5**
1742			97	**96**	**61**	**128**	**90**	**94**	**–5.8**
1743			85	104	66	102	99	105	4.9
1744			73	113	72	89	100	105	9.0
1798			82	111	59	95	101	107	14.4
1799			100	101	53	96	96	97	12.6
1800			157	**78**	**41**	**102**	**94**	**88**	**9.9**
1801			160	**73**	**38**	**108**	**87**	**82**	**5.8**
1802			91	96	50	104	99	116	11.9
1803			76	101	52	109	105	119	12.9
1804			80	014	54	94	105	108	17.1

Notes: Crisis years are in bold; preceding and succeeding years are shown for comparison. 'NI' = 'no information'.
Source: Campbell (2009: 44–5, tab. 1), reproduced with permission.

raiding out of Scotland into northern England and Ireland, and, after the crisis of human mortality passed, a cattle plague took hold that further decimated the rural economy (Jordan 1996; Kershaw 1973; Sharp 2013; Slavin 2014). It appears, though, that the desperate years of this decade were followed by a period of predominantly good harvests, which came to an abrupt end with further back-to-back harvest failures in 1349–51. Their existence has largely been concealed by the much greater, and coincidental, crisis of the Black Death. The arrival of a new – or, at least, reintroduced – disease into England conceals the gravity of the situation, for it is not possible to distinguish between deaths that might be attributed to starvation and those caused by plague. The evidence for a substantial shortfall in food supplies is plain enough but the overall level of mortality caused real wages to rise, a tendency that was answered by the Ordinance of Artificers of 1351. On Campbell's estimation, these were the last of the fourteenth-century famines. He identifies famines in 1437–38 and 1481–83, the former at a time when the population was probably close to its lowest in the late medieval depression and in the midst of a flight from tillage to pasture. The famine of 1437–40 has attracted much less attention than that of 110 years earlier. In southern England people were apparently reduced to eating poorer grains (peas, beans and barley) while there was a report that in the north people were eating fern roots. There were reports of a succession of wet summers, and flooding in the north that destroyed mills (Dyer 1989: 267–8; Pollard 1989: esp. 93–4, 103–4). Both these famines make the point that famine could occur when there was no shortage of land to cultivate. That of 1555–57 is another case of a famine that ran into a disease crisis, in this case a form of influenza that produced a very high mortality, running through into 1558 and 1559.

The crises of the 1590s have long been read as a Malthusian response to a long period of population growth. It is true that the episode takes some of the heat out of population growth but it also follows a period in which there are complaints of low grain prices. There was enough confidence in the food supply to repeal the early sixteenth-century legislation on enclosure in 1593. It was reinstated as a panic measure in 1597–98, quickly fell into abeyance and finally was repealed in 1621, just in advance of a further period of famine in 1622–23. This is the last period of famine found by Campbell in the seventeenth century. However, he finds two close together in the second quarter of the eighteenth century, at a time when it would normally be assumed that famine had disappeared from England, and a further period at the very end of the century, in 1800–01. On Wrigley and Schofield's figures, both 1728–29 and 1741–42 had a marked demographic impact, though there is little contemporary comment about famine (but there is a rash of food riots).

3   The Response to Famine

It should not be thought that contemporaries were hopeless in the face of either dearth or actual famine. On the contrary: they took positive steps to improve conditions and reduce suffering. The interventions we know about are very largely in urban society, however, and in particular London. We know little about how successful these relief efforts were in saving life.

Sharp has argued that many of the later devices for coping with famine arose in the policies implemented by Edward II's government after 1315. Some can be traced back earlier, though. The first, and most obvious, of these is that government made attempts to procure grain from abroad to make up local deficiencies. This was done in 1258, when Richard of Cornwall, king of Germany and brother of Henry III, purchased grain in Germany and had it sent to London. Attempts were made to procure grain from Gascony in 1315 and Spain in 1316. Ambitions by Edward III to buy Mediterranean grain in 1317 seem to have been largely abortive, and the grain was, in any case destined for the king's garrisons in the north in the years of vulnerability after Bannockburn. From that moment there is less evidence of royal initiatives in buying grain in international markets, the exception at the moment being 1527–28, when the government tried to secure grain in France, the Low Countries and Prussia (for 1258, see Keene 2011: 59; for 1317, see Sharp 2013: 640–2; for 1527–28, see Lee 2011: 74).

As the Crown withdrew from looking for famine supplies in international markets, others took over. The City of London certainly entered the market in 1391, 1429 and 1437–39 (Keene 2011: 60; Sharp 2013: 644–5). We know from later sources that a few second-rank towns also purchased grain in some years, sometimes as a corporate initiative, sometimes as an act of charity by richer individuals. So the mayor of Coventry procured grain for the city in 1520, the mayors of Exeter and Bristol for their towns in 1522. Worcester procured grain at Bristol in 1556–57 and we noted Shrewsbury seeking grain to buy in the hard years of both the 1580s and 1590s (Walter 1989: 116–17; Lee 2011: 74; Hoyle 2016). We should not be over-impressed by this: while the motivation may have been charitable, there is also every sign that the towns wanted their money back, and sold grain at cost rather than simply giving it away. The market was therefore allowed to set the price of grain. Experiments in price fixing by Edward II seem to have remained just that, were quickly repealed and were not repeated (though his ordnance is concerned with meat, poultry and eggs, not grain, and Sharp [2013: 631–4] is correctly sceptical as to whether it can be linked to the looming famine).

Instead, the concern of government in dearth years was very much to regulate supply and allow prices to find their own levels. The management of internal markets rested on deep-seated assumptions of profiteering and the withholding of grain. Forestalling was especially condemned in such years and the ideology that all grain should be exposed for sale enforced. Dearth years were invariably marked by attacks on the normal and otherwise unexceptional forms of the grain trade both by urban authorities and from the pulpit. An early example of this train of thought can be seen in Edward II's letter of 24 April 1316 addressed to the bishops. It admits that there had been rainstorms that had produced a scarcity of grain. Nonetheless, it then insisted that there was food being kept back in the barns and granges of the countryside. Both laity and clergy who had grain were instructed to bring it to the market, retaining only enough for their own needs. The same thinking occurs in 1321, when the lack of grain for sale in Gloucestershire, Worcestershire and Wiltshire was blamed on people withholding it to secure higher prices later in the season (Sharp 2013: 634–5, 637).

The conviction that dearth arose from middlemen playing the market for profit remained just as strong at the end of this period. It can be found, for example, in a letter to the Privy Council of 1586, in which the city of York held that the current 'great scarcities and dearth' were caused

chiefly by the greediness of the farmers and others having sufficient provision of corn in their barns and garners and yet of purpose to enhance and raise the prices do forbear to serve and furnish the market of such convenient quantities (cited by Lee 2011: 70).

Denouncing farmers, middlemen and traders and making them into the cause of dearth is a perennial denial of economic reality.

It is in this light that we should see periodic attacks on bakers in hard years and their closer regulation by some towns. In a variety of ways markets were often rigged against bakers and in favour of private individuals buying for their own consumption. Bakers were not to buy grain before private individuals. In dearth years there can be no doubt that they were more exactingly scrutinised and their profits squeezed (Lee 2011: 68, 72–3). Baking had to be allowed to continue, if under civic supervision, but malting could simply be suppressed so that barley in particular might be diverted into bread. This caused great problems in a town such as Stratford upon Avon in the 1590s, whose trade was largely malting (Fox 1990: xxi–xxiv). Magistrates also withdrew licences from peddlers and other resellers of small parcels of grain, the very people on whom the poor probably relied for their purchases (for the local administrative reaction to dearth, see Emmison [1976]: ch. 10; Walter and Wrightson [1976]).

The most familiar form of Tudor government activity was the census of grain, undertaken by JPs and returned to the Privy Council (the returns are often called 'corn certificates'; the key studies of government policy are Outhwaite [1981] and Slack [1992]). This was a strategy that emerged in the first half of Henry VIII's reign and continued to be implemented in hard years until the Civil War. The earliest known census of grain is that taken in Coventry in 1520, though it is not clear whether this was a government instruction or a civic initiative. But government certainly called for local censuses of grain to be taken in the last weeks of 1527 as part of a larger portfolio of crisis measures: commissioners were also to enforce the laws against beggars and vagabonds, unlawful games and alehouses. The instruction to make corn certificates then became a familiar part of the governmental toolbox.

The powers given to combat dearth were elaborated over time to include the power to regulate markets, give the poor the right to buy first in the market place, suppress brewing and withdraw the licences of badgers (itinerant peddlers of grain and foodstuffs). By the end of the century the making of starch was suspended as well. There appears to have been a rewriting of the orders in late 1586, when the orders were circulated for the first time as a printed pamphlet, the 'Book of Dearth Orders'. We know that the book was then reissued in 1594, 1595 (but renewed in the following two years), 1600, 1608, 1622 and 1630, all years in which famine was anticipated. The issue of the book is not evidence that there was any heightened mortality, however; indeed, if it was successfully implemented, then deaths might have been avoided (for the text of the 'Book of Dearth Orders' and examples of corn certificates, see Grey [1993]).

In theory, these 'corn certificates' allowed JPs to establish how big any shortfall was, and then to manage local markets by having the available food brought to them in a measured way. At the same time, the inspection (or declaration) of stocks limited the possibility for speculation and, in particular, playing the market by withholding stocks to take advantage of price rises later in the year. There are two criticisms that can be made of this policy. The first is that it generated not a single additional bushel of grain. Rather, by controlling market access it perhaps allowed those with less purchasing power to access the market on reasonably favourable terms when otherwise they might have been pushed to one side by richer individuals with deeper pockets. The management of markets by the gentry was perhaps even a statement of social solidarity with the poor at a time when there were fears that society would split apart. The second criticism, though, is that it created an element of localism. The question posed to the JPs was how far local stocks would extend to serve local needs. It was therefore in their interests to stop the movement of grain out of their jurisdiction to neighbouring towns or London. It is hardly surprising that we find conflicts between JPs charged with maintaining local peace and the food supply in their locality and the Privy Council, whose concern was to ensure an adequate supply of food to London and who were willing to accept rural disorder as the price for urban peace (Hipkin 2008). Likewise, grain riots, most obviously in the attempts to stop boats on the Severn in 1586 or to unload grain from boats sailing to the Low Countries from Maldon in 1629, were about impeding the movement of grain out of high-price areas into more distant markets (Sharp 1980: 15; Walter 1980).

Government also had another resource at its disposal, though its efficacy is very much to be doubted. The publication of an edition of state prayers issued at times of emergency (and celebration) has helped demark occasions when divine intervention was sought in the affairs of men. Prayers and fasts were offered both in periods of drought and of persisting rain. In 1675 and 1681 prayers were said in Scotland for the alleviation of drought; in the summer of 1661 in England for the cessation of rain; and in January following for the end of unseasonable weather (just how it was unseasonable is not explained). What lurked behind these addresses to the divine was the fear of famine: the explanation for inclement weather was invariably man's sinfulness and the need for moral reform. The 25 or so occasions on which prayers of this sort were instructed to be offered gives us some insight into the moments of anxiety, even panic, about what the near future might bring (Mears et al. 2013; also Hindle 2001).

If much of this seems crude posturing, there was rather more self-help than this might suggest. It was only in London, though, that the decision to erect a civic granary was taken, perhaps prompted by the famine of 1439. The building erected over the following years has been investigated archaeologically. The granary took the form of the two upper storeys of a larger civic complex (the Leadenhall), which included accommodation for specialist markets on the ground floor, a chapel, a college of priests and a school. Although it seems to have been well designed for the purpose and built of solid masonry to deter rodents, it had a fairly short life as a granary and was not normally used for that purpose in the sixteenth century (Keene 2011: 60–1; Lee 2011: 75). In fact, in 1512 the incoming mayor found that there was no grain in either the Leadenhall or the other building used for storage, the Bridgehouse (for what follows, Carmichael 2014).

The granary system in London was re-established in 1514. Thereafter the city increasingly passed the costs of the granaries onto the city livery companies, which contributed according to an agreed table of proportions. In the 1570s, after the city had suffered losses on its dealings in corn (which it looked to the livery companies to subvent), it passed the responsibility for acquiring and managing the corn (and the associated risks) over to the companies themselves. They were to store the grain at the Bridgehouse. The system remained under the control of the mayor and alderman but they were themselves supervised by the Privy Council. The companies bought grain on the Lord Mayor's precept, on occasion grain that the city itself had procured abroad; they released it onto the market on the mayor's instruction at a price below that prevailing. Individuals were allowed to buy only small parcels, to prevent the corn falling into the hands of corn dealers. By the early 1630s there were three granaries with a total storage capacity of 16,000 quarters, which, on one calculation, would serve to feed the city for a little over three months. The Privy Council thought that the city should hold 20,000 qr.; for a short period they tried to persuade it to hold 30,000 qr. of wheat, a proposal upon which the city dug in its heels. In 1631 doubts were expressed about the whole policy. Some of the food was being bought by country people, who carried it out of the city, and some by people of means, who sent poor people to buy it for them. As a result, the meal was not reaching the people at whom it was aimed. Further evidence of disillusionment with the system may be seen in the failure of some of the companies to buy their quotas in the early 1630s. The system remained in force through the 1630s but had fallen into disuse by the mid-1660s.

It is very hard to establish how much self-help there was in the countryside, whether local initiatives or charity from landlords or clergy. Schofield seems essentially pessimistic about the provision of charity in the late thirteenth- and early fourteenth-century countryside. The aspect of rural famine that it is easiest to access is the sudden increase in the land market as famished people sold land, quite possibly to secure the means for their immediate sustenance, to richer neighbours (Schofield 2008). Slavin may also be read as suggesting a lack of social solidarity in the Great Famine, with each landlord trying to maximise his income, and Smith has suggested that one of the key differences between the impact of famine then and in the 1590s was the emergence of local direction of markets, which made it much harder for those with grain to keep it back to sell in the highest market (Slavin 2014; Smith 2015).

For the later period we do have a few instances of initiatives in the countryside. Spufford has introduced us to Richard Greenham, the vicar of Dry Drayton in Cambridgeshire (1571–91), who, perhaps in 1586–87, persuaded his neighbours to establish a common granary and stock it with corn, from which it was sold at four groats (1s. 4d.) a bushel when the prevailing price was ten groats (3s. 4d.). Greenham's biographer records that this saved the poor (Spufford 1974: 51–2). How many such instances there were of the collective pooling of corn it is impossible to guess, or how many local initiatives to buy grain abroad and have it transported home. It is hard to establish the contribution of landowners to relief. It is possible to identify a rare figure such as Thomas Sackville, Lord Buckhurst and latterly earl of Dorset (d. 1608), who spent his own money on importing rye in 1597, and was sufficiently concerned by the prospects of future famines to leave in his will £1,000 to build a public granary in Lewes (Sussex) and £2,000 as a fund to supply it (Walter 1989: 108). Sir John Wynn tried to use his son, who was a merchant in Hamburg, to arrange for either Newcastle or Polish grain to be imported into north Wales to break the famine there in 1622–23, but it is not clear whether he succeeded (Wynn of Gwydir Papers nos. 1060, 1088, 1160). The most practical help, reported from a number of locations, was the willingness of farmers to sell to their neighbours at less than the marketplace rate and, as contemporaries would have seen it, 'to maintain hospitality'. Walter gathered a large number of examples of this a few years ago, but it is hard to assess whether kindly yeomen neighbours and a scattering of landlords with social consciences were capable of making a substantial difference to the course of a famine (Walter 1989).

4   The End of Famine in England

The 1640s and 1650s, two decades of civil war and then unstable government, are often seen as a 20-year intermission in accounts of the century. In economic terms, what emerged after 1660 was very different from what preceded 1640. After 1660 food supply ceased to be an issue for government. There are no more instances of the issue of the 'Book of Dearth Orders' in England, and, while this has sometimes been read as indicating a lack of confidence in the use of the prerogative, it seems likely that there were few or no occasions on which the book would have been needed. After 1660 rents and arable prices fall. There was increased specialisation as high-cost grain producers abandoned arable farming for beef production or dairying. Government in both England and Scotland turned from protecting domestic supply through bans on exports to encouraging exports through the payment of export premiums ('bounties'). This was a regime that lasted, broadly speaking, from the 1660s (or perhaps a few years earlier) to the 1750s, when England ceased to be self-sufficient in grain.

This is not to suggest that the essential variability of the harvest ceased. It is possible to identify years in which the prevailing direction of trade was reversed and England became a net importer again. The autobiography of the Lancaster merchant Leonard Stout is very clear on this. In 1729 and 1740 prices were so high that it was worth importing American flour; but in 1733, 1734 and 1735, when the domestic market was over-supplied, grain was exported on a large scale into the Mediterranean (Marshall 1967: 204, 229, 213, 217–18). What we do not see, even in the 1690s, is any evidence of a famine. There was certainly hardship. In high-price years a rash of food riots, aimed especially at the long-distance trade in foodstuffs, could be predicted; but not famine. Healey has recently considered this for Lancashire, which, it will be recalled, had been a famine-vulnerable area in both the early 1620s and late 1640s. But, while the difficulties of the 1670s certainly bit hard in the county, they did not produce an upsurge in deaths (Healey 2014: ch. 7). Stout noted a doubling of deaths in the high-price year of 1728, but he did not suggest famine. If we want to search for the final kick of famine in southern Britain, then we should look to Wales, where Jenkins has identified short but severe mortality crises in the years around 1700 (Jenkins 1990: 85–92).

Famine disappeared a little like the Cheshire Cat. Instead of a grin, what was left in high-price years were a few popular attempts to enforce a moral economy and just price, occasional popular searches for hoarders and disturbances aimed at impeding the movement of grain and bringing it to local markets. Unemployment and short-time working certainly grew in these years, so artisans were hit not only by rising prices and falling incomes, and the Poor Law stepped in to make up at least some of the widening gap between income and earnings in these years (Thompson 1971; Howell 2000: ch. 9; Randall 2006: chs. 4–5; Bohstedt 2010).

Explaining why famine disappeared from England is not simple. It is not enough to blame the change on weather. It seems likely that the weather did change after mid-century and become milder, giving a longer growing season; but it remained capable of surprises, as our account of conditions in Scotland will show. And it needs to be remembered that northern France also saw major harvest failures in the 1690s that coincided with the 'Seven Ill Years' in Scotland. Changing weather cannot be a total explanation for the English escape from famine.

Famine is less likely in economies that tend to overproduction in normal years. One of the reasons why the famine eased in England was simply that exports were switched into the domestic market in years of shortfall. It may be held that the implications of a shortfall in production in England were felt in the Low Countries rather than in England. It also seems quite plausible to suggest that the animals that felt the sharp end of high food prices were horses; that, as oats became expensive, one would expect the price of horses to fall and for many of them to be put on half-rations (in his account of 1741, Stout noted: 'Many horses die for want of fodder'). The oats released from animal provender could well have flowed back into human food (see also Slavin 2014: 20–2 for some comments on the treatment of horses in the Great Famine).

But this would be helpful only if there were mechanisms of regional redistribution in place whereby grain could be transported from areas of surplus to areas of need. This did not happen in the early 1620s, so far as we can tell. As we saw, it has been suggested that the problem of the north-west in that year was a lack of purchasing power to enter national or international markets. This may well be true, but, if so, it was not a problem in the 1670s and 1690s.

There is also some evidence of trading down, of people eating bread that had been part-made from poorer-quality grains instead of the favoured wheat bread. There is evidence too from the 1690s that oats were sown as a famine food (Hoyle 2013: 78–9).

All these factors certainly helped avoid famine, but what is perhaps crucial is the maintenance of purchasing power. It is suggested that this was possible because of the Poor Law. The uniqueness of the English (and Welsh) Poor Law, not just within the British Isles but also within Europe, has been much commented upon. It made one clear contribution to the relief of famine. By giving every person a settlement (a home parish responsible for his or her support), it prevented the movement of people on the roads looking for charity of the sort still found in Scotland and France. Poor people could apply to parish officials for aid, and, if refused, or dissatisfied, could appeal to the magistrates by petition. There was no advantage in moving to a local town to seek charity. And keeping the poor rooted may well have limited the spread of disease by mobile people or its appearance among displaced populations sheltering in insanitary conditions.

Healey has shown how the growth of poor relief in Lancashire was almost continuous after 1690, but shows clear spikes at the end of the 1690s, again around 1711 and most clearly around 1729 and 1742 (Healey 2014: ch. 7). Stout tells us that, in 1731, being a year of high prices 'increased the poor so our poor rate was advanced from £100 to £200' (Marshall 1967: 207). In our present state of knowledge it can be guessed that, in years of high prices, the numbers of people in receipt of relief increased; it is less certain that the per diem rate paid also increased. It seems likely that famine was prevented by subsidising household incomes.

There is a final possibility that is worth considering. Overton suggested some years ago that the climatic variability of the early eighteenth century might have encouraged the transfer of root crops from the garden to the field as an emergency fodder crop. In the first instance farmers were interested in the green leaf rather than the root, though it was this that, in time, became the key component of the Norfolk four-course system of husbandry (Overton 1996: 203). There are similar questions to be asked about the potato. The introduction and adoption of the potato has always remained obscure, not least because, as a bulky and low-value product, it had a local trade only. But Stout makes it clear that by the late 1720s it was a familiar part of the diet of the poor. In 1727 a shortage of grain in the south and east drained grain out of Lancashire, raising its price, but Stout comments that 'potatoes were plenty and cheap at 2s. 6d. to 3s. a load, which was a relief to the poor'. That said, the price of potatoes appears to have followed that of grain, so that in the hard year of 1730 potatoes were 10s. a load before the harvest but only 4s. afterwards (wheat went from 23s. to 12s.). In 1741 wheat again fetched 24s. and potatoes 10s. a load. Nonetheless, there remains the possibility that famine was avoided because potatoes, like oats, offered the possibility for people to trade down to cheaper, albeit less desirable, foodstuffs in high-price years (Marshall 1967: 201, 204, 230–1; Flinn 1977: 423).

5   The Scottish Experience

The disadvantages that Scotland laboured under were several. The north of the British Isles had been the most extensively glaciated part of the island and soil depth was accordingly less than in the south. Growing seasons were shorter. There was therefore a greater reliance on spring-sown grains in the north of England and Scotland generally, but possibly also a greater take-up of the potato in the later seventeenth and eighteenth centuries. To these natural disadvantages needs to be added a political one: the intermittent devastation caused by war, especially in the border zone with England, but more generally in the Cromwellian reconquest of Scotland. From the historian's point of view, the problem with Scotland – by comparison with England – is the relative poverty of its archives. Medieval estate archives are almost entirely lacking. The survival of parish registers before the mid-seventeenth century is very poor and there is some suggestion that they were rarely, if ever, kept in the Highlands and Islands before the nineteenth century. The extant parish register data were carefully gathered by a team under Flinn and an extensive discussion was published in 1977 (Flinn 1977). Central government was also more rudimentary and its reach more limited. The one advantage that Scotland has over

England is that annual, county-by-county, returns of corn prices, or fiars, were made from the mid-sixteenth century until 1973; the series through to the late eighteenth century have been gathered by Gibson and Smout (1995).

For these various reasons, little is known about medieval conditions. Our first firm data come from the second half of the sixteenth century, when it is possible to discern the Scottish Privy Council reacting to events outside its control. It is possible to identify years when the domestic harvest was so good that the council encouraged exports, and others in which it sought imports from the Baltic or from further south in the North Sea basin; these years were also associated with a tightening of market regulation. Lythe has identified periods of high prices in the early 1550s, in the early 1560s (marked by high levels of Baltic imports in 1563 and a period when John Knox referred to prices being three or four times their usual levels), 1567, 1571–73 (and perhaps longer), 1585–87 (when there was an especially heavy reliance on imported grain) and 1594–98 (when, again, Scots ships were very active in the Baltic trade). Aberdeen, for one, took the initiative in importing rye and rye meal in 1596. These dates will be familiar from our discussion of English conditions. Thereafter there seems to have been something of a respite (except in the Highlands, where there is evidence of famine conditions in 1602) until the early 1620s, when again there was a reliance on German and Polish grain. In the intervening periods – 1579–85, for instance, or the first 20 years of the seventeenth century – Scotland seems to have been a net exporter of grain (Lythe 1960: 15–23; Flinn 1977: 109).

The good years were brought to an end by a severe drought in the summer of 1621, broken by the arrival of persistent rain in early October, which ruined the harvest and produced at least some flooding. This calamity was answered by a rise in Scottish shipping returning with imports from the Baltic in 1622, but the harvest of that year failed as well, and in 1623 there was a full-blown famine with reports of high mortality, significant numbers of people on the road looking for relief and an influx into towns, most notably, of course, the capital, Edinburgh. The harvest of 1623 was adequate, but high mortality continued into the early months of 1624, after which prices fell, perhaps because markets relaxed once they were confident of a decent harvest in 1624 as the sowing of spring grains had proceeded without mishap. Flinn thought that the famine was general in Scotland south of the Great Glen, but he admitted that it was impossible to be certain of conditions in the central Highlands (Flinn 1977: 116–26; Stewart 2005).

There then appears to have been a run of decent, consistently good harvests in Lowland Scotland for a quarter-century. We have a graphic account of desperate conditions in Orkney and Shetland in the year following the 1633 harvest, word of which reached Edinburgh and in answer to which some relief was sent. The situation remained very poor in the early months of 1635. There were reports of mass migrations into Norway: food was sent from Ireland (which was suffering from its own poor harvest). There is a single reference to famine conditions in the Hebrides in 1636, and reports of a mass migration from the Moray Forth area into Ulster. Scattered evidence then points to a severe famine lasting over perhaps two harvest years in the Islands and on the far northern mainland of Scotland (Flinn 1977: 130–2).

The long run of good harvests broke with that of 1649. All the indications are that three successive years' harvests were inadequate. Reports of dearth are widespread. Comparisons were drawn with the harvest failure of 1623, but the demographic evidence is that these were not years of excessive mortality. Flinn thought that the parish register data perhaps showed a stronger fall in the number of baptisms than a rise in deaths. There is evidence of substantial imports of English grain. What is also interesting is that, when domestic grain prices settled down after the abundant harvest of 1653, they fell to levels not previously experienced. It was in reaction to this that the Scottish government moved to ban imports of grain in 1671. There is no point looking for a specifically Scottish explanation for this new regime (as Flinn did in 1977): it parallels the trajectory of change in England too (Flinn 1977: 150–3).

This essentially optimistic period was broken by a year of harvest failure in 1674 that seems to have been, essentially, a local phenomenon. Weather conditions were severe in the winter of 1674 in the Borders: there are reports of heavy losses of cattle and sheep, the sowing of spring grains was delayed and the grain was still green in some locations when the autumn weather closed in. The following year was marked by high prices but was not itself bad for agriculture. The major shortfall seems to have been in the Borders and south-west Lowlands. Imports of foodstuffs were licensed for these areas in 1675, and this continued after the 1675 harvest in some places. High prices had their inevitable echo of larger numbers of people on the roads, but the year seems to have passed without really high levels of mortality (Flinn 1977: 159–62).

Any belief that better conditions had returned for ever was dissipated by the later 1690s. It has long been appreciated that this was a period of persistent harvest failure in Scotland.

In most places outside the far north, the 'ill years' lasted from the harvest of 1695 until the harvest of 1700, although not all seasons were equally dear... [I]n most places there were three bad harvests caused by the weather and two barely adequate ones prevented from being good by a scarcity of seed and general agrarian disruption.

(Flinn 1977: 196–7)

It is impossible to give a full account here of one of the worst periods of Scottish history, and in British terms a calamity probably unseen since the years after 1315 (Flinn 1977:164–86 remains useful, but the standard study is now Cullen 2010). It was unexpected: despite some reports of adverse conditions in the far north, the problem faced by Scotland in the early 1690s was one of overproduction, and in 1695, at the very moment the good years came to an end, the Scottish parliament followed the English one in agreeing to pay bounties (subsidies) on grain exports. In 1696 the government went so far as to pay a bounty on imports in the expectation that the following harvest would be poor. The harvest of 1697 offered some respite. That of 1698 was worst of all: it would have been a poor harvest anyway, but it was washed out in autumn gales, rainstorms and, finally, snow. The fiar prices were the highest recorded in the second half of the century. Over the period large quantities of grain, meal and peas were imported, but attempts to secure more in the Baltic proved futile, for, as is well known, this was a northern European event, and not simply limited to northern Britain. In terms of dislocation the usual reports of men and women on the road begin early. In 1696 and 1698 the pressure of refugees in Edinburgh was sufficient for the city to try to corral them in Greyfriars kirkyard, and then place a guard on its perimeter to stop people escaping. Attempts were made to root people in their parishes by establishing rates (stents) for poor relief, but, as Mitchison and more recently Cullen have shown, this was far from universal (Cullen 2010: ch. 4). What may be unique to the worst years of this episode are the reports of men and women being found where they fell dead in the street or road: in Aberdeenshire it was ordered that the corpses of unknown people were to be buried where they were found. The progressive attrition of successive poor years resulted in not only the poor falling victim to the famine but also farmers and other families who had been of substance before the Ill Years. We have reports of a migration into Ulster, but also of farmers giving up their land or even being evicted for arrears of rent.

There are no really well founded estimates of the population loss of these years, only guesses, but an overall reduction of 10 per cent is not implausible and Cullen has suggested a higher figure. Finally, a national total is incalculable: we know little of the severity of the famine in the

Highlands and we have no record of those who died on the road or fled abroad. More locally, Tyson has argued for a loss of 21 per cent in Aberdeenshire as a whole, with the coastal parishes suffering least and those inland worst. Scots have always tended to look on these years with a touch of embarrassment (Cullen 2010: 188). The famine proved the inadequacy of both Scots agriculture and government: like the contemporaneous attempt to establish a Scottish colony on the Isthmus of Panama, it somehow seemed to be a national defeat that made the unification of the Crowns in 1707 inevitable. And yet it is hard to see what any northern European country could have done any better when so persistently battered by evil weather.

Our inability to discuss Scottish famines with demographic precision continues into the eighteenth century. It becomes much easier to say what was happening in the Lowlands and east, but events in the Highlands and Islands remain obscure and, frankly, one often fears the worst there. The extreme circumstances of 1739–40, which were also felt in Ireland and north-western England – extreme frost and cold from December 1739 to April 1740, a dry summer followed by a late harvest that had been incompletely gathered in when winter began – seem not to have prompted famine in Lowland Scotland. Parochial poor relief had developed far enough to provide a modicum of support. There were civic and private initiatives to bring in grain for sale at less than the market prices. There was a scatter of food riots on English lines, however (Flinn 1977: 216–23; Roessner 2011). The next great harvest failure in 1782–83 was marked by an even greater sophistication of response, with much greater government action, grants for the worst-affected areas in 1783 and public collections for relief efforts. In Aberdeenshire there was a concerted effort to manage the crisis, which included the planting of potatoes as well as commissioning imports of foodstuffs from abroad (Flinn 1977: 233–7).

The sting of famine was therefore taken from the Lowlands. We cannot have that confidence about the Highlands and Islands. Famine there may have been attenuated by the adoption of the potato, but, as is well known, the downside of this vegetable is that it not only encouraged a reliance on potato monoculture but allowed for greater population growth by breaking the ceiling on growth imposed by a climatically marginal, grain-growing economy. As it was, the potato was a benefit to the Highlands and Islands until it failed in 1846, with catastrophic results but no famine. Over the next few years the potato-growing societies of the west subsisted to a very large degree on a mixture of government aid, landlord assistance and charitable donation (Flinn 1977: 421–38; Devine and Orr 1992).

6   Conclusion: Famine as a Pan-National Phenomenon

With the emergence of potato blight, a new consideration came into famine. Until this time famine had essentially been a working out of abnormal weather patterns, whether too much rain, too much cold, or drought. Diseases of grain were certainly known, but, with the sudden discovery of the vulnerability of the potato to plant disease, a new autonomous factor appeared.

The driver of famine was weather. And weather, as we know, does not follow national boundaries. Historians for the most part do. In his account of 1528, the English chronicler Edward Hall tells a politically charged anecdote. The harvest of 1527 having been badly deficient, the mayor and alderman of London went to Cardinal Wolsey to express their fear of famine. Wolsey was not too concerned: the king of France had promised to victual England. The French wheat never arrived, though, and English ships in Normandy had the wheat they had laden seized. London was saved by the German merchants of the Steelyard (merchants of the Hanseatic League), who brought grain from Danzig, Bremen and Hamburg, and by merchants from Flanders, Holland and Frisland. In the end there was no crisis but 'the people said, "see how we had been served by the Frenchmen in our necessity if the Emperors' subjects had not helped us". For this kindness the common people loved the Emperor the better and all his subjects.' Other than confusing a trading opportunity with kindness, English opinion overlooked the dire state of the 1527 harvest in northern France (Hall 1809 [1548]: 736).

Let us offer another example of the way in which famine – or, at least, famine avoidance – in one country could have repercussions in another. In January 1566 Elizabeth I circulated a proclamation in response to rumours that she was going to issue licences for the export of grain. A few people were seeking to take advantage of this by engrossing grain, and prices had risen in an anxious market. The truth, the proclamation insisted, was that representatives of towns in the Spanish Netherlands had sought permission to export grain from England into Flanders. The queen was sympathetic. She acknowledged that the English had been reliant on imported grain in some years. But she had wanted to be reassured about the supply to the English market before she permitted exports, and finally she had decided not to allow any (Hughes and Larkin 1969: 276–8).

The call, then, is to look at famine as a phenomenon that crossed national boundaries and not just those of England, Scotland and Ireland. It may be suggested that famine in southern England was likely to be famine in northern France and the Low Countries too: 1124–26 serves as an example, 1315–17 as another. Famine in the north-west of England certainly coincided with famine in Scotland in the 1590s and 1620s (Flinn 1977: 116–26; Appleby 1978; Gillespie 1984: 10). The famine of 1586–87 in north-west England was also felt in northern France and the southern Low Countries (Clark 1985: 69–75, 80, 88–90). The hard years of the 1690s were found throughout northern Europe (but not, it would appear, in England – perhaps a comment on its precocious Poor Law). The famine of 1739–40 was desperately hard in Ireland, but felt in Scotland and the north-west of England too. Ideally, we want to define where agricultural production fell most sharply. All agricultural historians acknowledge the difficulty of doing this. If we take the severity of famine as our measure, then we may see only where relief was least adequate, where the market was least tamed, where government was most inactive. In looking at this natural phenomenon across national boundaries, there is much to be learnt about how the institutions of relief developed and coped, and how a common humanity asserted itself.

8   Ireland

Cormac Ó Gráda

Famines have been documented in Ireland since the late seventh century. The medieval text *Chronicum Scotorum (Chronicle of the Irish)*, which covers the period up to AD 1150, noted that in AD 699–700, on the heels of a cattle plague and a frost that caused 'the sea between Ireland and Scotland [to freeze] so that there was travelling between them on ice', there ensued a famine so severe that 'man ate man'. Similar short impressionistic accounts of many major famines in the following centuries survive. Yet the historical literature on famine before the eighteenth century is sparse, and the sources to study them are scarce. The public record is reticent and parish registers are lacking. And, although several of the lesser famines of the eighteenth and early nineteenth centuries have been the subject of specialist investigations (e.g. O'Neill 1966; Kelly 1988; 1992a; 1992b; Wells 1996), it is inevitable that any study of Irish famines must focus disproportionately on two more recent and better-documented famines: the massive famines of 1740–41 and the 1840s.

1   Chronology

Just as Cornelius Walford did for India and William Farr for England, Sir William Wilde, in his contribution to the analysis of famine deaths in the Irish population census of 1851, tried to infer the frequency of famines in the past in Ireland from documentary sources.[1] Certain familiar themes recur in the accounts reported by Wilde: parents selling their children for food, hunger-induced migration, war and pestilence as handmaidens of famine, excessive rainfall and cold as the causes of crop failure and, in a few cases, cannibalism (Ó Gráda 2015a). Examples of (presumably)

An earlier version of this chapter was presented at the first conference of the European Historical Demographic Society, Alghero, Italy, in September 2014. The comments of participants and of David Dickson, James Kelly, Padraig Lenihan and Peter Solar are much appreciated.

[1] Wilde's list has been reproduced in Crawford (1989b).

166

sky-high food prices begin to be reported from the early fourteenth century on – 'wheat for 23s. the cranock, and wine for 8d.' (1318), 'six pence of the old money for a cake of bread' (1545), 24s. for a peck of wheat (1552), 'potatoes 4s. 4d. a bushel' (1741), and so on. Unfortunately, non-crisis reference prices are usually not given, though a report from 1601 compares a price of 7.5 shillings per barrel for oats to the 'ordinary rate' of one shilling, and it was reported in February 1728 that 'oatmeal in many parts of this kingdom [was at] three times the customary price' (Boulter 1759: I, 222; Lyons 1989: 63; Crawford 1989b: 8). Nor is it recorded how long the high prices prevailed.

The uncertainties surrounding such famine chronologies have been summarised elsewhere (Ó Gráda 2009: 26). Even so, they have their uses, and Clarkson (1989) has disaggregated the data presented by Wilde, relying on his own judgement to distinguish between outright famine and less severe crises. By this reckoning the first half of the fourteenth, seventeenth and nineteenth centuries were the worst affected by subsistence crises. Wilde's chronology suggests a crisis or famine on average every 13 years, but famines in the strict sense were less frequent: by this reckoning there were only 29 during this 550-year period.

Some of these famines coincided with crises elsewhere. The Irish famine of the mid-1310s was part of a major crisis straddling the whole of north-western Europe (Jordan 1996). In Ireland the impact of poor harvests in those years was exacerbated by the scorched earth policy waged by the Scottish warlord Edward Bruce, to the extent that *do ithdais na daine cin amuras a cheli ar fod Erenn* ('undoubtedly men ate each other in Ireland'). Other famines, such as those of the 1580s, the early 1600s and 1649–52, were linked to colonial wars. The English poet Edmund Spenser was a witness to the famine of the 1580s and left an account of it in *A View of the Present State of Ireland* (1596). Sir William Petty, a more prosaic chronicler of famine during the Confederate and Cromwellian wars, reckoned in his *Political Anatomy of Ireland* that between 1641 and 1652 'about 504 M. of the Irish perished, or were wasted by the Sword, Plague, Famine, Hardship and Banishment'. Petty's demographic estimates were often cavalier and imprecise: his guesses at plague deaths are based on the premise that 'the Plague was no hotter in England than in Ireland' or, alternatively, that 'the Plague of London was but 2/3 as hot'! But his numbers tally with recent guesstimates that war-related losses reached 20 to 25 per cent of the population, mostly in 1649–52, since the latter combines deaths from plague and famine (Hull 1899: 150–1; Lenihan 1997; Smyth 2006: 158–61; Cronin and Lenihan forthcoming). Estimates, even of the most speculative sort, are impossible for earlier famines.

That the famine of the 1580s and those of the 1640s and early 1650s were linked to plausible accounts of cannibalism is an indication of their horrific extent (Ó Gráda 2015a: 26–9). Indeed, in relative terms, the carnage of 1649–53 may have dwarfed that linked to any other Irish disaster on record. In the 1640s deaths were more localised in Ulster and northeast Connacht, areas that were then more sparsely populated; thereafter the more densely settled areas to the south were worst affected, and the impact of war and famine was exacerbated by plague.

Both Spenser and Petty were very much part of the English colonial project in Ireland and the colonial links to the above famines were direct. Whether the associated land confiscations and 'soft' persecution of the native population also played some indirect role in subsequent eighteenth- and nineteenth-century famines remains a moot point. Perhaps they did, by skewing long-run demographic and socio-economic trajectories, but there is no guarantee that a different pattern of landholding or a different ruling elite would have rid Ireland of famine, given the susceptibility of early modern Europe to famine. Even so, suppose, for example, that the Irish landed elite had been as active in resisting the subdivision of holdings as their Scottish peers in the century or so before the 1840s: would that not have reduced the impact of *phytophthera infestans*? Scotland's clearances, cruel and ruthlessly executed though they were, help explain why the Scottish Highlands escaped lightly when the potato failed (Devine 1988): there was a trade-off between evictions before and during the 1840s. While variants of the colonial hypothesis have been proposed in other historical contexts (e.g. Sokoloff and Engerman 2000; Acemoglu, Johnson and Robinson 2001), they have not been much explored in Irish historiography (compare Dickson 2005: 497–8).

2   The Great Famine of 1740–41

The famine of 1740–41 and that of the 1840s were both the products of unprecedented exogenous shocks. The Great Frost of 1740–41 was one of the most severe climatic events to strike northern Europe during the past millennium. Its cause remains unclear: perhaps a volcanic eruption on the Kamchatka Peninsula in Russia's far east was responsible.[2] The arctic conditions led to the destruction of crops and livestock, extreme distress and increased mortality from infectious diseases across much of northern Europe (Post 1984; 1985; see too Engler et al. 2013).

[2] This eruption is included in the long list published by Russian specialists (Gusev et al. 2003: 9). A problem with this explanation is that the onset of the cold weather towards the very end of 1739 seems to have preceded an eruption in the peninsula's Tolbachik volcanic cluster in 1740.

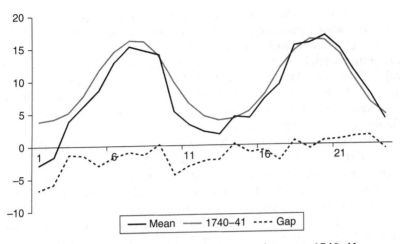

Figure 8.1 Monthly temperature versus the mean, 1740–41

Temperature data for Ireland are lacking, but in central England, where continuous monthly data are available from 1659 on, 1740 was the coldest year on record, with a mean temperature of only 6.8 degrees centigrade (Figure 8.1). January 1740, when the temperature was seven degrees below the mean, was the coldest month of all, but February 1740 also stands out. There is no comparable source for Ireland, but temperatures there cannot have been very different, and several accounts describing the extreme conditions in Ireland survive. In the initial phase lakes and rivers froze; fuel and provisions were scarce; and many people died of hypothermia. Contemporary accounts dwelt on mills that could not grind corn, horses 'heartless for want of oats', and potatoes trapped in the ground by the frozen earth.[3] The cold weather even prevented burials on occasion (Delamayne 1767: 11) and frozen soils disrupted crop sowing and economic activity more generally. The price of wheat had doubled by June 1740 and, as a result, the price of bread also doubled (Swift 1948: 370; Ní Úrdail and Ó Gráda 2015). Then a poor harvest meant that this high price level was maintained (Engler et al. 2013: 1173); potatoes remained 'locked in the frost'; famine followed. Nowhere in Europe did the icy weather wreak more havoc than in Ireland, where 1740–41 became known as *bliain an áir* ('the year of the slaughter'):

[3] British Library, Egmont Papers, Addl Mss. 46991, ffo. 4–5 (William Taylor to Lord Egmont 26 January 1740, 29 January 1740); National Library of Wales, Puleston Papers, Ms. 3582 fo. 46 (John? to Lord Barrymore, January 1740). I am very grateful to James Kelly for providing me with these references.

'[T]heir food was nettles and salt or some other vegetable if they were lucky, and after consuming such a meal their stomachs swole and they expired' (Ní Úrdail and Ó Gráda 2015: 38). Fever was so widespread that houses were boarded up as in times of plague in the past (Ó Gráda and Ó Muirithe 2010: 43–4; Ní Úrdail and Ó Gráda 2015). Indeed, if the Great Irish Famine of the 1840s was Europe's greatest famine of the nineteenth century, the Irish famine of 1740–41 may well have been, in relative terms, the eighteenth century's greatest.

In Ireland the famine lasted from early 1740 to mid-1741 (Dickson 1997). The 1741 harvest was a good one and grain prices soon returned to their pre-famine levels. But the famine was much more about potatoes than cereals. Its severity underlines the precocious dominance of the potato in the Irish diet, particularly in the southern province of Munster, where the famine and resultant mortality were most severe (Dickson 2005: 236–40). Although crop failures in 1740–41 were not confined to the potato, the Gaelic poetry[4] inspired by the famine – which is drawn primarily from the southern part of the country – attributes the disaster entirely to the failure of the potato. Already, by then, the potato was the main food of the poor – *is féidir 'rá ris gurb é dhá dtrian beatha innse Éire* ('it can be said of it that it provides two-thirds of the sustenance of the island of Ireland') – and was described variously as 'like manna from Egypt', 'Ireland's nourishment', 'the tree of life' and 'the cheapest nourishment of the Irish race'. Its great advantage was that it required 'neither harrow nor plough, neither sickle nor flail, nor protection against the wind, but went straight from the earth to the fire and dish'. But now, thanks to the frost, all that remained were 'a filthy crust and black streaks inside them'.

While cereal price data are available (Figure 8.2), we have only scattered quotations for potato prices in the 1740s. The Gaelic poetry of the time is silent on them. Even so, in the western county of Roscommon the barrel of potatoes that would have cost 3s. to 5s. a barrel in 1737 or 1738 cost 18s. in April 1741 (Ní Chinnéide 1957: 5, 16, 17). A quadrupling of the price of the staple crop suggests a very severe famine indeed. As in the 1840s, the price of potatoes rose much more than that of wheat.

The demographic toll of the 1740–41 famine can only be guessed at, since civil registration was still more than a century away and the evidence from parish registers is very limited (Drake 1968; Dickson, Ó Gráda and Daultrey, 1982: 164–9; Dickson 1997; Cullen 2012; Engler et al. 2013). An attempt at inferring excess mortality from the decline

---

[4] The extracts cited are taken from Ó Gráda and Ó Muirithe (2010). Compare Collins (2014).

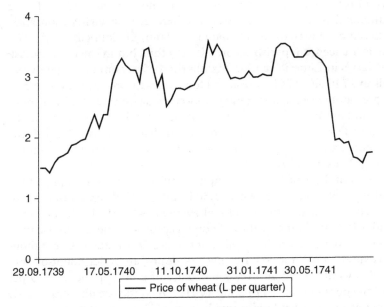

Figure 8.2 The price of wheat in Dublin, 1740–41

Source: Steven Engler, private communication.

in the number of hearths between 1732 and 1744 reckons that between 310,000 and 480,000 out of a population of about 2.4 million perished (Dickson, Ó Gráda and Daultrey 1982: 164–8; Dickson 1997: 69, 72). This is just an informed guess, and the implied proportionate mortality – up to 15 to 20 per cent of the population – is certainly very high. But a 'country gentleman' wrote to Anglican Lord Primate Hugh Boulter in 1741 that, 'by a moderate computation, very near one-third of the poor cottiers of Munster have perished by fevers, fluxes, and downright want' (cited in Creighton 1894: 242). That would tally with the 200,000 to 400,000 proposed by the anonymous author of *The Groans of Ireland*, though his political arithmetic is hardly conclusive (anon. 1741: 3–4):

If but one for every House in the Kingdom died (and that is very probable, when we consider that whole Families and Villages were swept off in many Parts together) the loss must be upwards of 400,000 Souls.

The Dublin physician John Rutty was presumably referring to *The Groans of Ireland* when he noted in his *Chronological History of the Weather and Seasons and of Prevailing Diseases in Dublin* a claim that one-fifth of the population perished, though he thought that to be an exaggeration

(Rutty 1770: 86). A medicinal practitioner who worked in Cork during the famine also argued for a lower number, 'at least eighty thousand', but offered no source to substantiate that claim (O'Connell 1746: 327).

The evidence from parish records is very thin, but in the urban parish of St Mary's in Limerick and in mainly rural Macroom in County Cork burials in 1740 and 1741 were about four times the average of the immediate pre-famine years; assuming a non-crisis death rate of 25 per thousand would imply an excess mortality of one-fifth. Even worse, in Cullen in County Tipperary a clergyman reckoned that nearly two-fifths of the inhabitants had perished of famine-related diseases by the late summer of 1741 (Dickson 1997: 66–9).

The Dublin Bills of Mortality imply significant excess mortality in the capital in 1740 and 1741, when 3,304 and 2,792 deaths, respectively, were recorded relative to the annual average of 2,189 deaths in 1735–39 and 1742–45. None of these figures captures all deaths in a city of 130,000 or so, however; the implied non-crisis death rate of 16 per thousand is surely much too low for that. Assuming an under-count of one-third, this would mean an excess mortality of 2,600 or so, about 3 per cent of the population, in 1740 and 1741.[5] Of course, death rates outside the capital were undoubtedly much higher. For the sake of comparison, in the 1840s the excess death rate in Dublin was about 4 per cent, whereas excess mortality in Ireland as a whole was about 11 to 12 per cent (Ó Gráda 1999: ch. 5). In 1740–41 suffering was worst in the south, west and midlands. Ulster, north Connacht and north Leinster, it would seem, escaped relatively lightly, perhaps because their poor were less reliant on the potato. The famine undoubtedly caused massive mortality, but we will probably never know its true extent (Dickson 1997: 62–9).[6]

Rutty's *Chronological History* is our best-known source on the causes of death in 1740–42. It mentions the standard causes of 'fever, dysentery, and famine', in that order (see too O'Connell 1746). Also noteworthy are Rutty's remarks about male mortality in 1741: 'Another notable circumstance seems worthy of being recorded, in relation to the subjects which this fever generally attacked, both here and in England viz. that they were generally men and those of a middle age, and strong, but few women; also children were but more rarely attacked' (Rutty 1770: 86–97). This age/gender pattern recalls that of the great influenza epidemic of 1918–19, and may well indicate that deaths from an influenza-like epidemic followed in the wake of classic famine mortality. The wealthy did not starve but they were not immune from fever (Delamayne 1767: 13).

[5] The calculation is [1.5 X (3,304 + 2,792 − 2,189 X 2)] = 2,600. See Rutty (1770: *passim*); Fagan (1991: 148).
[6] Compare Datta (1990: 102–8) on Bengal in 1770.

On the eve of the 1740–41 famine Ireland was sparsely populated compared to the mid-1840s; numbers rose from about 2.4 million to about 8.5 million in the interim. What this implies for living standards at the earlier date is far from clear. Cullen, rejecting the argument that the famine of 1740–41 was due to the weakness of the economy at the time, points instead to the tension between 'general amelioration' and 'a persistent and profoundly inegalitarian distribution of income' (Cullen 2010: 20).

3   A Gap in Famines?

At the height of the 1740–41 famine George Berkeley, the philosopher-bishop of Cloyne, feared that the 'nation probably will not recover this loss in a century'.[7] Yet between the mid-eighteenth century and 1821 Ireland's population grew from about 2.2 million c. 1750 to over 7 million, faster than anywhere else in western Europe. This implies a rather benign demographic regime by the standards of the day. In a classic and influential contribution, Connell (1950) attributes the rise in population mainly to increasing nuptiality and a consequent rise in the birth rate, but he also attributes some of it to a century-long 'gap in famines'. Connell links the 'gap' to the diffusion of the potato, which offered both insurance against harvest failure and a healthy food that made it easy for young couples to marry. The hypothesis oversimplifies, because it downplays a series of reasonably well documented, smaller, famines in 1756–57 ('agues were rife'), 1766, 1782–84, 1800–01 ('fever, dysentery, scarlatina, ophthalmia, and influenza'), 1816–18 ('a few unhappy sufferers are said to have died of absolute want of food'), 1822 ('extensive and alarming distress... [F]amine reported from various districts of the West') and 1831 ('some are now bleeding their starving cows...').[8] Even so, Dickson's analysis of a sample of north Leinster Catholic parishes – where, exceptionally, partial burial data survive – implies that there were no devastating famines in that region at least after the early 1740s (Dickson 1989: 102–3; see too Dickson 2014). And the excess mortality associated with the worst of these other famines – 40,000 in the case of 1800–01, perhaps 60,000 in 1816–18 – would have been insufficient to cancel out a rate of natural increase of about 75,000 annually. Note too that excess mortality in 1816–18 was far higher in parts of Italy, Switzerland, Austria-Hungary and Germany than in Ireland. That excess mortality in 1822 was relatively light is indicated by the silence of the

---

[7] Berkeley to Prior, 19 May 1741: Luce and Jessop (1956: VIII, 251–2).
[8] All quotations are from Crawford (1989b: 13–20).

Board of Health, which had been assembling data on fever deaths and would – most likely – have publicised any significant increases (O'Neill 1966; Ó Gráda 1993: 5).

These smaller famines struck in a context of rural proletarianisation and the increasing dominance of the potato. By the early 1840s that reliance was such that about one-third of the population consumed little else (Bourke 1993). Dependence on the potato was captured in the ditty *prátaí ar maidin, prátaí um nóin; is dá n-éireoinn meánoíche, prátaí a gheobhainn* ('potatoes in the morning, potatoes at noon; and if I rose at midnight, it would still be potatoes'). Why the potato achieved such dominance in the Irish diet has not been fully explained. Ireland's rather damp climate, which gave it a comparative advantage in potato cultivation, is part of the answer; so is the potato's role as a root crop (like the turnip in England) in an expanding acreage under grain. And, given Ireland's relative poverty, the potato's status as an 'inferior good' – as distinct from a Giffen good (compare Rosen 1999) – increased its appeal. The sharp drop in the price of potatoes relative to that of oats between the 1760s and the 1790s may also have been a factor (see Figure 8.3). But whether the diffusion caused the population to grow or was a response to that growth remains moot (compare Cullen 1968; Livi-Bacci 1981: 72–5; 1997; Mokyr 1981). Cullen describes its role as ancillary to grain, 'reflect[ing] the fact that cereal cultivation intensified in the 1750s and 1760s' (Cullen 2012: 111), but the evidence adduced above would argue for a more precocious dependence on the potato, especially in Munster. The potato harvest failed before 1845, but shortfalls before *phytophthera infestans* (potato blight) struck tended to be regionally uneven and once-off failures. Those of 1845, 1846 and after were unheralded ecological disasters.

4   Black '47

Like the famine of 1740–41, the Great Irish Famine of the 1840s was one of several famines that struck north-western Europe at the same time (Ó Gráda, Paping and Vanhaute 2007). And, like its predecessor, it was the worst of the lot. The 'Great Hunger', familiar to many worldwide through Woodham-Smith's eponymous classic, has been the focus of both specialist research and popular monographs (e.g. Edwards and Williams 1956; Mokyr 1985; Gray 1995; Ó Gráda 1999; Donnelly 2002; Nally 2011; Crowley, Murphy and Smith 2012; Delaney 2012; Ó Murchadha 2011; MacSuibhne 2013; Solar 2015). The outlines of the story are therefore familiar. The Great Famine, the product of repeated failures of the potato, was much more protracted than most famines.

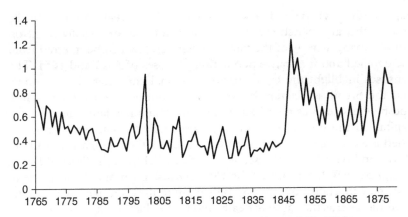

Figure 8.3 The ratio of potato to oats prices, 1765–1880

While deaths began to mount in the wake of the second attack of potato blight in autumn 1846, famine symptoms persisted in some areas until 1850 and even later. Although a precise count of famine deaths is impossible, there is now a broad consensus on the approximate death toll of about 1 million (or nearly one in eight of the entire population). Accounts differ as to how much a greater commitment to saving lives would have achieved, but all view the famine as due to a combination of economic backwardness, an ecological shock and an inadequate and, many would argue, callous official response.

Evictions, amounting in many places to significant mass clearances, were a feature of the period. Notorious examples include Toomevara in County Tipperary, where nearly 600 people were evicted by the Rev. Massey Dawson in May 1849; Moveen, in south-west Clare (highlighted in the *Illustrated London News*);[9] and Aghadrinagh, a townland[10] just outside Castlebar in County Mayo, where the population plummeted from 314 in 1841 to nine in 1851. Most of the 289 evicted by the Earl of Lucan in Aghadrinagh in May 1848 moved into the nearby town of Castlebar in the wake of the event; 44 emigrated to England and seven somehow made it to America. But their eventual fate is unknown (Hamrock 1998: 127–8, 147; O'Brien 2010; for more on evictions in these years, see O'Neill 2000; and Ó Murchadha 2011: 113–34).

The famine is well documented in official papers, in the press (which was relatively free at the time but did not circulate widely) and in private

---

[9] The much-reproduced sketch of unroofed cottages in Moveen appeared in 'Condition in Ireland: illustrations of the new poor law', 22 December 1849.
[10] A small geographical unit used in Ireland.

papers. Although Ireland lacked a system of civil registration of births and deaths, and parish register data are thin and are usually silent on burials, many aspects of the famine's demography can be inferred from the detailed and innovative population censuses of 1841 and 1851. The censuses highlight the highly uneven regional character of the famine, and the broad association between population loss, on the one hand, and markers such as poor housing, illiteracy and low land valuation per capita, on the other. However, they also indicate that some impoverished areas in the worst-affected west, such as the Iveragh Peninsula in Kerry and west Donegal, escaped relatively lightly. The *Tables of Death*, compiled by Wilde as part of the 1851 census, are an unreliable guide to aggregate mortality, but they usefully point to the dominant role of infectious diseases as the cause of death, and to the slight relative advantage of females (Mokyr and Ó Gráda 2002).

Mokyr's *Why Ireland Starved* pioneered econometric analysis of the famine. That wide-ranging classic invokes the 32 counties of Ireland as a pseudo-time series in attempts, using ordinary least squares regression, to account for material poverty on the eve of the famine and the variation in the death rate across the island between 1846 and 1851. Others have followed suit (McGregor 1989; Ó Gráda 1999: 30–4; Goodspeed 2013). Kelly and Ó Gráda (2015) use a different estimation approach to testing these two parameters with barony-level data (n > 300). Their finding that population growth in the pre-famine decades was fastest in marginal areas of poor land and where living standards were lowest corroborates Mokyr but runs contrary to the Malthusian presumption that population growth is an increasing function of incomes. In a review of Thomas Newenham's study of Irish population, Malthus (1808: 345) observed that, 'although it is quite certain that the population of Ireland cannot continue permanently to increase at its present rate, yet it is as certain that it will not suddenly come to a stop'. That was because 'both theory and experience uniformly instruct us that a less abundant supply of food operates with a gradually increasing pressure for a very long time before its progress is stopt'. The gradual reduction in living standards would reduce nuptiality and the birth rate, 'the habits necessary for an order of things in which the funds for the maintenance of labour are stationary'. But in pre-famine Ireland the kind of demographic adjustment posited by Malthus was slowest where it was required most. Had Malthus still been alive in the late 1840s he would doubtless have seen the Great Irish Famine as an example of the 'gigantic inevitable famine [which] stalks in the rear, and with one mighty blow levels the population with the food of the world' (Malthus 1798: ch. 7).

On the variation in death rates across Ireland, Kelly and Ó Gráda's analysis confirms the link between population loss during the famine decade (1841–51) and proxies for pre-famine poverty such as illiteracy and housing quality: areas heavily dependent on the land were also, not surprisingly, more likely to lose population during the famine decade.

5   Markets and Famines

At the height of the famine of 1727–29 the Anglican archbishop of Armagh, Hugh Boulter, described his efforts to relieve scarcity in the north of Ireland thus:

There has been set on foot a subscription here in Dublin, to buy corn from Munster, where it has been very cheap, to send it to the north, in order to keep the markets down; but though we have bought about £3000 of oats, oatmeal, and potatoes there, yet first by the continuance of easterly winds for three weeks, and since by the insurrections of the mob in those parts, not one boat load is yet arrived in the north... There have been tumults at Limerick, Cork, Waterford, Clonmel, and other places to prevent the corn we have bought from going to the north.

(Boulter 1759: I, 287; Kelly 1992a)

Boulter sanctioned severe measures against the rioters, but their effectiveness is not known. By preventing exports the rioters hoped to avert price increases in their own back yard. In so acting they were part of an old and universal tradition of 'moral economy' redressers (e.g. Eiríksson 1997; Bohstedt 2010). Boulter's motives in the 1720s were no doubt in part humanitarian; he would also spearhead relief efforts in Dublin in 1740–41. But they also had a sectarian tinge, since Boulter feared that hunger was forcing his co-religionists in Ulster to leave for America.

In 1740–41 the price of wheat more than doubled in Dublin, while it nearly doubled in England. However, while cereal prices began to fall back in England after mid-1740, they continued to rise in Ireland until mid-1741 (Figure 8.4). The subsequent decline was mainly the product of better harvest prospects, aided by imports from the American colonies, which began to arrive in significant quantities in the spring of 1741.

The markets for cereals functioned more or less as normal in Ireland during the 1840s, in the sense that movements in grain prices closely mimicked those across the Irish Sea. Data on the price of potatoes and cereals suggest that market failure, at least at wholesale level, bears little blame for excess mortality: markets functioned more or less as normal (Ó Gráda 2005). Figure 8.5, showing how potato prices rose much more than cereal prices and remained high after cereal prices began to fall, is another reminder that potatoes and cereal were imperfect substitutes. Because international grain markets were much more integrated in the

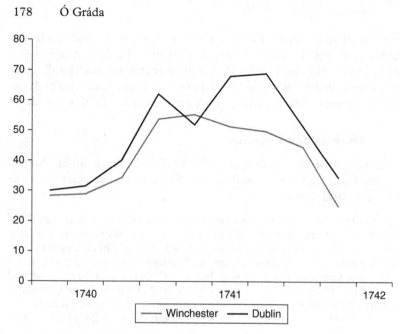

Figure 8.4 The price of wheat in Dublin and Winchester, 1739–41

Sources: Derived from Kennedy and Solar 2007; 'Monthly grain prices in England, 1270–1955' database, International Institute of Social History (www.iisg.nl/hpw/poynder-england.php); and data supplied by Steven Engler and Peter Solar.

1840s than a century earlier, price spikes in the 1840s reveal less about local harvest conditions than in the 1740s (compare Solar 2007). As for potatoes, markets on the eve of the famine carried a wide range of varieties, and were subject to rather regular seasonal price fluctuations. Once the blight struck, markets experienced a rush of supplies from nervous producers and merchants. And between early 1847 and the summer of 1848 potato markets essentially ceased to function in towns and cities. Two aspects bear noting. First, the seasonal tempo of supplies rules out hoarding on the part of sellers or panic buying on the part of consumers. Second, the telltale symptoms of potato blight enabled buyers and sellers to distinguish good potatoes from bad, so that prices adjusted to quality (Ó Gráda 1993: 111–21; 2006: 120).

6   Relief

While the role of famine relief is a key element in the literature on the Great Famine of the 1840s, it features little in that on the 1740s. John

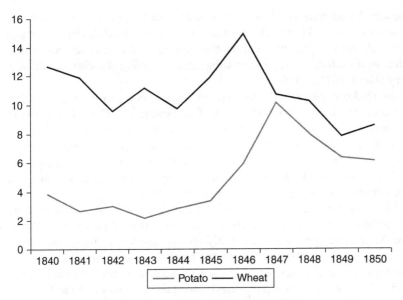

Figure 8.5 Potato and wheat prices, 1840–50

Note: Potato prices in pence per stone, wheat prices in shillings per cwt.
Sources: Derived from Kennedy and Solar 2007; 'Monthly grain prices in England, 1270–1955' database, International Institute of Social History (www.iisg.nl/hpw/poynder-england.php); and data supplied by Steven Engler and Peter Solar.

Post, the foremost historian of the European famine of 1740–41, has argued that that famine was particularly lethal in Ireland and in Norway, 'fundamentally because public administrations either neglected or failed to carry out the elementary welfare service of safeguarding the poor from hunger and starvation' (Post 1985: 145). True, Archbishop Boulter fed 2,500 Dubliners every morning and evening during the crisis (Anon. 1747), and it was claimed that 'but for the charity and humanity of Lord and Lady Mountjoy thousands would perish of the famine'. Again, the munificence of some southern grandees, including bishop-philosopher George Berkeley of Cloyne, are celebrated in the Gaelic poetry of the time (Ó Gráda and Ó Muirithe 2010).[11] But all those efforts relied on private philanthropy: contributions from the public purse were not forthcoming. At the same time, while Ireland's very limited system of

[11] See too Luce and Jessop (1956: VIII, 251). Berkeley had described the horrors of famine in *The Querist*, published in three parts between 1735 and 1737, but that work refers to an earlier famine, possibly that of the late 1720s.

parochial and municipal poor relief was ill-equipped to cope with the disaster of 1740–41, and the central authorities indeed did little – at any rate, relative to other times and other places – relief did become some-what more effective, at least in urban areas, during the eighteenth century (Kelly 2010; 2012).

As Dickson has noted, subsequent crises, though much less severe, left their mark on official responses. The famine of 1756–57 resulted in modest public funding of relief and a temporary embargo on distilling; that of 1782–84 in an embargo on grain exports; that of 1800–01 in the finance of emergency imports of rice and maize from the United States; and that of 1816–18 in publicly funded public works schemes and the importation of seed grain (Dickson 1989: 106–7).

Much of the literature on the Great Famine of the 1840s has focused on famine relief. Public expenditure on the crisis totalled about £10 million. While that sum almost certainly saved many lives, Mokyr and others have compared it unfavourably to the totals expended on compensating slave-owners in the West Indies in the 1820s and on the Crimean War of 1853–56. And these comparisons do not take into account the fact that most public expenditure on the famine was intended to be a loan, not a grant. It is also true that raising the funds placed the public finances under considerable pressure in 1847, but that was because the political will to increase direct taxation was lacking (O'Neill 1956: 255–6; Mokyr 1985: 292; Read 2016). So far nobody has attempted the daunting task of estimating how much excess mortality might have been avoided, given more generous and more effective relief – or, indeed, how many lives were saved by the relief that was granted. The literature has been content to highlight the inadequacy and, to some extent, the counterproductive character of public works schemes, and to criticise the over-reliance on relief within the workhouse system.

Public works are a common form of famine relief, and they were already familiar in Ireland before 1845–46. During the Great Famine, however, they were pursued on an unprecedented scale, in wintry weather, under conditions that were likely to spread disease, and that discriminated against the young, the aged and the weak. Workers were often paid on a piece-rate basis, and payments were hardly sufficient to sustain life (McGregor 2004). Oral historical accounts repeatedly refer to a daily rate of 4d. or even less on the public works, far below the wage of agricultural labourers before the potato failed (Póirtéir 1995: 153–65; 1996: 154–65). Nor were the workhouses equipped to cope with the challenge of famine: their capacity was inadequate, and they relied mainly on local funding, which made a mockery of the ability-to-pay principle. Indeed, the Irish workhouse system, which was never intended to cope with a catastrophe such as the famine, had been established as recently as 1838, and some workhouses had yet to open their doors for inmates when the blight struck. A high proportion of workhouse victims succumbed to infectious diseases, so much so that the risk of infection at the height of the crisis must have deterred all but the most desperate from entering. Mismanagement and corruption at local level compounded the inadequacies of this mode of relief (compare Kinealy 1989; McCabe and Ó Gráda 2009; Ó Gráda 2011). Nevertheless, the authorities imposed virtually the entire burden of famine relief on the workhouse system in the autumn of 1847. The publicly administered soup kitchens that provided food to over one-third of the population at their peak in July 1847 are usually awarded higher marks than the public works or the workhouses, but questions remain about the nutritional quality of the gruel administered (compare Crawford 1989c; Donnelly 2002: 90–2; Ó Murchadha 2011: 87–8).

Although migration is a standard feature of nearly all famines, and wandering beggars are often among its first victims, famine migrations are usually temporary. Survivors tend to return home after the worst is over. In this respect the great Irish potato famine of the 1840s was exceptional and unlike any previous Irish famine, in that it also spawned a massive permanent long-distant migration that would long outlast the famine, and that would have a big influence on Irish social, economic and indeed political history. Anbinder and McCaffrey's recent (2015) analysis of the county variation in the emigration rate to the United States during the famine and in its immediate wake (1846–54) reveals disproportionately large outflows from some midland counties, where migration had already been significant before the famine; an average outflow representing 11 per cent of the pre-famine population; but little from the devastated counties of Clare or Mayo. Although the forced character of that migration, and the hardships and deaths it entailed, were part of the tragedy, without mass migration the death toll in Ireland itself – and almost certainly in Britain too – would surely have been higher. To some extent the presence of North America as a distant safety valve let the authorities off the hook: without it, they would surely have been forced to stave off increased migration across the Irish Sea with more generous and timely relief in Ireland. Moreover, despite some deservedly notorious disasters, most of the migrants made it safely to the other side. Most stayed and, by the standards of what they had been used to, prospered (Ó Gráda and O'Rourke 1997). Note, however, that in the 1840s North America was beyond the reach of the poorest and the weakest.

Little is known about the impact on mortality in destination countries. Fernihough's recent estimate of Irish famine-induced excess mortality in Great Britain in the late 1840s – presumably due mainly to infectious diseases – yields the high figure of 150,000. This estimate is inferred from civil registration data; a more direct, archive-based estimate by the late Frank Neal returns a much lower figure (10,000 to 15,000) for 1847 alone (Neal 1998: 279–80; Ó Gráda 1999: 111–12; Fernihough 2014).

7   Conclusion

The impact of the Great Famine of the 1840s on post-famine economic and demographic patterns has been the subject of a good deal of analysis. The famine would seem to be an exception to the claim of Watkins and Menken (1985) that the demographic impact of famines is fleeting or temporary, though Crotty (1966: 35–83) argues, very much in the spirit of Watkins and Menken, that the Great Famine merely accelerated trends already under way since 1815. O'Rourke (1991) rejects this position, countering that the persistence of potato blight (through its impact on yields and prices dictating a shift to pastoral and mixed farming) and the impact of huge surge of emigration in the late 1840s and early 1850s (through the creation of networks that had their own added drawing power on subsequent outflows) meant that the famine did indeed 'matter'. In different ways, Connell (1957) and Guinnane (1997) have addressed the link between the famine and the subsequent huge decline in nuptiality and increase in mean marriage ages for both bride and grooms. Post-famine Ireland's status as Europe's demographic outlier, which lasted for a century and a half, had its roots in the Great Famine. By contrast, it would seem that the demographic vacuum created by the famine of the 1740s was quickly filled à la Watkins and Menken, so that *bliain an áir* ('the year of the slaughter', 1740–41) had little medium- or long-term impact on the economy.

In Ireland the era of major famines came to end with the Great Famine. A succession of poor harvests in the early 1860s, in 1879–80 and in the 1890s led to severe privation (Donnelly 1975: 251–5; 1976; O'Neill 1989; 1996). The rhetorical exaggeration of the *Irish Farmers' Gazette*'s claim in 1863 that 'the farming classes of this country are worse off in this season than they were in what are called "the famine years"' is lent some support by a contemporary economist's estimate in that same year that the equivalent of more than two years' rent had been wiped out by crop failures and accompanying declines in livestock numbers (Donnelly 1976: 33–4). The second crisis, during which there were several reports

Table 8.1 *Chronology of Irish famines*

Year(s)	Commentary
1310	Scarcity in Ireland. Wheat 20s. a bushel.
1315–18	Diseases, famine, murder, and incredible bad weather... Corpses eaten, women eat their children... Wheat 40s. a *crannoc* and in some places 4 marks and more a *crannoc*... '*do ithdais na daine cin amuras a cheli ar fod Erenn*' ('and undoubtedly men ate each other throughout Ireland').
1330–31	Famine – so humid, rainy and stormy that summer and autumn were converted into winter tempests.
1339	All the corn of Ireland destroyed: general famine.
1397	Famine – summer and autumn windy, wet and cold.
1410	Great famine in Ireland.
1433	*Samhradh na mearaithne* (the summer of fleeting acquaintances).
1447	Men were wont to eat all kinds of herbs.
1461	Great dearth.
1468	Great scarcity in Ireland.
1478	Hard, niggardly year.
1497	Great famine throughout Ireland... People ate food unbecoming to mention...
1523	Great famine in Ireland...
1586–89	Famine following Desmond rebellion; 'they did eat of the dead carrions, happy were they yf they could finde them, yea, and one another soone after...'.
1600–03	War-related famine.
1640s–1650s	Succession of war-related famines (see text); 'stealing; carrying off cats; dogs; eating humans; rotten leather; and undressed leather'.
1728–29	Oatmeal in March 1728 in many parts three times the customary price.
1740–41	Major famine (see text).
1756	Partial famine accompanied by influenza epidemic.
1782–84	Embargo placed on food exports June 1783–January 1784.
1799–1801	Potatoes scarcely to be procured for 7s. or 8s. per cwt.
1816–18	Mortality estimated at 40,000–60,000.
1822	Counties of the western seaboard particularly hit: little excess mortality [?].
1839	Potatoes 7d. a stone: little excess mortality [?].
1846–50	The Great Famine (see text).

of deaths from starvation in 1880,[12] was more severe; occurring during a peak of the Land War, it was overshadowed by political developments

[12] E.g. *Irish Times*, 'The distress in Ireland', 6 March 1880 (Moycullen); 'Alleged death of a farmer from starvation', 29 March 1880 (Araglen, Fermoy); 'The destitution in Loughrea: alleged death from starvation', 24 January 1880; 'The registrar-general's statement', 3 February 1880 (Parsonstown).

and largely overlooked by historians (see Geary 2014). O'Neill (1989) has rightly drawn attention to distress 'in restricted areas of a small number of counties' in 1890–91, 1894–95 and 1897–98, but the hardship he describes would qualify as 'crisis' rather than outright famine. And, although in both the early 1860s and in 1879–80 there were increases in workhouse admissions (particularly between 1861 and 1863) and in emigration to the United States and the colonies (which exceeded 100,000 annually in 1863–65 and in 1883),[13] excess mortality was low.

Why were earlier patterns not repeated? Part of the answer must be the massive depopulation caused by the Great Famine; as a result, the number of agricultural holdings of an acre or less fell from 140,000 c. 1845 to 88,000 in 1851 (Bourke 1993: 76), and the acreage under potatoes fell by almost a half (and potato output by much more, due to the lasting ravages of the potato blight). The net result was higher living standards and a more diversified diet for those survivors who stayed in Ireland. Donnelly (1976) also emphasises how reliance on maize outlasted the Great Famine, and that its spread was aided by the increasing commercialisation of rural Ireland. More generous relief mattered too. All the same, even though those crises are not usually described as famines by historians and were tiny even by the standards of 1799–1800 or 1816–17, by today's benchmarks they might be considered so: the crises of 2002 in Malawi and 2005 in Niger may well have cost fewer lives, but they made global headlines.

As other chapters in this volume attest, famines that kill more than 5 per cent of an extensive population are very rare. The Irish famines of 1740–41 and the 1840s stand out as exceptional in this respect.[14] The massive impacts of those crises are linked to both economic underdevelopment and inadequate responses from governing elites, but the unparalleled character of the shocks that attended them – the Great Frost of 1740 and potato blight in the 1840s – made them much worse.

---

[13] The data are reproduced in Schrier (1958: 157, 165).
[14] Compare Lappaleinen (2014) on Finland in the 1690s.

9 Nordic Europe

Martin Dribe, Mats Olsson and Patrick Svensson

Famines of different magnitudes have been reported in Nordic literature from the Middle Ages until the late nineteenth century. Most reports are based on contemporary sources that include qualitative statements on the causes and effects of the fatal events. Except for some Finnish famines in the seventeenth and nineteenth centuries and for a shorter period in early modern Sweden, Nordic famines have not been studied in detail. In this chapter, we focus on the Nordic countries from AD 536 to 1875.

The first part of this chapter aims at identifying the timing of famines in the Nordic countries since the Middle Ages. This identification is made by combining qualitative famine reports from the literature with price data and climate information. The second part aims to study regional famine patterns and their demographic characteristics in Sweden from 1750 to 1875. The focus here is to identify periods during which high food prices and excess mortality coincided at the county level and to make a deeper study of age- and sex-specific mortality as well as seasonal patterns in years of mortality crisis. In this part, we will use demographic data from the official statistics available from 1749 onwards.

The Nordic countries are Denmark, Sweden, Finland, Norway and Iceland. Denmark was the most populated country in Scandinavia from the Middle Ages to the sixteenth century. During this period Denmark also incorporated the provinces of Scania, Halland and Blekinge, which were lost to Sweden in 1658, as well as Schleswig-Holstein, lost to Germany in 1864. Denmark also ruled Norway from 1380 until 1814. Sweden and Finland constituted a united kingdom until 1809, when Finland became an autonomous grand duchy under Russia. During the seventeenth century Sweden conquered the above-mentioned southern provinces of Denmark as well as Jämtland and Härjedalen of Norway/Denmark. From 1814 to 1905 Sweden and Norway were in a union ruled by the Swedish king. Sweden also held provinces outside the Nordic realm, not included in this analysis. Finally, Iceland was settled by Norsemen in the ninth century but lost its independence in 1262 and was then under Danish rule until the twentieth century. In our discussion,

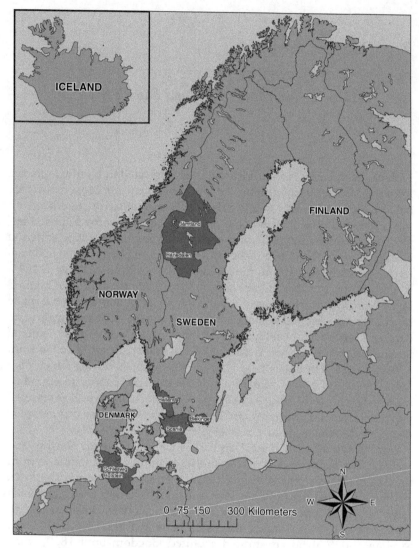

Figure 9.1 The Nordic countries

we treat the five countries as separate units but hold the internal Nordic divisions of provinces as they were at the time.

The Nordic countries are situated near the limit of possible crop farming. Central Sweden and Norway are at the same latitude as Alaska and southern Greenland, but the Gulf Stream has enabled cultivation in northern Scandinavia and even in Iceland. Whereas precipitation was important for agriculture in continental Europe and Great Britain, where drought or overly wet weather negatively affected food production, temperature appears to have been decisive for northern Europe (Utterström 1955: 5). There, agriculture's sensitivity to temperature shocks was not primarily due to low temperatures but, rather, to how long the winters were, which governed the length of the growing season. In this respect, the temperature and humidity in the spring and the short summer were also of importance. The summer was short but intense, and the interconnections between weather and harvests were complicated in this regard. When mapping bad harvest years in Scandinavia, hot and dry summers appear to have been as frequent as cold and wet ones, with the latter dominating before the eighteenth century and the former dominating thereafter (Utterström 1955; Edvinsson, Leijonhufvud and Söderberg 2009: 119–26).

Short-term climatic shocks may be caused by changes in annual weather systems but also by volcanic activity. Although only Iceland experienced volcanic eruptions within its territory, some of the major eruptions on other continents are likely to have affected harvests in the Nordic countries. The eruptions of Kaharoa in New Zealand in 1314 (±12 years), which lasted for four to five years, have been connected to the great famine of the 1310s (Nairn et al. 2004). In the same way, eruptions in 1453 (Kuwae in Vanuatu), in 1600 (Huaynaputina, Peru), in 1783 (Laki, Iceland) and in 1815 (Tambora, Indonesia) might have also affected growing conditions in the Nordic realm (Briffa et al. 1998). Another study shows that the 1600 eruption made the following summer the coldest of the past 1,500 summers in Scandinavia (de Silva and Zielinski 1998).

Long-term climatic changes have also affected the Nordic countries as they, both between and within countries, are situated on different latitudes; in Sweden, cultivation possibilities were quite different between the southern parts and the most northern parts, and conditions were of course very different between Denmark and Iceland. The so-called medieval warm period, stretching from approximately AD 1000 to the fifteenth/sixteenth century, meant that, even in the most northern parts of the Nordic countries, farming grain was possible (and even in Iceland and Greenland: Utterström 1955; Hybel and Poulsen 2007: 60–4). When average temperatures declined, during what is often called the Little Ice Age, grain farming was no longer possible, which implied that the Viking settlements on Greenland disappeared, and cereal production changed to animal herding and fishing in Iceland. Thus, temperature and the length of the growing season varied both in the short term and in the long term, and in the northernmost part of Europe this variation made agriculture, and thereby food provision, vulnerable and dictated population settlement (e.g. Solantie 1988).

1   Famines up to 1580

The first known famine in the Nordic countries was, until recently, quite unknown. Notwithstanding, it was probably the most profound and severe famine ever; it eradicated a large part of the Scandinavian population, and it has been suggested that it even changed the beliefs and the religion of those who survived (Gräslund 2007; Gräslund and Price 2012).

In 536 and 537 ashes darkened the sky, and the summer never came in either year. This major geological event, which emanated from volcanic eruptions or the impact of celestial objects, is well documented in Chinese and European late antique sources, and it has also been confirmed in dendrochronology and in ice core samples from both poles (Devroey and Jaubert 2011: 10). The Nordic countries were probably the hardest hit by the catastrophe, but, because written sources from this part of the world are lacking, the extent has not been registered (Gräslund 2007).

The preceding centuries can be characterised as the most expansive in Nordic prehistory (Pedersen and Widgren 2011: 52–9). Just at the time of this disaster, settlement and cultivation had reached their largest extent before the eighteenth century in many parts of Sweden. However, the expansion was abruptly broken in 536, with villages and farms being abandoned. The decline in human settlements are the hard facts that indicate that this probably was the most dramatic and sudden change in the cultural landscape of Sweden, southern Norway and the Baltic lands since the introduction of agriculture 6,000 years ago. Northern Norway appears to have fared better, perhaps because agriculture was often a supplement to fishing. The same was true for Finland, where agriculture was often combined with cattle rearing and foraging and where no decline in settlements can be observed in the sixth and seventh centuries. However, the crisis appears to have been devastating for areas in contemporary Estonia and Latvia (Tvauri 2014: 39–40).

Prior to this catastrophe, religious beliefs in the Nordic countries appear to have primarily revolved around fertility and the sun. Now, when the sun had failed with the result that perhaps half the population died, a new and much darker religion was established. This complex mythological world was populated by violent gods and giants who fought against each other, and it was prevalent from that point into the upcoming Viking age. In the myths about Ragnarök, the earth's destruction, the 'fimbul winter', was replicated – the years when summer never came (Gräslund and Price 2012). This event, hidden in the dim light of prehistory, does indeed indicate that agriculture in the Nordic countries was near the limit of where farming was possible.

We know very little about famines during the Viking age (793–1050) or the Nordic Middle Ages (1050–1520) and very little about their effects during even early modern times until 1750. At least for the early periods, designations of famines tend to correlate more with the preservation of letters and other writings, often with a political bias, than with high food prices or poor harvests. Even as late as during the reign of Gustav I of Sweden (1523–60), the king, to his annoyance, was held responsible by the peasants for years of distress (Andræ 1967: 468). Nevertheless, because the chronicles devoted much space to weather and harvests, indicating their importance for medieval society, and because they are almost the only existing sources, they have been used to assess whether common European famines also took place in the Nordic countries (Hybel and Poulsen 2007: 67–8). Hybel and Poulsen's point of departure is that it was primarily when bad weather affected larger areas and over a prolonged period, at least back-to-back harvest failures, that it resulted in famines. Combining the chronicles with other sparse narratives, they conclude that severe food crises most likely occurred in Denmark in 1099–1101, 1196–98 and 1225–26 and probably also 1310 and 1315–17 (Hybel and Poulsen 2007: 75).

The dating of these famines is in some cases doubtful, however. For example, the 1099–1101 famine is associated with King Olaf Hunger (1086–96), who came to power after his brother had been killed and was given his surname because Denmark was said to be haunted by famines during his reign. According to Saxo Grammaticus, this king even sacrificed his own life to end the torment of his land (Boisen 1985: bk. 12). So the case rests either upon the chronicles deliberately assigning the famines to his reign despite their actually taking place after his death to show what happens when an unrighteous king takes power, or on a false dating of the reign itself. Hybel and Poulsen base the famine of 1196–98 on evidence that surrounding areas were hit by famine and on notations in the chronicles of a tremor in Denmark. Likewise, the 1225–26 famines rest upon English grain exports to Denmark, despite bad harvests in England, and on one notation saying 'erra [sic] vastata est', which could be interpreted as 'the land is devastated' (Hybel and Poulsen 2007: 74).

However, for the famine in the 1310s, there are sources both in Sweden and Denmark indicating that this severe famine was also present in the Nordic countries; a now lost chronicle for the year 1315 was cited in a book printed in 1592 stating: '*Pluvia et tonitrua horrenda per totam aesta-tem; fames et pestis secutae, quibus tertia pars viventium absumta est*' ('Rain and thunder were horrible throughout the whole of the summer; famine and pestilence followed and a third of all living were struck') (Utterström 1955: 18). Furthermore, tithes were not paid in parts of Sweden in 1316–17 and 1319, cattle plague was mentioned for Sweden in 1316 and, from Danish sources, a drought appears to have taken place in 1310, then very wet years in 1315–17, though the chronicles disagree for these years (Myrdal 1999: 119, 174–6; Hybel and Poulsen 2007: 67–8, 75).

Because sources are rare, Hybel and Poulsen did not want to dismiss the possibility that other famines found for northern Europe – 1005–06, 1043–45, 1124–26, 1144–1147 and 1149–51 – also hit Denmark, though no records of this have been found. Ignoring the back-to-back criteria, the year 1283 also appears to have experienced a severe famine, according to Danish sources, whereas one chronicle from Sweden mentions 1291 as a famine year, caused by several years of drought (Myrdal 1999: 119; Hybel and Poulsen 2007: 74).

For Norway, Dybdahl (2010), using dendrochronology paired with statements in sagas and other narratives, finds several years when these sources match. These are, for example, 1021, 1182 and some years in the early thirteenth century, e.g. 1207 and 1211–13. There are also years when tree rings tell of bad weather but no narratives describing famines are found, for example for 1236–38. He also leans towards the posi-tion taken by Hybel and Poulsen that bad harvest years in the rest of Europe probably also hit Norway, particularly in the thirteenth century, when population pressure was high; 1258 is proposed to be one such year (Dybdahl 2010: 211).

As for Iceland, the famous Landnámabók (Book of Settlements) men-tions 'a great famine-winter in Iceland in heathen days, the severest there has been in Iceland. Men ate ravens then and foxes, and many abomina-ble things were eaten which ought not to be eaten, and some had the old and helpless killed and thrown over the cliff'. This was the winter of 975–76; Landnámabók also mentions 1057–58 and 1118 as major famine years (Tomasson 1977: 409). The frequent volcanic activity on the island caused devastation and famines; one of the most severe before the Laki disaster in 1783 was the eruption of Hekla in July 1300 (Thorarinsson 1944: 64–80).

For the Late Middle Ages, sources are even sparser, but the chronicles that do exist speak of years with very cold winters, creating ice passages between the islands of Denmark, e.g. 1323, 1431, 1452 and 1546 (Hybel and Poulsen, 2007: 76). Wet years are also recorded, and 1347 and 1489 stand out among these. However, none of these years can in any other way be related to famines, which is why Hybel and Poulsen ended up with no evidence of famines between 1315–17 and 1500 in Denmark. 1370 stands out in Norway as a potential famine year caused by harvest failure in the previous year (Dybdahl 2010: 213) while, for Sweden, some years during the reign of Christopher of Bavaria (1441–48) were hit by severe crop failures, resulting in his nickname 'King Bark' (Myrdal 1999: 193). However, Swedish sources also suggest that the period from the mid-fifteenth century to the second half of the sixteenth century appears to have experienced a better climate and no real famines; from 1460 to 1546 the south-western part of the Baltic was never completely frozen, and the vast number of preserved letters from King Gustav 1 (1521–60) speak of no severe famines during this period (Utterström 1955: 22–4). In addition, Norwegian data seem to indicate that the late fifteenth century and early sixteenth experienced relatively few famines (Dybdahl 2010: 213).

Another way to approach medieval famines is to use prices. It has been possible to construct a consumer price index for Sweden from 1290 onwards and for Denmark and Norway from the early sixteenth century. Figure 9.2 shows the annual logged deviations from a moving 25-year average. Because these are capital city prices, they can hardly reflect the fluctuations in all parts of the Nordic countries, but they are the best series we could obtain for before the eighteenth century.

There are some medieval years that stand out. None of them correspond with the worst years in England, as revealed by grain prices, tithe series and manorial grain yields (compare with Campbell 2009: 30). Apparently, there is no strong Swedish price effect from the crises that hit southern Scandinavia in the 1310s (Myrdal 2011: 79) or 1448, which in the Karl Chronicle is described as the worst famine year during the late Middle Ages. In the latter case, however, there are some indications from tithe records that the harvest was bad in a parish 70 kilometres to the north of Stockholm (Andræ 1967: 467), and the antecedent year exhibits 28 per cent higher grain prices than the surrounding years. The only Nordic high or late medieval year mentioned in Cornelius Waldorf's overview of the famines of the world is 1442; this and the surrounding years had low or normal consumer prices. The most spectacular sixteenth-century periods, in terms of inflation, are 1520–23 and 1571–74; however, these were due solely to monetary policies. In the first period both Christian II of Denmark and Gustav I of Sweden issued clipped coins with a very low silver value, immediately fuelling inflation, and in the second period the Swedish mark coin was debased (Edvinsson and Söderberg 2010: 425, 428). A similar depreciation of the Danish mark coin took place at the same time (Aakjaer 1936: 255).

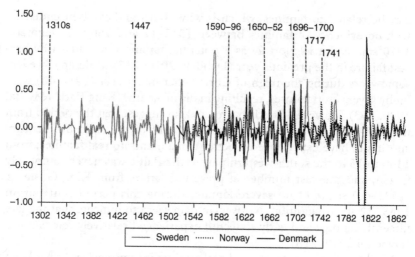

Figure 9.2 Scandinavian consumer prices, annual deviations from trend (25-year moving average), logarithmic values, 1302–1875

Note: Possible famine years, coinciding with CPI more than 0.3 log points above trend, are highlighted.
Sources: Edvinsson and Söderberg (2010), Abildgren (2010) and Grytten (2004) for prices; for possible famine years, see text.

2   Famines in the Early Modern Period

If it is hard to find evidence of major famines from around the 1320s to the second half of the sixteenth century, perhaps with the exception of 1370 in Norway and 1447–48 in Sweden, this is not the case for the subsequent two centuries. What Utterström (1955: 23) refers to as the European crisis of 1556 appears to have affected Denmark but not Sweden. However, the major famines before and after 1600 and in the 1690s, followed by a number of shorter crises in the eighteenth century including the early 1770s and 1780s, stand out in this period even if the effects differed across countries.

Local sources in Denmark indicate that the climate changed after approximately 1560–70. Flooding and storms hit western Denmark regularly but increased in intensity after 1570. From that year to 1661 the town of Ribe was hit by major storms no fewer than 43 times. The effects were severe both for the town itself and for the uplands, where meadows and fields were destroyed. Storms also swept sand in over the fields. After the flooding in 1593, Ribe was exempted from taxes for two years (Degn 1981: 410). Furthermore, local sources on climate, harvests and market price scales (*kapitelstakster*) from Ribe mention 1593, 1594, 1597 and 1601 as bad harvests and 1596–1600 as years with high prices and regulations that stopped grain from leaving the province around the town (Degn 1981: 414, 434). Population figures for the town show a 6 to 7 per cent lower population in 1590–99 compared to that in 1580–89 (Degn 1981: 439).

The famine of the late 1590s also hit south-eastern and western Sweden as well as southern Norway (Utterström 1955: 26). In the first years of the seventeenth century famine also affected central and northern Sweden. A foretaste of the long period of bad years came in 1591 in Norway and 1592–93 in western Denmark. After a few years with good harvests, the real difficulties started in mid-summer 1595, when a torrential rain destroyed the crops. Then followed two very wet years, with the second year also being very cold well into the summer. The year 1601 also appears to have been exceptionally bad. Two contemporary sources, one from south-eastern Sweden and one from western Sweden, described the weather and harvests as well as the effects on people and animals during the 1590s crisis (see Utterström 1955: 26–30). Both sources agreed on the very serious situation, with harvest failures leading to people eating 'mash, chaff, bark, buds, nettles, leaves, hay, straw, peat-moss, nutshells, peastalks, etc.', and even so 'an innumerable number of people died' (Utterström 1955: 27). A church book from Uppland, in central Sweden, also corroborates these statements, though dealing with the period 1601–03, thereby indicating the spread of the crisis to central Sweden (Heckscher 1936: 403). The prices in Figure 9.2 (see also Table 9.1) show that 1597 in Sweden, and the preceding years in Norway, were years of high prices, whereas the statement by Heckscher (1936: 403) that 1601–03 was a period of 'very high rye prices' is not corroborated. In Finland, 1601 was also described as a devastating year, and the famine of that year has been regarded as one of the most severe of the early modern period, aside from that in the late 1690s (Johanson 1924: 63; Holopainen and Helama 2009).

In the half-century following the 1590s/1600 crisis Sweden appears to have escaped famines, except in 1630 and 1633 (Heckscher 1936: 403–4). In 1630 reports from southern Sweden reveal that the bad harvest forced people to eat bark because food was lacking. For 1633–34 Sweden, Finland and the Swedish possessions in the Baltic countries were affected by a famine resulting in increased mortality, as shown both by narratives and in the low population level in the annual poll tax registers (Heckscher 1933; 1936: 404). The 1633–34 famine is also established from multiple sources (tithes, dendrochronology, prices and narratives) for Norway

Table 9.1 *Famine years in the Nordic countries: indications and prices, 536–1875*

Years	Countries affected	Sw.	De.	No.
536–37	Denmark, Sweden, Norway	–	–	–
975–76	Iceland	–	–	–
1021	Norway	–	–	–
1057–58	Iceland	–	–	–
1099–1101	Denmark	–	–	–
1118	Iceland	–	–	–
1182	Norway	–	–	–
1196–98	Denmark	–	–	–
1207–13	Norway	–	–	–
1225–26	Denmark	–	–	–
1300	Iceland	–	–	–
1310s	Denmark, Sweden	0.23	–	–
1370	Norway	–	–	–
1447–48	Sweden	0.23	–	–
1556	Denmark	–0.11	0.16	0.04
1590–96	Denmark, Sweden, Finland, Norway	–0.02*	0.10*	0.30*
1597	Denmark, Sweden, Finland, Norway	0.29	0.11	–0.13
1602–03	Denmark, Sweden, Finland, Norway	0.08	0.24	–0.07
1633–34	Sweden, Norway	0.28	–0.01	–0.06
1650–52	Sweden	0.37	0.26	0.10
1675–77	Denmark**, Sweden, Norway	0.21	0.22	0.08
1696–1700	Denmark**, Sweden, Finland, Norway	0.32	0.51	0.21
1709–10	Denmark**, Sweden, Finland	0.23	0.59	0.28
1717	Sweden	0.44	0.03	0.05
1719	Denmark**	0.66	0.04	0.05
1728–30	Denmark**	0.00	0.08	0.17
1740–43	Denmark**, Sweden, Norway	0.12	–0.01	0.37
1763–64	Denmark**	0.40	0.10	0.08
1771–73	Sweden, Finland, Norway	0.06	0.06	0.20
1783–87	Denmark, Norway, Iceland	0.03	0.13	0.06
1832–33	Finland	0.07	–0.01	0.05
1857–58	Finland	0.20	0.13	0.18
1866–68	Large parts of Finland, some counties in northern Sweden	0.06	0.07	0.08

Notes: The price indicators show year within periods with highest deviation from trend (25-year moving average), logarithmic values. *Average price for 1590–96, deviation from trend (25-year moving average), logarithmic values. **Characterised by Johansen (2002: 61) as Danish years with high mortality probably connected to famine.
Sources: See text and Figure 9.2.

(Dybdahl 2014: 266). For Denmark, the previously mentioned sources from Ribe show that the early 1620s contained a number of bad harvest years in a row: 1621–24 and 1648–51 were characterised by harvest failures and high prices (Degn 1981: 414). Rye prices from Zealand corroborate both these periods as high price years but also show that 1628–30 had high prices (Johansen 2002: 14). According to Johansen, the bad harvest years of the early 1620s did not manifest themselves in increased mortality, whereas there was increased mortality in 1628–30 (Johansen 2002: 24–5). The causes for this increase are unclear, however; for Jutland the invasion of German troops and records of typhus and dysentery might speak in favour of a famine, whereas for the rest of the country measles, smallpox or scarlet fever epidemics appear to be more likely causes of high mortality.

The high prices found in the early 1650s in Denmark and the records of bad harvests do not concur with the mortality pattern across the country. Because excess mortality occurred in different years of the 1650s for different parishes, Johansen interprets the increased mortality as primarily caused by epidemics, such as measles, rather than famine (Johansen 2002: 27–8, 35–6). The same conclusion can be drawn from sources in Norway, where the mortality crisis of 1650–51 appears to have primarily hit children and young people and was caused by epidemics (Mykland 1977: 150–60). In Sweden, on the contrary, 1650 and 1651 saw severe crop failures, resulting in very high prices in 1650 and 1652 as well as excess mortality in several parts of the country; a more than doubled crude death rate (CDR) is seen in the east of Sweden in 1650 and in 1651–52 in the north, middle and east of the country (Heckscher 1936: 405; Larsson 2006: 68, 90). All exports of grain were banned, and it is said that bakers in Stockholm fought by the toll gates to acquire any grain at all. Imports of grain now became substantial and necessary, above all those from the Baltic states (Myrdal 1999: 244).

The 1670s were also a difficult time in the Nordic countries. In 1675 famine struck northern and central Sweden, in 1676 it struck inland and coastal Norway and Denmark, and in 1677 it again struck Denmark. The primary reasons were harvest failures accompanied by high prices – 25 to 30 per cent higher than for surrounding years in both Sweden and Denmark. For Norway mortality data for the period are scarce, but for Sweden overall mortality more than doubled, whereas for Denmark mortality was approximately 37 per cent higher than normal in 1676 and only marginally lower the following year (Dyrvik, Mykland and Oldervoll 1976; Johansen 2002: 61–2; Larsson 2006: 68, 90). The primary causes of death in Denmark were typhus and dysentery, which both clearly depend on nutrition (Livi-Bacci 1991: 38).

The (in many aspects) troublesome seventeenth century ended with the 1690s crises that hit Finland and parts of Sweden worst but also affected other parts of the Nordic countries and the Baltic states. For Finland, mortality estimates following the 1696–97 harvest failures indicate that between a quarter and a third of the population died, with the higher number being more plausible (Jutikkala 1955: 53). Although people appear to have been dying from diarrhoea, caused by famine foods, already in 1696, the peak in mortality came in the spring and summer of 1697 with the spread of dysentery, typhus and typhoid fever (Lappalainen 2014). Harvests also failed in Sweden during these years, primarily in the northern and central parts of the country, with high food prices particularly in 1696 and 1697. According to Jutikkala, failed harvests were probably not reflected in a significant increase in mortality for 1697, but in 1698 some regions had mortality rates as high as 90 or even 160 per 1,000 (Jutikkala 1955: 56). However, according to subsequent research, the CDR more than doubled in northern and central Sweden in all three years 1696, 1697 and 1698 (Larsson 2006: 68, 90). Meanwhile, in the very south of Sweden, Scania had a mediocre harvest, which in fact resulted in a surplus that could be sent to adjacent Swedish counties (Jutikkala 1955: 56). Several hundred thousand barrels of grain were also imported to Sweden from the Baltics during these years to alleviate the famine (Myrdal 1999: 244). This famine has also been identified for major parts of Norway, at least in 1696. While the high mortality figures in 1695 were attributed to epidemics, the harvest in September that year was described as 'frozen away', which contributed to the demographic crisis the subsequent winter and spring (Dyrvik, Mykland and Oldervoll 1976; Mykland 1977: 150–60). In contrast, there are no figures indicating either high prices or excess mortality in Denmark during this period, aside from 1700 (Johansen 2002: 61). That year mortality was approximately 35 per cent higher than normal, and the year beforehand food prices had peaked, probably due to the harvest failure in 1699.

In eighteenth-century Sweden, excess mortality (equivalent to a doubling of the normal CDR) has been found in connection with reported harvest failures on four occasions between 1647 and 1775 (Larsson 2006: 68; 90): 1717 in the north and west of Sweden, 1740 in central Sweden, 1743 in northern and central Sweden and, finally, 1773 in central Sweden. In the south and east of Sweden, 1710 and 1711 were also years of excess mortality, but in these years the crop failure in 1709 interacted with a war in 1710 and the spread of the plague the same year. For the nineteenth century severe crop failures were recorded for 1812, 1816, 1826 and 1841, but the effects of these appear to have varied regionally and did not result in national famines (Sommarin 1917: 39–41). We will further investigate the national and regional patterns in mortality and food prices after the mid-eighteenth century for Sweden in the second part of this chapter, focusing on one of the most severe famines in early modern Sweden, that of 1772–73.

After the devastating famine during the final years of the seventeenth century, Finland also experienced famines in the eighteenth century, though they were less frequent and less severe than in the preceding century. Improved climatic conditions in general and the lower risk of coincident crop failures of rye and barley have been proposed as explanations for this change (Holopainen and Helama 2009: 220–1). Together with less spatial synchrony in this century, the large number of suggested years of famine – e.g. 26 years between 1749 and 1798 – probably reflected local crop failures rather than famines (Holopainen and Helama 2009: 222; see also Jutikkala [1971], who argues that crop failures leading to excess mortality were rare between 1722 and 1850). Nevertheless, the pattern found for Sweden was also to a large extent valid for Finland, namely 1709–10 and the 1770s.

Nineteenth-century Finland was exposed to four periods of elevated mortality: 1808–09, 1832–33, 1857–58 and the famine of the late 1860s. Excess mortality during the first of these, in 1808–09, was primarily caused by warfare and the spread of disease, though a bad harvest in 1807 and the war itself both caused food shortages (Pitkänen 2002: 76). The occupying army also provided rescue by importing food from Russia to relieve need, preventing a hunger-induced famine. The remaining years of high mortality were all caused by back-to-back harvest failures and hit large parts of Finland. In autumn 1832 and spring 1833 mortality increased substantially, doubling or tripling in affected areas, whereas the increase was somewhat smaller in 1857 (Pitkänen 2002: 71–3). Finally, during the 1860s consecutive harvest failures caused elevated mortality in both 1866 and 1867, but a dramatic increase occurred in 1868, with a CDR of approximately 78 and in some regions over 115, resulting in over 100,000 deaths (Kaukiainen 1984; Ó Gráda 2001; Pitkänen 2002: 75; Häkkinen and Forsberg 2015; Voutilainen 2015).

For Denmark, Johansen (2002: 61–3) lists all years from 1665 to 1775 with excess mortality over 30 per cent and discusses the possible causes. In 1710 the disastrous harvest the previous year caused both very high prices and excess mortality. Johansen claims that the same happened in 1728–30, 1740–42 and 1763–64, though the CPI fluctuations for these years are quite modest. In the latter period, 1763–64, famine was accompanied by an influenza epidemic. For 1719, the cause of the high mortality level was not mentioned in the sources (Johansen 2002: 63). The last famine in Denmark took place in 1786–87, when bad harvests in 1785 and 1786 and the subsequent high food prices led to excess mortality, with CDRs of 31 and 28 per thousand, respectively (Johansen 2002: 104). By permitting grain imports, Copenhagen was the least affected part of Denmark during this final famine.

The research on mortality crises in Norway has been very much centred on their causes in different parts of the country: are they due to starvation or epidemic diseases? The two major Norwegian mortality crises in the eighteenth century – 1742 and 1771–73 – were the subject of three doctoral theses in the late 1970s. Løvlien investigated the crises in 1742, comparing the landlocked, eastern parts of the country with the western parts, where fishing played a substantial role for subsistence. She concluded that all factors point in the direction of a deficit crisis in the east. Conversely, epidemic diseases appeared to have played the greatest role in the west. At the same time, Løvlien questioned the relationship between malnutrition and disease in this period. The same diseases ravaged the east and the west, apparently independently of whether there was a food shortage or not (Løvlien 1977: 125–6; 129–32).

Sogner found that the demographic crisis in 1773 in eastern Norway was preceded by three consecutive years of bad harvests. This area was characterised by irregular grain supply (this was a deficit area even in normal years, as was most of Norway), high grain prices (more than twice as high as normal), depression in many economic sectors and violent epidemics of typhus and dysentery. This picture is complemented by Aaraas, who has confirmed Sogner's finding that there was a major famine in the eastern part of the country in 1773. In the coastal districts in the west, there was also a food shortage after a long winter in 1771 and bad fishing and harvest failure in 1772, but people did not appear to have starved to death (Aaraas 1978: 107, 111). Sogner finally compared the 1773 crisis with the crisis in 1809, which hit only the more urban part of eastern Norway. This demographic crisis appeared to have been primarily due to reduced trade and grain imports because of the continental blockade during the Napoleonic War, which led to high grain prices throughout Europe. Often, the cause of death was also violence and nutrition-related epidemics (Sogner 1976: 108).

Combining tree ring dating, prices on grain and mortality for different regions in Norway, Dybdahl (2014: 273) finds that all sources indicate years of famine in the early 1740s, 1765, 1771–73 and around 1785. He refrains from discussing these in terms of either nutrition or disease and instead points to the interaction between famine and the spread of certain diseases during these years.

In June 1783 Mount Laki in south-western Iceland erupted. This event was followed by the Móðuharðindin, the Mist Hardship, in which a poisonous fog hit most of the island. The grasslands did not recover for three years, which killed 80 per cent of the livestock. The mortality in the subsequent famine was extremely high: 26 per cent of Iceland's population died during 1784 and 1785 (Vasey 1991: 343; 1996: 371–2). It must be noted that, despite the rich fishing waters surrounding the island, most Icelanders were in no position to substitute farming with fishing during the years of hardship. Fishing was tied to control of the land, and no fishing villages or activities were allowed to develop independently of the land rent system (Gunnarsson 1980: 14, 18).

3   Nordic Famines c. 500–1875: a Summary

By defining famines as periods of excess mortality caused by a shortage of food or low purchasing power, we have not addressed the causes of famines but, instead, sought to list and present the major famines occurring throughout the Nordic countries during the last millennium. The sources available for this quest differ in nature and in content over time. Before the seventeenth century, evidence of famines relies mostly on chronicles providing narratives on a lack of food, hunger and death. These sources, of course, make evaluations of when famines occurred and how severe they were highly uncertain. However, by using different sources and combining these with weather statements, previous research has proposed a number of such famines. From the seventeenth century onwards the growing bureaucracies of the Nordic kingdoms produced more solid source material. By examining tax records, church registers and population censuses and combining them with harvest evaluations and price data, we are better able to pinpoint the years of famine as well as their effects on mortality.

In general, crop failures seem to have appeared quite regularly during the last millennium, every 25 to 30 years, and even more often than that during certain periods. The seventeenth century appears to have been particularly bad, leading us to also look at long-term climatic changes as an important factor in the northern periphery. It is clear that not all crop failures resulted in famines. The consequences of a crop failure could be highly severe, as in the case of the late seventeenth-century famine in Finland, the late eighteenth-century famine in Sweden and the 1783 famine in Iceland. Potentially, earlier famines also increased mortality to horrendous levels. However, history is so far silent about this subject, apart from some contemporary statements such as the one on the late sixteenth-century famine in Sweden. It is not clear why some years of crop failures and/or high prices did not result in famines. However, it appears that, most often, more than one year of crop failure was needed to result in a famine with excess mortality. Moreover, over time, markets became more integrated and institutions distributing relief became more developed, leading to smaller effects from harvest failures, at least as long as they were regional. The differences between areas that normally produced a grain surplus, such as most of Denmark and Scania, and areas with production/consumption equilibrium or a grain deficit in normal years were huge. In the latter cases, a primary cause of a mortality crisis could be bad harvests, followed by outbreaks of hunger-related diseases such as typhus and dysentery. In the former case, bad harvests could also result in higher death rates, but the worst crisis years were the results of external factors such as plague and war-time diseases (Johansen 2002: 14, 45–6; Larsson 2006: 121–8; Gadd, Johansen and Lindkvist 2011: 270).

As a summary, Table 9.1 lists the years in which famine most likely occurred in the Nordic countries between c. 500 and 1875. In reality, there were major differences within countries as well as in the magnitude of the effects of each famine in terms of mortality. During some years entire countries, and even the entire Nordic region, appear to have been affected, but in most years regions fared differently. The price indicators for Stockholm, Copenhagen and Oslo are somewhat dubious because we do not know how well, in each and every case, they reflect the fluctuations in the affected areas. The differences in outcome might of course be related to geographic factors such as soil conditions, climate and location in terms of latitude, or to economic-political reasons such as distance to the central power. The regional pattern in itself is also interesting in terms of our perception of how often an area was in fact hit by a famine.

4   Famine in Sweden 1750–1875: National and Regional Patterns

We now turn to a disaggregated analysis to see whether we can find any event that looks like famine at the regional level in Sweden using county-level data. At that time Sweden was comprised of 24 counties plus the city of Stockholm. The following analysis was based on the 24 counties excluding the capital city because of problems of under-recording mortality.

Data on mortality were derived from the Tabular Commission, which published tables of vital events and population size for the period 1749–1859 (Sköld 2001), and from the official statistics (BiSOS) for the period 1860–75. County-level data were published in BiSOS, while county-level summaries are not readily available for the period 1749–1859 from the Tabular Commission. Instead, parish-level data were aggregated to the county level using data for homogeneous geographical units (usually parishes or groups of parishes). The aggregation was made based on a data

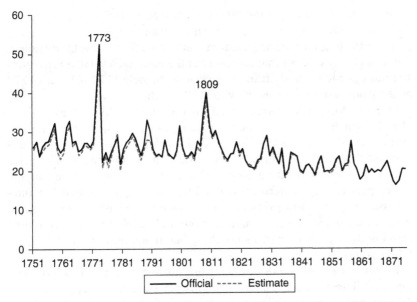

Figure 9.3 Comparison of the crude death rate according to official records (1751–1875) and estimated

Note: Deaths per thousand population.
Sources: Tabular Commission, DDB Umeå University own calculations for estimates; Statistics Sweden (1999: tab. 2.1) for official figures.

file supplied by the Demographic Database (DDB), Umeå University. The DDB has digitised all available parish-level tables from the Tabular Commission. There are also problems in this material, however, both with missing tables and double-counting, as well as with changes in geographical units (parishes or groups of parishes) over time. The total number of deaths in the Demographic Database is, for example, 20 per cent lower than the official summary for the entire country. These problems require great caution when using the data for aggregative purposes and long-term studies.

In this study, we used mortality rates (number of deaths divided by the mean population in a year) based only on geographical units with full information for both deaths and population at risk. Because population counts were available only every three to five years, while demographic events were available annually, we used the last census provided it was not more than five years before the year of the deaths. Based on these data, we aggregated county-level crude death rates. To check the reliability of this method, Figure 9.3 shows the aggregation of a national series using the same methodology compared to the official national-level series. Overall, the correspondence between the two series is very good, indicating that the aggregation method is reliable. From the graph, it is also clearly evident that mortality at the national level increased substantially above normal during two periods, namely 1772–73, with 1773 as the peak year, and 1808–09, with 1809 as the peak year.

Data on food prices were based on the series published by Jörberg (1972), which give information for most, but not all, counties for the entire period under study. We used the price of rye as an indicator because this was an important bread grain during the period. The price data were converted into a comparable unit (kronor/hectolitre) for the entire period. As we were primarily interested in the short-term fluctuations in prices and primarily large positive deviations from normal prices, we calculated the deviations from a Hodrick–Prescott smoothed trend of the log price (with a smoothing parameter of 6.25: see Ravn and Uhlig 2002).

Figure 9.4 shows the deviations from normal prices (HP trend) on a log scale. There are a few years when rye prices increased approximately 30 per cent or more above normal (log deviations greater than 0.25). One such year is 1771, when the price deviation at the national level was the largest during the entire period, amounting to roughly a 35 per cent price increase. Thus it appears that the high mortality observed in 1772–73 must at least be partly connected to high food prices, which most likely led to hunger and hunger-related diseases causing excess mortality. This picture is also confirmed in the literature. In 1771 there were widespread crop failures following a very dry summer and heavy rain during late summer and fall. In 1772 the difficult conditions continued, with crop failures in parts of middle and southern Sweden (Utterström 1957: I, 435; see also Larsson 2006: ch. 4; Statistics Sweden 1999: 50). According to Castenbrandt (2012: 68), approximately 50 per cent of the excess mortality in 1773 was due to dysentery, a disease usually considered to be highly nutrition-dependent (see Livi-Bacci 1991: 38; Larsson 2006: 105–7), which further supports the link between the high prices of food and the high mortality levels.

Turning to the other mortality peak in 1809, Figure 9.4 shows elevated rye prices in 1808, but not to any extreme levels (approximately 22 per cent above normal). In fact, there are a number of years with similar or higher levels of food prices when mortality did not increase to high levels, which makes it less likely that the mortality peak in 1809 was primarily caused by widespread hunger, even though we know it was a year with regional crop failures (Utterström 1957: I, 435). Instead, excess mortality in these years has often been connected to epidemic outbreaks of

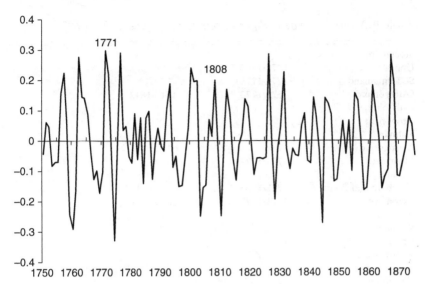

Figure 9.4 Deviations from normal in rye prices in Sweden (logarithmic values), 1750–1875

Notes: Deviations from Hodrick–Prescott trend of log values with a smoothing parameter of 6.25. The national price series is an unweighted mean of county prices.
Sources: Jörberg (1972) and own calculations.

dysentery and typhus following the war with Russia and troop movements contributing to contagion (e.g. Castenbrandt 2012: 31, 68).

Taken together, we could identify one case of likely famine in Sweden in the period after 1750, namely in 1772–73. In addition, mortality increased sharply in 1808–09, mainly as a result of epidemic outbreaks not primarily connected to high food prices and starvation, even though similar causes of death were involved and food prices were above normal. Later, these two periods of high mortality will be compared in terms of age-specific and seasonal mortality patterns.

Turning to the regional pattern, we looked at all counties for which we had data for both prices and mortality and identified years when high mortality coincided with high prices. We compared prices and mortality deviations from normal levels to detect periods when both rye prices and mortality rates were particularly high. We used 0.3 log units as the threshold, and famine years were defined as years when mortality was at least 0.3 log units above normal (roughly 35 per cent), and the price of rye was at least 0.3 log units above normal the same year, the year before

Table 9.2 *Famine years in different counties in Sweden, 1750–1875*

Stockholm			
Uppsala	1771/1773		
Södermanland	1771/1773		
Östergötland	1771/1773	1812/1812	
Jönköping			
Kronoberg			
Kalmar			
Kristianstad			
Malmöhus	1771/1772		
Halland			
Göteborg and Bohus	1762/1763		
Skaraborg	1771/1773	1806/1808	
Älvsborg			
Värmland	1772/1772,1773		
Örebro	1772/1773		
Västmanland	1771/1773		
Kopparberg	1756/1758	1771, 1772/1773	
Gävleborg	1771, 1772/1773		
Västernorrland			
Jämtland*	?/1773	1800/1801	1808/1809
Västerbotten*	1800/1800	1808/1809	1867/1868

Notes: Data available in Dribe, Olsson and Svensson, 2016. Left of '/': years of at least 35 per cent increase in prices. Right of '/': years of at least 35 per cent increase in crude death rates. So, for example, '1771/1773' refers to an increase in prices in 1771 followed by an increase in crude death rates in 1773. *No continuous price data before 1796, and thus the existence of famines as measured here cannot be established before this date.

or two years before, to allow for the maximum influence of prices. Thus, *food prices more than 35 per cent above normal leading to crude death rates increasing by at least 35 per cent within a two-year period* were considered to be famine years. This is a quite generous definition of famine, and years that do not qualify according to this definition can safely be ruled out as famine years.

Using this definition, we found a limited number of regional famines (see Table 9.2; all data are available in Dribe, Olsson and Svensson, 2016). What stands out from the table is that 1772–73 was a famine year in many regions, but not in all by far. Apart from this famine, there were regional famines in 1758 in Kopparberg County, in 1763 in Göteborg and Bohus County, in 1808 in Skaraborg County and in 1812 in Östergötland County. In addition, there was also a famine in Jämtland in 1800 and 1809 and in Västerbotten in 1801, 1809 and 1868. 1773 saw excess mortality in Jämtland but not in Västerbotten (due to a lack of price data, we do not know the price levels in this period for these two counties). It is interesting to note that, in 1809, there was only famine in Jämtland and Västerbotten, supporting the previous conclusion that the mortality peak in many places in this year was to a large extent the result of epidemic outbreaks not primarily connected to high food prices and widespread hunger, even though the dominant causes of death were partly the same as in the famine of 1772 (dysentery and other forms of diarrhoea; see Castenbrandt 2012: ch. 3).

In 1758 mortality was high in many other counties as well, following crop failures in several counties in 1756 and 1757 (Utterström 1957: II, app. 1), leading to food prices well above normal at the national level but not as high as in 1771 (see Figure 9.4). However, only in Kopparberg County were conditions severe enough to qualify as a famine by our definition.

In 1763 the situation was similar following bad harvests in several parts of the country, including Bohuslän (part of Göteborg and Bohus County) (Utterström 1957: II, app. 1). Several counties besides Göteborg and Bohus also observed mortality rates well above normal, for example Värmland, Örebro, Kopparberg, Gävleborg and Kalmar, which all showed crude death rates approximately 30 per cent above normal. Nonetheless, it was only Göteborg and Bohus County that showed a combination of rye prices and mortality at levels 35 per cent above normal.

Finally, in 1811 and 1812 crops failed in many parts of the country (Utterström 1957: II, app. 1), including Östergötland, but only in Östergötland did mortality increase to famine levels. In some other counties mortality was also elevated in this year, e.g. in the surrounding Södermanland and Jönköping Counties, with levels approximately 17 to 20 per cent above normal. There are also contemporary accounts supporting the finding of dire times in Östergötland in 1812 (Gullberg 1968: 98).

A number of counties were also largely unaffected by the famine of 1773, which allowed us to compare mortality development in a famine period between affected and non-affected regions. In addition, we also compared the more detailed mortality pattern in a period with high mortality not primarily caused by high food prices: 1808–09. Based on the CDR, we distinguish between counties with high mortality (> 0.3 log units above the HP trend) and medium/low mortality and compared the age-specific mortality between the two groups in the four different years. The results are displayed in Table 9.3.

As evident in panel A, mortality was higher in all age groups in high-mortality counties in all years. Overall mortality was 46 to 86 per cent

Table 9.3 *Mortality comparisons: Swedish counties, 1772–73 and 1808–09*

A *Mortality rates (per thousand)*

	1772			1773			1808			1809		
	(1) High	(2) Med./low	(3) (1)/(2)	(4) High	(5) Med./low	(6) (4)/(5)	(7) High	(8) Med./low	(9) (7)/(8)	(10) High	(11) Med./low	(12) (10)/(11)
Infants	339	283	1.20	367	300	1.22	252	237	1.06	239	216	1.11
Children (1–14)	39	21	1.88	68	26	2.62	44	17	2.54	48	24	2.05
Adults (25–49)	26	16	1.57	30	15	1.93	23	14	1.63	28	19	1.52
Old age (60–84)	133	101	1.32	151	85	1.79	130	88	1.48	133	98	1.36
Total	47	32	1.46	60	33	1.86	46	29	1.61	51	33	1.52
N (counties)	5	19		15	9		4	20		7	17	

B *Proportion of total deaths (per cent)*

	1772			1773			1808			1809		
	(1) High	(2) Med./low	(3) (1)/(2)	(4) High	(5) Med./low	(6) (4)/(5)	(7) High	(8) Med./low	(9) (7)/(8)	(10) High	(11) Med./low	(12) (10)/(11)
Infants	17	21	0.82	13	23	0.57	15	23	0.66	12	18	0.70
Children (1–14)	26	20	1.34	34	25	1.39	30	18	1.63	29	21	1.36
Adults (25–49)	17	16	1.05	16	15	1.05	16	16	1.01	18	18	1.00
Old age (60–84)	22	26	0.86	20	21	0.96	21	27	0.80	23	24	0.92
N (counties)	5	19		15	9		4	20		7	17	

Notes: High = high mortality: county-level mortality rate > 0.3 log points above HP trend. Med./low = medium or low mortality: county-level mortality rates < 0.3 log points above HP trend.

Sources: Tabular Commission and Demographic Database, Umeå University.

higher in high-mortality counties compared to low-mortality ones. We found the biggest difference for children: mortality in affected counties was 88 to 162 per cent higher than in non-affected counties, while the corresponding spans were 6 to 20 per cent for infants, 52 to 93 per cent for working-age adults and 32 to 79 per cent for the elderly. Looking at proportions of total deaths in each age group (panel B) confirms that children were the most affected of all age groups. High-mortality counties had 34 to 63 per cent higher proportions of child deaths than low-mortality counties, while proportions of infant deaths were considerably lower in the high-mortality counties than in the low-mortality ones. In the famine year of 1773 the difference between affected and non-affected counties was considerably larger than in 1772, while the same difference could not be observed when comparing 1808 and 1809. This age pattern in mortality during crises is consistent with the typical age pattern of mortality in dysentery and other types of diarrhoea (see Castenbrandt 2012: 76–9).

Table 9.4 shows a similar comparison regarding the seasonal pattern in mortality. In 1772 high-mortality counties showed a higher proportion of deaths in May, June and July compared to low-mortality counties and lower proportions in the winter months. In the famine year of 1773 the proportion of deaths in July, August and September was highest in the high-mortality counties relative to the low-mortality counties. This pattern is also consistent with the importance of dysentery for excess mortality, as dysentery often came in the summer and faded away during late autumn (Larsson 2006: 105–11; Castenbrandt 2012: 76–9). In 1808 and 1809 the difference in seasonality between high- and low-mortality counties was even larger, but the pattern was again expected given the importance of dysentery and typhoid fever related to epidemic outbreaks in the war camps (Larsson 2006: 105–11).

The age-specific and seasonal patterns are thus quite similar in high-mortality counties during periods with a dominance of child deaths during the late summer and early autumn. This similarity can be explained by similar causes of death being responsible for excess mortality regardless of the underlying cause, famine or war (possibly in combination with under-nutrition). Taken together, we have been able to identify only one clear and widespread famine in Sweden in the period after 1750, namely 1773. In addition, there are a couple of more regional famines in years when larger parts of the country were also affected by crop failures, high prices and increasing mortality, but not to levels here considered to be famines. The low frequency of famines, despite frequent crop failures, in this period reflects a high degree of market integration in Sweden as well as in other parts of Europe (see, for example, Bengtsson and Jörberg

Table 9.4 *Proportion of deaths by month: Svedish counties, 1772–73 and 1808–09*

	1772			1773			1808			1809		
	(1) High	(2) Med/low	(3) (1)/(2)	(4) High	(5) Med/low	(6) (4)/(5)	(7) High	(8) Med/low	(9) (7)/(8)	(10) High	(11) Med/low	(12) (10)/(11)
Jan.	5.6	6.7	0.83	7.5	10.2	0.74	4.6	7.6	0.61	9.2	11.3	0.81
Feb.	6.2	8.0	0.77	6.7	9.4	0.71	4.5	7.3	0.62	8.9	9.4	0.94
Mar.	9.1	9.9	0.93	7.3	8.8	0.83	6.1	8.8	0.69	8.3	10.4	0.80
Apr.	9.8	9.0	1.09	8.3	9.1	0.91	5.4	9.5	0.56	9.3	12.4	0.75
May	13.7	10.3	1.33	8.7	10.4	0.84	4.9	9.1	0.54	7.0	9.6	0.73
Jun.	9.6	8.3	1.15	7.9	6.6	1.19	4.1	7.0	0.59	7.4	7.4	1.00
Jul.	7.9	7.3	1.09	9.4	6.4	1.48	3.9	6.1	0.64	5.9	5.9	0.99
Aug.	8.5	7.9	1.08	13.1	9.6	1.36	11.7	6.0	1.95	8.6	5.3	1.63
Sep.	7.9	7.5	1.06	13.8	9.8	1.41	27.2	7.9	3.44	16.9	6.9	2.45
Oct.	8.3	7.3	1.14	7.9	8.5	0.93	15.2	9.8	1.55	8.9	7.3	1.21
Nov.	7.2	8.8	0.82	4.6	5.4	0.85	6.3	9.1	0.69	5.0	6.7	0.74
Dec.	6.0	9.0	0.67	4.8	5.9	0.81	6.0	11.7	0.52	4.6	7.3	0.64
Total	100.0	100.0		100.0	100.0		100.0	100.0		100.0	100.0	
Deaths	4,865	11,346		13,008	6,408		5,062	17,800		8,215	17,845	
Counties	5	19		15	9		4	20		7	17	

Notes: All ages; figures in percentages.
Sources: Tabular Commission and Demographic Database, Umeå University.

1975; Persson 1999), which implies that crop failures in some regions were relieved through trade with other regions and that famine occurred only in rare instances when crops failed in large parts of the country at the same time.

5   Conclusion

To chart the occurrence of famine in history without hard evidence about mortality rates and food prices or output is, of course, a bold task. In this chapter we have nevertheless aimed to address this issue, relying primarily on qualitative accounts based on contemporary reports and general historical writings. These qualitative sources have, when possible, been confronted with other indicators, such as prices, scattered population data or settlement patterns from archaeological evidence. From the middle of the eighteenth century we are on firmer ground, thanks to the emergence of reliable population statistics and price data.

We have presented the first attempt at a coherent historiography of famines in all the Nordic countries (see Jutikkala 1955; Sogner 1976; Dyrvik, Mykland and Oldervoll 1976; Larsson 2006; Hybel and Poulsen 2007; and Dybdahl 2010). Contemporary narrative sources often have a tendency to magnify bad or perhaps even normal years into veritable disasters. This may have had political or other motives, and, in the absence of conclusive evidence, Nordic historiography has been grappling with these stories. Furthermore, in general historical writings and textbooks these statements on suggested famines often have been repeated (Häger, Torell and Villius 1978; Häger, Norman and Villius 1980; Larsson 1999). Although we have not been able to completely support or dismiss them, we have modified the scope and timing of some of the proposed famines when comparing the narratives with other data, such as prices.

We have also for the first time systematically analysed the regional patterns of famines, using annual price and mortality data at the county level in Sweden. This not only enabled us to identify and shed new light on the last famines that took place in Sweden, but also helped us to demonstrate that some years with crop failures, designated by historians as widespread famines, in fact were of limited and regional nature. We have been able to do this after 1750, when data are available, but it is likely that some of the medieval and early modern Nordic famines mentioned in literature had a similar regional or local character.

Our survey has, thus, indicated that widespread famine was always a rare occurrence in the Nordic countries, despite frequent crop failures. Great famines of national character that we may regard as confirmed were as follows: 536 in virtually all parts of the Nordic countries that were dependent on agriculture; 1696 in Finland; 1773 in large parts of Sweden, eastern Norway and Finland; Iceland in 1783; and Finland again in 1866–68. There were also a number of medieval and early modern years with contemporary reports of famine, but we have not been able to substantiate their extent and depth. However, we have been able to establish co-variations between famine reports and high consumer prices in Sweden for the following years: 1597, 1633–34, 1650–52, 1697–98 and 1717. To discover whether the national death rates concealed deeper crises at the disaggregated level, we turned to a regional analysis going as far back as the data allowed. The results showed that 1773 probably was the last major famine in Sweden, though far from the entire country was affected. We recognised regional examples of increased mortality associated with high food prices, which also coincided with contemporary data on starvation and excess mortality. In addition to the 1773 famine, 1758, 1763, 1800, 1809, 1812 and 1868 were years when a regional famine could be detected, and, in most cases, only one county was seriously affected, though both mortality and prices were elevated in other counties as well but not to famine levels.

Examining the age-specific mortality and seasonality pattern in the two years of mortality crises in Sweden, one hunger-induced and one due more to epidemic outbreaks, we could show a highly similar pattern. This similarity could be explained by similar causes of death being involved: dysentery and typhus. All age groups were affected during the crisis, but children over the age of one were hit hardest. Mortality was highest during the summer and early autumn as epidemics spread rapidly through water and food.

Large parts of the Nordic countries are close to the climatological edge where agriculture is possible, with cold winters and frost on the ground until March and April. How has this location affected the frequency and intensity of famines? On average, this location has not had much of an effect, because population density in the long run tended to adapt to the carrying capacity of the land. The densely populated plains of Denmark and southern Sweden had almost continental climatological conditions, while areas less devoted to agriculture further north had considerably sparser populations. The survival strategies of these northern populations were more diversified, with fishing, gathering and nomadic grazing as supplementary activities.

However, on occasions when sudden and severe external shocks occurred, the Nordic countries were harder hit than regions in more southern latitudes. The clearest example is perhaps 536, when a long period of agricultural expansion was interrupted by extreme and prolonged weather deterioration, which led to an estimated half of the

Scandinavian population disappearing over the course of a few years. A local variant of this event was the Icelandic tragedy in 1783, which also had extreme death rates, but this event was due to the effects of volcanic activity on the island itself.

In most other years, and especially in the period after 1750, the market worked reasonably well to even out the supply of grain in different parts of the country, which lowered the impact of regional crop failures. A diversified agriculture also helped to minimise risks. At the same time, it should be stressed that mortality remained sensitive to short-term variations in grain prices and harvest outcomes well into the nineteenth century (e.g. Bengtsson and Ohlsson 1985; Bengtsson 2004; Bengtsson and Dribe 2005; Dribe, Olsson and Svensson 2012; 2017), and the same was true for fertility (Bengtsson and Dribe 2006: 2010). Thus, while people clearly were vulnerable to economic fluctuations, conditions rarely deteriorated to famine levels, which can be explained as a combination of a reasonably well-functioning market, a diversified economy, a population density in line with resource availability and the absence of serious political or war-related conditions conducive to famine.

10   Eastern Europe (Russia and the USSR)

Stephen Wheatcroft

Russia and the Soviet Union have endured a particularly large number of serious food crises over the last thousand years, and they persisted into the first half of the twentieth century. The scale and causes of these crises have been greatly disputed, with most recent evaluations of twentieth-century famines concentrating on short-term political factors. This chapter emphasises the need to include long-term historical-geographic factors in our explanation of these crises, and to consider the problematic nature of evaluating normal mortality when we attempt to assess excess mortality. The first two sections discuss these long-term factors in general and the specific problems of the reliability of statistical data once they became available in the modern period. Section 3 covers these food problems in three historic periods: from 1237 to 1613, from 1613 to 1917 and then the Soviet period.

1   The Geographical Problems of Russia in Relation to Food Production

The Black Earth soils of the lands covering the southern part of European Russia include some of the richest soils in the world. They produce good yields with little fertiliser and in the absence of crop rotations. To the north of this area the land becomes less favourable to agriculture.

The climate in eastern and northern Europe is more extreme than in western or southern Europe and far more problematic for agricultural production. Eastern Europe experiences more continental weather patterns, with hotter summers and colder winters. The northern part of the region has a relatively short growing season, making it vulnerable to extended periods of cold, which frequently reduces the length of the growing season so that grain cannot ripen. Southern parts are vulnerable to hot dry weather, which can cause a drought in the critical growing season from April to June, when moisture is needed for flowering and filling out the grain. In drought-affected years grain yields are greatly reduced. In addition to these factors, sudden excess rain in the harvesting season can lead to serious harvest losses as the damp grain rots, and unusual warm spells in March and April followed by severe frosts can kill off autumn-sown grain.

Reports of extreme weather are frequent in Russian history, but it is only from the late nineteenth century that modern meteorological data have become abundant. We now have access to data for 233 Russian weather stations, of which 12 have systematic daily data going back to 1881, 51 have data going back to 1891 and 101 have data going back to 1918 (Razuvaev, Apasova and Martuganov 2008). These stations provide data that enable us to model crop–weather relations for the relatively stable political period of 1883–1913. The model can then be used to produce indicators of agro-meteorologically induced harvest fluctuations for later years.[1]

2   Identifying Russian Famines

2.1   Historiography

Many Russian food problems, especially since 1889, have been described as famines, but the use of this term in Russian is problematic. The term 'famine', as distinct from 'hunger', did not exist in this language until the 1980s. In circumstances of normally high mortality and normally high levels of hunger, the Eastern Slavic community do not appear to have found it necessary to distinguish between different degrees of hunger in their vocabulary.

Different scholars have presented the nature of the food problems and the government's responses to them in different ways. Traditional Russian Marxist views saw the revolution as resulting from the increasing exploitation and the immiseration of the peasantry (Lyashchenko 1947). This view was argued in the West by scholars such as Dobb in Cambridge, and by Gershchenkron (1965) in Harvard. But from the 1970s there were a number of challenges to this view. The Russian-American historian Arcadius Kahan emphasised the importance of weather, low agricultural productivity, the increasing impact of drought as a result of southern expansion, deforestation and the temporal coincidence of several of these factors in contributing to Russian and Soviet famines. He was cautious in his attribution of importance to overall population growth and produced a table showing a relative decline in frequency of calamities as population growth increased (Kahan 1989: 127, 137–8). Simms (1977), Gregory (1982) and Wheatcroft (1991), in the West, and

---

[1] See Wheatcroft (1977) for an earlier attempt at such modelling and Wheatcroft (2017: app. 1) for a more recent effort.

Mironov (2010), in Russia, have all demonstrated that the empirical evidence does not support the traditional Marxist claims.

Recently the Russian historians Turchin and Nefedov (2009) have revived this debate when they emphasise the structural economic problems associated with population growth, which, in their view, produced a series of cyclical effects. They describe an early Muscovy cycle from 1460 to 1620, and a later Romanov cycle from 1620 to 1922. While their arguments may have some validity in the earlier period, the empirical evidence, as mentioned above, does not support these claims for the late nineteenth and twentieth centuries.

Although the collection of statistics on demography and food balances was greatly increased in the twentieth century, the Soviet government restricted access to these materials, and strictly controlled the amount of data published in order to give a highly distorted picture that denied the existence of famine in the USSR. This naturally led most commentators to ignore what data were published and to look for an explanation that emphasised the importance of political factors over other factors. The leading figure here was Conquest, who argued that the Soviet censuses were 'faked' and that the population registration system collapsed in the famine. He further claimed that there was no real economic problem in the USSR in the 1920s and that both the famines of 1921–22 and 1932–33 were caused primarily by Bolshevik policies (Conquest 1986: 55, 87, 326). Initially, at a time when the Soviet archives were inaccessible, and when the Soviet government was still denying that there had been a famine, he also argued that the famine had been caused on purpose. As is explained below, once Conquest became aware of the fuller picture emerging from the Soviet archives he changed his mind on this point, and ended up by denying that the famine was carried out on purpose. This has not stopped his authority from subsequently being used to support claims that these famines were acts of genocide.

2.2   The Reliability of Data

There is much confusion about the reliability of Soviet demographic data. Voznesenskii and other leading Soviet officials claimed in the late 1930s that the census and data on births and deaths had been distorted by the statisticians for political reasons. This led to the abandonment of the 1937 census and the execution of many statisticians and statistical officials on the charge of distorting figures. But these claims are false. Surprisingly, the surviving statisticians in TsSU and TsUNKhU (the Central Statistical Administration and the Central Administration of National-Economic Records that replaced it, respectively: essentially, the Soviet statistical service) were ultimately able to resist the extraordinary pressures to distort Soviet population data in order to conceal the famine and show a growth more similar to that included in the plans.[2]

When Conquest cited examples of the collapse of the conjunctural (early warning) statistical system he was unaware that there was a separate final reporting system that remained intact for all of the European USSR.[3] Andreev, Darskii and Kharkova (ADK), in their reworking of the statistical data in 1990, also claimed that the registration data were virtually useless, requiring corrections of 41 per cent for births and 98 per cent for deaths for 1933, and of 15 to 18 per cent for birth data and 45 to 47 per cent for death data for 1930–32 (Andreev, Darskii and Kharkova 1990: 56). There is little justification for these very large corrections, other than that they produced indicators of excess mortality as high as the 7 million figure claimed by Conquest, which they were instructed to support (Wheatcroft 2012). The effect of the ADK corrections was to extenuate the crisis and to focus it on 1933. Whereas the uncorrected data already imply a 23 per cent fall in births from 4,319 million in 1932 to 3,324 million in 1933, the ADK adjustments reduced the fall to a mere 300,000 (or 5 per cent), from 5,837 million in 1932 to 5,545 million in 1933. The extra 2.2 million unregistered children born in 1933 were subsequently presumed to have died in 1933, and this, together with the 98 per cent adjustment to 1933 mortality figures (in comparison with a 45 to 47 per cent adjustment for 1930–32), explains how an unadjusted surplus of 1.6 million deaths becomes 7 million.

All who had a political interest in claiming very large figures for the famine eagerly welcomed these early estimates, but in more specialist circles they were criticised at an academic conference in Toronto in 1995 in unpublished papers by Adamets and Shkolnikov, and by Wheatcroft. In 1998 ADK produced another set of statistics for the Russian Republic in which they repeated their calculations, and responded to Wheatcroft by denying that there was a significant real decline in births in 1933. They correctly noted that a decline in births associated with reduced conceptions in the first half of 1933 would reveal itself only as a reduction of births in 1934 (Andreev, Darskii and Kharkova 1998: 84–5). But that does not mean that there was no substantial decline in births in 1933. The data on massive increases in abortions in 1933 give adequate grounds to expect a massive collapse in the birth rate even prior to the knock-on effects of the famine itself (Wheatcroft 2001b).

---

[2] See Wheatcroft (2012) for the politics around these developments.
[3] It did collapse, however, in nomadic areas of Kazakhstan.

Recently, even more authoritative sets of calculations have been made by a joint French/Russian/Ukrainian team of demographers. Vallin et al. (2012: 25) claim a level of 2.6 million excess mortality for Ukraine in the 1930s, with an additional birth deficit of 1.1 million and a forced outmigration of 0.9 million. They accept the reliability of the Soviet censuses and state: '[T]he accuracy of the results of the two censuses...has hardly been challenged by specialists... Although the Kremlin authorities tried on many occasions to manipulate the published results of the censuses, everyone views the statistical literature preserved in the archives, now accessible, as reliable.' And they also accept that most of the registration data are reliable, with the possible exceptions of 1932 and 1933.[4]

This chapter argues that both natural and political factors need to be seen in perspective and also in relation to demographic factors. It also emphasises that Russia's historical strategic decisions to locate its capital in a region that is difficult to supply with food was a factor of very great importance. The growing urban population in the north of Russia was to become increasingly dependent upon distant supplies, which, when threatened in times of troubles in 1571, 1600–13, 1917–22, 1927–33 and 1941–47, would either cause famine or cause the government to take extreme measures in order to avoid famine.

3   Food Problems in Russia under Attack from Mongols, Tartars, Poles and Swedes: 1237–1613

The Mongol invasion of 1237–40 led to the centre of Eastern Slavic civilisation moving from the relatively mild and fertile region of Kiev to the harsher region of Moscow 850 kilometres to the north-east. There the power of Muscovy grew, but problems of food supply led to vulnerabilities that became apparent in the famines of 1567–1603.

The early civilisation of Kievan Rus had reached its peak in 1240 on the eve of the Mongol destruction of Kiev. At this time the population of Kiev is reported to have grown to over 50,000, very large for the thirteenth century. The city of Kiev was located in a fertile area, on good river communications, and food supply would normally not be a problem. But as the Mongols approached tens of thousands of people fled to the city, where the population doubled and where the food situation soon became desperate. The siege of Kiev lasted only nine days, from

---

[4] 'Although there was under-registration of deaths over the course of this period, in all likelihood it was not very significant, except perhaps during the two crisis years where the registration services really seem to have been snowed under, or perhaps manipulated to minimize the extent of the crisis' (Vallin et al. 2012: 16–17). See too Wheatcroft (2017: app. n. 3).

28 November to 6 December 1240, and it is reported that only 2,000 people out of 100,000 survived the slaughter. The city was burnt down, with only six out of 40 major buildings remaining (Halperin 1987).

The Mongols took most of the major cities of Rus, Novgorod and Minsk in the north-west being the main exceptions. The invaders slaughtered large numbers, but many more would have died prematurely as a result of the social dislocation, in which the disruption of food supplies would have played an important role. There was little that the remnants of the city states of Rus could do to defend themselves against food shortages, once they had lost the military conflict and their cities had been looted. Local leaders could petition the Great Khan to spare their lives. They could petition him to let them organise to defend themselves from other invaders, as Alexander Nevskii did when the Swedish and Lithuanians threatened his homeland. They could even petition him to let them collect taxes owed to him themselves, rather than through Mongol taxation agents, as the Grand Dukes of Muscovy did. But there was never any question of requesting the Khan for famine relief, or the return of their food.

The Slavic population that fell under Mongol control in these years had no reason to distinguish between famine and hunger in the way that many other populations did. The Russian Chronicles contain accounts of great 'hungers', which have been described as famines, but that terminology is a little misleading. Some early rulers engaged in acts of charity. But these were generally isolated and minor cases. There was not at this time the sense of obligation that relief action was required in times of disaster in the way that there was in the West. Signs of the beginning of the appearance of such an obligation came only after the overthrow of the Mongols in the major crises of the late sixteenth century that culminated in the 'Times of Troubles'.

Muscovy expanded because of its success at collaboration with the Khan. Alexander Nevskii's heirs were eventually rewarded with the title 'Grand Prince' in the reign of Ivan I. The period from the middle of the fifteenth century to the middle of the sixteenth is reputed to be the most tranquil and happiest time in Muscovy. Turchin and Nefedov (2009: 243) estimate that prices remained relatively low and that the population was to grow by about 50 per cent, to 9 to 10 million, in the first half of the sixteenth century. Ivan III, who took the title 'Tsar', had greatly consolidated power by taking possession of Novgorod (1470–78), Yaroslavl (1463) and Rostov (1474), and felt strong enough to stop paying tribute to the Great Khan in 1476. This was quickly followed by a military stand-off on the river Ugra in 1480, the retreat of the Khan and the collapse of the Golden Horde. In 1487 Kazan temporarily accepted vassalage to Russia. Ivan III's son Ivan IV (1533–84), after a shaky beginning, consolidated this position by removing all elements of opposition in Novgorod and Kazan, which now became totally subjugated to the Grand Princes of Muscovy. Only the Crimean Khanate remained independent, and would remain so until the end of the eighteenth century.

This period of stability and improvement was to change in the middle of the reign of Ivan IV with four devastating series of 'hunger'. The first came in 1548–49 in the north, and was followed by a more serious 'hunger' covering the Volga as well as the north in 1556–57. This resulted in mass peasant migration to the south, which led to much land along the river Dvina being left uncultivated. The third began with the poor harvest of 1567. The peasants would normally have had sufficient reserves to withstand one year of harvest failure, but the pressures on the peasantry to maintain the army required for defence against the Tartars in the south and the Poles and Livonians in the north made the harvest failure much more serious. Grain prices were reported to have increased by a factor of eight at this time. In 1568 the harvest failed again, and grain prices remained extraordinarily high. This continued into 1569 and 1570, when the plague struck, but the 'hunger' continued and cases of cannibalism were reported (Turchin and Nefedov 2009: 252). Hunger, plague and internal civil crisis caused by Ivan IV's *oprichniki* (1565–72) weakened the defence capabilities of the state, and in 1571 the Crimean Khan with a great host invaded Muscovy, burned Moscow, killed hundreds of thousands and took 100,000 prisoners to sell as slaves in the Crimea.

Turchin and Nefedov claim that the demographic disaster sparked by the 'hunger' of 1567–70 was greater than those of 1600–03 and the 'Times of Troubles' that followed them. However, the main specialists on the period claim that the demographic losses of 1600–03 were as much as one-third of the population and that this was the largest famine Russia ever experienced (Dunning 2001; Perrie 2006).

The population of Moscow city had grown in importance from a mere 10,000 to 15,000 in the early years of the Mongol rule in the mid-thirteenth century to over 100,000 at the end of the sixteenth century. This large population required the importation of at least 30,000 tons of grain annually, most of which came up the rivers Volga and Oka to Kolomna, where the river Moskva flowed into the Oka. In addition, food was needed for other northern towns and the Tsar's growing army. The acquisition of this large amount of food required great pressure to be placed on the peasantry. And when the peasants tried to escape these obligations they were forced into servitude.

The final and best-known stage of this crisis began with the anomalous cold-wet weather of 1600–03, which caused harvest failures in much of northern Europe. This famine coincided with a period of dynastic crisis and the usurpation of power by Boris Godunov. Godunov was anxious to win support and tried to avoid disturbances by providing food aid. This was probably the first time in Russian history, at least since the fall of Kiev, when the ruler acted as though he had an obligation to feed the population in times of food shortage. But, instead of calming the situation, Godunov simply made matters worse. Large numbers of destitutes were attracted to the Moscow food deficit region, and this intensified the supply problem. The swollen population of Moscow quickly used up all available reserves, and thousands died on the streets. Godunov was blamed. His attempts to resolve the food problem simply deepened the political problems. It was in this situation of aggravated disaffection caused by the famine that we see multiple internal and foreign challenges to the government emerging.

A devastating period of civil war between usurpers and pretenders, coupled with invasions by Poles and Swedes, resulted in Moscow and the northern towns being besieged and blockaded (Perrie 2006: 416–18). These places faced mass starvation. But, again, the word 'famine' tended not to be used. In times of civil war, invasion and mass social disruption mass starvation was inevitable, and, if there was no effective state to provide relief, there was really no need to distinguish between the deadly hunger that it produced and normal hunger.

Ultimately, sufficient domestic leadership was found to expel the invaders and make a new beginning with a newly elected Tsar. The massive decline in population, partly caused by the disaster of the 1570s, and reinforced by the famine of 1600–03 and the subsequent disasters, meant that the country was set for an extended period of growth. Curiously, at the same time that the political leadership had begun to move towards accepting that it had an obligation to feed the peasant in times of food shortage, it also moved towards binding the peasants into servile obligations to the Tsar's servitors. Part of the deal was that the serf owners would lose their serfs if they failed to care for them in times of severe hunger.

4 Famines in Russia and the Baltic, and Russian Colonial Expansion in the Seventeenth to Nineteenth Centuries

Under the early Romanovs Russia was able to avoid much of the terrible destabilisation that continued in other parts of north eastern and central Europe and that, ultimately, led to the collapse of the Swedish Empire and the disappearance of Poland and Lithuania. Large parts of central Europe were laid waste by the disasters associated with the Thirty Years

War (1618–48). Then the Polish/Lithuanian state faced further massive military disasters and social destabilisation with invasion from the Swedes, in what has become known as 'the Great Deluge' (1648–67). Sweden, a food deficit region in the north, would emerge out of all these disasters as the main victor. It was poised to place all of northern and eastern Europe – including Russia – under its control as it pushed south to control its necessary grain supplies.

In 1695–97 the Swedish-controlled eastern Baltic, comprising Finland, Estonia and Livonia, was affected again by extraordinary cold and wet weather (Neumann and Lindgrén 1979). It is claimed that between 25 and 33 per cent of the Finnish population died in this famine (see Chapter 9), together with 20 per cent of the population of Estonia and Livonia (Neumann and Lindgrén 1979). This great famine emphasised the need for the northern powers to have control over southern food supply regions. Although Sweden was victorious in the early stages of the Great Northern War (1700–6), it was ultimately defeated by Peter the Great at Poltava in 1709. Peter quickly moved to consolidate his position in the north by moving Russia's capital further to the north, to the shores of the Baltic, in 1713.

The decision to move the capital to St Petersburg is often presented as part of Peter's enlightened Westernism, to build a window on the West. But this is not the whole story. The supply complications of moving the capital from Moscow, already in a food deficit region, to St Petersburg, in an even greater food deficit region, which had recently (1695–97) experienced a massive famine, made it a major undertaking, which could only have been driven by military necessity. Unless Sweden was deprived of control over the eastern and southern Baltic, there would always be the risk of another Swedish 'deluge'. Overall, the Russian move northwards would add to food problems in Sweden, Finland, Lithuania and Russia itself throughout the eighteenth and nineteenth centuries, but it would destroy the Swedish military threat, which was more real at the time than is often presumed.

Comprehensive Russian price data can be traced back to the early eighteenth century (Wheatcroft 2017: app. 2). The differences between rye prices in the Northern Region (where St Petersburg is located), the Central Non-Black Earth Region (where Moscow is located) and the main agricultural Central Black Earth Region (CChZ) provide us with a striking indication of relative food scarcity in these regions over this period. In the eighteenth century rye prices in the north oscillated greatly from two to more than three times the level in the CChZ, but from the 1860s the level became more constant at about 50 per cent higher. Over the same period rye prices in the Northern Non-Black Earth Region

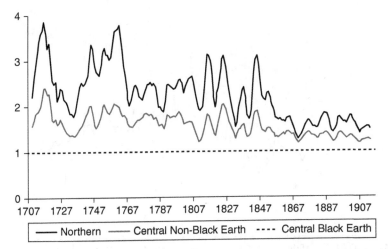

Figure 10.1 Rye prices in Northern and Central Non-Black Earth Regions in comparison with Central Black Earth Region, 1707–1913

(NChZ) varied at a much lower level, between 0 and 7 per cent above CChZ prices, and towards the end of this period they were fairly stable at about 30 per cent higher.

The price levels and fluctuations of rye in the Baltic provinces of Russia and in the west were similar to those in the north, with initially large differentials and amplitudes that decreased significantly in the late nineteenth century. Reliable data on per capita grain production in the different regions of Russia are available only for the period from the middle of the nineteenth century. If we bear in mind that average per capita grain consumption for food at this time was about 0.25 tons per person per year, that 10 per cent of the grain was needed for seed and that significant amounts of grain were used as feed, then any region producing less than 0.4 tons of grain per person per year would need to import grain. The food deficit regions of the north were becoming increasingly dependent upon external supplies of grain as their per capita grain production fell from 0.36 tons per head per year in the 1850s to about 0.3 in 1913. The traditional grain surplus regions of the centre were declining in importance as surplus providers as the centre's level of per capita production fell from about 0.6 tons per head per year in the 1850s to 0.5 in 1913. By contrast, per capita grain production in the south increased from about 0.4 tons per head per year to about 0.8 (see Wheatcroft 1991: 136–42 for regional grain production and population data grouped into five basic macro-regions). These were the surpluses

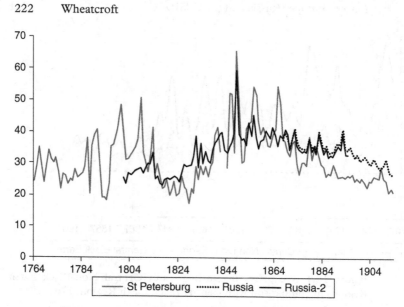

Figure 10.2 Crude death rate (CDR) in Russia and St Petersburg, 1764–1913

that fuelled the very large grain exports of the time (about 10 million tons per year).

Comprehensive sets of Russian mortality data are available only from the beginning of the nineteenth century. Data for St Petersburg go back to 1764, which is still after the period of great food shortages in the north in the first half of the eighteenth century (see Figure 10.2). There appears to have been a relatively favourable period in the early nineteenth century, a deterioration in mid-century and then a distinct improvement with less severe fluctuations after 1865. The incidence of epidemic diseases will have played a role in determining this dynamic, but the major decline in levels and in fluctuations from the 1870s coincided with the period when railways began to provide more certain food supplies.

The main reason why Russia avoided being more badly affected by food problems in the late eighteenth century and the nineteenth was its expansion into better agricultural regions to the south – first into the more 'black earth regions' of Tula, Ryazan, Kursk, Orlov, Voronezh, Tambov and Penza from the beginning of the seventeenth century, and then into Ukraine and the North Caucasus, after defeating the Crimean Khanate, from the late eighteenth and nineteenth centuries. This territorial expansion, and the later one eastward further into the North Caucasus and the Steppe (what we would now call Kazakhstan, the Ural Mountains and Western Siberia), would all greatly assist the regular food supply to the Russian north. Over this period the north became greatly dependent upon these external supplies, and most of the more serious later famines will be associated with the breakdown of these supply channels.

The magnitude of the 1891–92 demographic crisis in Russia, which is associated with the 'famine' of 1891–92, is very minor in comparison with the pre-1870s crises, or later crises. Yet the literature on the episode suggests that 1891–92 was the greatest famine of the nineteenth century. The perception of this crisis differed from the earlier ones primarily because it came in a period of modern record keeping when normal mortality rates had begun to decline and when society was used to the idea of progress.

The series of harvest failures of 1889–91 in the Volga which caused the famine of 1891–92 were the first serious harvest failures that were acknowledged as famines. But it is doubtful whether the food shortages were much worse than the crises of the 1840s, the early 1870s or the early 1880s. These earlier crises had occurred at a time when statistics were not available[5] and when the community was less inclined to take shortages seriously. The 1891 crisis came when society was more inclined to recognise the famine and to demand that something be done about it. The Tsarist government's response to the famine was actually far better than the British responses to famine in Ireland and India in the nineteenth century (Robbins 1975). At its height over 5 million people were receiving food aid, but the government received little acknowledgement for the success of its actions. Instead, more attention was placed on the disgrace of having high levels of mortality in the late nineteenth century.

The chronology of the mortality in 1892, which peaked in July and August, after the harvest, instead of in April to June, prior to the harvest, would suggest that most mortality at this time was a result of the concurrent cholera epidemic, rather than of famine as such (Wheatcroft 1992). The levels of excess mortality and deficit births over the problematic 1889–92 period, in comparison with the immediately previous year, show that signs of strain were apparent in 1889, when birth rates fell by 0.8 per cent and death rates increased by 8.2 per cent. At the same time infant mortality rose by 19 per cent while mortality in the 1+ age group rose by just 4.6 per cent. Then in 1892, the main famine year, we can see a much larger decline in birth rates and increases in mortality. Birth rates fell by 7.8 per cent while deaths rates increased by 16.1 per cent and, again, infant mortality rose more rapidly than 1+ mortality, by 31.1 per

---

[5] It was the crisis of the early 1880s that led to the Tsarist Central Statistical Committee being created and to a series of regular harvesting statistics becoming available from 1881.

cent in comparison with 10.5 per cent. In absolute figures we can calculate a birth deficit of about 0.5 million and excess deaths of 1.1 million, of which 0.7 million were infants and 0.4 million in the 1+ age group (see Wheatcroft 2017: app. 3).

5   Famine and Food Problems in the First Half of the Twentieth Century

Supplying the northern capitals with food from the south became much more problematic in the first half of the twentieth century. The population of the northern cities, which had been growing at an accelerating rate in the late nineteenth century, was to grow at an even faster pace in the twentieth century despite the collapse of the revolutionary period.[6] Military aggression was to result in significant losses and disruptions on two occasions. And there were to be major political changes, which greatly affected the quality and amount of statistical data that was published. Famines occurred in three periods: 1917–22, 1928–33 and 1941–48.

1917–22

The famine of 1917–22 can best be understood as two separate but related famines, which had complex causes in which Bolshevik policy played a far less important role than is often presumed.

(1)   The northern urban famine of 1918–20 was largely the result of the civil war on top of the collapse of the state procurement system. Together they deprived the Northern Consumer Region (NCR), which includes the industrial regions of Moscow and St Petersburg/ Leningrad, of the 5 million tons of grain that it needed to import annually from regions that were no longer under Bolshevik control. This famine was associated with a massive loss in population from the main northern cities, which reached a low point in January 1921.

(2)   The southern rural famine of 1921–22 was triggered by the drought of late spring and early summer 1921, coming at a time when the countryside was bereft of reserves. This famine began when the northern cities were already beginning to recover their populations,

---

[6] While Moscow's population doubled from a quarter of a million to half a million in the 50 years from 1820 to 1870, it doubled again to reach 1 million in the next 27 years, then doubled again in the next 18 years, reaching more than 2 million in February 1917. In the next 24 years it tripled, to reach 6.4 million in 1941. See Wheatcroft (2017: app. 1).

and when the government had partly restored the grain collection mechanism and was in the process of changing its procurement policy. This shift in importance between the northern and southern famines is clearly indicated in the price and food consumption data (Wheatcroft 2017).

In terms of policy, Lih has described how the Tsarist government, the Provisional government and the Bolshevik government all struggled with procurement in these troubled times, and that they were all forced to move from what he describes as an enlistment solution to an increasingly forced 'gubernatorial' system, whereby local governors or commissars tried to impose their plans on the population (Lih 1990: 248). In a sense, this is common for all war economies, whatever their ideology. At first the Bolsheviks blamed the failures of their radical enlistment system on saboteurs and wreckers, but eventually they learned that in a time of troubles it was necessary to force the rebuilding of state structures and to ensure that producers had an incentive to produce. When the food crisis ameliorated a little in early 1921 they tried to replace requisitioning with a tax in kind, but the severe drought of that year made it impossible. The first consequence of the change in policy was to remove large numbers of people from rations, just as the famine in the south was intensifying. It was the drought of the spring and summer of 1921, after the announcement of the change in policy, that caused the harvest failure in the normally grain surplus areas of the Volga and that caused a peak in famine mortality in the first half of 1922.

I have described above that traditional Marxist accounts of the famine tend to see it as part of the deep-seated revolutionary crisis, though detailed works on national income levels (Gregory 1982), welfare levels (Wheatcroft 1991; Mironov 2010) and on policy (Lih 1990) show that this is not the case. Conquest tends to blame both the famine and the revolution on the culpability of the revolutionaries in causing these upheavals and he also denies the importance of the weather in 1921: '[T]he weather though bad, was not at the disaster level' (Conquest 1986: 55). The basis of this assessment is not stated. Dronin and Bellinger (2005), who have looked at this question in detail, state: 'Historians perhaps underestimated the scale of food crises in Russia in the 1920s. There was no agricultural policy for analysis in terms of failure or success, but rather a series of dramatic, and in some ways spontaneous, events, bringing the country to a state of continuing mass famine.' They use the word 'catastrophic' to describe the weather, causing crop failures in both 1920 and 1921, and emphasise that it was crop failures in a row of years aggravated by policy that underlay the famine crisis (Dronin and Bellinger 2005: 108).[7]

The regional figures on grain collections provide a striking indication of where the grain was coming from and whether it was large enough to provide the 4 to 5 million tons of grain that were normally required by the consumer regions in pre-war years. Just prior to the drought, in the 1920–21 agricultural year, 6 million tons of grain were collected, and this was sufficient to allow for the abandonment of requisitioning and the move to a tax. But the drought and harvest failure of 1921–22 led to a reduction of collections to a slim 3.8 million tons (with over 1 million tons of that coming from the NCR itself).

The collection of just 3.8 million tons of grain in 1921 was minimal for sustaining the recovery of the two consumer regions, and left few resources for famine relief to the Volga. Without international support very little relief would have been available for the Volga, Urals and parts of North Caucasus and Ukraine affected by the drought. Even with the provision of massive international relief[8] the consequences of this famine in 1921–22 were very serious and ranked at the time as the largest famine in modern history.

On the basis of pre-revolutionary Zemstvo (local government) budget studies, the statisticians in TsSU pioneered a mass network of food consumption studies in urban and rural areas that began in 1918. These provide some of the most detailed indicators of food consumption during a famine period. They show the extraordinarily low levels of food consumption in Petrograd in 1918, and the very low levels reached in rural areas in the Volga in 1921 (Wheatcroft 1992).

The most dramatic and most significant consequence of the early stages of the famine was the extraordinary de-urbanisation of the population, especially in the north and in Petrograd, where the population on 1 January 1921 fell to only a third of that on 1 January 1917 (Table 10.2).

This scale of de-urbanisation would be matched in 1941–44, but not in 1931–33. Much of this de-urbanisation was a result of the population fleeing the northern cities and heading for food surplus regions, but a large part was also the consequence of the very high level of mortality in these years. We can get a sense of the timing and location of this increased mortality by looking at monthly mortality for the major towns

---

[7] Wheatcroft calculates the poor weather effect in 1920 and 1921 to have been −1.32 and −1.07, respectively, or an average of −1.20, which was the fourth lowest on record and lower than either 1890 and 1891 (−1.07) or 1891 and 1892 (−0.95) (see Wheatcroft 2017: app. 1).

[8] The American Relief Administration (ARA) alone was providing over 10 million meals a day at its peak (Fisher 1927).

Table 10.1 *Central grain collections, in million tons, 1916/17–1922/23*

| | Consumer regions | | Producer regions | | | | |
	NCR	SCR	SPR	CPR	EPR	All	All USSR
1916/17	0.4	0.1	4.0	2.8	1.0	7.8	8.3
1917/18	0.0	0	0.4	0.3	0.4	1.1	1.2
1918/19	0.2	0	0	1.5	0	1.5	1.8
1919/20	0.4	0	0	2.1	1.0	3.2	3.5
1920/21	0.5	0.2	2.2	1.6	1.6	5.4	6.0
1921/22	1.0	0.1	1.4	0.5	0.9	2.8	3.8
1922/23	1.2	0.1	2.3	1.6	0.8	4.7	5.9

Notes: NCR = Northern Consumer Region, which includes Moscow and St Petersburg/Leningrad Industrial Regions; SCR = Southern Consumer Region, which includes the Transcaucasus area and central Asia; SPR = Southern Producer Region (Ukraine and North Caucasus); CPR = Central Producer Region (Central Black Earth Region and the Volga); EPR = Eastern Producer Region (Urals, Siberia, Russian Far East and Kazakhstan). *Source:* Calculated from data in *Itogi desyatiletiya sovetskoi vlasti v tsifrakh 1917–1927* (1927), p. 379.

Table 10.2 *The population of Petrograd, Moscow, Kiev and Saratov, in thousands, 1916–23*

| | Northern cities | | Ukraine | Volga |
	Petrograd	Moscow	Kiev	Saratov
1916	2,410	1,890	541	228
1917	2,360	1,940	512	218
1918	1,890	1,770	480	207
1919	1,190	1,550	545	202
1920	820	1,270	455	195
1921	790	1,150	379	189
1922	900	1,280	402	185
1923	1,030	1,500	425	187
Year of max. decline	1921	1921	1921	1922
1921/1916	33%	61%	70%	83%

Source: Wheatcroft (1976b).

where civil registration had been introduced before the revolution. Rural data are available for Saratov *krai* (district) in 1919, and for a number of other central provinces from 1922. The following figures provide indications of monthly and annual mortality for the major northern cities of

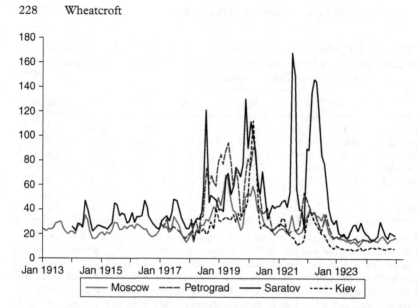

Figure 10.3 Mortality in deaths per thousand in annual equivalent, January 1913–December 1924

Moscow and Leningrad and for Saratov, the main city in the Volga at this time, and for Kiev, the major city in Ukraine.

Petrograd and Moscow suffered their highest levels of mortality in 1919, when they registered levels of 72.6 per thousand in Petrograd, which was 338 per cent of its 1914 level, and 44.8 per thousand in Moscow, which was 193 per cent of its 1914 level. By 1922 mortality in these two cities was much lower, at 29.2 per thousand in Petrograd (136 per cent of its 1914 level) and 29.4 per thousand in Moscow (126 per cent of its 1914 level). By contrast, Saratov in the Volga registered in 1919 69.8 per thousand (238 per cent of its 1914 level), and a higher level in 1922, with 81.5 per thousand (278 per cent of its 1914 level).

The major decline in natality during the war and revolution has the effect of reducing the relative share of infants, and therefore infant mortality, in the total figures for mortality. This, in its turn, has the effect of masking a significant increase in mortality in older age groups when we look at crude death rates undifferentiated by age.

For Saratov, infant mortality rate was at its height in 1916 and fell during the subsequent famine years. In Leningrad it rose to almost double its pre-war rate in the famine, while in Moscow and Kiev it rose by 50 per cent. Meanwhile, for the older 1+ age group mortality rose by a much larger factor of five or more in the famine. Moscow and Leningrad in the north had a single peak in 1919 while Saratov and Kiev would rise again after the 1919 peak to an even higher one in 1922.

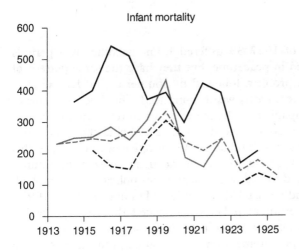

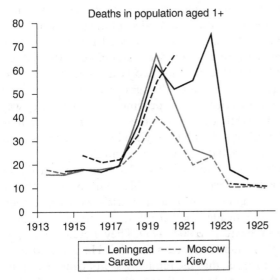

Figure 10.4 Infant mortality per thousand births and deaths in population aged 1+ per thousand population, 1913–25

Total excess civilian mortality for this period may well have been about 8 million, with about 5 million in the 1915–20 period and 3 million in 1921–22 (Wheatcroft 2017: app. 3). The similarity in mortality patterns across the country in both traditional deficit and traditional surplus regions was the effect of the large pandemics that were raging at this time (Wheatcroft 1976a). We will see below that the pandemic aspect was far less marked in all later famines.

1927–33

The food problems of 1927–33 differed from the other two periods because they occurred in peacetime, but they have the same pattern of northern urban food problem followed by southern rural famine after harvest failures that were partly weather-induced. The food problems of this time were accompanied by the major agrarian revolution of collectivisation, and some accounts see the famine as being the direct consequence of collectivisation. The main authoritative accounts trace this tragic history back to the food crisis in the northern cities in the autumn of 1927, which resulted in extreme procurement policies being applied. (Lewin 1968; Carr and Davies 1974; Danilov, Manning and Viola 1999). They argue that government policies aggravated the already existing economic problem. Collectivisation in 1930 was a policy applied in the midst of this series of procurement crises in an attempt to ensure that the peasantry would continue growing grain when they were getting so few rewards from doing so. It was not the initial cause of the problem.

It was the drought of 1931 that played the crucial role in turning a northern urban crisis into a southern rural one, but, unlike in 1921, there was not just one year of harvest failure but two years. The first harvest failure, in 1931, was caused by a serious drought in the Volga, and the second, in 1932, centred on Kiev *oblast* (province) and Ukraine, was caused by a very damp harvesting time, which resulted in massive harvest losses turning a relatively good biological yield into a disastrous barn yield. Again, the meteorological data are very clear on this matter.[9]

Davies and Wheatcroft reviewed the available data and concluded that Stalin's 'policies towards the peasants were ruthless and brutal' but the Soviet leadership 'was struggling with a famine crisis which had been caused partly by their wrongheaded policies, but was unexpected and undesirable' (Davies and Wheatcroft 2004: 441). They therefore disagree with Conquest's claim that Stalin 'wanted a famine'. Having read their book, Conquest appears to agree that the famine was not caused on purpose. He wrote stating that he no longer disagreed with them, and asked them to make clear to their readers that he [Conquest] no longer thought that Stalin wanted the famine and had caused it on purpose (Davies and Wheatcroft 2004: 441, no. 145).

Data on grain collections, transportation, prices and food consumption show a more nuanced picture, with different areas suffering the most

---

[9] See Wheatcroft (1977) and Davies and Wheatcroft (2004), and the latest estimates of Wheatcroft and Bishop (2017), where 1931 has the lowest ranking, at –2.88, out of 110 years of data.

Table 10.3a *Grain collections, excluding milling levy (garnts), in million tons, 1927–32*

	NCR	SCR	All CR	SPR	CPR	EPR	All PRs	USSR
1927	0.2	0.03	0.2	5.5	2.8	2.5	10.8	11.1
1928	0.2	0.2	0.4	2.4	3.0	3.5	8.9	9.3
1929	0.9	0.4	1.3	6.2	3.7	2.5	12.4	13.8
1930	1.3	0.3	1.6	9.1	5.4	3.8	17.8	19.8
1931	1.6	0.3	1.9	10.3	5.7	3.3	19.3	21.2
1932	1.3	0.3	1.6	9.4	5.9	3.7	19.0	20.5

Table 10.3b *Regional utilisation of collected grain, in million tons, 1927/28–1932/33*

	NCR	SCR	All CR	SPR	CPR	EPR	All PRs	USSR
1927/28	3.3	0.9	4.2	2.2	0.8	1.3	4.3	8.5
1928/29	2.8	0.7	3.5	2.0	0.5	1.3	3.8	7.3
1929/30	3.1	1.2	4.3	2.6	1.5	2.4	6.5	10.9
1930/31	3.8	1.6	5.4	3.0	1.7	2.7	7.4	12.8
1931/32	4.2	1.4	5.6	3.5	2.2	4.0	9.7	15.2
1932/33	3.4	1.3	4.7	3.8	1.7	3.1	8.6	13.4

Table 10.3c *Transfers of grain, in million tons (+ = received, – = exported), 1927/28–1932/33*

	NCR	SCR	All CR	SPR	CPR	EPR	All PRs	USSR
1927/28	3.1	0.9	4.0	–3.3	–2.0	–1.2	–6.5	–2.6
1928/29	2.6	0.5	3.1	–0.4	–2.5	–2.2	–5.1	–2.0
1929/30	2.2	0.8	3.0	–3.6	–2.2	–0.1	–5.9	–2.9
1930/31	2.5	1.3	3.8	–6.1	–3.7	–1.1	–10.9	–7.0
1931/32	2.6	1.1	3.7	–6.8	–3.5	0.7	–9.6	–6.0
1932/33	2.1	1.0	3.2	–5.6	–4.2	–0.6	–10.4	–7.1

Note: See Table 10.1 for definition of regions.

at different times; Ukraine was relatively sheltered in the early stages of the crisis, 1927–31, and became the major victim only at later stages, when the situation was spiralling out of control. By the early 1930s the grain collections system had expanded to cover local supplies that had earlier been handled by private trade, so therefore we need to consider the utilisation of collected grain as well as its collection.

These transfers show the relatively poor performance of the Southern Producer Region of Ukraine and the North Caucasus, which in the decade before the revolution had been consistently exporting over 10 million tons of grain per year. In 1927 and 1928 Ukraine suffered from very severe winter killing of autumn-sown grains, and this partly explains the low production and collections of these years. But even in the favourable year of 1930 the SPR was only able to export 6 million tons. This placed great strain on other supply regions. After four years of heavy procurement the Central Producer Region (CPR, including Central Black Earth and Volga) and the Eastern Producer Region (EPR, including the Urals, Siberia, Russian Far East and Kazakhstan) began to falter in the drought year of 1931, and grain had to be imported into the EPR. It was only at this time that greater attention began to be directed towards the SPR. Large procurements were eventually enforced despite the indications of relatively poor harvests in 1931 and 1932, and this is what caused the major famine in Ukraine.

The reason why Kiev *oblast* was the worst-affected region is that it suffered the most from the internal reduction in allocations of grain from central collections. These reductions in allocations were ordered once it became clear that the grain collection plan was not going to be fulfilled. At this time most of the urban grain consumers in Kiev city were struck off central grain allocation plans, which concentrated on large industrial enterprises. This forced the Kiev authorities to collect grain in a decentralised fashion from within the rural grain producing areas of Kiev *oblast*. As a result of these activities, rural mortality in Kiev *oblast* rose to 99 per thousand[10] while mortality rates in Kiev city were still very high, but were kept significantly lower at 38 per thousand (Wheatcroft, Garnaut and Leiken 2013).

Food consumption surveys results are available for a number of regions from the beginning of 1933, including from Kiev *oblast*, the worst-affected region in Ukraine and of all the USSR. The data for kolkhoz (collective farm) peasants in the surveyed households in Kiev *oblast* show catastrophically low food consumption (Wheatcroft 1993). It is highly likely that the returns came from households that were better off than normal, and that totally collapsed households were not returning results; nevertheless, the information we have is quite revealing of a catastrophic situation. Of course, these surveys were all classified at the time.

The major distinction between this set of famines and the 1918–22 ones is that the Soviet government was successful in providing the

---

[10] Tetivskii *raion* (administrative division) registered a death rate of 244 per thousand, a birth rate of 12 per thousand and an infant mortality rate of 319 per thousand births. Volodarskii *raion* registered a crude death rate of 206.1 per thousand, a crude birth rate of 7.3 per thousand and an infant mortality rate of an incredible 958 per thousand.

northern deficit regions with sufficient grain to avoid famine and de-urbanisation. But the extraction of grain from the normally surplus-producing regions was so intense that it caused the famine to be redirected from the northern deficit regions to the producer regions. This occurred predominantly in the second half of the 1932–33 crop year – i.e. in the first half of 1933.

Mortality data are available for these years for both urban and rural areas. Urban mortality was much lower than rural mortality, in general and particularly in the Northern Consumer Region. In the food surplus areas where grain was often directed out of the region, mortality for the urban population was higher, especially in the Central Producer Region. Monthly mortality reached a peak of 316 per thousand in annual equivalents in June 1933 in such areas, 196 per thousand for all of Ukraine, 133 per thousand in lower Volga, 92.1 per thousand in North Caucasus and 44.3 per thousand in all of Soviet Russia (RSFSR) (Davies and Wheatcroft 2004: 511).

Excess mortality for the registered civil population in 1929–33 can be calculated to have been about 3 million, with more than a half of that in the SPR and less than 300,000 in the NCR. The figures for Soviet Russia alone are about 850,000 overall, with 248,000 urban and 606,000 rural. These were, respectively, 49 per cent for all Soviet Russia, 58 per cent for the urban population and 45 per cent for the rural. But when we look at age differentiation amongst excess mortality we see that only 19 per cent relate to infant deaths and 59 per cent to deaths in the older (1+) age group. Despite these very high levels of mortality, there was relatively little increase in infectious disease.[11]

1941–47

This section groups together the wartime food problems and famine with the post-war famine because they are linked, in a similar way to the urban and rural food problems and the famines of 1918–22 and 1927–33. All these cases began as complex food problems mainly affecting the northern urban areas, which then turned into southern rural famines after a complex of factors including weather-induced harvest failures. The major difference are that by 1941 the USSR had reached a much lower level of normal mortality (Wheatcroft 2017: app. 2); that the problems were more complex; and that the latter stages of this famine coincided with a global food crisis. We can identify four separate but related problems.

---

[11] There was no cholera and some increase in typhus, and other diseases, but considerably less than in 1918–22.

(1) A northern urban food problem during 1941–45, caused by German occupation of grain surplus-producing regions.
(2) An eastern urban food problem, caused by the evacuation and establishment of industry in the east without adequate food supply.
(3) A rural crisis in parts of the formerly surplus areas when very poor weather produced a harvest failure in 1946 and a famine in the first half of 1947.
(4) A genocidal policy carried out by the Germans in occupied and besieged areas. Here I will deal primarily with the first three parts of the problem. The last part is discussed in more detail in Chapter 11.

In the final years of the 1930s, and in 1940 and 1941, the scale of grain required by the Russian Northern Consumer Region increased greatly. Instead of the 4 to 5 million tons per year required from late Tsarist times up to the mid-1930s, now up to 8 million tons of grain were imported into the NCR. This was partly a consequence of increased rates of urbanisation in the northern towns, but also the consequence of the addition of the food deficit Baltic states to this region.

In the first year of the war the German army did not take advantage of Soviet food vulnerabilities. The German invasion was delayed by the need to help Mussolini in Greece, and this enabled the USSR to collect a large proportion of the 1941 harvest. Then, bolstered with overconfidence, the German army made a direct attack on the main food deficit regions, instead of targeting the food surplus regions in order to deprive Moscow of its food supply. Furthermore, a large part of the urban populations of Moscow and Leningrad was evacuated to parts of the CPR, with many government offices going to Kuibyshev. This was a belated attempt to reduce the level of population in the NCR and to ease the regional food balance.

In the second year of the war, after a defeat before Moscow, the Germans adopted a more strategic approach by retreating from the deficit region of Moscow, Tula and Kalinin *oblasts* and attacking other food surplus regions in the South and North Caucasus and central Volga. This effectively returned a large food deficit region back to the Soviet government, while German forces occupied an even larger food surplus region. The food deficit regions could now be supplied with grain only from the EPR and about two-thirds of the CPR.

Fortunately, the USSR had exceptionally good weather for all the war years from the 1941 harvest to the 1945 harvest, with only slightly poorer than average weather in 1943. According to crop/weather models based on meteorological data, the CPR had exceptionally good weather

Table 10.4a *Grain collections and grain stocks, in million tons, 1939/40–1947/48*

	Grain collections	Grain stocks, end of year (30 June)
1939/40	21.1	5.1
1940/41	25.1	6.4
1941/42	19.5	9.4
1942/43	11.2	5.2
1943/44	8.9	3.0
1944/45	16.1	6.3
1945/46	15.1	5.7
1946/47	13.2	3.3
1947/48	18.2	7.4

Sources: The data of the State Committee on Collections (KomZag) for grain and grain produce collected or held in KomZag stores: Russian State Archives of the Economy (RGAE) 8040/6/360, ll. 34–7.

Table 10.4b *Grain transportation from regions, in million tons, 1940–48*

	1940 (a)	1941	1942 (b)	1943 (b)	1944 (b)	1945 (a)	1946 (a)	1947 (a)	1948 (a)
NCR	-8.0	n.a.	-2.7	-2.0	-3.3	-3.1	-5.4	-4.0	-5.7
SCR	-0.8	n.a.	-0.4	0.2	0.1	-0.5	-0.1	0.44	-0.3
SPR	5.7	n.a.	0.4	0	3.3	6.1	2.9	3.2	6.5
CPR	1.1	n.a.	1.7	0.7	-0.3	-0.4	0.6	-0.1	-0.7
EPR	1.6	n.a.	0.8	1.0	0.2	-2.0	-0.1	-0.1	-1.5
Balance	-0.4	n.a.	-0.3	-0.2	0	0.9	-2.1	-1.5	-1.6

Notes: The table is compiled from two distinct sources. When they can be compared, the regional receipts for both series are similar, with those coming from source (b) being about 0.3 million tons less. The data may exclude military allocations. A negative value in the balance indicates that grain was being withdrawn. For additional information, see Wheatcroft (2017).
Sources: (a) for 1940 and 1945–50: Gruzooborot zhel. dor. po respublike, krai I ob za 1940 I 1945–50g. Materialy po stat zhd transporta, vyp. 245, M. 1952 RGAE 1562/329/4685, ll. 29–192; (b) for 1942–44 (no regional data are available for 1941): RGAE, F1884, op. 61, dd.37, 43, 53, 78, 122.

in 1942 (resulting in a deviation of +2.31 *tsentners* – or 231 kg – of grain production from trend) and 1944 (+3.09). The SPR was exceptional in 1941 (+2.80) and in 1945 (+2.09). The average for these five years was the highest on record. After all these good years the weather deteriorated dramatically in 1946. Within the SPR the situation deteriorated progressively from east to west. The Military Don district in North Caucasus registered +1.46, Kiev registered 0.07 and Kishinev in Moldova registered −5.42, which was much lower than all other values it had registered before the revolution or after World War II (Wheatcroft 2017: app. 1). Tables 10.4a and 10.4b indicate how the Soviet government succeeded in collecting and controlling grain in these years.

In 1941–42 the Soviet government collected a relatively large amount of grain (almost 20 million tons). Given the reduced population and tight controls over the distribution of grain, the level of grain stocks held by state collectors increased by 3 million tons to over 9 million at the end of the first year of the war. This high level of stocks would then be drawn down in the following, difficult years. In 1942–43 the level of grain collection from a much smaller harvest area fell to 11.2 million tons. This was the beginning of a very difficult two-year period, when end-of-year stocks were gradually reduced to a level of 3 million tons on 1 July 1944. The regional dimension of the grain transport problem can be seen from Table 10.4b.

The loss of 5 million tons of grain from the SPR in 1942 and 1943 resulted in a reduction of net imports into the NCR of 5 million tons, with about 2 million tons being pumped out of the CPR and the EPR. The local food supplies in these regions were greatly strained by these exports. 1944 remained strained but now the SPR was able to provide 3.3 million tons to the NCR (2.3 million tons from Ukraine and 1 million tons from North Caucasus), and the burden of the strain could be relieved from the CPR and the EPR. In 1945 these two normally surplus regions imported 2.4 million tons of grain. Fortunately, by 1944 the German army had been defeated and was slowly retreating from the USSR. But the German retreat did not bring as much relief as was commonly expected, as it added many additional millions to the population that needed to be fed. Although this population was in areas that had previously been food surplus regions, their ability to generate food surpluses was greatly reduced.

Fortunately, other supplies became available from the United States. Goldman and Filtzer (2015: 324–9) have recently provided a good overview of the scale and significance of US supplies to the Soviet Union at this time. They distinguish between two periods and conclude that in 1943 'Lend-Lease did little to help the civilian population and went almost entirely to preventing hunger and malnutrition in the military'. However, this changed in 1944, when 'Lend-Lease food aid provided critical assistance for those at the margins of debility or death. It kept many urban civilians from dying during the first half of the year and helped to eliminate starvation disease almost entirely from mid-1944 onward.'

Apart from the wartime problems in the traditional deficit regions of the north, there were also problems in the east, where large numbers of evacuees were transported, with initially insufficient food supplies. Filtzer (2010) points out that these areas began suffering from serious famine in 1942 and 1943. From the transportation data cited above it looks as though a very conscious attempt was made to improve the situation in the EPR in 1945 by shipping 2 million tons of grain into this region.

Moskoff (1990) and Goldman and Filtzer (2015) emphasise how ancillary agricultural production by factory workers and townspeople played an important role by producing potatoes on spare or unused ground. In desperate wartime circumstances the government was prepared to allow these necessary relaxations in control over food production to occur, but after the war Stalin was keen to reinforce measures to limit the spread of these forms of activities. This change in policy undoubtedly caused additional problems in the immediate post-war period.[12]

The poor harvest of 1946 stopped the continued growth in central grain stocks. As Table 10.4a indicates, grain stocks had begun to increase in 1944/45 and had reached 6.3 million tons on 1 July 1945, but by 1 July 1946, on the eve of the harvest for the drought year, they had already fallen to 5.7 million tons, and by the end of 1946/47 they had fallen to 3.3 million tons.[13]

The claims made by Zima (1996), and repeated by Zubkova (1993) and Filtzer (2002), that there was plenty of grain available, and that Stalin's refusal to supply grain to the peasantry was a sign of his antagonism to them, are not supported by these records on grain collections and stocks. In 1946–47 grain collections fell by almost 2 million tons when compared with 1945–46 levels and the level of stocks held by state organisations at the end of 1946–47 fell by 2.4 million to reach a low point of 3.3 million tons. This was lower than any wartime year apart from the very lowest level of 3 million tons on 1 July 1944. And there was no longer Lend-Lease to supplement it. Ellman correctly notes this fall in grain stocks, but rashly argues that there was still enough grain to allow further releases (Ellman 2000).

The main factor causing this disaster was undoubtedly the drought of 1946, which was particularly severe in Moldova and the south-west, where it was the second of two harvest failure years (Wheatcroft 2012). The worst-affected areas were those that had recently undergone enemy occupation[14] and were suffering as a consequence. Some assistance was provided by the

---

[12] Famine in the occupied regions and the besieged city of Leningrad is discussed in Chapter 11.

[13] This was a level 10 per cent higher than they had been in July 1943. However, we should note that the population of the USSR at this time was more than 20 per cent lower than at the end of 1945.

[14] In the Moldavian Soviet Socialist Republic, by Romanian, and not German, forces.

Table 10.5 *Moldovan grain balance, million tons and tons per head per year, 1944–47*

	Population (millions)	Grain production		Per capita	Net exports	Grain available	Per capita
		Plan	Actual				
1944	2.00		1.27	0.64			
1945	2.02	1.608	0.99	0.49	0.161	0.83	0.41
1946	2.1	1.645	0.38	0.18	−0.093	0.48	0.23
1947	2.17	1.676	1.49	0.69	−0.196	1.68	0.78

Sources: Based on materials in RGAE 1562/324/5299, 1562/329/4685 and Moldovan State Archives (MGA).

United Nations Relief and Rehabilitation Administration (UNRRA), but it was much less the Lend-Lease aid, which had ended in 1945. In many areas Stalin's attempted re-enforcement of controls over the kolkhoz can be assigned some share of the blame. But in newly occupied regions, such as western Moldova, mass collectivisation had not yet been introduced. Here the outcome was primarily a consequence of drought reducing yields in an impoverished society at a time when insufficient relief was available. Transport data show that some grain was shipped into Moldova in 1946–47, but, clearly, not enough to avoid a massive famine.

To conclude this brief analysis of the 1941–47 period, something should be said about the overall demographic consequences of the famine. For non-occupied and non-besieged areas, crude mortality and infant mortality indicators show a major elevation in both city and country during the winter of 1941–42. From 1942 onwards crude mortality and infant mortality indicators are much lower. As Filtzer has pointed out, these indicators are potentially misleading, because this period – like that of 1933, discussed above – experienced a great reduction of births, which would have changed the age structure of the population, reducing the number of infants and very young (under the age of five). Filtzer goes as far as to identify two periods of famine during the war: the famine of the first year of the war, which largely affected young children, and that of the second and additional years of the war, which largely affected adults, who found themselves carrying out extreme levels of work on very low rations.

Excess mortality for the civilian population can be estimated at over 10 million for 1940–47, with most of this falling in the period 1940–45. Excess mortality for the 1946–47 famine could be as high as 1 million, depending upon what was assumed to be normal mortality (Wheatcroft

2017: app. 3). Again, the level of infectious disease was surprisingly low throughout the USSR during the war, and especially in 1946–47. It is noteworthy, however, that Moldova, which experienced exceptionally high mortality in 1946–47, was also exceptional in 1943–44 in having the highest rates of typhus in the USSR.

6   General Conclusions

This chapter has surveyed the history of famines in Russia and the USSR. It has drawn attention to the fact that the major urban areas of Russia were located in a large food deficit region of northern Russia, which required quite extensive supply arrangements. The collapse of these supply arrangements in the 'Times of Troubles' led to massive famines in the beginning of the seventeenth century. The additional strain of moving the capital to St Petersburg in the beginning of the eighteenth century caused decades of supply problems until the canals were built and modernised in the late eighteenth century. The opening up of large new supply areas in the south and the east, and the revolution in transport provided by the late nineteenth century, led to far more grain exports than could be consumed by the north, and large amounts of grain (up to 10 million tons per year) were exported to western Europe. As long as the country remained intact and the markets remained operational there was plenty of grain to feed the northern towns. Problems would emerge when civil war or international war stopped the regular flow of grain from the surplus regions to the deficit ones, or when extreme industrialisation plans combined with unanticipated changes in domestic grain utilisation placed extreme strain on the system. The major famines of 1918–22 and 1927–33 began with challenges to this food supply, which led to the government taking extreme measures in an attempt to modify the crisis. In the 1918–20 period the government was unsuccessful in avoiding a famine in the north, which was accompanied by mass de-urbanisation. In 1927–33 the government was able to protect the northern cities, but at the expense of famine in the rural south. In 1941 the USSR faced a massive genocidal attack from the most powerful military force ever assembled. It immediately lost control over many of its supply areas. Besieged Leningrad faced serious famine, as did the occupied areas. Within the rest of the country the northern towns narrowly avoided mass famine by evacuating much of their population, by severely controlling food supplies, by seeking additional ancillary food production and, in 1943 and 1944, by using US Lend-Lease food. The drought of 1946–47 combined with the cessation of Lend-Lease caused famine in the worst-affected regions of the west.

11 The European Famines of World Wars I and II

Stephen Wheatcroft and Cormac Ó Gráda

This chapter considers the regional and chronological aspects of the serious food crises during and after World Wars I and II, which among some groups of the population in certain regions at certain times reached famine proportions. It is divided into three parts. The first two consider the food supply problems associated with these crises and their immediate demographic consequences. The third part considers the longer-term health consequences of the crises and, in particular, their effect on foetal origins.

Both in 1914–18 and in 1939–45 the food supply for armies, capital cities and major urban industrial locations were the major concerns for the state. Challenges to these supplies would often lead to extraordinary state measures, which would divert the food problem away from groups and regions favoured by the state onto groups and regions less valued, or even viewed with hostility. Unfortunately, the historical record tends to follow state interests (especially of the victors), and so the fate of poor peasants and ration-less groups in central and eastern Europe is often less well documented.

International relief played a role in supplying some individual regions and groups, when they lacked adequate state protection. This is particularly the case after military occupation or the end of warfare, when normal state authority has collapsed. The levels of relief needed were generally much greater than had been appreciated before these wars. The prospect of Communist states emerging out of wartime collapse and famine resulted in other states, fearful of the spread of Communism, being motivated by more than humanitarianism when responding to these crises. Without the large amount of external aid provided, there would have been significantly greater levels of famine than actually occurred after both World War I and II. Herbert Hoover, who had more direct experience of these problems than anyone else, described the situation after both world wars as reaching levels of crisis unparalleled in Europe since the famine and destruction of the Thirty Years War (Hoover 1951: 287).

The immediate demographic consequences of these crises are difficult to identify in the complex circumstances of post-war chaos. This is especially the case for Russia and eastern Europe, which were the worst-affected regions, and where there was until recently little access to archives. Now that we have access to Soviet and east European archival material it is possible to get a better idea of the level of demographic crisis in these worst-affected regions. The Section 2 of this chapter incorporates material from Soviet, Ukrainian, Moldovan, Polish and Baltic archives into our analysis.

1   World War I

1.1   Food Supply Problems

On the eve of World War I the European food system could be divided into four distinct macro-regions with at least seven different zones. The United Kingdom and western continental Europe (WCE), the more urbanised and industrialised parts of Europe, were the main grain-importing regions. The less industrialised parts of Europe – eastern continental Europe (ECE) and Russia/USSR – were overall grain exporters, though within them we can identify separate surplus and deficit zones.

The United Kingdom, the region most dependent upon external food supplies, was also the most industrialised and urbanised. It had a population of about 45 million, of which about 80 per cent was urban, and it imported more than 10 million tons of grain per year, or about 60 per cent of its basic grain requirements.[1] This large dependence on foreign grain was accompanied with relatively low domestic stocks of grain; Britain purposely imported grain from several different regions (North America, Russia and Australia) so that grain would arrive at different times of the year. This would appear to make UK supplies even more insecure in times of war.

Most of the countries in western continental Europe were following the United Kingdom into industrialisation, urbanisation and increased external food dependence. They varied between the most dependent countries, such as Belgium and the Netherlands, with levels of dependence similar to UK levels, and others such as protectionist Germany and France, with lower levels of external dependence. The WCE area, with 188 million people, was importing an annual total of about 16 million tons, or about 15 per cent of its needs. The urban (mainly western) zone of the ECE area was also a net importer, of probably as much as 2.4 million tons of grain, which was provided by the large surpluses of its

---

[1] The data on which these figures are based are given in Wheatcroft and Ó Gráda (2016).

own eastern Danubian zone. Much further to the east, in the Northern Consumer Region (NCR) zone of Russia, we find the fourth main deficit zone, with about 33 million people, which needed to import about 5 million tons of grain per year or about 29 per cent of the grain that it consumed. These four food deficit zones had a combined population of about 300 million[2] and imported a total of around 33 million tons of grain per year, or about 0.11 tons per person. This was roughly one-third of the grain consumed per person.

Russia/USSR was the largest grain surplus-producing region, not only in Europe but also in the world. The 5 million tons per year required by its own NCR was largely produced by its traditional Central Producer Region (CPR) zone (the Volga and Black Earth Regions), and an additional 10 million tons of grain per year were exported from its New World zone – the Southern Producer Region (SPR) of Ukraine and the North Caucasus. In ECE the Danubian zone provided about 3 million tons of grain per year to its industrial and urban zones, as well as exporting 2.6 million tons per year to WCE.

World War I greatly disturbed these complex European supply patterns. The major problems emerged in the less developed parts of eastern Europe, in the Russian and Danubian regions. Despite the drama of the U-boat attacks on British shipping, which tends to attract most attention in the West, the most significant factors disturbing the pre-war pattern of supply were the disruption of Russian and Danubian grain exports, and the British naval blockade of enemy and occupied Europe. The United States and Argentina continued to supply grain to the neutral countries, but, even here, the British navy controlled the amount of grain going to these countries to ensure that there was no extra grain imported that could be transshipped to the Central Powers or to the countries occupied by them.

The supply of occupied areas presented particular problems in both the west and the east of Europe. In the west, Belgium, with a particularly large dependence on foreign overseas grain, presented the main problem when it was occupied and pillaged by the German army in the early stages of the war. On the Eastern Front, Russian troops occupied parts of Austrian Poland throughout the war and parts of Prussian Poland until 1915, when the Germans advanced to occupy the Russian Kingdom of Poland and large parts of Russia. Many of the formerly Austrian regions of Poland had previously received grain supplies from the Danube countries, which were now cut off, and it was likewise for the formerly Russian areas of Poland previously reliant on Russian grain. Overall, central

[2] UK 45 million, WCE 188 million, Western urban areas of ECE 36 million and NCR of Russia 33 million.

Europe probably gained from this situation. Danubian supplies flowed westwards rather than northwards into Russian-occupied Austrian Poland, or eastwards into the Black Sea. But the level of Danubian production declined sharply during the war.

Further south, Serbia, which had started the war, was occupied by the Austrians, and was also experiencing severe supply problems. And in the south-east the Ottoman Empire was also facing supply problems: bereft of Russian supplies, it was dependent on supplies from the Danube, Iraq, Iran and Syria. The latter three regions were soon engulfed in war, which hindered the amount of supplies getting through to Turkey.

The British attitude to the problems faced by civilians and neutrals, championed by First Lord of the Admiralty Winston Churchill, was that the blockade directed against the Central Powers should also include Belgium and Poland. It was argued that the German army had requisitioned as much food as it could, and that Germany should be held responsible for feeding the population that it occupied, rather than benefit from their food supplies (Beckett 2007: 367). The German government disputed this, and, in circumstances in which it was experiencing food shortages, was in no position to provide assistance to these occupied countries. The fate of the Belgians, the Poles and all occupied peoples looked grim.

In these dire circumstances the American businessman Herbert Hoover was invited to help the Belgians to escape from this predicament, and was successful in saving the Belgians from famine. He was able to persuade the British government to lift the food embargo on Belgium, on the grounds that US representatives would distribute the food delivered by American ships directly to Belgian children. At the same time he persuaded the German government not to requisition local grain and to let his representatives operate in Belgium to receive and deliver the food.[3] When the United States joined the war, in 1917, Hoover persuaded both sides to accept other neutral intermediaries, from Spain and Sweden, to replace the Americans. A similar scheme was proposed for the Kingdom of Poland, after the Russian retreat of 1915, when the Rockefeller Foundation had tried to provide relief, but in this case it proved impossible to get an agreement between British, Russian and German authorities that would allow American relief to be provided (see Rockefeller Foundation (1915: 300–85) and Gay and Fisher (1929: ch. 11)).

In his report to Woodrow Wilson on the success of his activities Hoover stated that a population of 7.5 million Belgians and 2.5 million French in

---

[3] For well-documented accounts of this extraordinary story, see Gay and Fisher (1929), Hoover (1951) and Lyons (1964).

occupied Belgium and northern France 'had been preserved. The population is undiminished in numbers.' He went on to explain (with some exaggeration) that '[t]he proof of necessity of the Commission lies in the parallel loss of 25 per cent to 50 per cent of the populations of Serbia and Poland, countries of larger proportionate agricultural resources but of no relief'.[4] Later, it could be argued, Hoover and the American Relief Administration (ARA) were going to play an even greater role in alleviating famine in central and eastern Europe and in Russia after the war.

Offer (1989) explains in some detail the development of German policy in regard to disrupting British food supplies, and how they came to make the fateful decision that brought the United States into the war by moving to unrestricted U-boat warfare in early 1917. The German navy persuaded the Kaiser and the German government that it would be able to starve Britain into surrender before the Americans could arrive. Although the German navy sank as much shipping as it had planned, Britain was easily able to survive, partly because the German naval claims had been excessive (Offer 1989: 361–2), but mainly because Britain was able to greatly increase its domestic production of grain in 1917.

Britain had greatly reduced its domestic sowings of grain after the repeal of the Corn Laws in 1846. In 1914 the tilled area at 7.7 million hectares was only 75 per cent of the 1873 level (10.4 million acres), but a combination of high prices and compulsory tillage drove it back to 10.4 million acres by 1918 (Murray 1955: 370). The yields on this semi-virgin pastureland were also fairly high, and so British domestic production of grain grew significantly.[5] By contrast, countries such as Germany, more self-sufficient in grain, were already sowing a large area and using a large amount of fertiliser to maintain high yields. They were unable to increase this area; instead, due to labour shortages, the sown area was greatly reduced. Furthermore, a large proportion of the fertilisers that had previously been used had been imported from Britain, and was no longer available. Domestic fertiliser production could not make up the loss since the nitrates and sulphates were diverted to munitions manufacturing. The result was a disastrous decline in local grain production (Table 11.1). The winter of 1916–17 was particularly bad, when the population of Germany and much of central east Europe had to survive on turnips and livestock feed (Woodward 2003: 29).

When the European governments concentrated their attention on directing scarce food resources to their armies and armaments

---

[4] See Commission for Relief in Belgium, Document no. 110, Hoover to Wilson, Washington, 21 October 1918, http://net.lib.byu.edu/estu/wwi/comment/CRB/CRB1-3b.htm.

[5] UK grain production rose from 5.2 million tons in 1914 to 6.8 million tons in 1918: Mitchell (1975: 266).

Table 11.1 *Grain production in the United Kingdom and Germany relative to 1914, 1913–19*

	1913	1914	1915	1916	1917	1918	1919
Germany	116	100	81	82	56	57	54
United Kingdom		100	100	93	100	131	106

manufacturers it was the civilian population that suffered. Hoover was correct when he argued that the blockade affected, above all, civilian women and children, because the governments would always ensure that the army and munitions workers would be well fed. But this civilian catastrophe was not necessarily without political effect. The civilian food crisis of February 1917 in Petrograd undoubtedly had great importance in setting in track the complex of developments that moved from the February to the October Revolution, the collapse of state power, the civil war and the famines that indisputably followed (see Chapter 10). And in Germany and Austria the terrible 'turnip winter' of 1916–17 did eventually lead into the great civil distress, revolution and food crisis of the immediate post-war period. But the extent to which this was famine remains controversial. The rationing system undoubtedly broke down as the blockade intensified after the armistice, and, as discussed below, there was a deadly four-month delay before relief was allowed to penetrate the blockade.

In addition to the diversion of food away from the civilian population in general, there were parts of the population that were singled out for special treatment. Almost all countries introduced special regulations for enemy aliens, which required at least registration, and often transfer to a controlled location or camp, where, in theory, they were to be provided for. Prisoners of war were also located in camps, where they were supposed to receive food and shelter. In most cases during World War I these basic provisions were met. But there were some countries where parts of the domestic population, which the government or the military commanders felt to be disloyal, were treated badly. Some were forcibly relocated to camps in other areas, and some of these relocation operations failed to provide adequate food and shelter for the expelled population. At least one of these operations appears to have descended into genocide.

The Temporary Law of Deportation (the Tehcir law) enacted on 29 May 1915 gave the Ottoman government and military authorities permission to deport anyone they considered to be a threat to national security. This legislation was quickly applied to the Armenian population, living in north-east Turkey, who were suspected of sympathy with Russia, and the entire Armenian population was forced into death marches into the Syrian desert. Most died of starvation on the way, or in isolated locations such as Deir ez-Zor. Other indigenous Christian groups, such as the Assyrians and Ottoman Greeks, were similarly targeted. The Russian army took a similarly motivated, but less deadly, action when it retreated from Galicia in September 1915, and forcibly dispossessed the local Jewish population, whom it accused of sympathy with the Germans. Mortality levels certainly increased, but in Russia the refugees were given aid (Stone 1975; Gatrell 1999; Akçam 2012).

Hoover and the Committee for Relief in Belgium were successful in relieving Belgium throughout World War I, but, as the United States entered the war and the war showed signs of coming to an end, it became clear to Hoover and President Wilson that significantly more aid would be needed after the war to avoid an immediate catastrophe. In April 1917 in Britain Sir George Paish was predicting massive famine unless the war ended and more grain was sown.[6] Hoover had a more realistic understanding of the great possibilities for American agriculture to expand to meet the growing needs of Europe, but he saw the problems to be in transporting the grain to Europe and in paying for it. In his memoirs Hoover (1951: 259) describes his fears in the early part of 1918 that the Allies would run out of grain, explaining: 'We [the Allied Food Council] quickly completed a survey of British, French, Italian, Belgian and neutral food needs for the forthcoming year [1918], the sources of available food supply and the available shipping to transport it. Our estimate for the allied civilians was 2 million tons a month of food, clothing and medical supplies.'

Hoover was confident that the United States and Canada could provide these supplies, but the problem was transport. The US military commander, General Pershing, needed shipping to bring in more American troops and their supplies. At first Pershing told Hoover that his supplies would have to be reduced to 1.2 million tons of shipping per month. But as the troop build-up began the military requirements for shipping were increased and the amount left for Hoover and civilian supply was reduced to a mere 700,000 tons per month – about one-third of the initially stated requirement. Hoover thought that he could manage the first reduction to 1.2 million tons per month if the Allies overdrew on their summer crops and animal feed consumption, but he argued that this

---

[6] Memorandum by Sir George Paish on 'The World Crisis' to the War Cabinet, 27 April 1917, the National Archives of the UK (TNA), CAB 24/14.

'would create a dangerous vacuum during the spring months' (Hoover 1951: 259–60). The additional reduction to 700,000 tons per month was unsustainable, however, in Hoover's view, and would have led the Allies into a major food crisis and famine had the war not been quickly terminated: 'Our salvation came from a quarter which we had hardly dared to consider. That was the American victories followed by the Armistice of November 1918, after which ships were available' (Hoover 1951: 260). Hoover's biographer, Eugene Lyons (1964: 112), then describes the situation at the end of the war:

Food reserves on the Continent were at vanishing point as the Armistice approached, with the next harvest ten months away. An exceptionally harsh winter blanketed Europe. Already starvation was reaping its own harvest of death and disease. In the eighteen enemy and liberated countries ten to twelve million children...were in a state of advanced undernourishment.

When Hoover arrived back in Europe to try to ameliorate the crisis he was surprised to discover that his British, French and Italian confreres didn't seem to be disturbed by this unfolding humanitarian disaster. While Hoover was anxious to get food into central and eastern Europe as soon as possible, they were determined to maintain the blockade until the peace treaty was signed. Part of the reason for this might well have been for humanitarian reasons to help the wretched civilian population, but there was also the case of large amounts of US agricultural produce accumulated in the docks that Hoover wanted to liquidate (Perren 2005: 226) and a fear of the spread of Communism among the famished population. In the end it took four months before Wilson and Hoover could get Lloyd George, Clemenceau and the Australian prime minister, William Hughes, to agree to lift the blockade on food, in March 1919.

The extent to which Germany, Austria, Poland, Hungary, Romania, Bulgaria and Yugoslavia and the Ottoman Empire experienced famine at this time remains unclear and is highly controversial. Offer (1989; but compare Howard 1993 and Cox 2015) claims that, although Germany faced real hunger, it 'did not really starve' and that its demographic data show a less serious situation than in France. He disputes the claims of German official sources that the blockade caused the deaths of 700,000 civilians. Winter, on the other hand, looking simply at the data for the city of Berlin, claims that there is a basis for arguing that there were 478,500 excess deaths, if the Berlin figures were extrapolated to cover all of Germany. However, he agrees that the standardised death rates for Berlin seemed to be lower than for Paris (Winter 1997: 494–7). The situations in central and eastern Europe, Russia and the Ottoman Empire were considerably worse than this.

In the former Ottoman Empire, apart from the hundreds of thousands of Armenians who died of starvation in 1916 on the roads towards Damascus or Deir ez-Zor, there are also reports of famine in Lebanon from 1915 to 1918 (Ghazai 2015). And after the war food shortages and disturbances continued, especially in Iran, where repeated military requisitioning and looting by Ottoman, Russian and British armies caused great suffering. The retreat of Ottoman and Russian armies in 1917 and 1918 was followed by a more systematic attempt by British military authorities to requisition food to supply the army of occupation in southern Russia and Baku. This appears to have completely destroyed the internal grain market in Iran and may have led to millions of deaths, albeit significantly fewer than the 9 million claimed by Majd (2003). Finally, there was very widespread and well-documented famine in Russia, beginning in the urban areas of the Northern Consumer Region in 1918–20, and spreading to the normal surplus-producing regions of the centre and south following the drought of 1921. This is discussed at length in Chapter 10.

1.2   Demographic Consequences Related to Food Shortages and Famine

There is an enormous variability in the quality and quantity of demographic data available for different regions in this period, and the main problem is that the worst-affected regions are generally those with the least reliable data. The United Kingdom and western continental Europe are fairly well covered, but the data for eastern continental Europe and Russia are usually far more problematic. In this analysis infant mortality indicators, when available, have been given most weight, as they are generally far more robust than other indicators.[7]

Data on infant mortality for the United Kingdom and Ireland show no significant signs of elevated mortality during the World War I period that would indicate famine. Crude death rate figures show a slight rise of mortality in 1915 and another in 1918, which extended through to 1919 in Ireland. However, the 1918 rise was undoubtedly a result of the Spanish flu pandemic, which affected older aged groups more than younger ones (Taubenberger and Morens 2006). The most significant increases in infant mortality in the early stages of the war occurred in Austria and Hungary (see Figure 11.1): 1915, 1916, 1917 and 1918 levels were all more than

---

[7] Infant mortality is an indicator of deaths of children aged up to one per thousand life births per year. It can be calculated solely from registration data and does not need to be deflated by a separate calculation of the population size. It is therefore more generally available, and is less likely to suffer from separate non-comparable indicators.

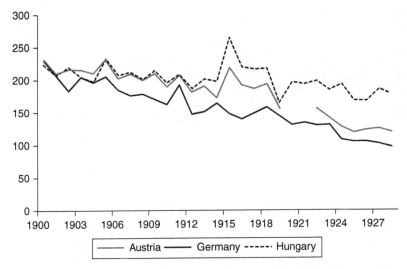

Figure 11.1 Infant mortality (per thousand births) in Germany, Austria and Hungary, 1900–28

10 per cent above the trend level, with 1915 up to 30 per cent above trend. Germany, by contrast, recorded levels that were below trend in 1915 and 1916 and rose only to 3 per cent above trend in 1917, 12 per cent in 1918 and 6 per cent in 1919. Belgium, which had been occupied by German forces but had been allowed to receive US aid, fared slightly better. It recorded levels of infant mortality that were only slightly above trend in 1914; exactly on trend in 1915; slightly below trend in 1916 (–16 per cent); then significantly above trend in 1917 and 1918 (+16 and +13 per cent, respectively); and, finally, significantly below trend in 1919 (–15 per cent). The dynamic of infant mortality was fairly similar in the unoccupied Netherlands, though it experienced a far less sharp decline in trend.

Figure 11.2 highlights the impact of war on the Western Front. The decline in French infant mortality failed to keep pace with that for England and Wales through the war and immediate post-war years, and, overall, there was a marked difference between the least affected countries (England and Wales and the Netherlands) and those more affected (France and Belgium).

In eastern continental Europe the generally available data sets[8] are far less complete for these years and data for the USSR, Poland and Romania are normally excluded. For Russia we have infant mortality

[8] Mitchell (1975: 127–34); and the 'Human Mortality' database (www.mortality.org).

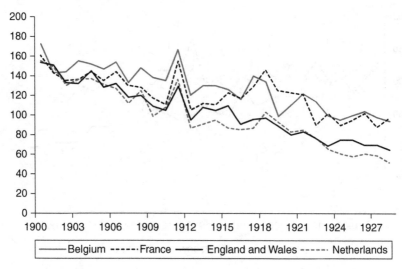

Figure 11.2 Infant mortality in England and Wales, France and the Low Countries, 1900–28

data for some cities, which show a very large rise in 1919 to above 300 per thousand, which was much higher than the Hungarian peak of 260 per thousand in the figure below (Figure 11.3).

Crude death rate data are also available for three major regions of Poland of this period: the Kingdom of Poland, with Warsaw in Russia; western Poland, including Poznan in Prussia; and Galicia, with Krakow and Lvov in Austria (Davies 1994: 104–8). All three regions show an increase in mortality in the war years, which extended into 1920. Available data for Russian cities show mortality peaks in 1919 that far exceeded the Spanish flu peaks of 1918 experienced in all countries (also see Chapter 10, Figure 10.4).

In sum, there are no indications of excess mortality from food shortages in the United Kingdom. There are some signs, albeit disputed, of excess mortality in Germany and Austria. There are signs of significant population losses in Poland, Serbia, Russia and the Ottoman Empire. Urban population indicators for Moscow, Petrograd and Saratov also show extremely high levels of mortality (see Chapter 10).

With regard to forced population relocations into food-strained areas, the Turkish relocation of its Armenian population in 1915 led to the death of as many as 1 million Armenians, many of whom would have died from famine. Losses in Poland and Serbia, though not quantifiable, were also very high. The level of excess mortality in Russia needs to be extended from the northern urban famine of 1918–20 to the southern

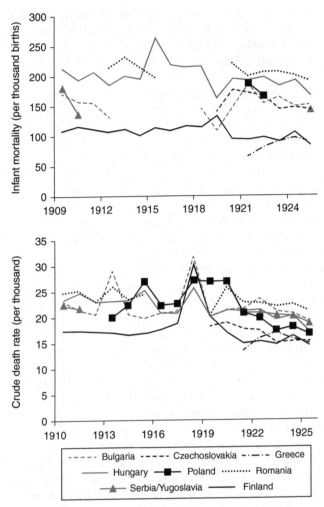

Figure 11.3 Mortality in eastern Europe, 1909–25

rural famine of 1921–22, and in both cases, and especially in the south, it covered much larger numbers.

2   World War II

2.1   Food Supplies

The major changes in food supplies from the eve of World War I to the eve of World War II were (1) that Europe had become even more industrialised and generally more dependent upon external grain; (2) that

Russia/USSR, which had supplied over a half of all grain surpluses before World War I, was now only covering its own requirements, with some small exports to Germany; and (3) that Germany had taken further steps to protect its own agriculture and to limit its external dependence on grain.

The United Kingdom remained the largest importer of grain. The requirements of western continental Europe had increased, especially in Belgium and the Netherlands, though Germany and Italy had both taken steps to try to reduce their dependence on external grain. In the USSR the Northern Consumer Region had become far more dependent on external supplies, but these were no longer provided by the Central Producer Region, which had itself become dependent on external supplies, so the surpluses were provided by regions to the south and east. Following the September 1939 Soviet–German trade agreement a few million tons of grain were exported to Germany in 1939–41, but there were no longer large amounts of grain to be exported.

As far as foodstuffs were concerned, the major difference in the nature of the war was on the Eastern Front. The initial alliance between Germany and the Soviet Union to some extent provided Germany with the additional food resources that it required. The breach of this alliance in June 1941 was followed by the German occupation of the food surplus areas of Ukraine and North Caucasus, and by the attempt to destroy the occupied Slavic and Jewish populations by starvation.

As had already happened during World War I, the U-boat blockade of Britain was unsuccessful, and the British blockade of occupied Europe fell most heavily on the occupied countries, which were being looted by the German army. In 1941 Greece was threatened by the same collateral damage as occurred in Belgium in 1914, and ultimately was relieved by the same kind of humanitarian operation, but only after suffering significant famine mortality (Hionidou 2006; Voglis 2006; Clogg 2008). Again Britain demonstrated the flexibility of being able to increase its domestic grain production by greatly expanding its sown area to levels only previously seen in 1873 and 1918. Germany, most of continental Europe and the Soviet Union lacked this ability, though allotments appeared in all towns.

Thanks to the early introduction of compulsory tillage, the increase in the acreage under grain in Britain in World War II was much more rapid than in World War I. It rose by 25 per cent in the first year of World War II, in comparison with only 5 per cent in World War I. In 1918 the area under grain was only 36 per cent above 1913 levels. In World War II grain sowings exceeded pre-war levels by 70 per cent in 1943 and 1944, and were reduced – somewhat prematurely, as it turned out – to 58 per cent

Table 11.2 *Grain production in the United Kingdom and Germany relative to 1939, 1873–1945*

Year	1873	1914	1939	1940	1941	1942	1943	1944	1945
United Kingdom									
Sown area	173	131	100	125	147	156	172	171	158
Production			100	123	139	167	181	175	167
Germany									
Production		127	100	86	86	84	87	78	

Notes: UK figures exclude Eire. German 1914 grain production figure refers to 1913.
Sources: Murray (1955: 371) for UK sown area; Mitchell (1975: 254, 266) for UK and German and grain production.

above 1939 levels in 1945. The growth of grain production in the United Kingdom again contrasted sharply with what happened in western continental Europe, where there was a decline in production in most regions, and particularly in Germany. Germany did, however, reduce its deficits by forcing contributions from WCE, ECE and the occupied USSR.

The food situation in ECE and the occupied USSR was extremely bad, as these territories experienced both large decreases in production and very severe policies of extracting food, which alternated between extreme and genocidal. Some Reichskommissars and military commanders of occupied territories were apparently still behaving with a degree of restraint in trying to preserve the population under their control. But they received short shrift from Goering:

> For God's sake, you haven't been sent there to work for the well-being of the peoples entrusted to you, but to get hold of as much as you can for the German people. I expect you to devote your energies to that. This continual concern for aliens must come to an end once and for all... I could not care less when you say that people under your administration are dying of hunger. Let them perish so long as no German starves.

(Mazower 1993)

The most serious famines again occurred in the east, where the German army was in any case prepared to implement the Hunger Plan, which, as promoted by Herbert Backe, involved the diversion of Ukrainian and North Caucasus grain surpluses away from the towns of the Northern Consumer Region of the USSR to support the urban population in the Reich and Fortress Europe. This would inevitably lead to the starvation and collapse of the northern towns. The unwanted Slavic population of these areas designated for German colonisation was considered to be redundant, and would either be relocated east of the Urals or would die from starvation.

No towns would be needed in the occupied areas, just a small population of slaves to run the local farms, until German colonists could take over. This policy was effectively put in place in the occupied areas, where the local population was systematically starved (Berkhoff 2004; Collingham 2011).

German policy in the west was normally not as harsh. As we will see below, foreign aid was eventually allowed for the Greek population following the German occupation of Greece in May 1941. The main exception in the west was with the Jews, who were identified as an alien population, eventually associated with Soviet Communism, and they were systematically transferred to the hungry and violent lands of the east, where they were starved and killed together with east European Jews and Slavs.

Western relief was eventually allowed for Greece, following the precedent set by Belgium in World War I. Following Italy's failed invasion of Greece in October 1940, Germany, with little preparation, came to the assistance of its ally in April 1941, and conquered all of Greece by June 1941. The German, Italian and Bulgarian armies fed off the land, which in any case was deficient in basic foodstuffs and dependent on trading olives and fish produce to import one-third of the grain that it consumed. A British embargo on occupied Greece contributed to the severe food shortage of 1941–42, in which 40,000 people are estimated to have died in the Athens–Piraeus area and as many as 300,000 in the country as a whole (Voglis 2006).

Little aid or relief could be provided to Jewish or Slavic groups in the east. In the final stages of the war, with the delayed liberation of the Netherlands, another famine developed in the west Netherlands in the winter of 1944–45 (van der Zee 1998). Part of the problem here was the deliberate sabotage of the Dutch rail network in anticipation of imminent liberation. The problem of whether the Dutch resistance could have done more to get the rails restored to help relief supplies is still a controversial topic. Some food supplies were parachuted into the country, but, generally, relief from famine came only with the liberation of the country in May 1945.

In the changed circumstances after the war Britain tried to maintain its predominant position. If Winston Churchill, Britain's wartime prime minister, and Franklin Roosevelt, US president till he died in April 1945, had still been in control, the old wartime alliance might have counted for more. But in the changed political circumstances (the Labour Party, led by Clement Attlee, won the British general election of July 1945 by a landslide and Harry Truman became US president on Roosevelt's death) the United States quickly realised that it was not necessarily in its interests to preserve British supremacy in Europe and the world. Initially the idea of a Carthaginian peace, associated with US Secretary of the Treasury Henry Morgenthau, continued to hold sway, and it seemed as though there might be a continuation of wartime priorities, with old military allies such as Britain and her dependencies being favoured above the old enemies of Germany, Austria, Bulgaria and Japan, but this was soon to change. The privileged position of the USSR in receiving US aid changed in 1945 almost as soon as the fighting had stopped. This was not helped by Stalin's secrecy over his supply situation, which tended to make both the British and the Americans think that he might have reserves available to export.

In February 1945 the British minister of food notified the British War Cabinet: 'The year 1945 will be a critical year for the world in food.' But he was mainly worried about meat, canned fish, fats, sugar and dairy produce. He stated, inaccurately, 'Of the chief foods only wheat will be available in abundance.'[9] Realisation that there would also be a serious grain problem came later.

In a memorandum to the British Cabinet of 27 December 1945, the Ministry of Food warned: 'Requirements of importing countries for 6 months July–December 1945 will substantially be met but for the next 6 months January–June 1946 there will be a deficit of 7 million tons of grain with 11.7 to 12.3 million tons of wheat & flour (in wheat equivalent) available with stated import requirements of 19 million tons.'

The British ministry complained that the Combined Food Board was failing to make the appropriate cuts to bring demand in line with supply, and it therefore made its own recommendations. However, the British-recommended cuts would have resulted in the allocations to the United Kingdom being reduced by a considerably smaller proportion than for those for other regions. The earliest draft seems to have envisaged a drop of only 3 per cent for the United Kingdom and of 13 per cent for the London Food Committee group of regions (which covered a wide range of British Commonwealth and other dependencies), when total allocations were almost halved. Later drafts were more realistic, envisaging a fall of 18 per cent for the United Kingdom, from 2.57 to 2.1 million tons, and by only 11 per cent for the whole London Food Committee group, from 4.6 to 3.1 million tons.[10] Meanwhile, proposed allocations for all

---

[9] War Cabinet papers, 28 February 1945, W.P. (45) 109, p. 77.
[10] The allocation to India would eventually be increased, narrowly avoiding a reappearance of the 1943 Bengal famine there. By January 1946 the gap still appeared to be about 5 million tons (TNA, War Cabinet papers, 31 January 1946, C.M. (46) Cabinet 10 Conclusions, p. 70).

other areas would fall by considerably more. The initial British proposal was for Germany and Austria to be reduced from 2.6 million tons to a mere 72,000 tons, and the countries receiving UNRRA aid (a group that included Italy, Greece, Yugoslavia, Poland, Czechoslovakia, Albania, Austria and China) from 3 million tons to 1.3 million tons.

On their food missions to Washington, Ernest Bevin, British foreign secretary, and Sir Ben Smith, minister of food, appeared initially to get Truman's acceptance for deflecting much of the impact of the shortage onto Germany and Austria, where they expected famine to occur.

The areas that will suffer most from the proposed allocation will be UK, US & French Zones of Germany and Austria and the UNRRA countries... So far as Germany and Austria are concerned the cut will be severe...of the 2,525,000 tons required the maximum wheat that can be made available is 1,490,000 tons... *The President and I both recognize that this will mean famine conditions and serious privation but more wheat cannot be found. It will be for the military commanders to consult and decide how best the available supplies can be used by making pro rata reductions for their respective areas.*[11]

The Americans initially agreed with these British proposals, when the Morgenthau plan was in favour, but then their own military commanders protested about the proposal that they preside over mass starvation, and insisted for security reasons that their areas be better fed. At the Combined Food Board[12] meeting in Washington, Smith's statement that Germany and Japan should be put on a diet of 1,000 calories a day is believed to have won considerable support, but the US military authorities appear to have clung to their own estimate that 1,500 calories a day were necessary to prevent 'disease and unrest' (Bullen and Pelly 1999: 197). Attlee wrote directly to Truman asking the Americans to share part of the burden to help out the situation in Asia, concluding gloomily that a period of 'great strain and hardship' was in store before the next harvest: 'I fear that thousands may die of starvation and many more thousands may suffer severely from hunger.'[13]

---

[11] Bullen and Pelly (1987: 29–34, emphasis added), British Foreign Mission (Washington) to Mr Bevin (received 11 January 1946 at 12:00 p.m.). Footnote 14 on p. 32 notes that the United Kingdom would be suffering a 9 per cent reduction, as opposed to 30 per cent for UNRRA countries and over 40 per cent for Germany and Austria.

[12] The Combined Food Board was set up by Roosevelt and Churchill in 1942 to allocate the combined food resources of the United States and Britain. In November 1942 Canada became a board member. Later, in 1946, it was expanded to become the International Emergency Food Council.

[13] Bevin to Halifax, 4 February 1946, containing text of telegram from Attlee to Truman, 4 February 1946, ibid., pp. 82–4. Ernest Bevin was British foreign secretary from 1945 to 1951, and Lord Halifax, foreign secretary from 1938 to 1940, was British ambassador to Washington from 1941 to 1946.

This initial agreement between the British and the Americans, that the Germans should be the last in line when it came to receiving relief, soon changed, and decisions about the receipt of American relief began to fall in line with US strategic interests. The Americans began to favour areas under their own control, with the result that areas not under US administration began to suffer. In the last quarter of 1946, of the 565,000 tons of US grain that were allocated for Germany, the US Zone received 425,000, while the British Zone, which was arguably more dependent on external grain supplies, received only 140,000 tons. On 29 October 1946 Air Marshal Sir Sholto Douglas, head of the Control Commission for the British Zone in Germany, wrote to his superiors warning that the continued 'prolonged semi-starvation' of the population of the UK Zone would lead to consequences. To avoid such consequences the British government sought to combine the British and US Zones of Germany, so that areas for which they were in control would receive the same treatment.

Because the Americans held most of the resources their decisions ultimately became the most important. The US population was encouraged to be frugal, but there was to be no real control or rationing of US consumption. During the war Britain had been the gateway for all US and Canadian supplies, but after the war it would lose this privileged position, and it was forced to reduce its reserves and introduce grain rationing – something that it had always previously avoided.[14] US commanders in Germany and Japan argued that, to maintain security, they needed to ensure that the populations for whom they were responsible were well fed. In the end 1947 was a hungry year all over Europe and Asia, and famine was diverted from Germany and Japan, which received US protection, and instead occurred in the relatively unprotected populations of eastern Europe, Romania, Moldova, western Ukraine and Belarus (Ellman 2000; Wheatcroft 2012; Slaveski 2013).

The USSR received Lend-Lease aid during the war, including some high-nutrient foodstuffs (mainly canned meat), which was of particular value for military personnel, but insufficient to make a major difference to civilian supply. At first, in 1945 and early 1946, there was little appreciation in the West of food shortages in the USSR, to the point that in early 1946 Attlee was requesting Truman to use his good services to see if Britain could receive Soviet grain exports.

---

[14] Throughout World Wars I and II bread was not rationed, but meat, dairy produce, sugar and other more expensive foods were. Bread rationing was introduced only in July 1946 (Collingham 2011: 472).

2.2   Demographic Consequences Related to Food Shortage and Famine

In the 20 years between the end of World War I and the beginning of World War II overall mortality levels had fallen considerably in all parts of Europe. Normal infant mortality rates – a sensitive barometer of health, on which data are widely available – were now less than 100 per thousand births in the United Kingdom and western continental Europe, instead of up to 200 per thousand, and they were below 200 per thousand in eastern continental Europe, instead of below 300 per thousand. Crude death rates in all of Europe were below 20 per thousand on the eve of World War II, instead of below 25 on the eve of World War I. Again, there is a very sharp difference between the way that the war was experienced in the United Kingdom and Ireland in comparison with WCE, and even more of a difference between WCE, ECE and the USSR.

The United Kingdom experienced an initial increase in infant mortality in 1939–41, but then a fairly major decrease, which is often attributed to the greater availability of milk for pregnant women and infants (Collingham 2011: 395–9). Ireland experienced an increase until 1943 and then a decline. Crude death rates in the United Kingdom and Ireland tended to follow the trend of infant mortality. Infant mortality in western Europe followed a very different path, with a major leap upwards in 1945. In the Netherlands this is associated with the food problems and famine that we described above. Similar sudden elevations in infant mortality in France and Belgium, and even higher levels for Austria, must reflect the less familiar but very difficult supply situation in the months following liberation. Figures for the different parts of Germany are not readily available, but we would expect them and other regions in central and eastern Europe to have been facing similar problems.

Further east, data are less reliable (Figure 11.4). Infant mortality rates were clearly higher, however. In Romania the rate oscillated between 160 and 180 per thousand births, and rose to a peak of 200 in 1947. As we will see below, this is compatible with the 1946–47 famine in Moldova. Hungary, Czechoslovakia and Bulgaria all tended to peak earlier, in 1945, in a similar pattern to WCE. Crude death rates were high in Greece in 1941 and 1942, and in Bulgaria in 1943 and 1944. They peaked in Hungary and Czechoslovakia in 1945 and, again, Romania suffered a much-delayed peak in 1947. Poland, the worst-affected region throughout this period, is very poorly covered by statistics before 1948.

The desperate situation in the USSR in this period has been discussed in some detail in Chapter 10. Here, we need to add that the history of the occupied parts of the USSR was similar to, though probably slightly worse than, that in other parts of occupied eastern continental Europe,

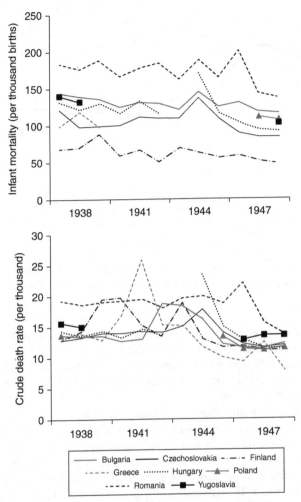

Figure 11.4 Mortality in eastern Europe, 1938–49

but the situation in besieged Leningrad was considerably worse. It was more comparable with the Warsaw Ghetto, but on a larger scale.

In besieged Leningrad the blockade lasted for 872 days, from 18 September 1941 to 27 January 1944, during which time up to 1.5 million people died, mainly from starvation. The population fell from 2.8 million on 1 June 1941 to 1 million on 1 January 1942 and to 641,000 on 1 January 1943. It is possible to make a monthly estimate of increased mortality and decreased natality over this period, but because of the scale

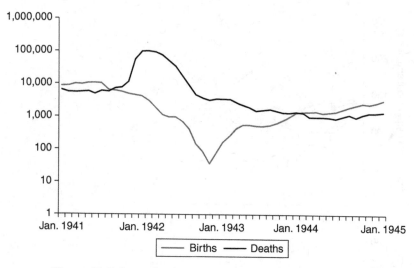

Figure 11.5 Annualised monthly births and deaths in Leningrad per thousand of the population (logarithmic values), January 1941–January 1945

of these indicators they need to be presented on a logarithmic graph to capture the overall pattern (Figure 11.5). At the peak, in January and February 1942, almost 100,000 people were dying monthly, with 2,734 dying suddenly (*skoropostizhno*) on the streets in January and 2,105 in February (Lomagin 2002: II, 300).

The situation in Moldova and the western parts of Ukraine in 1946–47 was also strikingly different from and worse than anywhere else in Europe at that time. The situation in Romania is the only part of Europe that may have come close to it. The problem in these regions was the double impact of a general food shortage combined with a very severe drought (Wheatcroft 2012). In Moldova grain production in 1946 was very low. According to official harvest reports, grain production in the Moldavian Soviet Socialist Republic fell from 1.81 million tons in 1940 to 1.06 million tons in 1941, and to 0.99 million tons in 1945. It was planned to be increased to 1.65 million tons in 1946, with a yield of 10.5 *tsentners* (= 100 kg) per hectare, but instead it plummeted to a disastrous 0.38 million tons, with a yield of just 2.4 *tsentners* per hectare (RGAE 1562/324/5299, ll. 10, 12, 178, 184–5). In per capita terms this meant a reduction from 0.78 tons per head in 1940 to 0.49 tons per head in 1945, a plan to return to 0.78 tons per head in 1946, but instead a level of production of 0.18 tons per head – about a half of the per capita food consumption level.

Table 11.3 *Grain balance in Moldova, in million tons, millions of population and tons per head per year, 1945–47*

Year	Population	Grain production	Per capita	Exports	Net	Net per capita
1945	2.02	0.99	0.49	0.16	0.83	0.41
1946	2.10	0.38	0.18	−0.09	0.48	0.23
1947	2.17	1.49	0.69	−0.20	1.68	0.78

Sources: See production figures given above. Collections data from *Golod v Moldovii*; transportation data from RGAE 1562/329/4571.

State procurements had initially been set at 0.279 million tons in 1945 but only 0.176 million tons were collected. They were further reduced to 0.165 million tons for 1946, but with the disastrous harvest almost nothing was collected and 93 thousand tons were imported in calendar year 1946, with an additional 196 thousand tons in calendar year 1947 (of course, both these sums really refer to the single agricultural crop year of 1946–47). The extent to which grain transportation affected overall availability in Moldova is indicated in Table 11.3. The additional shipping of 0.29 million tons of grain in 1946–47 may have slightly alleviated a desperate situation, but it was clearly insufficient to stop the tragedy from unfolding.

Mortality and infant mortality rates in Moldova reached very high levels. Mortality peaked at an annualised rate of about 160 per thousand in February, March and June in 1947, and was much higher than in the epidemic crisis of early 1945. The infant mortality data also show two peaks, in February and July 1947, but they were lower than the epidemic peak in March 1945.

During the famine of 1946–47 the level of epidemic illness in Moldova was reported to have been very low, but it is significant that this region had previously, immediately after liberation in 1944–45, experienced the worst pandemics endured in the USSR at this time. The morbidity statistics show that these pandemics did not return in 1946–47, but it is possible that they had weakened the ability of the population to withstand the immediate ordeal of famine.

Among the Jewish and Slavic populations that experienced German occupation there were mass executions and attempted genocide. In many cases famine was an integral component of these genocides. It is difficult, if not impossible, to identify the extent of famine in genocide, but it is necessary to point out that it was a component.

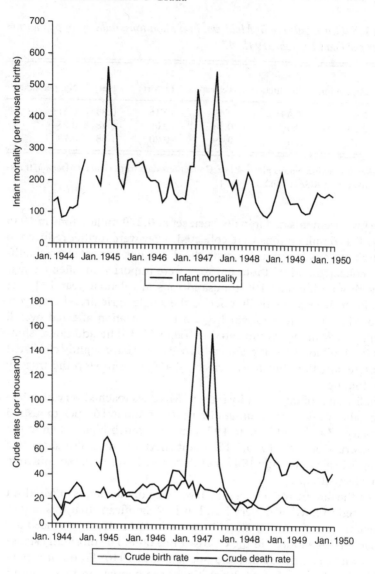

Figure 11.6 Mortality in Moldova, January 1944–January 1950

Again, there are no signs of excess mortality in the United Kingdom, and infant health may well have improved as a consequence of improved rationed supplies of milk to infants. Within WCE there are few signs of excess mortality until the outbreak of famine in the western Netherlands in late 1944–45. During the war Germany did not experience food shortages on the scale of World War I. In ECE the situation was significantly worse, with famine in Greece in the early years of the war (1941–42), and famine was constantly present in occupied areas of Poland, Ukraine, Belorussia and Russia, where it was part of the genocidal policies being applied. There were also isolated cases of famine in other areas of the USSR in 1942, and a very severe famine in besieged Leningrad, as mentioned above. The forcible relocation of Jews from western as well as eastern Europe, and their concentration in poorly supplied locations, contributed to the mass killing and genocide of the Jews. Soviet prisoners of war were also starved to death.

Following the war, food supplies throughout Europe deteriorated. In the United Kingdom and western continental Europe this was accompanied by effective rationing (the first time that bread had been rationed in the United Kingdom), which largely limited the mortal consequences of the food crisis. Good health provisions also contributed to this benign outcome. In eastern Europe the situation was worse, and it was particularly bad in Romania, Moldova and western Ukraine.

3   Famine and the Foetal Origins Hypothesis

It was inevitable that famines, as a form of 'natural experiment', would attract interest as a testing ground for the foetal origins hypothesis (FOH) – i.e. the claim that foetal and early childhood nutrition are linked to adult health, variously defined. Thanks in part to the insight of two South African epidemiologists, the so-called Dutch *Hongerwinter* (Hunger Winter) is the *locus classicus* for famine-related research on the link between foetal exposure to malnutrition, on the one hand, and adult health and disease susceptibility, on the other. The Dutch famine is far better documented and more extensively researched than any other historical episode employed as a 'natural experiment'. Even allowing for the broad interest in the FOH, the extent of the specialist literature based on the *Hongerwinter* is extraordinary.

Research using famines as testing grounds for the FOH has since spread globally. The long-term consequences of being born towards the end of World War II, or in its wake, have been the focus of particular attention. These studies have investigated health (physical and mental), education and employment outcomes; all claim to have identified a long-run impact of famine.

Some of this research is inspired by the pioneering work of David Barker and his collaborators (Barker et al. 1989; Barker 1995). They initially highlighted the foetal origins of heart disease later in life. The story of an alternative or complementary link – that between foetal origins and cognitive development – began in the early 1970s with the publication of work by the South-Africa-born husband-and-wife team of Zena Stein and Ezra Susser. In 1967 Stein and Susser had the bright idea that the subjects of Clarence Smith's analysis of foetal growth during the Dutch *Hongerwinter* of 1944–45 (Smith 1947) would by then have reached adulthood. In this way, a 'small' famine in the western Netherlands in 1944–45 gave rise to an influential literature on the foetal origins hypothesis, which continues to expand.

The Dutch famine struck towards the end of World War II, when access to outside food supplies in the German-occupied, heavily urbanised western Netherlands was severely restricted for several months (Banning 1946; Dols and van Arcken 1946; Sellin 1946; Smith 1947; Hart 1993; Trienekens 2000). There is some slight ambiguity about precisely how long the accompanying famine lasted, but Figure 11.7, based on data in Stein et al. (1975: 244–6), tracks birth weights by month and offers quite a precise guide to the famine's duration and intensity.

Although mortality was already rising before the famine, which makes estimating excess mortality tricky, it is likely that the famine resulted in about 20,000 excess deaths in a population of 4.5 million. Age and gender were better predictors of death during the famine than socio-economic class. Thus in The Hague, for example, nearly four-fifths of all deaths from malnutrition in the first half of 1945 were of people aged 55 years and above. Those aged 20–39 years accounted for less than 4 per cent of the total (Banning 1946). This must not be taken as evidence that the elderly suffered relatively more; the contrary is true, since they were also more vulnerable in non-crisis years.

Moreover, nearly two-thirds of those who died in The Hague at the famine's peak during the first three months of 1945 were male. The gender gap in mortality was much greater than usual during famines. The wartime context must partly account for the marked male disadvantage. There was a class aspect to the famine too; in The Hague the female share of deaths was 31.5 per cent in working-class households, 40.2 per cent in middle-class households and 46.8 per cent in the relatively small number of upper-class households. Those who suffered most, relatively speaking, were prime-age males from working-class households. Deaths in working-class households were also more likely to be from malnutrition, though the share of all deaths in The Hague due to malnutrition was also significant in middle-class households, reaching two-fifths at the peak in April (Banning 1946; 'Human mortality' database).

Food ration entitlements before and during the Hunger Winter are well documented, but a shortcoming of Dutch research on the FOH is

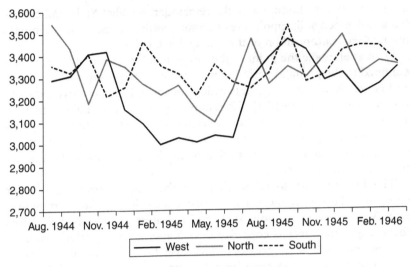

Figure 11.7 Birth weight by month, 1944–46

that individual-level consumption levels at different stages of the famine
are not. That the average mother was malnourished may be inferred by
the low weights of full-term births during the famine but there is no hard
evidence on how badly off individual mothers were. This is a quite serious but unavoidable shortcoming of the Dutch studies. As Lumey and
van Poppel (2010) complain, it is 'difficult' to establish the validity of
such self-recall measures of individual-level nutrition, but they are a key
feature of other studies described later.

The Susser–Stein project yielded its first fruits in 1972, and the
much-cited *Famine and Human Development: The Dutch Hunger Winter
of 1944–1945* followed in 1975. These works compare measures of cognitive development for Dutch conscripts exposed to famine *in utero* to
conscripts born before and after the famine and to conscripts born in
non-famine regions of the Netherlands. *Famine and Human Development*
concludes with an acceptance that 'poor prenatal nutrition cannot be
considered a factor in the social distribution of mental competence
among surviving adults in industrial societies' (Stein et al. 1975: 236), an
outcome that Stein et al. describe as 'negative'. But they attribute their
finding that 18-year-old army recruits conceived during the famine were
more intelligent than both recruits from non-famine areas and recruits
born just before and after the famine in the affected area to selection
bias. This was because more resilient and better-resourced households,
whose children were on average brighter, experienced less of a fertility

decline during the famine than the remainder. So what Stein and Susser initially deemed a disappointing outcome was due to the famine's impact on the social composition of the famine birth cohort.

Stein et al. make the point at the outset that '[n]utritional deprivation confined to the prenatal period may be too brief to produce much effect' and conclude that 'post-natal learning [might be] an attractive explanation for a great part of [the] differences among social strata' (Stein et al. 1975: 236). However, the short duration of the Dutch famine is critical for research purposes, because it permits analysis of the impact of exposure by trimester, a feature that research on the Hunger Winter has focused on from the start.

The literature on foetal origins and the Dutch famine is by now enormous. However, the list of robust conclusions is not commensurate. A recent, very cautious survey of the literature rejects claims that foetal exposure affected cognitive development; self-reported health or depression; and blood pressure. The case for coronary heart disease is also 'inconclusive', having been 'reported for only one of the birth cohort studies for the Netherlands' (Lumey, Stein and Susser 2011). But claims linking foetal origins with height, diabetes and schizophrenia are more robust (Lumey and van Poppel 2013). In addition, Heijmans et al. (2008) and Tobi et al. (2009) found that foetuses exposed to famine early in pregnancy had lower rates of DNA methylation – a biochemical process that is important in the development of most kinds of cancer – than their same-sex siblings. There is also a case for likely epigenetic effects, first proposed by Lumey and Stein (1997), whose comparison of birth weights of siblings born to mothers exposed (or not) during the Hunger Winter led them to speculate that there might be 'long-term biological effects, even into the next generation, of maternal intrauterine nutrition, which do not correspond to the effects on the mothers' own birthweights'.

In their study of the siege of Leningrad (1941–44) Stanner and Yudkin (2001) failed to find any effect on glucose tolerance, blood pressure or insulin concentration, but they claimed to have found evidence of endothelial dysfunction (which precedes atherosclerosis) and a 'stronger interaction between adult obesity and blood pressure' (compare Vågerö et al. 2013 and Kozlov and Samsonova 2005).

Juerges (2013) has invoked 1970 West German census data to show that men and women born between November 1945 and May 1946 had 'significantly and substantially lower educational attainment and occupational status than cohorts born shortly before or after'. He deems this a confirmation of the FOH, and invokes Austrian data to corroborate. A study of the long-run impact of early life exposure to the Greek famine of 1941–42 also claims that exposure exacted an educational penalty, which was worse in urban than in rural areas, and more extreme for those aged up to one year than either those *in utero* or aged one year at the height of the famine (Neelson and Stratmann 2011).

Two recent studies take a multi-country approach to the impact of World War II, using the retrospective Survey on Health, Aging, and Retirement in Europe (SHARE). Kesternich et al. (2014) have identified a link between exposure to war in 1939–45 and the likelihood of heart disease, diabetes, depression and health generally. In the most extensive study so far on the impact of twentieth-century wars on adult health outcomes, Havari and Peracchi (2014) also show that living in a war zone during childhood or adolescence in 1939–45 was linked to worse physical and mental health in later life. They too found an impact on life satisfaction, though not on happiness. Living in a war zone impacted more strongly on females than on males in these respects, and the impact also increased with the length of the exposure. In an attempt to identify the pathways to these adverse outcomes, Kesternich et al. found that hunger, persecution, dispossession and an absent father had strong explanatory power.

To summarise: research on the Dutch *Hongerwinter* has moved from the 'not proven' verdict of those who were first to invoke it in the early 1970s, through a growing number of competing and conflicting claims by rival medical researchers, to the tempered understanding represented by Lumey and van Poppel (2013), which highlights both the limitations of famines as natural experiments and the robustness of a small number of findings. The databases underpinning recent research by economists, who tend to be more sensitive to selection issues, broadly corroborate, while devoting particular attention to the impact of health insults *in utero* or in early childhood on economic well-being in adulthood.

4   General Conclusions

Although famines had largely disappeared in Europe by the late nineteenth century, the exceptional circumstances of modern total war, with deliberate attempts to disrupt food supplies, and to place parts of the population in less well provided circumstances, contributed to the re-emergence of major famines during both World War I and World War II. Because the victors had appeared to be most vulnerable to disruptions of food supply, and because they had been able to overcome this vulnerability, there has been a tendency to underestimate the significance of the possible damage (direct and collateral) caused by the difficult food situation elsewhere. The levels of famine experienced in eastern Europe and in Russia/USSR in these periods were quite significant and need to be recognised as some of the consequences of these wars.

The chapter has highlighted the importance of both international aspects of food supply to Europe in these years and of intra-regional aspects of food distribution within individual European states. The major problem, as seen by the state, was the concern with supplying the non-food-producing groups, and especially the army. Farmers in western Europe tended to be better fed than urban non-food producers. This is because they retained control over much of their produce, some of which entered the black market at very high prices. But the situation in eastern Europe was very different. There the controls over the peasant producers were much greater, and the rural peasantry often suffered more than the ration-protected urban population. Worst of all, of course, were the non-rationed non-food producers, whose exchange entitlements to food were the lowest.

It should also be realised that, even in the West, the threat of massive continental mortality caused by food shortages was only narrowly averted by an unusually active international aid policy. At the time, both in 1919 and 1946, Hoover complained that politicians were ignoring the largest threat to European health and security in centuries. It is to be hoped that historians will not continue to act in a similar way.

Bibliography

Aakjaer, S. 1936. 'Maal, vaegt og taxter i Danmark', in *Nordisk Kultur 30: Mått och vikt*. Stockholm: Albert Bonniers Förlag.

Aaraas, O. 1978. 'Befolkningskrisa i Norge 1770–74: sult eller sykdom?', PhD thesis: University of Bergen.

Abel, W. 1935. *Agrarkrisen und Agrarkonjunktur in Mitteleuropa vom 13. bis zum 19. Jahrhundert*. Berlin: Parey.

1974. *Massenarmut und Hungerkrisen im vorindustriellen Europa: Versuch einer Synopsis*. Berlin: Parey.

Aberth, J. 2013. *From the Brink of the Apocalypse: Confronting Famine, War, Plague and Death in the Later Middle Ages*, 2nd edn. London: Routledge.

Abildgren, K. 2010. 'Consumer prices in Denmark 1502–2007'. *Scandinavian Economic History Review* 58: 2–24.

Acemoglu, D., Johnson, S., and Robinson, J. A. 2001. 'The colonial origins of comparative development: an empirical investigation'. *American Economic Review* 91: 1369–401.

Adamets, S. 2002. 'Famine in nineteenth- and twentieth-century Russia: mortality by age, cause, and gender', in Dyson, T., and Ó Gráda, C. (eds.). *Famine Demography: Perspectives from the Past and Present*. Oxford: Oxford University Press, pp. 158–80.

Akçam, T. 2012. *The Young Turks' Crime against Humanity: The Armenian Genocide and Ethnic Cleansing in the Ottoman Empire*. Princeton, NJ: Princeton University Press.

Alfani, G. 2007. 'Population and environment in northern Italy during the XVIth century'. *Population* 4: 1–37.

2010. 'Climate, population and famine in northern Italy: general tendencies and Malthusian crisis, ca. 1450–1800'. *Annales de Démographie Historique* 120: 23–53.

2011. 'The famine of the 1590s in Northern Italy: an analysis of the greatest "system shock" of the sixteenth century'. *Histoire et Mesure* 26: 17–49.

2012. 'Ambiente fisico, colture, insediamento e reti socio-economiche: il case study del Canavese sul lunghissimo periodo', in Alfani, G., Di Tullio, M., and Mocarelli, L. (eds.). *Storia economica e ambiente italiano (ca. 1400–1850)*. Milan: Franco Angeli, pp. 168–87.

2013a. *Calamities and the Economy in Renaissance Italy: The Grand Tour of the Horsemen of the Apocalypse*. Basingstoke: Palgrave.

2013b. 'Plague in seventeenth century Europe and the decline of Italy: an epidemiological hypothesis'. *European Review of Economic History* 17: 408–30.

2013c. 'Population dynamics, Malthusian crises and Boserupian innovation in pre-industrial societies: the case study of Northern Italy (ca. 1450–1800) in the light of Lee's "dynamic synthesis"', in Malanima, P., and Chiarini, B. (eds.). *From Malthus's Stagnation to Sustained Growth*. Basingstoke: Palgrave, pp. 18–51.

2015. 'Famines in late medieval and early modern Italy: a test for an advanced economy', Working Paper no. 82. Milan: Dondena Centre for Research on Social Dynamics and Public Policy, Bocconi University.

Alfani, G., Dalla Zuanna, G., and Rosina, A. 2009. 'Introduzione: differenze demografiche all'alba dell'era moderna'. *Popolazione e Storia* 10: 9–17.

Alfani, G., and Melegaro, A. 2010. *Pandemie d'Italia: dalla peste nera all'influenza suina: l'impatto sulla società*. Milan: Egea.

Alfani, G., and Rizzo, M. 2013. 'Politiche annonarie, provvedimenti demografici e capitale umano nelle città assediate dell'Europa moderna', in *Nella morsa della guerra: Assedi, occupazioni militari e saccheggi in età preindustriale*. Milan: Franco Angeli, pp. 15–45.

Alifano, E. 1996. *Il grano e la politica annonaria a Napoli nel settecento*. Naples: Edizioni Scientifiche Italiane.

Allen, R. C. 2001. 'The great divergence in European wages and prices from the Middle Ages to the first World War'. *Explorations in Economic History* 38: 411–47.

Allen, R. C., Bassino J.-P., Debin, M., Moll-Murata, C., and van Zanden, J. L. 2011. 'Wages, prices, and living standards in China, 1738–1925: in comparison with Europe, Japan, and India'. *Economic History Review* 64: 8–38.

Anbinder, T., and McCaffrey, H. 2015. 'Which Irish men and women immigrated to the United States during the Great Famine migration of 1846–54?'. *Irish Historical Studies* 39: 620–42.

Andræ, C. G. 1967. 'Nödår', in *Kulturhistoriskt lexikon för Nordisk medeltid*, vol. XII. Malmö: Allhems Förlag, pp. 467–8.

Andreev, E. M., Darskii, L. E., and Kharkova, T. L. 1990. *Istoriya naseleniya SSSR 1920–1959gg*. Moscow: Goskomstat.

1998. *Demograficheskaya istoriya Rossii: 1927–1959*. Moscow: Goskomstat.

Anes, G. 1968. 'Los pósitos en la España del siglo XVIII'. *Moneda y Crédito* 105: 39–69.

1970a. *Las crisis agrarias en la España moderna*. Madrid: Taurus.

1970b. 'La economía española (1782–1829)', in *El Banco de España: Una historia económica*. Madrid: Banco de España, pp. 233–60.

1970c. *Economía e ilustración en la España del siglo XVIII*. Barcelona: Ariel.

1974. 'Antecedentes próximos del motín contra Esquilache'. *Moneda y Crédito* 128: 219–24.

Anon. 1741. *The Groans of Ireland: In a Letter to a Member of Parliament*. Dublin: Georg Faulkner.

1747. 'Life of the Right Reverend Hugh Boulter D.D., Archbishop of Armagh'. *London Magazine* October: 397–405.

Appleby, A. B. 1978. *Famine in Tudor and Stuart England*. Liverpool: Liverpool University Press.

Arizcun Cela, A. 1988. *Economía y sociedad en un valle pirenaico de Antiguo Régimen: Baztán, 1600–1841*. Pamplona: Institución Príncipe de Viana.

Auchmann, R., Brönnimann, S., Breda, L., Bühler, M., Spadin, R., and Stickler, A. 2012. 'Extreme climate, not extreme weather: the summer of 1816 in Geneva, Switzerland'. *Climate of the Past* 8: 325–35.

Bade, K. 2000. *Europa in Bewegung: Migration vom späten 18. Jahrhundert bis zur Gegenwart.* Munich: Beck.

Baehrel, R. 1961. *Une croissance: la Basse-Provence rurale de la fin du XVIe siècle à 1789.* Paris: Sevpen.

Bailey, M. 1998. 'Peasant welfare in England, 1290–1348'. *Economic History Review* 51: 223–51.

Banning, C. 1946. 'Food shortage and public health, first half of 1945: the Netherlands during German occupation'. *Annals of the American Academy of Political and Social Science* 245: 93–110.

Barber, J., and Dzeniskevich, A. (eds.) 2001. *Zhizn' ismert' v blokirovannom Leningrade: Istoriko-meditsinskii aspect.* St Petersburg: Akedimiya Voenno-Istoricheskikh Nauk.

   (eds.) 2005. *Life and Death in Besieged Leningrad, 1941–44.* London: Palgrave Macmillan.

Bardet, J.-P. 1983. *Rouen aux XVIIe et XVIIIe siècles: Les mutations d'un espace social.* Paris: Sedes.

Barker, D. J. 1995. 'Foetal origins of coronary heart disease'. *British Medical Journal* 311: 171–4.

Barker, D. J., Winter, P. D., Osmond, C., Margetts, B., and Simmonds, S. J. 1989. 'Weight in infancy and death from ischaemic heart disease'. *Lancet* 2: 577–80.

Barker, F., and Cheyne, J. 1821. *An Account of the Rise, Progress and Decline of the Fever Lately Epidemical in Ireland,* 2 vols. London: Baldwin, Craddock, and Joy.

Basini, G. L. 1970. *L'uomo e il pane: Risorse, consumi e carenze alimentari della popolazione modenese nel cinque e seicento.* Milan: Giuffrè.

Bass, H.-H. 1991. *Hungerkrisen in Preussen während der ersten Hälfte des 19. Jahrhunderts.* St. Katharinen, Germany: Scripta Mercaturae Verlag.

   2007. 'The crisis in Prussia', in Ó Gráda, Paping and Vanhaute (eds.), pp. 185–212.

Baulant, M. 1968. 'Le prix des grains à Paris de 1431 à 1788'. *Annales ESC* 23: 520–40.

Béaur, G. 1984. *Le marché foncier à la veille de la Révolution: Les mouvements de propriété beaucerons dans les régions de Maintenon et de Janville de 1761 à 1790.* Paris: Éd. de l'EHESS.

   2000. *Histoire agraire de la France au XVIIIe siècle: Inerties et changements dans les campagnes françaises à la fin de l'époque moderne (jusqu'en 1815).* Paris: SEDES.

   2007. 'La soudure n'est plus ce qu'elle était: contribution à l'étude du mouvement saisonnier du marché du blé et du marché de la terre d'après le cas de la région de Chartres au XVIIIe siècle', in Chauvard, J.-F., and Laboulais, I. (eds.). *Les fruits de la récolte: Études offertes à Jean-Michel Boehler.* Strasbourg: Presses Universitaires de Strasbourg, pp. 93–107.

   Forthcoming. 'Le niveau de vie des populations rurales et urbaines dans la France de l'Ancien Régime'. *Revue d'Histoire Moderne et Contemporaine.*

Forthcoming. 'Une révolution des objets, ene révolution industrieuse? Meaux et ses campagnes, aux 17e et 18e siècles'. *Revue d'Histoire Moderne et Contemporaine.*

Béaur, G., Chevet, J.-M., Ó Gráda, C., and Pérez-Picazo, M. T. (eds.) 2011. *Histoire et Mesure* 26 (special issue), *Revisiter Le Crises.*

Beckett, F. W. 2007. *The Great War 1914–1918.* London: Routledge.

Behringer, W. 1995. 'Weather, hunger and fear: origins of the European witch-hunts in climate, society and mentality'. *German History* 13: 1–27.

Behringer, W., Lehmann, H., and Pfister, C. (eds.) 2005. *Kulturelle Konsequenzen der 'Kleinen Eiszeit': Cultural Consequences of the 'Little Ice Age'.* Göttingen: Vandenhoeck & Ruprecht.

Bellettini, A. 1987. *La popolazione italiana: Un profilo storico.* Turin: Einaudi.

Benedictow, O. J. 2004. *The Black Death 1346–1353: The Complete History.* Woodbridge, UK: Boydell & Brewer.

Bengtsson, T. 2004. 'Living standards and economic stress', in Bengtsson, T., Campbell, C., and Lee, J. Z. (eds.). *Life under Pressure: Mortality and Living Standards in Europe and Asia, 1700–1900.* Cambridge, MA: MIT Press, pp. 27–59.

Bengtsson, T., and Dribe, M. 2005. 'New evidence on the standard of living in Sweden during the eighteenth and nineteenth centuries: long-term development of the demographic response to short-term economic stress', in Allen, R. C., Bengtsson, T., and Dribe, M. (eds.). *Living Standards in the Past: New Perspectives on Well-Being in Asia and Europe.* Oxford: Oxford University Press, pp. 341–72.

2006. 'Deliberate control in a natural fertility population: southern Sweden, 1766–1894'. *Demography* 43: 727–46.

2010. 'Economic stress and reproductive responses', in Tsuya, N. O., Feng, W., and Lee, J. (eds.). *Prudence and Pressure: Reproduction and Human Agency in Europe and Asia, 1700–1900.* Cambridge, MA: MIT Press, pp. 97–128.

Bengtsson, T., and Jörberg, L. 1975. 'Market integration in Sweden during the 18th and 19th centuries: spectral analysis of grain prices'. *Economy and History* 18: 93–106.

Bengtsson, T., and Ohlsson, R. 1985. 'Age-specific mortality and short-term changes in the standard of living: Sweden, 1751–1859'. *European Journal of Population* 1: 309–26.

Berger, H., and Spoerer, M. 2001. 'Economic crises and the European revolutions of 1848'. *Journal of Economic History* 61: 293–326.

Berkhoff, K. 2004. *Harvest of the Despair: Life and Death in the Ukraine under Nazi Rule.* Cambridge, MA: Harvard University Press.

Bernat i Martí, S., and Badenes Martín, M. A. 1988. 'Cronología, intensidad y extensión de las crisis demográficas en el País Valencià (siglos XVII–XIX)', in Pérez Aparicio, C. (ed.). *Estudios sobre la població del País Valenciá,* vol. I. Valencia: Alfons el Magnànim, pp. 537–57.

Berthe, M. 1984. *Famines et épidémies dans les campagnes navarraises à la fin du Moyen Âge.* Paris: Sfied [Catalan version: 1991. *Fams i epidèmies al camp navarrès als segles XIV i XV.* Barcelona: L'Avenç].

Betrán, J. L. 1996. *La peste en la Barcelona de los Austrias.* Lleida, Spain: Milenio.

Biraben, J.-N. 1975. *Les hommes et la peste en France et dans les pays européens et méditerranéens,* 2 vols. Paris: Mouton.

1977. 'La mortalité des évêques siégeant entre 1220 et 1458 sur le territoire actuel de la France'. *Population* 32: 467–80.

Black, R. C. D. 1960. *Economic Thought and the Irish Question 1817–1870* Cambridge: Cambridge University Press.

Blanco García, F. 1987. 'Crisis meseteña de principios del siglo XIX', unpublished PhD thesis. Complutense University of Madrid.

Blaschke, K. 1967. *Bevölkerungsgeschichte von Sachsen bis zur industriellen Revolution*. Weimar: Böhlau.

Blockmans, W., Pieters, G., Prevenier, W., and Van Schaïk, R., 1980. 'Tussen crisis en welvaart: sociale veranderingen, 1300–1500', in *Algemene Geschiedenis der Nederlanden*, vol. IV, *Middeleeuwen*. Haarlem: Fibula-Van Dishoeck, pp. 42–86.

Bohstedt, J. 2010. *The Politics of Provisions: Food Riots, Moral Economy, and Market Transition in England, c. 1500–1850*. Farnham, UK: Ashgate.

Boisen, M. 1985. *Saxos Danmarks krönike 2*. Copenhagen: Peter Asschenfeldt's Forlag.

Boserup, E. 1965. *The Conditions of Agricultural Growth: The Economics of Agrarian Change under Population Pressure*. London: Allen & Unwin.

1981. *Population and Technological Change: A Study of Long-Term Trends*. Oxford: Blackwell.

Boudia, Y. 2000. 'Mortaliteit en pest in het kwartier van Gent: testregio: de kasselrij Kortrijk, de Oudburg en de stad Gent (c. 1350–1500)', unpublished MA thesis. Ghent University.

Boulter, H. 1759. *Letters Written by His Excellency Hugh Boulter D. D. ... from 1724 to 1738*, 2 vols. Oxford: Clarendon Press.

Bourin, M., Drendel, J., and Menant, F. (eds.) 2011. *Les disettes dans la conjoncture de 1300 en Méditerranée occidentale*. Rome: Collection de l'École Française de Rome.

Bourke, A. 1993. *The Visitation of God? The Potato and the Irish Famine*. Dublin: Lilliput Press.

Bouton, C. A. 1993. *The Flour War: Gender, Class and Community in Late Ancien Régime French Society*. University Park, PA: Pennsylvania State University Press.

Boutruche, R. 1963. *La crise d'une société: Seigneurs et paysans du Bordelais pendant la Guerre de Cent Ans*. Paris: Les Belles Lettres.

Bradley, R. S., and Jones, P. D. (eds.) 1992. *Climate since A.D. 1500*. London: Routledge.

Brandenberger, A. 2004. *Ausbruch aus der 'Malthusianischen Falle': Versorgungslage und Wirtschaftsentwicklung im Staate Bern 1755–1797*. Bern: Peter Lang.

Brandt, K., Shiller, O., and Ahlgrimm, F. 1953. *Management of Agriculture and Food in the German-Occupied and Other Areas of Fortress Europe: A Study in Military Government*. Stanford, CA: Stanford University Press.

Bräuer, H. 2002. 'Reflexionen über den Hunger im Erzgebirge um 1700', in Hettling, M., Shirmer, U., Schötz, S., and Zwahr, H. (eds.). *Figuren und Strukturen: Historische Essays für Hartmut Zwahr zum 65. Geburtstag*. Munich: Saur, pp. 225–39.

Brázdil, R., Valásek, H., Luterbacher, J., and Macková, J. 2001. 'Die Hungerjahre 1770–1772 in den böhmischen Ländern: Verlauf, meteorologische Ursachen und Auswirkungen'. *Österreichische Zeitschrift für Geschichtswissenschaften* 12: 44–78.

Briffa, K. R., Jones, P. D., Schweingruber, F. H., and Osborn, T. J. 1998. 'Influence of volcanic eruptions on Northern Hemisphere summer temperature over the past 600 years'. *Nature* 393: 450–5.

Britnell, R. 2004. *Britain and Ireland 1050-1530: An Economic and Social History*. Oxford: Oxford University Press.

Broadberry, S., and Gupta, B. 2006. 'The early modern Great Divergence: wages, prices and economic development in Europe and Asia, 1500–1800'. *Economic History Review* 59: 2–31.

Brönnimann, S., and Krämer, D., 'Tambora and the "Year Without a Summer" of 1816', *Geographica Bernensia* 690.

Bruegel, M., Chevet, J.-M., Lecocq, S., and Robin, J.-M. 2013. 'Explaining the food purchases of the convent school at Saint-Cyr, 1703–1788'. *Annals of Economics and Statistics* 109/110: 63–91.

Brumont, F. 1988. 'Le pain et la peste: épidémie et subsistances en Vieille-Castille à la fin du XVIe siècle'. *Annales de Démographie Historique*: 207–20.

Bruneel, C. 1977. *La mortalité dans les campagnes: Le Duché de Brabant aux XVIIe et XVIII siècles*. Louvain, Belgium: Éditions Nauwelaerts.

Brusselle, E. 1997. 'Demografische ontwikkeling, doopnaamgeving, kerkelijk leven, volksonderwijs en alfabetisatie in enkel parochies van het Brugse Vrije', unpublished MA thesis, 2 vols. University of Louvain.

Buat, N. 2010. 'Marchés et spéculation à Paris pendant la disette de 1692–1694: une approche par les prix'. *Histoire et Mesure* 25: 55–93.

Buchner, T., and Hoffmann-Rehnitz, P. (eds.) 2011. *Shadow Economies and Irregular Work in Urban Europe: 16th to Early 20th Centuries*. Vienna: LIT Verlag.

Bulgarelli Lukacs, A. 2009. 'La popolazione del regno di Napoli nel primo seicento (1595–1648): analisi differenziale degli effetti redistributivi della crisi e ipotesi di quantificazione delle perdite demografiche'. *Popolazione e Storia* 10: 77–114.

Bullen, R., and Pelly, M. E. (eds.) 1987. *Documents on British Policy Overseas*, series 2, vol. II. London: HMSO.

(eds.) 1999. *Documents on British Policy Overseas*, series 1, vol. IV. London: HMSO.

Burger, G., Stanstead, H., and Drummond, J. 1948. *Malnutrition and Starvation in Western Netherlands, September 1944-45*, parts I and II. The Hague: General State Printing Office.

Cabourdin, G., and Biraben, J.-N. 1988. 'Les crises démographiques', in Dupâquier, J. (ed.), *Histoire de la population française*, vol. II, *De la Renaissance à 1789*. Paris: Presses Universitaires de France, pp. 175–91.

Campbell, B. M. S. 2009. 'Four famines and a pestilence: harvest, price, and wage variations in England, 13th to 19th centuries', in Liljewall, B., Flygare, I. A., Ulrich, L., Ljunggren, L., and Söderberg, J. (eds.). *Agrarhistoria på många sätt: 28 studier om människan och jorden*. Stockholm: Kungl. Skogs-och Lantbruksakademien, pp. 23–56.

2010a. 'Cause and effect? Physical shocks and biological hazards', in Cavaciocchi (ed.), pp. 13–32.

2010b. 'Nature as historical protagonist: environment and society in pre-industrial England'. *Economic History Review* 63: 281–314.

Campbell, B. M. S., and Ó Gráda, C. 2011. 'Harvest shortfalls, grain prices, and famines in preindustrial England'. *Journal of Economic History* 71: 859–86.

Camuffo, D., and Enzi, S. 1992. 'Reconstructing the climate of northern Italy from archive sources', in Bradley and Jones (eds.), pp. 143–54.

Caravale, M., and Caracciolo, A. 1978. *Lo Stato pontificio da Martino V a Pio IX*. Turin: UTET.

Carbajo Isla, M. F. 1987. *La población de la villa de Madrid: Desde finales del siglo XVI hasta mediados del siglo XIX*. Madrid: Siglo XXI.

Carmichael, D. J. S. 2014. 'Feeding and supporting the poor of London in the early seventeenth century: the City's response to crisis', unpublished PhD thesis. University of London.

Carmona, J. I. 2000. *Crónica urbana del malvivir (s. XIV–XVII): Insalubridad, desamparo y hambre en Sevilla*. Seville: University of Seville.

Carpentier, E. 1962. 'Autour de la Peste Noire: famines et épidémies dans l'histoire du XIVe siècle'. *Annales ESC* 17: 1062–92.

Carr, E. H., and Davies, R. W. 1974. *The Foundations of a Planned Economy 1926–29*. London: Macmillan.

Castells, I. 1970. 'El rebomboris del pa de 1789 a Barcelona'. *Recerques* 1: 51–81.

Castenbrandt, H. 2012. 'Rödsot i Sverige 1750–1900: en sjukdoms demografiska och medicinska historia', unpublished PhD thesis. University of Gothenburg.

Cattini, M. 1983. 'Per la storia della popolazione emiliana nel Cinquecento', in Borelli, G. (ed.). *Studi in onore di Gino Barbieri: problemi e metodi di storia ed economia*, vol. I. Pisa: IPEM, pp. 449–67.

Cavaciocchi, S. (ed.) 2010. *Le interazioni fra economia e ambiente biologico nell'Europa preindustriale*. Florence: Florence University Press.

Cerisier, P. 2004. 'Le commerce des grains dans la France du nord, fin XVIIe–1790 (Artois, Flandre, Hainaut, Cambrésis)', unpublished PhD thesis. University of Lille 3.

Chen, S., and Kung, J. K.-S. 2016. 'Of maize and men: the effect of a new crop on population and economic growth in China'. *Journal of Economic Growth* 21: 71–99.

Chevet, J.-M. 1984. 'Le Marquisat d'Ormesson: essai d'analyse économique', unpublished PhD thesis. EHESS Paris.

1993. 'Les crises démographiques en France à la fin du XVIIe siècle et au XVIIIe siècle: un essai de mesure'. *Histoire et Mesure* 8: 117–44.

Chevet, J.-M., and Ó Gráda, C. 2004. 'Revisiting subsistence crises: the characteristics of French demographic crises in the first half of the nineteenth century'. *Food and Foodways* 12: 165–95.

2007. 'Crisis: what crisis? Price and mortality in France in 1846', in Ó Gráda, Paping and Vanhaute (eds.), pp. 247–65.

Chuprov, A. I., and Posnikov, A. S. (eds.) 1897. *Vliianie urozhaev i khlebnykh tsen na nekotorye storony russkogo narodnogo khoziaistva*, 2 vols. St Petersburg.

Clark, G. 2007. *A Farewell to Alms: A Brief Economic History of the World*. Princeton, NJ: Princeton University Press.

Clark, P. (ed.) 1985. *The European Crisis of the 1590s: Essays in Comparative History*. London: HarperCollins.

Clarke, P. 2014. 'Let them pay for their starvation: the imposition of income tax in Ireland (1853)', unpublished communication presented at the annual conference of the Irish Accounting and Finance Association, Belfast, 30 May.

Clarkson, L. A. 1989. 'Conclusion: famine and Irish history', in Crawford (ed.), pp. 220–36.

Clogg, R. (ed.) 2008. *Bearing Gifts to Greeks: Humanitarian Aid to Greece in the 1940s*. London: Palgrave Macmillan.

Cohn, S. K. 2002. *The Black Death Transformed*. London: Arnold.

Collantes de Terán, A. 1977. *Sevilla en la Baja Edad Media: La ciudad y sus hombres*. Seville: Publicaciones del Exmo, Sevilla.

Collet, D. 2010. 'Storage and starvation: public granaries as agents of "food security" in early modern Europe'. *Historical Social Research* 35: 234–53.

2011. '"Moral economy" von oben? Getreidesperren als territoriale und soziale Grenzen während der Hungerkrise 1770–72'. *Jahrbuch für Regionalgeschichte* 29: 45–61.

2014a. 'Hungern und Herrschen: umweltgeschichtliche Verflechtungen der Ersten Teilung Polens und der europäischen Hungerkrise 1770–72'. *Jahrbücher für Geschichte Osteuropas* 62: 237–54.

2014b. 'Predicting the past? Integrating vulnerability, climate and culture during historical famines', in Tischler, J., and Gresche, H. (eds.). *Grounding Global Climate Change: Contributions from the Social and the Cultural Sciences*. Dordrecht: Springer, pp. 39–58.

2015. 'Mitleid Machen: die Nutzung von Emotionen in der Hungersnot 1770–72'. *Historische Anthropologie* 23: 54–69.

Collingham, L. 2011. *The Taste of War: World War Two and the Battle for Food*. London: Allen Lane.

Collins, L. 2014. 'The frosty winters of Ireland: poems of climate crisis 1739–41'. *Journal of Ecocriticism* 5: 1–11.

Colmenares, D. de 1969 [1637]. *Historia de la insigne ciudad de Segovia y compendio de las historias de Castilla*, 2 vols. Segovia: Academia de Historia y Arte de San Quirce.

Coniglio, G. 1940. 'Annona e calmieri durante la dominazione spagnola'. *Archivio storico della Provincia di Napoli* 26: 105–53.

Connell, K. H. 1950. *The Population of Ireland 1750–1845*. Oxford: Oxford University Press.

1957. 'Peasant marriage in Ireland after the Great Famine'. *Past and Present* 12: 76–91.

Conquest, R. 1986. *The Harvest of Sorrow: Soviet Collectivization and the Terror Famine*. London: Hutchinson.

Corradi, A. 1973 [1865–94]. *Annali delle epidemie occorse in Italia dalle prime memorie fino al 1850*, 2 vols. Bologna: Forni.

Corritore, R. 2007. 'La costituzione di scorte granarie pubbliche e la politica economica degli Stati in Età pre-industriale', in Lopane, I., and Ritrovato, E. (eds.). *Tra vecchi e nuovi equilibri: domanda e offerta di servizi in Italia in età moderna e contemporanea*. Bari: Cacucci, pp. 490–4.

Cox, M. E. 2015. 'Hunger games: or how the Allied blockade in World War I deprived German children of nutrition, and Allied food aid subsequently saved them'. *Economic History Review* 68: 600–31.

Crawford, E. M. (ed.) 1989a. *Famine: The Irish Experience*. Edinburgh: John Donald.

1989b. 'William Wilde's table of Irish famines 900–1850', in Crawford (ed.), pp. 1–30.

1989c. 'Subsistence crises and famines in Ireland: a nutritionist's view', in Crawford (ed.), pp. 199–219.

Creighton, C. 1894. *A History of Epidemics in Britain*, vol. II, *From the Extinction of Plague to the Present Time*. Cambridge: Cambridge University Press.

Cronin, J., and Lenihan, P. Forthcoming. 'The war for Ireland, 1641–1691', in Ohlmeyer, J. (ed.). *The Cambridge History of Ireland*, vol. II, *Early Modern Ireland, 1550–1730*. Cambridge: Cambridge University Press.

Crotty, R. 1966. *Irish Agricultural Production: Its Volume and Structure*. Cork: Cork University Press.

Crowley, J., Murphy, M., and Smith, W. J. (eds.) 2012. *The Atlas of the Great Irish Famine*. Cork: Cork University Press.

Crowley, T. J., and Lowery, T. S. 2000. 'How warm was the Medieval Warm Period?'. *Ambio* 29: 51–4.

Cullen, K. 2010. *Famine in Scotland: The 'Ill Years' of the 1690s*. Edinburgh: Edinburgh University Press.

Cullen, L. M. 1968. 'Irish history without the potato'. *Past and Present* 11: 72–83.

2010. 'The food crises of the early 1740s: the economic conjuncture'. *Irish Economic and Social History* 37: 1–23.

2012. *Economy, Trade, and Irish Merchants at Home and Abroad, 1600–1988*. Dublin: Four Courts Press.

Curran, D., Kuciuk, L., and Newby, A. G. 2015. *Famines in European Economic History: The Last Great European Famines Reconsidered*. London: Routledge.

Curschmann, F. (ed.) 1900. *Hungersnöte im Mittelalter: Ein Beitrag zur deutschen Wirtschaftsgeschichte des 8. bis 13. Jahrhunderts*. Leipzig: B. G. Teubner.

Curtis, D. 2014. 'The impact of land accumulation and consolidation on population trends in the pre-industrial period: two contrasting cases in the Low Countries'. *Historical Research* 87: 194–228.

Curtis, D., and Campopiano, M. 2014. 'Medieval land reclamation and the creation of new societies: comparing Holland and the Po Valley, 800–1500'. *Journal of Historical Geography* 44: 93–103.

D'Haenens, A. 1959. 'Les mutations monétaire du XIVe siècle et leur incidence sur les finances des abbayes bénédictines: le budget de Saint-Martin de Tournai de 1321 à 1348'. *Revue belge de philologie et d'histoire* 37: 317–42.

Dalle, D. 1963. *De bevolking van Veurne-Ambacht in de 17de en 18de eeuw*. Brussels: Paleis der Academiën.

Danilov, V., Manning, R., and Viola, L. (eds.). 1999. *The Tragedy of the Soviet Village: Collectivization and Dekulakization: Documents and Materials*, vol. I, May, *1927 – November, 1929*. Moscow: Rosspen.

(eds.). 2001. *The Tragedy of the Soviet Village: Collectivization and Dekulakization: Documents and Materials*, vol. III, *1931–1933*. Moscow: Rosspen.

Datta, R. 1990. 'Rural Bengal: social structure and agrarian economy in the late eighteenth century', unpublished PhD thesis. University of London.

Davies, N. 1994. *Boże igrzysko: Historia Polski*, vol. I. Krakow: Wydawnictwo Znak.

Davies, R. W., and Wheatcroft, S. G. 1974. 'Further thoughts on the first Soviet Five-Year Plan'. *Slavic Review* 4: 790–802.

2004. *The Years of Hunger: Soviet Agriculture, 1931–33*. London: Palgrave.

Davies, R. W., Harrison, M., and Wheatcroft, S. G. 1994. *The Economic Transformation of the Soviet Union, 1913–1945*. Cambridge: Cambridge University Press.

De Boer, D. 1978. *Graaf en grafiek: Sociale en economische ontwikkelingen in het middeleeuwse 'Noordholland' tussen 1345 en 1415*. Leiden: New Rhine Publishers.

De La Roncière, C.-M. 2011. 'Les famines à Florence de 1280 à 1350', in Bourin, M., Menant, F., and Drendel, J. (eds.). *Les disettes dans la conjoncture de 1300 en Méditerranée occidentale*. Rome: École Française de Rome, pp. 225–46.

De Maddalena, A. 1949. *Prezzi e aspetti di mercato in Milano durante il secolo XVII*. Milan: Malfasi.

De Ram, P. (ed.) 1861. *Joannis Molani in Academia Lovaniensi s. theologiae et professoris Historiae Lovanensium, libri XIV*, 2 vols. Brussels: Commission Royale d'Histoire.

De Silva, S. L., and Zielinski, G. A. 1998. 'Global influence of the AD 1600 eruption of Huaynaputina, Peru'. *Nature* 393: 455–8.

De Visscher, M. 1978. 'Het hongerjaar 1698'. *Annales de la Société belge d'Histoire des Hôpitaux* 23: 3–22.

De Vries, J., and Van der Woude, A. 1997. *The First Modern Economy: Success, Failure, and Perseverance of the Dutch Economy, 1500–1815*. Cambridge: Cambridge University Press.

Degn, O. 1981. *Rig og fattig i Ribe*. Aarhus, Denmark: Universitetsforlaget.

Dehaeck, S. 2004. 'Voedselconsumptie in het Brugse Sint-Jans Hospitaal tijdens de Middeleeuwen (1280–1440)'. *Handelingen van het Genootschap voor Geschiedenis* 141: 332–64.

Del Panta, L. 1980. *Le epidemie nella storia demografica italiana*. Turin: Loescher.

Del Panta, L., and Livi Bacci, M. 1977. 'Chronologie, intensité et diffusion des crises de mortalité en Italie: 1600–1850'. *Population* 32: 401–46.

Delamayne, T. H. 1767. *To Francis Bindon, Esq., on a Picture of His Grace Dr. Hugh Boulter*. London: Williams.

Delaney, E. 2012. *The Curse of Reason: The Great Irish Famine*. Dublin: Gill & Macmillan.

Delumeau, J. 1957–59. *Vie économique et sociale de Rome dans la seconde moitié du XVIe siècle*, 2 vols. Paris: Boccard.

Demerson, P. de 1969. 'La distribución de sopas económicas por la Real Sociedad Matritense en 1803–1804'. *Boletín de la Real Academia de la Historia* 164: 119–37.

Desai, M. 1993. 'The agrarian crisis in medieval England: a Malthusian tragedy or a failure of entitlements?'. *Bulletin of Economic Research* 43: 223–58.

Devine, T. M. 1988. *The Great Highland Famine: Hunger, Emigration and the Scottish Highlands in the Nineteenth Century*. Edinburgh: John Donald.

1995. 'Why the Highlands did not starve: Ireland and Highland Scotland in the Potato Famine', in Morris, R. J., Houston, R., and Connolly, S. (eds.).

Conflict, Identity and Economic Development: Ireland and Scotland, 1600–1939. Preston, UK: Carnegie Publications, pp. 77–88.

Devroey, J.-P., and Jaubert, A. N. 2011. 'Family, income and labour around the North Sea, 500–1000', in Vanhaute, E., Devos, I., and, Lambrecht, T. (eds.). *Making a Living: Family, Income and Labour: Rural Economy and Society in North-Western Europe, 500–2000*. Turnhout, Belgium: Brepols, pp. 5–44.

Deyon, P. 1967, *Amiens, capitale provinciale: Étude sur la société urbaine au 17e siècle*. Paris: Mouton.

Díaz Marín, P. 2003. 'Crisis de subsistencia y protesta popular: los motines de 1847'. *Historia Agraria* 30: 31–62.

  2006. 'Subsistence crisis and popular protest in Spain: the motines of 1847', in Ó Gráda, Paping and Vanhaute (eds.), pp. 267–92.

Dickson, D. 1989. 'The gap in famines: a useful myth?', in Crawford (ed.), pp. 96–111.

  1997. *Arctic Ireland: The Extraordinary Story of the Great Frost and Forgotten Famine of 1740–41*. Belfast: White Row Press.

  2005. *Old World Colony: Cork and South Munster 1630–1830*. Cork: Cork University Press.

  2014. 'Famine and economic change in eighteenth-century Ireland', in Jackson, A. (ed.). *The Oxford Handbook of Modern Irish History*. Oxford: Oxford University Press, pp. 422–38.

Dickson, D., Ó Gráda, C., and Daultrey. S. 1982. 'Hearth-tax, household size and population change, 1672–1821'. *Proceedings of the Royal Irish Academy* 82C: 125–81.

Diederiks, H. 1982. *Een stad in verval: Amsterdam omstreeks 1800: demografisch, economisch, ruimtelijk*. Amsterdam: Historisch Seminarium Universiteit van Amsterdam.

Dijkman, J. 2011. *Shaping Medieval Markets: The Organisation of Commodity Markets in Holland, c. 1200 – c. 1450*. Leiden: Brill.

Dodds, B., and Liddy, C. D. (eds.) 2011. *Commercial Activity, Markets and Entrepreneurs in the Middle Ages: Essays in Honour of Richard Britnell*. Woodbridge, UK: Boydell & Brewer.

Dols, M. J. L., and van Arcken, J. A. M. 1946. 'Food supply and nutrition in the Netherlands during and immediately after World War II'. *Milbank Memorial Fund Quarterly* 24: 319–58.

Dombrecht, K. 2014. 'Plattelandsgemeenschappen, lokale elites en ongelijkheid in het Vlaamse kustgebied (14de – 16de eeuw): case-study: Dudzele ambacht', unpublished PhD thesis. Ghent University.

Domínguez Ortiz, A. 1969. 'La crisis de Castilla en 1677–1687', in *Crisis y decadencia de la España de los Austrias*. Barcelona: Ariel, pp. 195–217.

  1976. *Sociedad y Estado en el siglo XVIII español*. Barcelona: Ariel.

Donnelly, J. S. 1975. *The Land and the People of Nineteenth-Century Cork*. London: Routledge & Kegan Paul.

  1976. 'The Irish agricultural depression of 1859–64'. *Irish Economic and Social History* 3: 33–54.

  2002. *The Great Irish Potato Famine*. London: Sutton.

Dontenwill, S. 1973. 'Mutations foncières lors des crises de 1652 et 1709 dans l'élection de Roanne: un exemple d'utilisation des sources notariales dans l'analyse d'une crise sociale', in *Actes du 98e Congrès National des Sociétés Savantes*, vol. II. Saint-Étienne: Histoire Moderne, pp. 29–42.

Drake, M. 1968. 'The Irish demographic crisis of 1740–41', in Moody, T. W. (ed.). *Historical Studies*. London: Routledge & Kegan Paul, pp. 101–24.

Dribe, M., Olsson, M., and Svensson, P. 2012. 'Was the manorial system an efficient insurance institution? Economic stress and demographic response in Sweden, 1749–1859'. *European Review of Economic History* 16: 292–310.

2016. 'Famines in the Nordic Countries, AD 536–1875'. *Lund Papers in Economic History* 138. Lund: Department of Economic History, Lund University.

2017. 'The agricultural revolution and the conditions of the rural poor, Southern Sweden 1750–1860'. *The Economic History Review* 70: 483–508.

Dronin, N. M., and Bellinger, E. G. 2005. *Climate Dependence and Food Problems in Russia, 1900–1990*. Budapest: CEU Press.

Dunning, C. S. L. 2001. *Russia's First Civil War: The Time of Troubles and the Founding of the Romanov Dynasty*. Philadelphia: Pennsylvania University Press.

Dupâquier, J. (ed.). 1988. *Histoire de La Population Française*. Paris: PUF.

Dupâquier, J. 1989. 'Demographic crises and subsistence crises in France, 1650–1725', in Walter, J., and Schofield, R. S. (eds.). *Famine, Disease and the Social Order in Early Modern Society*. Cambridge: Cambridge University Press, pp. 189–99.

Dybdahl, A. 2010. 'Klima og demografiske kriser i Norge i middelalder og tidlig nytid'. *Historisk Tidsskrift* 89: 183–222.

2014. 'Klimatiske sjokk, uår, sykdom og demografiske kriser i Trøndelag på 1600- og 1700-tallet'. *Historisk Tidsskrift* 93: 243–75.

Dyer, C. 1989. *Standards of Living in the Later Middle Ages: Social Change in England, c. 1200–1520*. Cambridge: Cambridge University Press.

Dyrvik, S., Mykland, K., and Oldervoll, J. 1976. *The Demographic Crises in Norway in the 17th and 18th centuries: Some Data and Interpretations*. Bergen: Universitetsforlaget.

Edvinsson, R., and Söderberg, J. 2010. 'The evolution of Swedish consumer prices 1290–2008', in *Exchange Rates, Prices, and Wages, 1277–2008*. Stockholm: Sveriges Riksbank, Ekerlids Förlag, pp. 412–52.

Edvinsson, R., Leijonhufvud, L., and Söderberg, J. 2009. 'Väder, skördar och priser i Sverige', in Liljewall, B. (ed.). *Agrarhistoria på många sätt: 28 studier om människan och jorden*. Stockholm: Kungl. Skogs- och Lantbruksakademien, pp. 115–36.

Edwards, R. D., and Williams, T. D. (eds.) 1956. *The Great Famine: Essays in Irish History*. Dublin: Browne and Nolan.

Egido López, T. 1980. 'El motín madrileño de 1699'. *Investigaciones Históricas: Época Moderna y Contemporánea* 2: 253–94.

Eiríksson, A. 1997. 'Food supply and food riots', in Ó Gráda, C. (ed.). *Famine 150: Commemorative Lecture Series*. Dublin: Teagasc, pp. 67–93.

Ellison, G. T., and Kelly, M. 2005. 'Growth of Jersey schoolchildren during the 1940–1945 German occupation: comparison with schoolchildren on mainland Britain'. *Human Biology* 77: 761–72.

Ellman, M. 2000. 'The 1947 Soviet famine and the entitlement approach to famines'. *Cambridge Journal of Economics* 24: 603–30.

Emmison, F. G. 1976. *Elizabethan Life: Home, Work and Land.* Chelmsford, UK: Essex Country Council.

Engler, S., Mauelshagen, F., Werner, J., and Luterbacher, J. 2013. 'The Irish famine of 1740–1741: famine vulnerability and "climate migration"'. *Climate of the Past* 9: 1161–79.

Epstein, S. R. 2001. 'The late medieval crisis as an "integration crisis"', in Prak, M. (ed.). *Early Modern Capitalism: Economic and Social Change in Europe, 1400–1800.* London: Routledge, pp. 25–50.

Ermolov, A. S. 1909. *Nashineurozhai i prodovol'stvennyivopros,* 2 vols. St Petersburg.

Espadas Burgos, M. 1968. 'El hambre de 1812 en Madrid'. *Hispania* 110: 594–623.

1972. 'Hambre, mendicidad y epidemia en Madrid (1812–1823)'. *Anales del Instituto de Estudios Madrileños* 8: 371–93.

Faber, J. A. 1976. *Dure tijden en hongersnoden in pre-industrieel Nederland.* Amsterdam: Rodopi.

Fagan, B. 2000. *The Little Ice Age: How Climate Made History, 1300–1850.* New York: Basic Books.

Fagan, P. 1991. 'The population of Dublin in the eighteenth century with particular reference to the proportions of Protestants and Catholics'. *Eighteenth-Century Ireland* 6: 121–56.

Falchi, L., Pastura, R., and Sinisi, D. 1995. 'L'Annona di Roma nel secolo XVI', in *Gli archivi per la storia dell'alimentazione.* Rome: Ministero per i Beni Culturali e Ambientali, pp. 568–89.

Fazio, I. 1993. *La politica del grano: Annona e controllo del territorio in Sicilia nel settecento.* Milan: Franco Angeli.

Federico, G. 2005. *Feeding the World: An Economic History of World Agriculture 1800–2000.* Princeton, NJ: Princeton University Press.

Fernández Hidalgo, M. C., and García Ruipérez, M. 1989. 'La crisis agraria de 1802–1806 en la provincia de Toledo a través de los precios del trigo'. *Revista de Historia Económica* 7: 323–53.

Fernihough, A. 2014. 'Famine mortality in Britain', unpublished manuscript.

Ferreira Rodrigues, T. (ed.) 2008. *História da população Portuguesa: Das longas permanências à conquista da modernidade.* Porto: Ed. Afrontamento.

2009. 'Deteção e análise dos períodos de sobremortalidade em Portugal (séculos XVI a XIX) balanço de duas décadas de investigação', in Godinho, P., Pereira Bastos, S., and Fonseca, I. (eds.). *Homenagem a Jorge Crespo.* Lisbon: 100 Luz, pp. 627–64.

Filtzer, D. 2002. *Soviet Workers and Late Stalinism: Labour and the Restoration of the Stalinist System after World War II.* Cambridge: Cambridge University Press.

2010. *The Hazards of Urban Life in Late Stalinist Russia: Health, Hygiene, and Living Standards, 1943–1953.* Cambridge: Cambridge University Press.

Finzi, R. 1986. 'Il sole, la pioggia, il pane e il lavoro: note su clima, raccolto, calendario agrario nel Bolognese durante il secolo XVIII', in *Le meteore e il frumento: Clima, agricoltura e meteorologia a Bologna nel '700.* Bologna: Il Mulino, pp. 347–87.

2009. *'Sazia assai ma dà poco fiato': Il mais nell'economia e nella vita rurale italiane, secoli XVI–XX.* Bologna: CLUEB.

Fisher, H. H. 1927. *The Famine in Soviet Russia, 1919–1923: The Operations of the American Relief Administration.* Stanford, CA: Stanford University Press.

Flinn, M. (ed.) 1977. *Scottish Population History from the Seventeenth Century to the 1930s*. Cambridge: Cambridge University Press.

Floutard, G. 1972. 'La crise de 1709–1713 à Albi'. *Annales du Midi* 84: 117–50.

Fogel, R. W. 1992. 'Second thoughts on the European escape from hunger: famines, price elasticities, entitlements, chronic malnutrition, and mortality rates', in Osmani, S. R. (ed.). *Nutrition and Poverty*. Oxford: Clarendon Press, pp. 243–86.

  2004. *The Escape from Hunger and Premature Death, 1700–2100*. Cambridge: Cambridge University Press.

Fossier, R. 1968. *La terre et les hommes en Picardie jusqu'à la fin du XIIIe siècle*, 2 vols. Paris: Béatrice-Nauwelaerts.

Fossier, R., and Fossier, L. 1955. 'Aspects de la crise frumentaire en Artois et en Flandres gallicante', in *Recueil des travaux offerts a M. Clovis Brunel par ses amis, collègues et élèves*. Paris: Société de l'École des Chartes, pp. 436–47.

Fourquin, G. 1964. *Les campagnes de la région parisienne à la fin du Moyen Âge*. Paris: Presses Universitaires de France.

Fox, L. (ed.) 1990. *Minutes and Accounts of the Corporation of Stratford-upon-Avon and Other Records*, vol. V, *1593–98*. Warwick, UK: Dugdale Society.

Fraser, R. 2006. *La maldita guerra de España: Historia social de la Guerra de la Independencia, 1808–1814*. Barcelona: Crítica.

Frêche, G. 1974. *Toulouse et la région Midi-Pyrénées au siècle des lumières, vers 1670–1789*. Paris: Éd. Cujas.

Friis, A. 1953. 'The two crises in the Netherlands in 1557'. *Scandinavian Economic History Review* 1: 193–241.

Furió Diego, A. 2010. 'La crisis de la Baja Edad Media: una revisión', in *Las crisis a lo largo de la historia*. Valladolid, Spain: University of Valladolid, pp. 13–45.

  2011. 'Disettes et famines en temps de croissance: une révision de la crise autour 1300: le royaume de Valence dans la première moitié du XIVe siècle', in Bourin, M., Menant, F., and Drendel, J. (eds.). *Les disettes dans la conjoncture de 1300 en Méditerranée occidentale*. Rome: École Française de Rome, pp. 343–416.

Gadd, C.-J., Johansen, H. C., and Lindkvist, T. 2011. 'Scandinavia 1000–1750', in Vanhaute, E., Devos, I., and Lambrecht, T. (eds.). *Making a Living: Family, Income and Labour: Rural Economy and Society in North-Western Europe, 500–2000*. Turnhout, Belgium: Brepols, pp. 265–291.

Gailus, M. 2001. 'Die Erfindung des "Korn-Juden": zur Erfindung eines antijüdischen Feindbildes des 18. und frühen 19. Jahrhunderts'. *Historische Zeitschrift* 272: 597–622.

García-Sanz, A. 1977. *Desarrollo y crisis del Antiguo Régimen en Castilla la Vieja: Economía y sociedad en tierras de Segovia, 1500–1814*. Madrid: Akal.

García-Sanz Marcoteguy. 1985. *Demografía y sociedad de la Barranca de Navarra (1760–1860)*. Pamplona: Institución Príncipe de Viana.

García-Sanz Marcotegui, A., and Zabalza Cruchaga, M. A. 1983. 'Consecuencias demográficas de la Guerra de la Convención en Navarra: la crisis de mortalidad en 1794–1795'. *Príncipe de Viana* 44: 63–87.

Gascon, R., and Latta, C. 1963. 'Une crise urbaine au XVIIe siècle: la crise de 1693–1694 à Lyon. Quelques aspects démographiques et sociaux'. *Cahiers d'Histoire* 1: 371–404.

Gatrell, P. 1999. *A Whole Empire Walking: Refugees in Russia during World War I*. Bloomington, IN: Indiana University Press.

Gauvard, C. 2005. *Violence et ordre public au Moyen Âge*. Paris: Picard.

Gay, G. I., and Fisher, H. H. (eds.) 1929. *Public Relations of the Commission for Relief in Belgium: Documents*. Stanford, CA: Stanford University Press, http://net.lib.byu.edu/estu/wwi/comment/CRB/CRB2-11.htm#1 (accessed 14 August 2015).

Geary, L. 2014. '"Waiting and watching for food the live long day": famine and fever in Ireland, 1879–1880', unpublished manuscript.

Gehrmann, R. 2000. *Bevölkerungsgeschichte Norddeutschlands zwischen Aufklärung und Vormärz*. Berlin: A. Spitz.

Georgelin, J. 1982. 'L'écologie du froment en Europe occidentale', in Goy, J., and Le Roy Ladurie, E. (eds.). *Prestations paysannes, dîmes, rente foncière et mouvement de la production agricole à l'époque préindustrielle*, vol. II. Paris: Mouton, pp. 569–82.

Gerhard, H. J., and Engel, A. 2006. *Preisgeschichte der vorindustriellen Zeit: Ein Kompendium auf Basis ausgewählter Hamburger Materialien*. Stuttgart: Steiner.

Gerritsma, B. 1981. 'Pauperisme, kriminaliteit en konjunktuur: Amsterdam 1771/1772'. *Tijdschrift voor Sociale Geschiedenis* 7: 374–91.

Gerschenkron, A. 1965. 'Agrarian policies and Russian industrialization', in Habakkuk, H. J., and Poston, M. M. (eds.). *The Cambridge Economic History of Europe*, vol. VI, *The Industrial Revolutions and After: Incomes, Population and Technological Change*. Cambridge: Cambridge University Press, pp. 706–800.

Gestrich, A. 2003. 'Religion in der Hungerkrise von 1816/1817', in Jakubowski-Tiessen, M., and Lehmann, H. (eds.). *Um Himmels Willen: Religion in Katastrophenzeiten*. Göttingen: Ruprecht & Vandenhoeck, pp. 275–93.

Ghazai, R. 2015. 'Lebanon's dark days of hunger: the Great Famine of 1915–18', *The National* 14 April, www.thenational.ae/world/middle-east/lebanons-dark-days-of-hunger-the-great-famine-of-1915-18.

Gibson, A. J. S., and Smout, T. C. 1995. *Prices, Food and Wages in Scotland, 1550–1780*. Cambridge: Cambridge University Press.

Gillespie, R. 1984. 'Harvest crisis in early seventeenth-century Ireland'. *Irish Economic and Social History* 11: 5–18.

Glaser, R. 2008. *Klimageschichte Mitteleuropas: 1000 Jahre Wetter, Klima, Katastrophen*. Darmstadt: Primus.

Goldman, D., and Filtzer, W. Z. 2015. *Hunger and War: Food Provisioning in the Soviet Union during World War II*. Bloomington, IN: Indiana University Press.

Gómez Mampaso, M.V. 1975. 'La peste en el reinado de los Reyes Católicos: contribución al estudio de la demografía española de 1474 a 1516', unpublished PhD thesis. Complutense University, Madrid.

Gómez Moreno, M., and de Mata Carriazo, J. (eds.) 1962. *Memorias del reinado de los Reyes Católicos que escribía el bachiller Andrés Bernáldez, cura de los Palacios*. Madrid: Real Academia de la Historia.

Goodspeed, T. B. 2013. 'Famine, finance, and adjustment to environmental shock: microcredit and the Great Famine in Ireland', unpublished manuscript.

Goody, J. 2006. *The Theft of History*. Cambridge: Cambridge University Press.

Goubert, P. 1960. *Beauvais et le Beauvaisis de 1600 à 1730: Contribution à l'histoire sociale de la France du XVIIe siècle*, 2 vols. Paris: EPHE.

1967. *L'Avènement du Roi-Soleil: 1661*. Paris: Julliard.

Goudriaan, K., and Ibelings, B. J. 2002. 'Een menigte poorters en inwoners', in Abels, P. H. A. M., Goudriaan, K., Habermehl, N. D. B., and Kompagnie, J. K. (eds.). *Duizend jaar Gouda: Een stadsgeschiedenis*. Hilversum, Netherlands: Verloren, pp. 37–49.

Goy, J. 1968. 'Dîmes, rendements, états de récoltes et revenu réel'. *Studi storici* 3/4: 794–811.

1982. 'Les rendements du blé au pays d'Arles XVIIe–XVIIIe siècles', in Goy, J., and Le Roy Ladurie, E. (eds.). *Prestations paysannes, dîmes, rente foncière et mouvement de la production agricole à l'époque préindustrielle*, vol. II. Paris: Mouton, pp. 245–54.

Grabbe, H.-J. 2001. *Vor der grossen Flut: Die europäische Migration in die Vereinigten Staaten von Amerika 1783–1820*. Stuttgart: Franz Steiner Verlag.

Graber, R. 2010. 'Wohlstandswahrung für wenige oder Nahrungssicherung für alle? Armut, Tugenddiskurs und Krisenbekämpfungskonzepte im Kontext der Hungerkrise 1770/71 auf der Zürcher Landschaft', in Holenstein, A., Rohr, C., and Schmidt, H. R. (eds.). *Reichtum und Armut in den schweizerischen Republiken des 18. Jahrhunderts*. Geneva: Slatkine, pp. 195–213.

Gräslund, B. 2007. 'Fimbulvintern, Ragnarök och klimatkrisen år 536–537 e. Kr', in *Saga och sed. Kungl. Gustav Adolfs akademiens årsbok: Annales Academiae Regiae Gustavi Adolphi*. Uppsala: Kungl. Gustav Adolfs Akademien, pp. 93–123.

Gräslund, B., and Price, N. 2012. 'Twilight of the gods? The "dust veil event" of AD 536 in critical perspective'. *Antiquity* 86: 428–43.

Gray, P. 1995. *The Irish Famine*. London: Thames & Hudson.

2007. 'The European food crisis and the relief of Irish famine, 1845–1850', in Ó Gráda, Paping and Vanhaute (eds.), pp. 95–107.

Gregory, P. R. 1982. *Russian National Income, 1885–1913*. Cambridge: Cambridge University Press.

Grenier, J.-Y. 1985. *Séries économiques françaises (XVIe–XVIIIe siècles)*. Paris: Éd. de l'EHESS.

1996. 'Vaches maigres, vaches grasses: une reconstitution des données climatiques en France du Nord (1758–1789)'. *Histoire et Sociétés Rurales* 6: 77–93.

Grey, T. (ed.) 1993. *Harvest Failure in Cornwall and Devon: The Book of Orders and the Corn Surveys of 1623 and 1630–1*. Redruth, UK: Institute of Cornish Studies.

Groman, V. G. 1927. *Vliyanie neurozhaev na narodnoe khozyaistvo Rossii*. Moscow.

Grupo Complutense de Historia Económica Moderna 2013. 'La mortalidad catastrófica y su papel en el declive de la mortalidad general en las dos Castillas, 1700–1864', unpublished communication.

Grytten, O. 2004. 'A consumer price index for Norway 1516–2003', in Eitrheim, Ø., Klovland, J. T., and Qvigstad, J. F. (eds.). *Historical Monetary Statistics for Norway*. Oslo: Norges Bank, pp. 47–98.

Guenzi, A. 1978. 'Un mercato regolato: pane e fornai a Bologna nell'età moderna'. *Quaderni Storici* 37: 370–97.

1979. 'Processo popolare in piazza Maggiore: la carestia del 1648 a Bologna'. *L'Archiginnasio* 74: 161–79.

1995. 'Le magistrature e le istituzioni alimentari', in *Gli archivi per la storia dell'alimentazione*. Rome: Ministero per i Beni Culturali e Ambientali, pp. 285–301.

Guinnane, T. W. 1997. *The Vanishing Irish: Households, Migration, and the Rural Economy in Ireland, 1850–1914*. Princeton, NJ: Princeton University Press.

Gullberg, E. 1968. *Norrköpings historia*, vol. VIII, *Norrköpings kommunalstyrelse 1719–1862*. Stockholm: P. A. Norstedts & Söner.

Gunnarsson, G. 1980. 'A study of causal relations in climate and history: with an emphasis on the Icelandic experience', Paper no. 1980/17. Lund: Department of Economic History, Lund University.

Gusev, A. A., Ponomareva, V. V., Braitseva, O. A., Melekestsev, I. V., and Sulerzhitsky, L. D. 2003. 'Great explosive eruptions on Kamchatka during the last 10,000 years: self-similar irregularity of the output of volcanic products'. *Journal of Geophysical Research* 108: 1–18.

Gutiérrez Alonso, A. 1989. *Estudio sobre la decadencia de Castilla: La ciudad de Valladolid en el siglo XVII*. Valladolid, Spain: University of Valladolid.

Gutmann, M. P. 1980. *War and Rural Life in the Early Modern Low Countries*. Princeton, NJ: Princeton University Press.

Häger, O., Norman, J.-H., and Villius, H. 1980. *1000 år: En svensk historia*. Uppsala: Brombergs.

Häger, O., Torell, C., and Villius, H. 1978. *Ett satans år: Norrland 1867*. Stockholm: Sveriges Radio Libris.

Häkkinen, A., and Forsberg, H., 2015. 'Finland's famine years in the 1860s: a nineteenth-century perspective', in Curran, D., Luciuk, L., and Newby, A. (eds.). *Famines in European Economic History: The Last Great European Famines Reconsidered*. Abingdon, UK: Routledge, pp. 99–123.

Hall, E. 1809 [1548]. *Hall's Chronicle*. London: J. Johnson etc.

Halperin, C. 1987. *Russia and the Golden Horde: The Mongol Impact on Medieval Russian History*. Bloomington, IN: Indiana University Press.

Hamilton, E. J. 1934. *American Treasure and the Price Revolution in Spain, 1501–1650*. New York: Octagon Books.

1969. *War and Prices in Spain 1651–1800*. New York: Russell & Russell.

Hamrock, I. (ed.) 1998. *The Famine in Mayo 1845–1850: A Portrait from Contemporary Sources*. Castlebar, Ireland: Mayo County Council.

Harrison, M. (ed.) 1994. *The Economics of World War II: Six Great Powers in International Comparison*. Cambridge: Cambridge University Press.

Hart, N. 1993. 'Famine, maternal nutrition and infant mortality: a re-examination of the Dutch Hunger Winter'. *Population Studies* 47: 27–46.

't Hart, P. D. 1983. *De stad Utrecht en haar inwoners: Een onderzoek naar samenhangen tussen sociaal-economische ontwikkelingen en de demografische geschiedenis van de stad Utrecht 1771–1825*, PhD dissertation. Utrecht University.

Havari, E., and Peracchi, F. 2014. 'Growing up in wartime: evidence from the era of two world wars', Working Paper no. 05/14. Rome: Einaudi Institute for Economics and Finance.

Healey, J. 2014. *The First Century of Welfare: Poverty and Poor Relief in Lancashire, 1620–1730*. Woodbridge, UK: Boydell & Brewer.

Hecht, M. 2003. 'Teuerungsproteste 1846/47 in Frankreich und Preussen: vergleichende Untersuchung ihrer Bedingungsfaktoren'. *Francia: Forschungen zur Westeuropäischen Geschichte* 30: 115–42.

2012. 'Handeln in Hungerkrisen 1846/47: Nahrungsproteste und "Krisenmanagement" in Preussen', in Collet, D., Lassen, T., and Schanbacher, A. (eds.). *Handeln in Hungerkrisen: Neue Perspektiven auf soziale und klimatische Vulnerabilität*. Göttingen: Universitätsverlag, pp. 131–50.

286   Bibliography

Hecker, J. F. C. 1839. *Geschichte der neueren Heilkunde*. Berlin: Enslin.

Heckscher, E. F. 1933. 'En mätare på svenska folkets välståndsutveckling: den mantalsskrivna befolkningen 1634–1820'. *Historisk Tidskrift*: 365–402.

1936. *Sveriges ekonomiska historia från GustavVasa*. Stockholm: Albers Bonniers Förlag.

Heerma van Voss, L., and Van Leeuwen, M. H. D. 2012. 'Charity in the Dutch Republic: an introduction'. *Continuity and Change* 27: 175–97.

Heijmans, B. T., Tobi, E. W., Stein, A. D., Putter, H., Blauw, G. J., Susser, E. S., Slagboom, P. E., and Lumey, L. H. 2008. 'Persistent epigenetic differences associated with prenatal exposure to famine in humans'. *Proceedings of the National Academy of Sciences* 105: 17046–9.

Herlihy, D. 1967. *Medieval and Renaissance Pistoia*. New Haven, CT: Yale University Press.

Hindle, S. 2001. 'Dearth, fasting and alms: the campaign for general hospitality in late Elizabethan England'. *Past and Present* 172: 44–86.

2008. 'Dearth and the English revolution: the harvest crisis of 1647–50'. *Economic History Review* 61 (suppl.): 64–98.

Hionidou, V. 2006. *Famine and Death in Occupied Greece 1941–1944*. Cambridge: Cambridge University Press.

Hipkin, S. 2008. 'The structure, development and politics of the Kent grain trade, 1552–1647'. *Economic History Review* 61 (suppl.): 99–139.

Hippel, W. von 1984. *Auswanderung aus Süddeutschland: Studien zur württembergischen Auswanderung und Auswanderungspolitik im 18. und 19. Jahrhundert*. Stuttgart: Klett-Cotta.

Hochedlinger, M., and Tanter, A. (eds.) 2005. ' "…der größteTeil der Untertanen lebt elend und mühselig": die Berichte des Hofkriegsrates zur sozialen und wirtschaftlichen Lage der Habsburgermonarchie 1770–1771', Mitteilungen des österreichischen Staatsarchivs Special Volume no. 8. Vienna: Studien Verlag.

Holopainen, J., and Helama, S. 2009. 'Little Ice Age farming in Finland: preindustrial agriculture on the edge of the grim reaper's scythe'. *Human Ecology* 37: 213–25.

Holt, J. S. 2013. 'A new view of the Fells: Sarah Fell of Swarthmoor and her cashbook', in Hoyle, R. W. (ed.). *The Farmer in England: 1650–1980*. Farnham, UK: Ashgate, pp. 43–68.

Hoover, H. 1951. *The Memoirs of Herbert Hoover*, vol. I, *Years of Adventure, 1874–1920*. New York: Macmillan.

Horrox, R., and Hammond, P. W. 1980. *British Library Harleian Manuscript 433*, vol. II. Upminster, UK: Richard III Society.

Howard, N. P. 1993. 'The social and political consequences of the Allied food blockade of Germany, 1918–19'. *German History* 11: 161–88.

Howell, D. W. 2000. *The Rural Poor in Eighteenth-CenturyWales*. Cardiff: University of Wales Press.

Hoyle, R. W. 2010. 'Famine as agricultural catastrophe: the crisis of 1622–3 in east Lancashire'. *Economic History Review* 63: 974–1002.

2013. 'Why was there no crisis in England in the 1690s?', in *The Farmer in England: 1650–1980*. Farnham, UK: Ashgate, pp. 69–100.

2016. 'Shrewsbury: the famines of 1586–87 and 1595–97 in England and extreme weather', unpublished paper.

Hruschka, R. 1940. 'Die Hungersnot 1771–72 im Fladinger Raum'. *Zeitschrift des deutschen Vereins für die Geschichte Mährens und Schlesiens* 42: 74–7.

Hughes, P. L., and Larkin, J. F. (eds.) 1969. *Tudor Royal Proclamations*, vol. II, *The Later Tudors, 1553–1587*. New Haven, CT: Yale University Press.

Huhn, M. 1987. 'Zwischen Teuerungspolitik und Freiheit des Getreidehandels: staatliche und städtische Maßnahmen 1770–1847', in Teuteberg, H. J. (ed.). *Durchbruch zum modernen Massenkonsum: Lebensmittelmärkte und Lebensmittelqualität im Städtewachstum des Industriezeitalters.* Münster, Germany: Franz Steiner, pp. 37–89.

Hull, C. H. (ed.) 1899. *The Economic Writings of Sir William Petty...*, vol. I. Cambridge: Cambridge University Press.

Hybel, N., and Poulsen B. 2007. *The Danish Resources c. 1000–1550: Growth and Recession.* Amsterdam: Brill.

Ibarra Rodríguez, E. 1944. *El problema cerealista en España durante el reinado de los Reyes Católicos (1475–1516).* Madrid: Consejo Superior de Investigaciones Científicas.

Jacks, D. S. 2004. 'Market integration in the North and Baltic Seas, 1500–1800'. *Journal of European Economic History* 33: 285–329.

Jacquart, J. 1974. *La crise rurale en Ile-de-France 1550–1670.* Paris: Armand Colin.

Jäger, G. 2010. *Schwarzer Himmel – kalte Erde – weißer Tod: Wanderheuschrecken, Hagelschläge, Kältewellen und Lawinenkatastrophen im 'Land der Gebirge': Eine kleine Agrar- und Klimageschichte von Tirol.* Innsbruck: Universitätsverlag Wagner.

Jahn, P. M. 2010. *Vom Roboter zum Schulpropheten: Hanso Nepila (1766–1856).* Bautzen, Germany: Domowina.

Jansen, H., and Janse, A. (eds.) 1991. *Kroniek van het klooster Bloemhof te Wittewierum.* Hilversum, Netherlands: Verloren.

Jansen, P. C., and De Meere, J. M. M. 1982. 'Het sterftepatroon in Amsterdam 1774–1930: een analyse van de doodsoorzaken'. *Tijdschrift voor Sociale Geschiedenis* 8: 180–223.

Jenkins, D. 1990. 'The demography of late Stuart Montgomeryshire, c. 1660–1720'. *Montgomery Collections* 78: 73–113.

Johansen, H. C. 2002. *Danish Population History: 1600–1939.* Odense: University Press of Southern Denmark.

Johanson, V. F. 1924. *Finlands agrarpolitiska historia: En skildring av det finländska lantbrukets ekonomiska betingelser*, vol. I, *Från 1600-talet till år 1870.* Helsinki: Lantbruksvetenskapliga Samfundet.

Jones, R. E. 2013. *Bread upon the Waters: The St Petersburg Grain Trade and the Russian Economy, 1703–1811.* Pittsburgh: University of Pittsburgh Press.

Jörberg, L. 1972. *A History of Prices in Sweden 1732–1914*, vol. 1, *Sources, Methods, Tables.* Lund, Sweden: Gleerup.

Jordan, W. C. 1996. *The Great Famine: Northern Europe in the Early Fourteenth Century.* Princeton, NJ: Princeton University Press.

Jörg, C. 2008. *Teure, Hunger, Grosses Sterben: Hungersnöte und Versorgungskrisen in den Städten des Reiches während des 15. Jahrhunderts.* Stuttgart: Anton Hiersemann.

2010. 'Die Besänftigung göttlichen Zorns in karolingischer Zeit: kaiserliche Vorgaben zu Fasten, Gebet und Buße im zeitlichen Umfeld der Hungersnot von 805/06'. *Das Mittelalter* 15: 38–51.

Juerges, H. 2013. 'Collateral damage: the German food crisis, educational attainment and labor market outcomes of German post-war cohorts'. *Journal of Health Economics* 32: 286–303.

Jutikkala, E. 1955. 'The great Finnish famine in 1696–97'. *Scandinavian Economic History Review* 3: 48–63.

1971. 'The structure of mortality during catastrophic years in a pre-industrial society'. *Population Studies* 25: 283–5.

Jütte, R. 2005. 'Klimabedingte Teuerungen und Hungersnöte: Bettelverbote und Armenfürsorge als Krisenmanagement', in Behringer, W., Lehmann, H., and Pfister, C. (eds.). *Kulturelle Konsequenzen der 'Kleinen Eiszeit': Cultural Consequences of the 'Little Ice Age'*. Göttingen: Vandenhoeck & Ruprecht, pp. 225–37.

Kahan, A. 1989. *Russian Economic History: The Nineteenth Century*. Chicago: University of Chicago Press.

Kamen, H. 1974. *La Guerra de Sucesión en España 1700–1715*. Barcelona: Grijalbo.

Kaplan, S. 1976. *Bread, Politics and Political Economics in the Reign of Louis XV*. The Hague: Nijhoff.

1982. *Le complot de famine: Histoire d'une rumeur au XVIIIe siècle*. Paris: A. Colin.

Kaukiainen, Y. 1984. 'Harvest fluctuations and mortality in agrarian Finland (1810–1870)', in Bengtsson, T., Fridlizius, G., and Ohlsson, R. (eds.). *Pre-Industrial Population Change: The Mortality Decline and Short-Term Population Movements*. Stockholm: Almqvist & Wiksell International, pp. 235–54.

Kay, A. J. 2006. 'Germany's Staatssekretäre, mass starvation and the meeting of 2 May 1941'. *Journal of Contemporary History* 41: 685–700.

Keene, D. 2011. 'Crisis management in London's food supply, 1250–1500', in Dodds and Liddy (eds.), pp. 45–62.

Kelly, J. 1988. 'The resumption of emigration from Ireland after the American War of Independence, 1783–1787'. *Studia Hibernica* 24: 61–88.

1992a. 'Harvests and hardship: famine and scarcity in Ireland in the late 1720s'. *Studia Hibernica* 26: 65–105.

1992b. 'Scarcity and poor relief in eighteenth-century Ireland: the subsistence crisis of 1782–4'. *Irish Historical Studies* 28: 38–62.

2010. 'Charitable societies: their genesis and development, 1720–1800', in Kelly, J., and Powell, M. J. (eds.). *Clubs and Societies in Eighteenth-Century Ireland*. Dublin: Four Courts Press, pp. 89–108.

2012. 'Coping with crisis: the response to the famine of 1740–41'. *Eighteenth-Century Ireland* 27: 99–122.

Kelly, M., and Ó Gráda, C. 2013. 'The waning of the Little Ice Age'. *Journal of Interdisciplinary History* 44: 301–25.

2014a. 'Change points and temporal dependence in reconstructions of annual temperature: did Europe experience a Little Ice Age?'. *Annals of Applied Statistics* 8: 1372–94.

2014b. 'Living standards and mortality since the Middle Ages'. *Economic History Review* 67: 358–81.

2015. '*Why Ireland Starved* after three decades: the Great Famine in cross-section reconsidered'. *Irish Economic and Social History* 42: 53–61.

Kennedy, L., and Solar, P. M. 2007. *Irish Agriculture: A Price History from the Mid-Eighteenth Century to the Eve of the First World War*. Dublin: Royal Irish Academy.

Kerr, D. 1996. *The Catholic Church and the Famine*. Dublin: Columba Press

Kershaw, I. 1973. 'The Great Famine and the agrarian crisis in England'. *Past and Present* 59: 3–50.

Kesternich, I., Siflinger, B., Smith, J. P., and Winter, J. K. 2014. 'The effects of World War II on economic and health outcomes across Europe'. *Review of Economics and Statistics* 96: 103–18.

Kinealy, C. 1989. 'The poor law during the Great Famine: an administration in crisis', in Crawford (ed.), pp. 157–75.

Kluge, U. 1987. 'Hunger, Armut und soziale Devianz im 18. Jahrhundert: Hungerkrisen, Randgruppen und absolutistischer Staat in Preußen'. *Freiburger Universitätsblätter* 26: 61–91.

Kondrashin, V. V. (ed.) 2011–13. *Golod v SSSR, 1928–34*, 3 vols. Moscow.

Kondrat'ev, N. D. 1991 [1922]. *Rynok khlebov i ego regulirovaniye vo vremya voiny i revolyutsii*. Moscow: Nauka.

Kozlov, I., and Samsonova, A. 2005. 'The impact of the siege on the physical development of children', in Barber and Dzeniskevich (eds.), pp. 1174–96.

Krämer, D. 2015. *'Menschen grasten nun mit dem Vieh': Die letzte grosse Hungerkrise der Schweiz*. Basel: Schwabe.

Kurmann, F. 2011. 'Hungersnöte'. Historisches Lexikon der Schweiz, www.hls-dhs-dss.ch (accessed 16 February 2011).

Kuttner, E. 1949. *Het Hongerjaar 1566*. Amsterdam: NV Amsterdamsche Boeken Courantmaatschappij.

Kuys, J. (ed.) 1983. *De Tielse kroniek: Een geschiedenis van de Lage Landen van de volksverhuizingen tot het midden van het vijftiende eeuw, met een vervolg over de jaren 1552–1566*. Amsterdam: Verloren.

Labrousse, E. 1933. *Esquisse du mouvement des prix et des revenus en France au XVIIIe siècle*. Paris: Librairie Dalloz.

1944. *La crise de l'économie française à la fin de l'Ancien Régime et au début de la Révolution*. Paris: Presses Universitaires de France.

Lachiver, M. 1969. *La population de Meulan du XVIIe au XIXe siècle (vers 1600– 1870): Étude de démographie historique*. Paris: EPHE.

1991. *Les années de misère: La famine au temps du Grand Roi, 1680–1720*. Paris: Fayard.

Ladan, R. 2012. *Gezondheidszorg in Leiden in de late Middeleeuwen*. Hilversum, Netherlands: Verloren.

Ladero Quesada, M. A. 2014. 'La población de reinos y ciudades en la Baja Edad Media española (de finales del siglo XIII a comienzos del XVI)'. *Boletín de la Real Academia de la Historia* 211: 37–78.

Laliena Corbera, C. 2011. 'Dévelopment économique, marché céréalier et disettes en Aragon et en Navarre, 1280–1340', in Bourin, M., Menant, F., and Drendel, J. (eds.). *Les disettes dans la conjoncture de 1300 en Méditerranée occidentale*. Rome: École Française de Rome, pp. 277–308.

Lamb, H. H. 1982. *Climate, History and the Modern World*. London: Routledge.

Landsteiner, E. 2005. 'Wenig Brot und saurer Wein: Kontinuität und Wandel in der zentraleuropäischen Ernährungskultur im letzten Drittel des 16. Jahrhunderts', in Behringer, W., Lehmann, H., and Pfister, C. (eds.). *Kulturelle Konsequenzen der 'Kleinen Eiszeit': Cultural Consequences of the 'Little Ice Age'*. Göttingen: Vandenhoeck & Ruprecht, pp. 87–147.

Lappalainen, M. 2014. 'Death and disease during the Great Finnish Famine 1695–1697'. *Scandinavian Journal of History* 39: 425–47.

Larsson, D. 2006. 'Den dolda transitionen: om ett demografiskt brytningsskede i det tidiga 1700-talets Sverige', unpublished PhD thesis. University of Gothenburg.

Larsson, H. A. 1999. *Boken om Sveriges historia*. Stockholm: Forum.

Laurénaudie, M.-J. 1952. 'Les famines en Languedoc au XIVe et XVe siècles'. *Annales du Midi* 64: 23–35.

Lázaro Ruiz, M. 1994. *La población de la ciudad de Logroño durante el Antiguo Régimen (1500–1833)*. Logroño, Spain: Instituto de Estudios Riojanos.

Lázaro Ruiz, M., and Gurría García, P. A. 1989. *Las crisis de mortalidad en La Rioja (siglos XVI–XVIII)*. Logroño, Spain: Instituto de Estudios Riojanos.

Le Mée, R. (ed.) 1980. 'Bibliographie des monographies paroissiales'. *Bulletin d'information de la Société de Démographie Historique* 30 (special issue).

Le Roy Ladurie, E. 1969. 'L'Aménorrhée de famine (XVIIe–XXe siècles)'. *Annales: Économies, Sociétés, Civilisations* 24: 1589–601.

1974. 'Homme–animal, nature–culture: les problèmes de l'équilibre démographique', in Morin, E., and Piattelli-Palmarini, M. (eds.). *L'Unité de l'homme*, vol. III, *Pour une anthropologie fondamentale*. Paris: Seuil, pp. 87–128.

1978. 'L'Histoire immobile', in *Le territoire de l'historien*, vol. II. Paris: Gallimard, pp. 7–34.

1983. *Histoire du climat depuis l'an mil*, 2nd edn. Paris: Flammarion.

2006. *Histoire humaine et comparée du climat*, vol. II, *Disettes et révolutions*. Paris: Fayard.

2007. 'Fluctuations météorologiques: retentissement sur la vie et la santé humaines (XIVe–XXIe siècles)'. *Presse thermale et climatique* 144: 95–102.

Lee, J. J. 1973. *The Modernization of Irish Society 1848–1921*. Dublin: Gill & Macmillan.

Lee, J. S. 2011. 'Grain shortages in late medieval towns', in Dodds and Liddy (eds.), pp. 63–80.

Lehmann, H. 1981. *Das Zeitalter des Absolutismus: Gottesgnadentum und Kriegsnot*. Stuttgart: Kohlhammer.

Lenihan, P. 1997. 'War and population, 1649–1652'. *Irish Economic and Social History* 24: 1–21.

Levasseur, E. 1893. *Les prix: Aperçu de l'histoire économique de la valeur et du revenu de la terre en France, du commencement du XIIIe siècle au XVIIIe siècle*. Paris: Typographie Chamerot et Renouard.

Lewin, M. 1968. *Russian Peasants and Soviet Power*. London: George Allen & Unwin.

Lih, L. T. 1990. *Bread and Authority in Russia, 1914–1921*. Berkeley, CA: University of California Press.

Livi Bacci, M. 1968. 'Fertility and nuptiality changes in Spain from the 18th to the early 20th century'. *Population Studies* 22: 83–102.

1981. *A Concise History of World Population*. Cambridge: Cambridge University Press.

1991. *Population and Nutrition: An Essay on European Demographic History*. Cambridge: Cambridge University Press.

1997. 'Population, constraint and adaptation: a historical outlook', in Dorfman, R., and Rogers, P. P. (eds.). *Science with a Human Face: In Honor of Roger Randall Revelle*. Cambridge, MA: Harvard University Press, pp. 207–25.

2000. *The Population of Europe*. Oxford: Blackwell.

Llopis Agelán, E., and Abarca, V. 2014. 'El retroceso de la mortalidad catastrófica y su papel en la moderación de la mortalidad general en la España interior en los siglos XVIII y XIX', unpublished communication.

Llopis Agelán, E., and Sánchez Salazar, F. 2014. 'La crisis de 1803–1805 en las dos Castillas: subsistencias, mortalidad y colapso institucional', unpublished paper. XVI Seminario de Historia Económica. Bernardos (Segovia).

Llopis Agelán, E., García-Hiernaux, A., García Montero, H., González Mariscal, M., and Hernández García, R. 2007. 'Índices de precios de tres ciudades españolas, 1680–1800: Palencia, Madrid y Sevilla'. *América Latina en la Historia Económica* 32: 31–80.

Llopis Agelán, E., Pérez Moreda, V., and Sebastián Amarilla, J. A. 2015. 'Algunas sombras en el *Siglo de las Luces*: la sobremortalidad adulta en el interior castellano a mediados del setecientos', in García Ruiz, J. L., and Ortiz-Villajos, J. M. (eds.). *Ensayos de historia y pensamiento económicos: En homenaje al profesor Juan Hernández Andreu*. Madrid: Universidad Complutense, pp. 69–82.

Lo Cascio, E., and Malanima, P. 2005. 'Cycles and stability: Italian population before the demographic transition'. *Rivista di Storia Economica* 3: 197–232.

Lomagin, N. 2002. *Neizvestnaya blokada*, 2 vols. St Petersburg: Neva.

Lorcin, M.-T. 1981. *Vivre et mourir en Lyonnais à la fin du Moyen Age*. Paris: CNRS.

Lorimer, F. 1946. *The Population of the Soviet Union: History and Prospects*. Geneva: League of Nations.

Løvlien, A. 1977. 'Dødelighetskrisa på 1740-tallet: en sammenligning mellom to norske landsdeler', PhD thesis. University of Bergen.

Löwe, H.-D. 1986. 'Teuerungsrevolten, Teuerungspolitik und Marktregulierung im 18. Jahrhundert in England, Frankreich und Deutschland'. *Saeculum* 37: 291–312.

Lucas, H. 1930. 'The Great European Famine of 1315, 1316, and 1317'. *Speculum* 5: 343–77.

Luce, A. A., and Jessop, T. E. (eds.) 1956. *The Works of George Berkeley, Bishop of Cloyne*, 9 vols. London: Thomas Nelson.

Lumey, L. H., and Stein, A. D. 1997. 'Offspring birth weights after maternal intrauterine undernutrition: a comparison within sibships'. *American Journal of Epidemiology* 146: 810–19.

Lumey, L. H., and Vaiserman, A. (eds.) 2013. *Early Life Nutrition and Adult Health and Development: Lessons from Changing Dietary Patterns, Famines and Experimental Studies*. New York: Nova Science.

Lumey, L. H. and van Poppel, F. W. A. 2013. 'The Dutch famine of 1944–45 as a human laboratory: changes in the early life environment and adult health', in Lumey and Vaiserman (eds.), pp. 59–76.

Lumey, L. H., Stein, A. D., Kahn H. S., van der Pal-de Bruin K. M., Blauw G. J., Zybert P. A., and Susser, E. S. 2007. 'Cohort profile: the Dutch Hunger Winter families study'. *International Journal of Epidemiology* 36: 1196–204.

Lumey, L. H., Stein, A. D., and Susser, E. S. 2011. 'Prenatal famine and adult health'. *Annual Reviews of Public Health* 32: 237–62.

Lundh, C. 2003. 'Den regionala befolkningsstatistiken i Tabellverket: en data-beskrivning', Paper in Economic History no. 91. Lund, Sweden: Department of Economic History, Lund University.

Luterbacher, J., and Pfister, C. 2015. 'The year without a summer'. *Nature Geoscience* 8: 246–8.

Luterbacher, J., García-Herrera, R., Akcer-On, S., Allan, R., Alvarez-Castro, M. C., and Benito, G. 2012. 'A review of 2000 years of paleoclimatic evidence in the Mediterranean: the climate of the Mediterranean region', in Lionello, P. (ed.). *The Climate of the Mediterranean Region*. New York: Elsevier, pp. 87–183.

Lyashchenko, P. I. 1947. *Istoriya Narodnogo Khozyaistvo SSSR*. Leningrad.

Lyons, E. 1964. *Herbert Hoover: A Biography*. Garden City, NY: Doubleday.

Lyons, M. C. 1989. 'Weather, famine, pestilence, and plague in Ireland, 900–1500', in Crawford (ed.), pp. 31–74.

Lythe, S. G. E. 1960. *The Economy of Scotland, 1550–1625*. Edinburgh: Oliver and Boyd.

McCabe, D., and Ó Gráda, C. 2009. 'Destitution, human agency, and relief: Enniskillen workhouse during the Irish Famine', in Denie, M., and Farrell, S. (eds.). *Power and Popular Culture in Modern Ireland: Essays in Honour of James S. Donnelly, Jr.* Dublin: Irish Academic Press, pp. 7–30.

McGregor, P. P. L. 1989. 'Demographic pressure and the Irish famine: Malthus after Mokyr'. *Land Economics* 65: 228–38.

　2004. '"Insufficient for the support of a family?" Wages on the public works during the Great Irish Famine'. *Economic and Social Review* 35: 219–39.

MacSuibhne, B. 2013. 'A jig in the poorhouse'. *Dublin Review of Books* 32: www.drb.ie/essays/a-jig-in-the-poorhouse.

Mahlerwein, G. 2007. 'The consequences of the potato blight in south Germany', in Ó Gráda, Paping and Vanhaute (eds.), pp. 213–21.

Majd, M. G. 2003. *The Great Famine and Genocide in Persia, 1917–1919*. Lanham, MD: University Press of America.

Malanima, P. 2013. 'Prezzi e salari', in Malanima, P., and Ostuni, N. (eds.). *Il Mezzogiorno prima dell'Unità: Fonti, dati, storiografia*. Soveria Mannelli, Italy: Rubbettino, pp. 339–94.

Malthus, T. R. 1798. *An Essay on the Principle of Population, as It Affects the Future Improvement of Society*. London: Johnson.

　1808. 'Newenham and others on the state of Ireland'. *Edinburgh Review* 12: 336–45.

Marin, B., and Virlouvet, C. (eds.) 2003. *Nourrir les cités de Méditerranée: Antiquité – temps modernes*. Paris: Maisonneuve & Larose.

Marshall, J. D. (ed.) 1967. *The Autobiography of William Stout of Lancaster, 1665–1752*. Manchester: Manchester University Press.

Martin, J. 2007. *Medieval Russia, 980–1584*. Cambridge: Cambridge University Press

Mattmüller, M. 1982. 'Die Hungersnot der Jahre 1770/71 in der Basler Landschaft', in Nicolai, B., and Quirinus, R. (eds.). *Gesellschaft und Gesellschaften: Festschrift zum 65. Geburtstag von Prof. Dr. Ulrich Im Hof*. Bern: Wyss, pp. 271–91.

1987. *Bevölkerungsgeschichte der Schweiz*, vol. I, *Die Frühe Neuzeit 1500–1700*. Basel: Helbing Lichtenhahn.

Mauelshagen, F. 2010. *Klimageschichte der Neuzeit*. Darmstadt: WBG.

Mazower, M. 1993. *Inside Hitler's Greece: The Experience of Occupation, 1941–44*. New Haven, CT: Yale University Press.

Mears, N., Raffe, A., Taylor, S., and Williamson, P. 2013. *National Prayers: Special Worship since the Reformation*, vol. I, *Special Prayers, Fasts and Thanksgivings in the British Isles, 1533–1688*. Woodbridge, UK: Boydell & Brewer.

Medick, H. 1985. 'Teuerung, Hunger und "moralische Ökonomie von oben": die Hungerkrise der Jahre 1816–17 in Württemberg'. *Beiträge zur Historischen Sozialkunde* 2: 39–44.

Meister, A. (ed.) 1901. 'Niederdeutsche Chroniken aus dem XV. Jahrhundert'. *Annalen des Historischen Vereins für den Niederrhein* 70: 43–64.

Mentink, G. J., and van der Woude, A. M. 1965. *De demografische ontwikkeling te Rotterdam en Cool in de 17e en 18e eeuw*. Rotterdam: Gemeentearchief Rotterdam.

Mestayer, M. 1963. 'Prix du blé et de l'avoine de 1329 à 1793'. *Revue du Nord* 45: 157–76.

Meuvret, J. 1946. 'Les crises de subsistances et la démographie de la France d'Ancien Régime'. *Population* 1: 643–50.

1977. *Le problème des subsistances à l'époque Louis XIV*, 2 vols. Paris: Éd. de l'EHESS-Mouton.

Militzer, S. 1998. 'Sachsen: Klimatatsachen und Umriß von Klimawirkungen im 17. Jahrhundert', in Schirmer, U. (ed.). *Sachsen im 17. Jahrhundert: Krise, Krieg und Neubeginn*. Brandis, Germany: Sax-Verlag, pp. 69–100.

Miller, J. A. 1999. *Mastering the Market: The State and the Grain Trade in Northern France, 1700–1860*. Cambridge: Cambridge University Press.

Mironov, B. N. 1985. *Khlebnietseny v Rossiizadvastoletiya (XVIII–XIX gg)*. Leningrad.

2010. *Blagosostoyanie naseleniya i revolyutsii v imperskoi Rossii: XVIII – nachalo XX veka*. Moscow: Novyi Khronograf.

Mitchell, B. R. 1975. *European Historical Statistics*. London: Macmillan.

Mocarelli, L. 2012. 'Le crisi alimentari nello Stato di Milano tra metà Settecento e Restaurazione: una realtà di eccezione?', in David, T., Mathieu, J., Schaufelbuehl, J. M., and Straumann, T. (eds.). *Krisen: Ursachen, Deutungen und Folgen: Crises: Causes, interprétations et conséquences*. Zurich: Chronos Verlag, pp. 97–109.

2015. 'Ripensare le crisi alimentari: lo Stato di Milano nel secondo Settecento', in Ferrari, M. L., and Vaquero Piñeiro, M. (eds.). *"Moia La Carestia". La Scarsità Alimentare in Età Preindustriale*. Bologna: Il Mulino, pp. 35–54.

Mokyr, J. 1981. 'Irish history with the potato'. *Irish Economic and Social History* 8: 8–29.

1985. *Why Ireland Starved: A Quantitative and Analytical History of the Irish Economy 1800–1850*, 2nd edn. London: Allen & Unwin.

Mokyr, J., and Ó Gráda, C. 2002. 'Famine disease and famine mortality: lessons from the Irish experience, 1845–50', in Dyson, T., and Ó Gráda, C. (eds.). *Famine Demography: Perspectives from the Past and Present*. Oxford: Oxford University Press, pp. 19–43.

Molinier, A. 1985. *Stagnations et croissance: Le Vivarais aux XVIIe–XVIIIe siècles*. Paris: Éd. de l'EHESS.

Moltmann, G. (ed.) 1989. *Aufbruch nach Amerika: Die Auswanderungswelle von 1816/17*. Stuttgart: Metzlersche Verlagsbuchhandlung.

Monahan, G. W. 1993. *Year of Sorrows: The Great Famine of 1709 in Lyon*. Columbus, OH: Ohio State University Press.

Moreno Lázaro, J. 2009. *Los hermanos de Rebeca: Motines y amotinados a mediados del siglo XIX en Castilla la Vieja y León*. Palencia, Spain: Región Editorial.

Moriceau, J.-M., and Postel-Vinay, G. 1992. *Ferme, entreprise, famille: Grande exploitation et changements agricoles: Les Chartier XVIIe–XIXe siècles*. Paris: Éd. de l'EHESS.

Morineau, M. 1970a. *Les faux-semblants d'un démarrage économique: Agriculture et démographie en France au XVIIIe siècle*. Paris: Armand Colin.

1970b. 'Cendrillon devenue fée? La pomme de terre au XVIIIe siècle'. *Annales: Économies, Sociétés, Civilisations* 6: 1767–85.

Moskoff, W. 1990. *The Bread of Affliction: Food Supply in the USSR during World War II*. Cambridge: Cambridge University Press.

Müller, G. 1998. *Hunger in Bayern 1816–1818: Politik und Gesellschaft in einer Staatskrise des frühen 19. Jahrhunderts*. Frankfurt: Peter Lang.

Murray, K. A. H. 1955. *Agriculture*. London: HMSO.

Mus, F. 1984. 'De historisch-demografische ontwikkeling van Aarsele tijdens de nieuwe tijd, 1627–1795', unpublished MA thesis. University of Louvain.

Mykland, K. 1977. *Norges historie*, vol. VII, *Gjennom nødsår og krig: 1648–1720*. Oslo: Cappelen.

Myrdal, J. 1999. *Jordbruket under feodalismen 1000–1700*. Stockholm: Natur och Kultur.

2011. 'Farming and feudalism', in Myrdal, J., and Morell, M. (eds.). *The Agrarian History of Sweden*. Lund, Sweden: Nordic Academic Press, pp. 72–117.

Nadal i Oller, J. 1991. 'Las grandes crisis de mortalidad de los años 1793–1812: los efectos a largo plazo en la población catalana'. *Boletín de la Asociación de Demografía Histórica* 8: 37–49.

Nadal i Oller, J., and Giralt, E. 1960. *La population catalane de 1553 à 1717: L'Immigration française et les autres facteurs de son développement*. Paris: Sevpen.

Nairn, I. A., Shane, P. R., Cole, J. W., Leonard, G. J., Self, S., and Pearson, N. 2004. 'Rhyolite magma processes of the ~AD1315 Kaharoa eruption episode, Tarawera volcano, New Zealand'. *Journal of Volcanology and Geothermal Research* 131: 265–94.

Nally, D. P. 2011. *Human Encumbrances: Political Violence and the Great Irish Famine*. South Bend, IN: University of Notre Dame Press.

Nassiet, M. 1998. 'La diffusion du blé noir en France à l'époque moderne'. *Histoire et Sociétés Rurales* 9: 59–77.

Neal, F. 1998. *Black '47: Britain and the Famine Irish*. London: Palgrave Macmillan.

Neelsen, S., and Stratmann, T. 2011. 'Effects of prenatal and early life malnutrition: evidence from the Greek famine'. *Journal of Health Economics* 30: 479–88.

Netting, R. 1981. *Balancing on an Alp: Ecological Change and Continuity in a Swiss Mountain Community*. Cambridge: Cambridge University Press.

Neumann, J., and Lindgrén, S. 1979. 'Great historical events that were significantly affected by the weather: 4, the Great Famines in Finland and Estonia, 1695–97'. *Bulletin of American Meteorological Society* 60: 775–87.

Neveux, H. 1980. *Vie et déclin d'une structure économique: Les grains du Cambrésis, fin du 14e – début du 17e siècle*. Paris: Mouton.

Neveux, H., and Tits-Dieuaide, M.-J. 1979. 'Étude structurelle des fluctuations courtes des rendements céréaliers dans l'Europe du Nord-Ouest (XIVe–XVIe siècles)'. *Cahiers des Annales de Normandie* 11: 17–42.

Ní Chinnéide, S. 1957. 'Dialann Í Chonchubhair'. *Galvia* 4: 4–17.

Ní Urdail, M., and Ó Gráda, C. 2015. 'Tadhg Ó Neachtain agus Muiris Ó Conaill ag trácht ar bhlianta an áir, 1739–42', in Ó Ciosáin, N., and Cunningham, J. (eds.). *Culture and Society in Ireland since 1750: Essays in Honour of Gearóid O Tuathaigh*. Dublin: Lilliput Press, pp. 33–43.

Nicholas, D. 1992. *Medieval Flanders*. New York: Longman.

Nicolai, N. M. 1803. *Memorie, leggi ed osservazioni sulle campagne e sull'Annona di Roma*, vol. III. Rome: Stamperia Pagliarini.

Nifontov, A. 1973. *Zernovoeproizvodstvo v Rossiivovtoroy XIX veka*. Moscow.

Noordam, D. J. 1986. *Leven in Maasland: Een hoogontwikkelde plattelandssamenleving in de achttiende en het begin van de negentiende eeuw*. Hilversum, Netherlands: Verloren.

Noordegraaf, L. 1980. 'Levensstandaard en levensmiddelenpolitiek in Alkmaar vanaf het eind van de 16de tot in het begin van de 19de eeuw'. *Alkmaarse Historische Reeks* 4: 55–100.

1985a. 'Dearth, famine and social policy in the Dutch Republic at the end of the sixteenth century', in Clark, P. (ed.). *The European Crisis of the 1590s: Essays in Comparative History*. London: George Allen & Unwin, pp. 67–83.

1985b. *Hollands welvaren? Levensstandaard in Holland 1450–1650*. Bergen: Octavo.

Noordegraaf, L., and Valk, G. 1988. *De gave Gods: De pest in Holland vanaf de late middeleeuwen*. Amsterdam: Bert Bakker.

Ó Gráda, C. 1993. *Ireland Before and After the Famine: Explorations in Economic History*, 2nd edn. Manchester: Manchester University Press.

1994. *An Drochshaol: Béaloideas agus Amhráin*. Dublin: Coiscéim.

(ed.) 1997. *Famine 150: Commemorative Lecture Series*. Dublin: Teagasc.

1999. *Black '47: The Great Irish Famine in History, Economy, and Memory*. Princeton, NJ: Princeton University Press.

2001. 'Markets and famines: evidence from nineteenth-century Finland'. *Economic Development and Cultural Change* 49: 575–90.

2005. 'Markets and famines in pre-industrial Europe'. *Journal of Interdisciplinary History* 36: 143–66.

2006. *Ireland's Great Famine: Interdisciplinary Perspectives*. Dublin: UCD Press.

2009. *Famine: A Short History*. Princeton, NJ: Princeton University Press.

2011. 'Yardsticks for workhouse management during the Great Famine', in Crossman, V., and Gray, P. (eds.). *Poverty and Welfare in Ireland 1838–1948*. Dublin: Irish Academic Press, pp. 69–96.

2015a. *Eating People Is Wrong and Other Essays on the History and Future of Famine*. Princeton, NJ: Princeton University Press.

2015b. 'Neither feast nor famine: England before the Industrial Revolution', in Nye, J., Greif, A., and Kiesling, L. (eds.). *Institutions, Industrialization, and Innovation*. Princeton, NJ: Princeton University Press, pp. 1–31.

Ó Gráda, C., and Chevet, J.-M. 2002. 'Famine and market in Ancien Régime France'. *Journal of Economic History* 62: 706–33.

Ó Gráda, C., and Ó Muirithe, D. 2010. 'The Irish famine of 1740–41 in Gaelic poetry'. *Éire – Ireland* 45: 41–62.

Ó Gráda, C., and O'Rourke, K. H. 1997. 'Mass migration as disaster relief: lessons from the Great Irish Famine'. *European Review of Economic History* 1: 3–27.

Ó Gráda, C., Paping, R., and Vanhaute, E. (eds.) 2007. *When the Potato Failed: Causes and Effects of the Last European Subsistence Crisis, 1845–1850*. Turnhout, Belgium: Brepols.

Ó Murchadha, C. 2011. *The Great Famine: Ireland's Agony 1845–1852*. London: Bloomsbury.

O'Brien, H. 2010. *The Famine Clearance in Toomevara, County Tipperary*. Dublin: Four Courts Press.

O'Connell, M. 1746. *Observationes Medicinales*. Dublin: Kelly & Faulkner.

O'Neill, T. P. 1956. 'The organization and administration of relief, 1845–52', in Edwards and Williams (eds.), pp. 209–59.

1966. 'The famine of 1822', unpublished MA thesis. University College Dublin.

1989. 'The food crisis of the 1890s', in Crawford (ed.), pp. 176–97.

1996. 'Minor famines and relief in Galway, 1815–1925', in Moran, G., and Gillespie, R. (eds.). *Galway: History and Society*. Dublin: Geography Publications, pp. 445–87.

2000. 'Famine evictions', in King, C. (ed.). *Famine, Land and Culture in Ireland*. Dublin: UCD Press, pp. 29–70.

O'Rourke, K. H. 1991. 'Did the Great Famine matter?'. *Journal of Economic History* 51: 1–22.

Odenwälder, N. 2008. *Nahrungsproteste und moralische Ökonomie: Das Alte Reich von 1600 bis 1789*. Saarbrücken, Germany: Müller.

Offer, A. 1989. *The First World War: An Agrarian Interpretation*. Oxford: Oxford University Press.

Offermans, P. H. M. G. 1972. *Arbeid en levensstandaard in Nijmegen omstreeks de Reductie, 1550–1600*. Zutphen, Netherlands: De Walburg Pers.

Oliver-Smith, A. 2004. 'Theorizing vulnerability in a globalized world: a political ecological perspective', in Bankoff, G., Frerks, G., and Hillhorst, D. (eds.). *Mapping Vulnerability: Disasters, Development and People*. London: Earthscan, pp. 10–24.

Oman, L., Roback, A., Stenchikov, G. L., and Thordarson, T. 2006. 'High-latitude eruptions cast shadow over the African monsoon and the flow of the Nile'. *Geophysical Research Letters* 33: http://onlinelibrary.wiley.com/doi/10.1029/2006GL027665/full.

Orlandi, G. 1996. 'Il regno di Napoli nel settecento: il mondo di S. Alfonso Maria de Liguori'. *Spicilegium Historicum Congregationis SSmi Redemptoris* 44: 5–389.

Ostrom, E. 1990. *Governing the Commons: The Evolution of Institutions for Collective Action.* Cambridge: Cambridge University Press.

Otterness, P. 2004. *Becoming German: The 1709 Palatine Migration to New York.* Ithaca, NY: Cornell University Press.

Outhwaite, R. B. 1981, 'Dearth and government intervention in English grain markets, 1590–1700'. *Economic History Review* 34: 389–406.

  1991. *Dearth, Public Policy and Social Disturbance in England, 1550–1800.* Cambridge: Cambridge University Press.

Overton, M. 1996. *Agricultural Revolution in England: The Transformation of the Agrarian Economy, 1500–1800.* Cambridge: Cambridge University Press.

Palermo, L. 1990. *Mercati del grano a Roma tra Medioevo e Rinascimento,* vol. I, *Il mercato distrettuale del grano in età comunale.* Rome: Istituto nazionale di studi romani.

  1997. *Sviluppo economico e società preindustriali: Cicli strutture e congiunture in Europa dal medioevo alla prima età moderna.* Rome: Viella.

Palermo, L., and Strangio, D. 1997. 'Politiche dell'alimentazione e carestie nello Stato della Chiesa: un modello di lungo periodo (secoli XIV–XVIII)', in Cavaciocchi, S. (ed.). *Alimentazione e nutrizione.* Florence: Le Monnier, pp. 325–38.

Pallach, U.-C. (ed.). 1986. *Hunger: Quellen zu einem Alltagsproblem Quellen seit dem Dreissigjährigen Krieg, mit einem Ausblick auf die Dritte Welt.* Munich: Deutscher Taschenbuch-Verlag.

Paping, R. 1995. *Voor een handvol stuivers: De levensstandaard van boeren, arbeiders en middenstanders op de Groninger klei, 1770–1860.* Groningen, Netherlands: NEHI.

  2004. 'Family strategies, wage labour and the family life cycle in the Groningen countryside, c. 1850–1910', in Kooij, P., and Paping, R. (eds.). *Where the Twain Meet Again: New Results of the Dutch–Russian Project on Regional Development 1750–1917.* Wageningen, Netherlands: NEHI, pp. 147–67.

Paping, R., and Tassenaar, V. 2007. 'The consequences of the potato disease in the Netherlands, 1845–60: a regional approach', in Ó Gráda, Paping and Vanhaute (eds.), pp. 149–84.

Parker, G. 2013. *Global Crisis: War, Climate Change and Catastrophe in the Seventeenth Century.* New Haven, CT: Yale University Press.

Parziale, L. 2009. *Nutrire la città: Produzione e commercio alimentare a Milano tra cinquecento e seicento.* Milan: Franco Angeli.

Pedersen, E. A., and Widgren, M. 2011. *Agriculture in Sweden: 800 BC – AD 100,* in Myrdal, J., and Morell, M. (eds.). *The Agrarian History of Sweden.* Lund, Sweden: Nordic Academic Press, pp. 46–71.

Peña Sánchez, D., and Sánchez-Albornoz, N. 1983. *Dependencia dinámica entre precios agrícolas: El trigo en España, 1857–1890: Un estudio empírico.* Madrid: Banco de España.

Pérez Moreda, V. 1980. *Las crisis de mortalidad en la España interior (siglos XVI–XIX).* Madrid: Siglo XXI.

1984. 'Crisis demográficas y crisis agrarias: paludismo y agricultura en España a fines del siglo XVIII', in *Congreso de historia rural: Siglos XIV al XIX*. Madrid: Casa de Velázquez Universidad Complutense, pp. 333–54.

1985. 'Consum deficitari, fam i crisis demogràfiques a l'Espanya dels segles XVI-XIX'. *Estudis d'Història Agrària* 5: 7–24.

1998. 'El final de la expansión demográfica: las crisis de mortalidad de los años 90', in Ribot García, L. A., and Belenguer Cebrià, E. (eds.). *Las sociedades ibéricas y el mar a finales del siglo XVI*, vol. IV, *La corona de Castilla*. Madrid: Comisaría General de España en la Expo de Lisboa 98, pp. 5–23.

2010a. 'Las crisis demográficas del periodo napoleónico en España', in La Parra López, E. (ed.). *La Guerra de Napoleón en España: Reacciones, imágenes, consecuencias*. Alicante: Universidad de Alicante Casa de Velázquez, pp. 305–32.

2010b. 'Una nueva interpretación de las relaciones entre mortalidad y economía: pruebas históricas contra el modelo de las "crisis de subsistencias"', in Cavaciocchi (ed.), pp. 181–218.

Pérez Serrano, J. 1992. *Cádiz, la ciudad desnuda: Cambio económico y modelo demográfico en la formación de la Andalucía contemporánea*. Cadiz: Universidad de Cádiz.

Perren, R. 2005. 'Farmers and consumers under strain: Allied meat supplies in the First World War'. *Agricultural History Review* 53: 212–28.

Perrie, M. 2006. 'The Time of Troubles (1603–1613)', in *The Cambridge History of Russia*, vol. I, *From Early Rus' to 1689*. Cambridge: Cambridge University Press, pp. 409–32.

Perrot, J.-C. 1984. 'L'Analyse dynamique des crises au XVIIIe siècle', in Croix, A., Jacquart, J., and Lebrun, F. (eds.). *Études réunies en l'honneur de Pierre Goubert*. Toulouse: Privat, pp. 543–51.

Persson, K. G. 1999. *Grain Markets in Europe 1500–1900: Integration and Deregulation*. Cambridge: Cambridge University Press.

Peset, J. L., and de Carvalho, J. A. 1972. 'Hambre y enfermedad en Salamanca: estudio d la repercusión de la "crisis de subsistencias" de 1803–1805 en Salamanca'. *Asclepio* 24: 225–66.

Pfister, C. 1984. *Das Klima der Schweiz von 1525-1860 und seine Bedeutung in der Geschichte von Bevölkerung und Landwirtschaft*, 2 vols. Bern: Haupt.

1990. 'Food supply in the Swiss canton of Bern, 1850', in Newman, L. F. (ed.). *Hunger in History: Food Shortage, Poverty, and Deprivation*. Oxford: Blackwell, pp. 281–303.

1999a. *Wetternachhersage: 500 Jahre Klimavariationen und Naturkatastrophen (1496–1995)*. Bern: Haupt.

1999b. 'Wanderungsgewinne und -verluste 1764–1990', in Pfister, C., and Egli, H.-R. (eds.). *Historisch-Statistischer Atlas des Kantons Bern 1750–1995: Umwelt – Bevölkerung –Wirtschaft – Politik*. Bern: Historischer Verein, pp. 62–3.

2005. 'Weeping in the snow: the second period of Little Ice Age-type impacts, 1570–1630', in Behringer, W., Lehmann, H., and Pfister, C. (eds.). *Kulturelle Konsequenzen der 'Kleinen Eiszeit': Cultural Consequences of the 'Little Ice Age'*. Göttingen: Vandenhoeck & Ruprecht, pp. 31–86.

2007a. *Bevölkerungsgeschichte und Historische Demographie 1500–1800*, vol. II. Munich: Oldenbourg.

2007b. 'Climatic extremes, recurrent crises and witch hunts: strategies of European societies in coping with exogenous shocks in the late sixteenth and early seventeenth centuries'. *Medieval History Journal* 10: 33–73.

Pfister, C., and Brázdil, R. 2006. 'Social vulnerability to climate in the "Little Ice Age": an example from central Europe in the early 1770s'. *Climate of the Past* 2: 115–29.

Pfister, U., and Fertig, G. 2010. 'The population history of Germany: research strategy and preliminary results', Working Paper no. 2010-035. Rostock, Germany: Max Planck Institute for Demographic Research.

Pfrenzinger, A. 1941. *Die Mainfränkische Auswanderung nach Ungarn und den Österr: Erbländern im 18. Jahrhundert.* Vienna: Melchior.

Pinto, G. 1978. *Il libro del biadaiolo: Carestie ed annona a Firenze dalla metà del '200 al 1348.* Florence: Olschki.

1996. 'Dalla tarda antichità alla metà del XVI secolo', in Del Panta, L., Livi Bacci, M., Pinto, G., and Sonnino, E. (eds.). *La popolazione italiana dal Medioevo ad oggi.* Rome: Laterza, pp. 17–71.

2012. 'Food security', in Montanari, M. (ed.). *A Cultural History of Food in the Medieval Age.* London: Berg, pp. 57–71.

Piquero, S. 1991. *Demografía guipuzcoana en el Antiguo Régimen.* Bilbao: Universidad del País Vasco.

Pitkänen, K. J. 2002. 'Famine mortality in nineteenth-century Finland: is there a sex bias?', in Dyson, T., and Ó Gráda, C. (eds.). *Famine Demography: Perspectives from the Past and Present.* Oxford: Oxford University Press, pp. 65–92.

Piuz, A.-M., and Zumkeller, D. 1985. 'La politique de stockage des grains à Genève au XVIIIe siècle', in Gast, M., and Sigaut, F. (eds.). *Les techniques de conservation des grains à long terme: Leur rôle dans la dynamique des systèmes de cultures et des sociétés*, vol. II. Paris: Éditions du Centre National de la Recherche Scientifique, pp. 579–95.

Póirtéir, C. 1995. *Famine Echoes.* Dublin: Gill & Macmillan.

1996. *Glórtha ón Ghorta: Béaloideas na Gaeilge agus an Gorta Mór.* Dublin: Coiscéim.

Pollard, A. J. 1989. 'The north-eastern economy and the agrarian crisis of 1438–1440'. *Northern History* 25: 88–105.

Pomeranz, K. 2005. *The Great Divergence: China, Europe, and the Making of the Modern World Economy.* Princeton, NJ: Princeton University Press.

Post, J. D. 1977. *The Last Great Subsistence Crisis in the Western World.* Baltimore: Johns Hopkins University Press.

1984. 'Climatic variability and the European mortality wave of the early 1740s'. *Journal of Interdisciplinary History* 15: 1–30.

1985. *Food Shortage, Climatic Variability, and Epidemic Disease in Preindustrial Europe: The Mortality Peak in the Early 1740s.* Ithaca, NY: Cornell University Press.

1990. 'The mortality crisis of the early 1770s and European demographic trends'. *Journal of Interdisciplinary History* 21: 29–62.

Posthumus, N. W. 1964. *Nederlandse prijsgeschiedenis*, 2 vols. Leiden: Brill.

Priewer, H., Göbler, W., and Priewer, M. 2002. 'Subsistenzkrisen im Kirchspiel Rückeroth/Ww. vom 17. bis zum 19: Jahrhundert aus historisch-demographischer Sicht'. *Nassauische Annalen* 113: 331–40.

Prims, F. 1933. *Geschiedenis van Antwerpen: onder Hertog Jan de Derde (1312–1355), politieke en economische orde*, vol. IV, part 1. Antwerp: N.V. Standaard Boekhandel.

Pult Quaglia, A. M. 1982. 'Sistema annonario e commercio dei prodotti agricoli: riflessioni su alcuni temi di ricerca'. *Società e Storia* 15: 181–98.

Queipo de Llano y Ruiz de Saravia, J. M. [7th Count of Toreno] 1839. *Historia del levantamiento, guerra y revolución de España*, vol. III. Madrid: Imprenta del Diario.

Randall, A. 2006. *Riotous Assemblies: Popular Protest in Hanoverian England*. Oxford: Oxford University Press.

Rankl, H. 2005. 'Die bayerische Politik in der europäischen Hungerkrise 1770–1773'. *Zeitschrift für bayerische Landesgeschichte* 68: 745–79.

Rashin, A. G. 1956. *Naselenie Rossiiza 100 let (1811–1913gg): Statisticheskiy ocherki*. Moscow: Gos.

Ravn, M. O., and Uhlig, H. 2002. 'On adjusting the Hodrick–Prescott filter for the frequency of observations'. *Review of Economics and Statistics* 84: 371–6.

Razuvaev, V. N., Apasova, E. G., and Martuganov, R. A. 2008. 'Daily temperature and precipitation data for 223 former-USSR stations', ORNL/CDIAC-56, NDP-040. Oak Ridge, TN: Carbon Dioxide Information Analysis Center, US Department of Energy, http://cdiac.ornl.gov/ndps/ndp040.html.

Read, C. 2016. 'Laissez-faire, the Irish famine, and British financial crisis'. *Economic History Review* 69: 411–34.

Reglero, C. 2011. 'Les disettes dans le Royaume de Castille (entre 1250 et 1348)', in Bourin, M., Menant, F., and Drendel, J. (eds.). *Les disettes dans la conjoncture de 1300 en Méditerranée occidentale*. Rome: École Française de Rome, pp. 309–42.

Reher, D. S. 1991. 'Dinámicas demográficas en Castilla la Nueva, 1500–1900: un ensayo de reconstrucción', in Nadal i Oller, J. (ed.). *La evolución demográfica bajo los Austrias*. Alicante: Instituto de Cultura Juan Gil-Albert, pp. 17–75.

1980. 'La crisis de 1804 y sus repercusiones demográficas: Cuenca (1775–1825)'. *Moneda y Crédito* 154: 35–72.

Reinhardt, V. 1991. *Überleben in der frühneuzeitlichen Stadt: Annona und Getreideversorgung in Rom 1563–1797*. Tübingen, Germany: Bibliothek des Deutschen Historischen Instituts in Rom.

Reith, R. 2011. *Umweltgeschichte der Frühen Neuzeit (Enzyklopädie deutscher Geschichte 89)*. Munich: Oldenbourg.

Revel, J. 1972. 'Le grain de Rome et la crise de l'Annone dans la seconde moitié du XVIIIe siècle'. *Mélanges de l'École Française de Rome: Moyen Age, Temps Modernes* 84: 201–81.

1975. 'Les privilèges d'une capitale: l'approvisionnement de Rome à l'époque moderne'. *Mélanges de l'École Française de Rome: Moyen Age, Temps Modernes* 87: 460–93.

1982. 'Rendements, production et productivité agricoles: les grands domaines de la campagne romaine, XVIIe–XVIIIe siècles', in Goy, J., and Le Roy

Ladurie, E. (eds.). *Prestation paysannes, dîmes, rente foncière et mouvement de la production agricole à l'époque préindustrielle*, vol. I. Paris: Mouton, pp. 226–36.

Riera Melis, A. 2009. 'El aprovisionamiento urbano de cereales en las ciudades de la Corona de Aragón durante la Baja Edad Media', in Sesma, A (ed.). *La Corona de Aragón en el centro de su historia, 1208–1458: Aspectos económicos y sociales*. Zaragoza: Departamento de Educación, Cultura y Deporte, Gobierno Aragón, pp. 233–77.

Ritzmann-Blickenstorfer, H. 1997. *Alternative Neue Welt: Die Ursachen der schweizerischen Überseeauswanderung im 19. und frühen 20. Jahrhundert*. Zurich: Chronos.

Robbins, R. G. 1975. *Famine in Russia, 1891–92*. New York: Columbia University Press.

Rockefeller Foundation 1915. *Annual Report 1915*. New York: Rockefeller Foundation, www.rockefellerfoundation.org/app/uploads/RF-Annual-Report-1915.pdf.

Rodríguez, L. 1973. 'The Spanish riots of 1766'. *Past and Present* 52: 76–136.

Roeck, B. 1987. *Bäcker, Brot und Getreide in Augsburg*. Sigmaringen, Germany: Jan Thorbecke.

Roessingh, H. 1976. 'Het begin van de aardappelteelt en de aardappelconsumptie in Gelderland'. *Gelders Oudheidkundig Contactbericht* 68: 1–9.

Roessner, P. R. 2011. 'The 1738–41 harvest crisis in Scotland'. *Scottish Historical Review* 90: 27–63.

Rolf, G. 2010. 'Wohlstandswahrung für wenige oder Nahrungssicherung für alle? Armut, Tugenddiskurs und Krisenbekämpfungskonzepte im Kontext der Hungerkrise 1770/1771 auf der Zürcher Landschaft', in Holenstein, A., Kapossy, B., and Tosato-Rigo, D. (eds.). *Reichtum und Armut in schweizerischen Republiken*. Geneva: Slatkine, pp. 195–213.

Rommes, R. 1990. 'Pest in perspectief: Aspecten van een gevreesde ziekte in de vroegmoderne tijd'. *Tijdschrift voor sociale geschiedenis* 16: 244–66.

——— 1991. 'Op het spoor van de dood: de pest in en rond Utrecht', in Vereniging Oud-Utrecht (ed.). *Jaarboek Oud-Utrecht 1991*. Utrecht: Vereniging Oud-Utrecht, pp. 93–121.

Rosen, S. 1999. 'Potato paradoxes'. *Journal of Political Economy* 107: 294–313.

Rotberg, R. I., and Rabb, T. K. (eds.) 1985. *Hunger and History: The Impact of Changing Food Production and Consumption Patterns on Society*. Cambridge: Cambridge University Press.

Rubio Vela, A. 1982. 'A propósito del "mal any primer": dificultades cerealísticas en la Corona de Aragón en los años treinta del siglo XIV', in *Estudios dedicados a Juan Peset Aleixandre*, vol. III. Valencia: Universidad de Valencia, pp. 477–87.

Rutty, J. 1770. *Chronological History of the Weather and Seasons and of Prevailing Diseases in Dublin*. Dublin: Sleator.

Ruwet, J. 1954. 'Crises démographiques: problèmes économiques ou crises morales? Le pays de Liège sous l'Ancien Régime'. *Population* 9: 451–76.

Salmelli, D. 1986. 'L'alluvione e il freddo: il 1705 e il 1709', in Finzi (ed.), pp. 17–97.

Salzmann, M. 1978. *Die Wirtschaftskrise im Kanton Zürich 1845 bis 1848: Ihre Stellung und Wertung im Rahmen der wirtschaftlich-sozialen Entwicklung in der ersten Hälfte des 19. Jahrhunderts*. Bern: Peter Lang.

Sánchez-Albornoz, N. 1968. 'La Crisis de Subsistencia de 1857', in *España hace un siglo: Una economía dual*. Barcelona: Península, pp. 57–134.

Santa Cruz, A. de (ed. de Mata Carriazo, J.) 1927 [1552]. *Crónica de los Reyes Católicos*, 2 vols. Madrid: Espasa-Calpe.

Savy, P. 2011. 'Les disettes en Lombardie d'après les sources narratives (fin XIIIe – début XIVe siècle)', in Bourin, M., Menant, F., and Drendel, J. (eds.). *Les disettes dans la conjoncture de 1300 en Méditerranée occidentale*. Rome: École Française de Rome, pp. 181–205.

Sax, P. (ed. Panten, A.) 1986 [1636]. *Nova, totius Frisiae septentrionalis, Descriptio*.... St. Peter Ording, Germany: Nordfriisk Instituut.

Schanbacher, A. 2012. 'Vulnerabilität, Kartoffelkrankheit und Nahrungskrise vor Ort: das Fürstentum Osnabrück 1845–1847', in Collet, D., Lassen, T., and Schanbacher, A. (eds.). *Handeln in Hungerkrisen: Neue Perspektiven auf soziale und klimatische Vulnerabilität*. Göttingen: Universitätsverlag, pp. 111–30.

2015. 'Kartoffelkrankheit und Nahrungskrise in Nordwestdeutschland 1845–1849/61', unpublished thesis. University of Göttingen.

Schlöder, C. 2014. *Bonn im 18. Jahrhundert: Die Bevölkerung einer geistlichen Residenzstadt*. Cologne: Böhlau.

Schmahl, H. 2001. 'Innerlicher Mangel und Äusserliche Nahrungshoffnung: Aspekte der Auswanderung aus Kurmainz im 18. Jahrhundert', in Hartmann, P. C. (ed.). *Reichskirche – Mainzer Kurstaat – Reichserzkanzler*. Frankfurt: Peter Lang, pp. 121–44.

Schmidt, G. 1991. 'Die frühneuzeitlichen Hungerrevolten: soziale Konflikte und Wirtschaftspolitik im Alten Reich'. *Zeitschrift für Historische Forschung* 18: 257–80.

Schofield, P. R. 1997. 'Dearth, debt and the local land market in a thirteenth-century village community'. *Agricultural History Review* 45: 1–17.

2008. 'The social economy of the medieval village in the early fourteenth century'. *Economic History Review* 61 (suppl.): 38–63.

Scholliers, E. 1960. *De levensstandaard in de XVe en XVIe eeuw te Antwerpen*. Antwerp: De Sikkel NV.

Schrier, A. 1958. *Ireland and the American Emigration 1850–1900*. Minneapolis: University of Minnesota Press.

Schulte Beerbühl, M. 2004. 'Frühneuzeitliche Flüchtlingshilfe in Großbritannien und das Schicksal der Pfälzer Auswanderer von 1709', in Beer, M., and Dahlmann, D. (eds.). *Über die trockene Grenze und über das offene Meer: Binneneuropäische und transatlantische Migrationen im 18. und 19. Jahrhundert*. Essen: Klartext, pp. 303–28.

Sellin, T. 1946. 'The Netherlands during German occupation'. *Annals of the American Academy of Political and Social Science* 245: 1–180.

Sen, A. 1981. *Poverty and Famines: An Essay on Entitlement and Deprivation*. Oxford: Clarendon Press.

Sentrie, P. 2007. 'Een demografische schets van West-Vlaanderen 1500–1850', unpublished MA thesis. Ghent University.

Sesma Muñoz, J. A., and Laliena Corbera, C. (eds.) 2004. *La población de Aragón en la Edad Media (siglos XIII–XIV): Estudios de demografía histórica*. Zaragoza: Leyere editorial.

Sharp, B. 1980. *In Contempt of All Authority: Rural Artisans and Riot in the West of England, 1586–1660*. Berkeley, CA: University of California Press.

2013. 'Royal paternalism and the moral economy in the reign of Edward II: the response to the Great Famine'. *Economic History Review* 66: 628–47.

Sieglerschmidt, J. 1992. 'Untersuchungen zur Teuerung in Südwestdeutschland 1816/17', in Hagenmaier, M., and Holtz, S. (eds.). *Krisenbewusstsein und Krisenbewältigung in der Frühen Neuzeit: Crisis in Early Modern Europe: Festschrift für Hans-Christoph Rublack*. Frankfurt: Peter Lang, pp. 113–44.

Simms, J. Y. 1977. 'The crisis in Russian agriculture at the end of the nineteenth century: a different view'. *Slavic Review* 36: 377–98.

Sköld, P. 2001. 'Kunskap och kontroll: den svenska befolkningsstatistikens historia', Demographic Database Report no. 17. Umeå, Sweden: Umeå University.

Slack, P. 1992. 'Dearth and social policy in early modern England'. *Social History of Medicine* 5: 1–17.

Slaveski, F. 2013. 'The occupiers' burden: tackling food shortage and related health problems in post-war Germany, 1945–47', in Lumey and Vaiserman (eds.), pp. 187–206.

Slavin, P. 2014. 'Market failure during the Great Famine in England and Wales (1315–1317)'. *Past and Present* 222: 9–49.

Slicher van Bath, B. H. 1970. 'Welvaart op wankele basis: de sociaal-econo-mische omstandigheden gedurende de middeleeuwen', in *Geschiedenis van Overijssel*. Deventer: Kluwer, pp. 93–105.

1977. 'Agriculture in the vital revolution', in Rich, E. E., and Wilson, C. H. (eds.). *The Cambridge Economic History of Europe*, vol. V, *The Economic Organization of Early Modern Europe*. Cambridge: Cambridge University Press, pp. 42–132.

Smith, A. 1976 [1776]. *An Inquiry into the Nature and Causes of the Wealth of Nations*. Oxford: Oxford University Press.

Smith, C. A. 1947. 'Effects of wartime starvation in Holland on pregnancy and its products'. *American Journal of Obstetrics and Gynecology* 53: 599–608.

Smith, R. M. 2015. 'Dearth and local political responses: 1280–1325 and 1580–1596/7 compared', in Kowaleski, M., Langdon, J., and Schofield, P. R. (eds.). *Peasants and Lords in the Medieval English Economy: Essays in Honour of Bruce M. S. Campbell*. Turnhout, Belgium: Brepols, pp. 377–406.

Smyth, W. J. 2006. *Map-Making, Landscapes and Memory: A Geography of Colonial and Early Modern Ireland c. 1530–1750*. Cork: Cork University Press.

Soden, J. von 1828. *Die annonarische Gesetzgebung: Versuch eines Systems...Nebst einer annonarischen Bibliothek*. Nuremberg: Riegel & Wießner.

Soens, T. 2009. *De spade in de dijk? Waterbeheer en rurale samenleving in de Vlaamse kustvlakte, 1280–1580*. Ghent: Academia Press.

Soens, T., and Thoen, E. 2010. 'Vegetarians or carnivores? Standards of living and diet in late medieval Flanders', in Cavaciocchi (ed.), pp. 495–527.

Sogner, S. 1976. *Folkevekst og flytting: En historisk-demografisk studie i 1700-årenes Øst-Norge*. Oslo: Universitetsforlaget.

Sokoloff, K., and Engerman, S. L. 2000. 'History lessons: institutions, land endowment, and paths of development in the New World'. *Journal of Economic Perspectives* 14: 217–32.

Solantie, R. 1988. 'Climatic conditions for the cultivation of rye with reference to the history of settlement in Finland'. *Fennoscandia Archaelogica* 5: 3–20.

Solar, P. M. 1989. 'The Great Famine was no ordinary subsistence crisis', in Crawford (ed.), pp. 112–33.

 2007. 'The crisis of the late 1840s: what can be learned from prices?', in Ó Gráda, Paping and Vanhaute (eds.), pp. 79–93.

 2015. '*Why Ireland Starved* and the big issues in pre-famine Irish economic history'. *Irish Economic and Social History* 42: 62–75.

Sommarin, E. 1917. *Det skånska jordbrukets ekonomiska utveckling 1801–1914*, vol. I. Lund, Sweden: Berlingska Boktryckeriet.

Sommer, D. 2013. *Eine baltisch-adlige Missionarin bewegt Europa: Barbara Juliane v. Krüdener, geb. v. Vietinghoff gen Scheel (1764–1824)*. Göttingen: Francke.

Sparén, P., Vågerö, D., Shestov, D. B., Plavinskaja, S., Parfenova, N., Hoptiar, V., Paturot, D., and Galanti, M. R. 2003. 'Long term mortality after severe starvation during the siege of Leningrad: prospective cohort study'. *British Medical Journal* 328: doi: 10.1136/bmj.37942.603970.9A.

Spufford, M. 1974. *Contrasting Communities: English Villages in the Sixteenth and Seventeenth Centuries*. Cambridge: Cambridge University Press.

Stanner, S. A., and Yudkin, J. S. 2001. 'Fetal programming and the Leningrad Siege study'. *Twin Research* 4: 287–92.

Statistics Sweden 1999. *Befolkningsutvecklingen under 250 år: Historisk statistik för Sverige*. Stockholm: Statistika Centralbyrån.

Stauter-Halsted, K. 2001. *The Nation in the Village: The Genesis of Peasant National Identity in Austrian Poland, 1848–1914*. Ithaca, NY: Cornell University Press.

Stein, Z. A., Susser, M., Saenger, G., and Marolla, F. 1975. *Famine and Human Development: The Dutch Hunger Winter of 1944/45*. Oxford: Oxford University Press.

Stewart, L. A. M. 2005, 'Poor relief in Edinburgh and the famine of 1621–24'. *International Review of Scottish Studies* 30: 5–40.

Stöger, G. 2012. *Sekundäre Märkte: Zum Wiener und Salzburger Gebrauchtwarenhandel im 17. und 18. Jahrhundert*. Munich: Oldenbourg.

Stone, N. 1975. *The Eastern Front 1914–1917*. London: Macmillan.

Strangio, D. 1998. 'Di fronte alla carestia in età preindustriale'. *Rivista di Storia Economica* 14: 161–92.

 1999. *Crisi alimentari e politica annonaria a Roma nel settecento*. Rome: Istituto Nazionale di Studi Romani.

 2013. 'Papal debt in the Papal State, sixteenth to eighteenth century'. *Journal of Interdisciplinary History* 43: 511–37.

Strömmer, E. 2003. *Klima-Geschichte: Methoden der Rekonstruktion und historische Perspektive: Ostösterreich 1700 bis 1830*. Vienna: Deuticke.

Struick, E. 1981. 'Utrechts Beziehungen zum flachen Land im Mittelalter'. *Hansisch Geschichtsblätter* 99: 1–10.

Studer, R. 2008. 'Market integration and economic development: a comparative study of India and Europe, 1700–1900', unpublished PhD thesis. University of Oxford.

2015. *The Great Divergence Reconsidered: Europe, India, and the Rise to Global Economic Power.* Cambridge: Cambridge University Press.

Studer, R., and Schuppli, P. 2008. 'Deflating Swiss prices over the past five centuries'. *Historical Methods: A Journal of Quantitative and Interdisciplinary Methods* 41: 137–53.

Surface, F. M. 1926. *American Pork Production in the World War.* Chicago: Shaw.

Swift, J. 1948. *History of the Dublin Bakers and Others.* Dublin: Irish Bakers, Confectionery and Allied Workers Union.

Szöllösi-Janze, M. 1997. 'Notdurft – Bedürfnis: historische Dimensionen eines Begriffswandels'. *Geschichte in Wissenschaft und Unterricht* 48: 653–73.

Taubenberger, J. K., and Morens, D. M. 2006. '1918 influenza: the mother of all pandemics'. *Emerging Infectious Diseases* 12: 15–20.

Teuteberg, H. J., and Wiegelmann, G. 1986. 'Einführung und Nutzung der Kartoffel in Deutschland', in *Unsere tägliche Kost: Geschichte und regionale Prägung.* Münster, Germany: Coppenrath, pp. 93–134.

Thoen, E. 1988. *Landbouwekonomie en bevolking in Vlaanderen gedurende de late Middeleeuwen en het begin van de Moderne Tijden: Testregio: De kasselrijen van Oudenaarde en Aalst, eind 13de – eerste helft 16de eeuw,* 2 vols. Ghent: Belgisch Centrum voor Landelijke Geschiedenis.

1995. 'Historical demography in late medieval rural Flanders: recent results and hypotheses', in Duvosquel, J.-M., and Thoen, E. (eds.). *Peasants and Townsmen in Medieval Europe: Studia in honorem Adriaan Verhulst.* Ghent: Snoeck-Ducaju, pp. 573–82.

Thompson, E. P. 1971. 'The moral economy of the English crowd in the 18th century'. *Past and Present* 50: 76–136.

Thorarinsson, S. 1944. *Tefrokronologiska studier på Island: Þjórsárdalur och dess förödelse.* Stockholm: Geografiska Annaler.

Tijms, W. 1977. *Prijzen van granen en peulvruchten te Arnhem, Breda, Deventer, 's-Hertogenbosch, Kampen, Koevorden, Maastricht en Nijmegen,* 2 vols. Groningen: Nederlands Agronomisch Historisch Instituut.

1989. 'De effractie van Sint Andries te Roermond'. *Studies over de sociaal-economische geschiedenis van Limburg* 34: 112–63.

2000. *Groninger graanprijzen: De prijzen van agrarische producten tussen 1546 en 1990.* Groningen: Nederlands Agronomisch Historisch Instituut.

Tilly, L. A. 1972. 'La révolte frumentaire, forme de conflit politique en France'. *Annales: Économies, Sociétés, Civilisations* 27: 731–57 [translation of (1971) 'The food riot as a form of political conflict in France'. *Journal of Interdisciplinary History* 2: 23–57].

1983. 'Food entitlement, famine, and conflict'. *Journal of Interdisciplinary History* 14: 333–49.

1985. 'Food entitlement, famine, and conflict', in Rotberg and Rabb (eds.), pp. 135–51.

Tits-Dieuaide, M.-J. 1975. *La formation des prix céréaliers en Brabant et en Flandre au XVe siècle.* Brussels: Édition de l'Université de Bruxelles.

Tobi, E. W., Lumey, L. H., Talens, R. P., Kremer, D., Putter, H., Stein, A. D., Slagboom P. E., and Heijmans, B. T. 2009. 'DNA methylation differences after exposure to prenatal famine are common and timing- and sex-specific'. *Human Molecular Genetics* 18: 4046–53.

Tomasson, R. 1977. 'A millennium of misery: the demography of the Icelander'. *Population Studies* 31: 405–27.

Trienekens, G. 2000. 'The food supply in the Netherlands during the Second World War', in Smith, D. F., and Phillips, J. (eds.). *Food, Science, Policy and Regulation in the Twentieth Century.* London: Routledge, pp. 117–34.

Turchin, P., and Nefedov, S. A. 2009. *Secular Cycles.* Princeton, NJ: Princeton University Press.

Tvauri, A. 2014. 'The impact of the climate catastrophe of 536–537 AD in Estonia and neighbouring areas'. *Estonian Journal of Archaeology* 18: 30–56.

Uebele, M., Grünebaum, T., and Kopsidis, M. 2013. 'King's law and food storage in Saxony, c. 1790–1830', Working Paper no. 2613. Münster, Germany: Center for Quantitative Economics, University of Münster.

Ulbrich, C. 1993. 'Zwischen Resignation und Aufbegehren: Frauen, Armut und Hunger im vorindustriellen Europa', in Klein, G. (ed.). *Begehren und Entbehren: Bochumer Beiträge zur Geschlechterforschung.* Pfaffenweiler, Germany: Centaurus, pp. 167–83.

Unger, W. S. 1916. 'De Hollandsche graanhandel en de graanhandelspolitiek in de middeleeuwen'. *De Economist* 65: 243–70, 337–87, 461–87.

Utterström, G. 1955. 'Climatic fluctuations and population problems in early modern history'. *Scandinavian Economic History Review* 3: 3–47.

1957. *Jordbrukets arbetare: Levnadsvillkor och arbetsliv på landsbygden från frihetstiden till mitten av 1800-talet,* 2 vols. Stockholm: Tidens Förlag.

Vågerö, D., Koupil, I., Parfenova, N., and Sparén, P. 2013. 'Long-term health consequences following the siege of Leningrad', in Lumey and Vaiserman (eds.), pp. 207–26.

Valdeón, J. 1969. 'Aspectos de la crisis castellana de la primera mitad del siglo XIV'. *Hispania* 29: 5–24.

1984. 'Reflexiones sobre la crisis bajomedieval en Castilla', in *En la España medieval IV: Estudios dedicados al profesor D. Ángel Ferrari Núñez,* vol. II. Madrid: Universidad Complutense, pp. 1047–60.

Vallin, J., Meslé, F., Adamets, S., and Pyrozhkov, S. 2012. 'The crisis of the 1930s', in Meslé, F., and Vallin, J. (eds.). *Mortality and Causes of Death in 20th-Century Ukraine.* New York: Springer, pp. 13–38.

Van Bavel, B. 2010. *Manors and Markets: Economy and Society in the Low Countries, 500–1600.* Oxford: Oxford University Press.

Van Bavel, B., and Van Zanden, J. L. 2004. 'The jump-start of the Holland economy during the late-medieval crisis, c. 1350 – c. 1500'. *Economic History Review* 57: 503–32.

Van Bavel, B., and Rijpma, A. 2016. 'How important were formalized charity and social spending before the rise of the welfare state? A long-run analysis of selected western European cases, 1400–1850'. *Economic History Review* 69: 159–87.

Van der Wee, H. 1966. 'De handelsbetrekkingen tussen Antwerpen en de Noordelijke Nederlanden tijdens de 14e, 15e en 16e eeuw'. *Bijdragen voor de Geschiedenis der Nederlanden* 20: 268–85.

Van der Woude, A. M. 1972. *Het Noorderkwartier: Een regionaal-historisch onderzoek in de demografische en economische geschiedenis van westelijk Nederland van de late Middeleeuwen tot het begin van de negentiende eeuw.* Wageningen, Netherlands: Veenman.

Van der Zee, H. A. 1998. *The Hunger Winter: Occupied Holland 1944–1945.* Lincoln, NE: University of Nebraska Press.

Van Osta, M.-H. 1969. 'Het hongerjaar 1709: een onderzoek naar de prijsmechanismen van een crisisjaar en naar de toestand en de reacties van de bevolking in Vlaanderen en Brabant', unpublished MA thesis. Ghent University.

Van Schaïk, R. 1978. 'Prijs- en levensmiddelenpolitiek in de Noordelijke Nederlanden van de 14e tot de 17e eeuw: bronnen en problemen'. *Tijdschrift voor Geschiedenis* 91: 214–55.

1987. *Belasting, bevolking en bezit in Gelre en Zutphen, 1350–1550.* Hilversum, Netherlands: Verloren.

Van Tielhof, M. 1995. *De Hollandse graanhandel 1470–1570: Koren op de Amsterdamse molen.* The Hague: Stichting Hollandse Historische Reeks.

Van Tielhof, M. 2002. *The 'Mother of All Trades': The Baltic Grain Trade in Amsterdam from the Late 16th to the Early 19th Century.* Leiden: Brill.

Van Werveke, H. 1959. 'La famine de l'an 1315 en Flandre et dans les régions voisines'. *Revue du Nord* 41: 5–14.

Van Zanden, J. L. 2009. *The Long Road to the Industrial Revolution: The European Economy in a Global Perspective, 1000–1800.* Leiden: Brill.

Vandenbroeke, C. 1975. *Agriculture et alimentation.* Ghent: Belgisch Centrum voor Landelijke Geschiedenis.

Vanhaute, E. 2007. '"So worthy an example to Ireland": the subsistence and industrial crisis of 1845–1850 in Flanders', in Ó Gráda, Paping and Vanhaute (eds.), pp. 123–48.

Vanhaute, E., and Lambrecht, T. 2011. 'Famine, exchange networks and the village community: a comparative analysis of the subsistence crises of the 1740s and the 1840s in Flanders'. *Continuity and Change* 26: 155–86.

Vasey, D. E. 1991. 'Population, agriculture, and famine: Iceland, 1784–1785'. *Human Ecology* 19: 323–50.

1996. 'Population regulation, ecology, and political economy in preindustrial Iceland'. *American Ethnologist* 23: 366–92.

Vasold, M. 2008. 'Die Hunger- und Sterblichkeitskrise von 1770/73 und der Niedergang des Ancien Régime'. *Saeculum* 59: 107–42.

Verhaeghe, F. 1984. 'The late medieval crisis in the Low Countries: the archaeological viewpoint', in Seibt, F., and Eberhard, W. (eds.). *Die Krise des Spätmittelalters.* Stuttgart: Klett-Cotta, pp. 146–71.

Verhulst, A. 1965. 'Prijzen van granen, boter en kaas te Brugge volgens de slag van het Sint-Donatiaanskapittel (1348–1801)', in Verlinden, C., and Scholliers, E. (eds.). *Dokumenten voor de geschiedenis van prijzen en lonen in Vlaanderen en Brabant,* vol. II. Bruges: Thempelhof, pp. 3–70.

Vilar, P. 1969. *Oro y moneda en la historia (1450–1920).* Barcelona: Ariel.

1972. 'El Motín de Esquilache y las crisis del Antiguo Régimen'. *Revista de Occidente* 107: 199–249.

Villalba, J. de 1803. *Epidemiología española, o historia cronológica de las pestes, contagios, epidemias y epizootias que han acaecido en España...hasta el año 1801,* 2 vols. Madrid: Imprenta de D. Fermín Villalpando.

Vincent, C. P. 1985. *The Politics of Hunger: The Allied Blockade of Germany, 1915– 1919.* Athens, OH: Ohio University Press.

Vivier, N. 2007. 'The crisis in France: a memorable crisis but not a potato crisis', in Ó Gráda, Paping and Vanhaute (eds.), pp. 223–45.

Voglis, P. 2006. 'Surviving hunger: life in the cities and the countryside during the Occupation', in Gildea, R., Wievorka, O., and Warring, A. (eds.). *Surviving Hitler and Mussolini: Daily Life in Occupied Europe*. Oxford: Berg, pp. 16–41.

Voutilainen, M. 2015. 'Feeding the famine: social vulnerability and dislocation during the Finnish famine of the 1860s', in Curran, D., Luciuk, L., and Newby, A. (eds.). *Famines in European Economic History: The Last Great European Famines Reconsidered*. Abingdon, UK: Routledge, pp. 124–44.

Walford, C. 1878. The famines of the world: past and present. *Journal of the Statistical Society of London* 41: 433–535.

Walter, J. 1980. 'Grain riots and popular attitudes to the law: Maldon and the crisis of 1629', in Brewer, J., and Styles, J. (eds.). *An Ungovernable People: The English and Their Law in the Seventeenth and Eighteenth Centuries*. London: Hutchinson, pp. 47–84.

1989. 'The social economy of dearth in early modern England', in Walter, J., and Schofield, R. S. (eds.). *Famine, Disease and the Social Order in Early Modern Society*. Cambridge: Cambridge University Press, pp. 75–128.

Walter, J., and Schofield, R. S. 1989, 'Famine, disease and crisis mortality in early modern society', in *Famine, Disease and the Social Order in Early Modern Society*. Cambridge: Cambridge University Press, pp. 1–74.

Walter, J., and Wrightson, K. 1976. 'Dearth and the social order in early modern England'. *Past and Present* 71: 22–42.

Watkins, S. C., and Menken, J. 1985. 'Famines in historical perspective'. *Population and Development Review* 11: 647–75.

Weber, E. 2005. *Untiefen, Flut und Flauten: Der Güterverkehr auf dem Rhein zwischen 1750 und 1850: Die Modernisierung der vorindustriellen Rheinschifffahrt aus einer wirtschafts-, sozial- und umweltgeschichtlichen Perspektive betrachtet*, PhD dissertation. University of Bern.

Weber, S. 2012. 'Migration als Herrschaftsproblem: die Maßnahmen der kurmainzischen Landesregierung gegen die Emigration von Untertanen 1763–1774', in Rebitsch, R., Taddei, E., and Müller, M. (eds.). *Migration und Reisen: Mobilität in der Neuzeit*. Innsbruck: Studien Verlag, pp. 309–22.

Weiler, P. (ed.) 1935. *Urkundenbuch des Stiftes Xanten*, vol. I, *(Vor 590) bis 1359*. Bonn: Röhrscheid.

Weir, D. R. 1984. 'Life under pressure: France and England, 1670–1870'. *Journal of Economic History* 44: 27–47.

1989. 'Markets and mortality in France, 1600–1789', in Walter, J., and Schofield, R. S. (eds.). *Famine, Disease and the Social Order in Early Modern Society*. Cambridge: Cambridge University Press, pp. 201–34.

Wells, R. 1996. 'The Irish famine of 1799–1801: market culture, moral economies and social protest', in Randall, A., and Charlesworth, A. (eds.). *Markets, Market Culture and Popular Protest in Eighteenth-Century Britain and Ireland*. Liverpool: Liverpool University Press, pp. 163–95.

Wheatcroft, S. G. 1976a. 'Population dynamic and factors affecting it, in the USSR in the 1920s and 1930s, part I', Soviet Industrialisation Project

Series Discussion Paper no. 1. Birmingham: Centre for Russian and East European Studies, University of Birmingham.

1976b. 'Population dynamic and factors affecting it, in the USSR in the 1920s and 1930s, part II, statistical appendices', Soviet Industrialisation Project Series Discussion Paper no. 2. Birmingham: Centre for Russian and East European Studies, University of Birmingham.

1977. 'The significance of climatic and weather change on Soviet agriculture (with particular reference to the 1920s and the 1930s)', Soviet Industrialisation Project Series Discussion Paper no. 11. Birmingham: Centre for Russian and East European Studies, University of Birmingham.

1981a. 'Famine and factors affecting mortality in the USSR: the demographic crises of 1914–1922 and 1930–1933', Soviet Industrialisation Project Series Discussion Paper no. 20. Birmingham: Centre for Russian and East European Studies, University of Birmingham.

1981b. 'Famine and factors affecting mortality in the USSR: the demographic crises of 1914–1922 and 1930–1933, statistical appendices', Soviet Industrialisation Project Series Discussion Paper no. 21. Birmingham: Centre for Russian and East European Studies, University of Birmingham.

1983. 'Famine and epidemic crises in Russia, 1918–1922: the case of Saratov'. *Annales de Demographie Historique*: 329–52.

1991. 'Crises and the condition of the peasantry in late imperial Russia', in Kingston-Mann, E., and Mixter, T. (eds.). *Peasant Economy, Culture, and Politics of European Russia, 1800–1921*. Princeton, NJ: Princeton University Press, pp. 128–74.

1992. 'The 1891–92 famine in Russia: towards a more detailed analysis of its scale and demographic significance', in Edmondson, L., and Waldron, P. (eds.). *Economy and Society in Russia and the Soviet Union, 1860–1930*. Basingstoke: Palgrave-Macmillan, pp. 44–64.

1993. 'Famine and food consumption records in early Soviet history 1917–25', in Geissler, C., and Oddy, D. J. (eds.). *Food Diet and Economic Change: Past and Present*. Leicester: Leicester University Press, pp. 151–74.

2001a. 'On grain harvests and evaluations of yield in USSR in 1931–33', in Danilov, Manning and Viola (eds.), pp. 842–65.

2001b. 'On demographic evidence of the tragedy of the Soviet village, 1931–33', in Danilov, Manning and Viola (eds.), pp. 866–87.

2004. 'Towards explaining the Soviet famine of 1931–3: political and natural factors in perspective'. *Food and Foodways* 12: 107–36.

2009. 'The first 35 years of Soviet living standards: secular growth and conjunctural crises in a time of famines'. *Explorations in Economic History* 46: 24–52.

2012. 'The Soviet famine of 1946–1947, the weather and human agency in historical perspective'. *Europe-Asia Studies* 64: 987–1015.

2013. 'Pokazateli demograficheskogo krizisa v period goloda', in Kondrashin, V. (ed.). *Golod v SSSR, 1929–1934: Dokumenty*, vol. III, *Leto 1933–1934*, bk. 2. Moscow: MFD, pp. 719–71 [a fuller version is available on the website of the Russian State archives Administration (Gosarkhiv): www.rusarchives.ru/publication/wheatcroft-pokazateli-demografy-crizis-golod-sssr].

(ed.) 2017. 'Famines in Russia and the USSR', working paper. Melbourne: Melbourne University.

Wheatcroft, S. G., and Bishop, I. 2017. 'A crop weather model for the USSR', in Wheatcroft (ed.).

Wheatcroft, S. G., and Ó Gráda, C. 2017. 'The European famines of World Wars 1 and 2: causes and consequences', working paper (with data appendix).

Wheatcroft, S. G., Garnaut, A., and Leikin, I. 2013. 'Mapping crude death rates in Ukraine in 1933 and explaining the raion patterns', in *Golod v Ukraini y pershiipolovini XX stolittya: Prichini ta naslidki (1921–1923, 1932–1933, 1946–1947): Materiali mizhnarodnoi naukovoi konferentsii*. Kiev: Institut istorii Ukraini, pp. 219–25.

White, S. 2013. 'The Little Ice Age crisis of the Ottoman Empire: a conjuncture in Middle East environmental history', in Mikhail, A. (ed.). *Water on Sand: Environmental Histories of the Middle East and North Africa*. Oxford: Oxford University Press, pp. 71–90.

Winter, J. 1997. 'Surviving the war: life expectation, illness and mortality rates in Paris, London, and Berlin 1914–1919', in Winter, J., and Robert, J.-L. (eds.). *Capital Cities at War: Paris, London, Berlin 1914–1919*. Cambridge: Cambridge University Press, pp. 487–523.

Wood, G. 2014. *Tambora: The Eruption that Changed the World*. Princeton, NJ: Princeton University Press.

Woodham-Smith, C. 1962. *The Great Hunger*. London: Hamish Hamilton.

Woodward, D. R. 2003. *Trial by Friendship: Anglo-American Relations, 1917–1918*. Lexington, KY: University of Kentucky Press.

Wrigley, E. A., and Schofield, R. S. 1981. *The Population History of England 1541–1871: A Reconstruction*. Cambridge: Cambridge University Press.

Wyffels, A. 1985. 'Het kwalitatief en kwantitatief aspekt van het graanverbuik in Vlaanderen in de 16de en 17de eeuw'. *Bijdragen tot de Prijzengeschiedenis* 3: 113–20.

Zanetti, D. 1964. *Problemi alimentari di una economia pre-industriale: Cereali a Pavia dal 1398 al 1700*. Turin: Bollati Boringhieri.

Zima, V. F. 1996. *Golod v SSSR 1946–1947 godov: Proiskhozhdenie i posledstviya*. Moscow: Institut rossiiskoi istorii RAN.

Zimmermann, C. 1987. '"Noth und Theuerung" im badischen Unterland: Reformkurs und Krisenmanagement unter dem aufgeklärten Absolutismus'. *Aufklärung* 2: 95–119.

1994. 'Obrigkeitliche Krisenregulierung und kommunale Interessen: das Beispiel Württemberg 1770/71', in Gailus, M., and Volkmann, H. (eds.). *Der Kampf um das tägliche Brot: Nahrungsmangel, Versorgungspolitik und Protest 1770–1990*. Opladen, Germany: Westdeutscher Verlag, pp. 107–31.

Zubkova, E. 1993. *Russia after the War: Hopes, Illusions, and Disappointments, 1945–1957*. Armonk, NY: M. E. Sharpe.

Zürcher, E. J. 2004. *Turkey: A Modern History*. London: I. B. Tauris.

Index

Aakjaer, S., 191
Aaraas, O., 198
Abarca, V., 59n. 2
Abel, W., 6, 73, 101, 102n. 1, 104n. 6,
    107n. 11, 117t. 5.1
Aberdeen, 160
Aberdeenshire, 162, 163
Aberth, J., 13, 121
Abildgren, K., 192f. 9.2
Acemoglu, D., 168
Africa, 52
Aghadrinagh, 175
agrarian innovation, 12, 24, 47, 95, 99,
    112, 159, 173
agriculture, 73, 131, 134, 141, 163, 187,
    188, 189, 210, 211, 212, 246, see also
    barley; maize; potato; rice; rye; wheat
Akçam, T., 246
Alaska, 186
Albacete, 59, 67
Albania, 256
Albi, 79, 91, 92f. 4.6, 93
Alfani, G., 3, 11, 12, 14, 17, 18, 19, 21, 26,
    27t. 2.1, 28, 29, 30t. 2.2, 31, 32t. 2.3,
    33, 35, 36, 40t. 2.5, 41, 42, 43, 44,
    44f. 2.3, 45, 46, 47, 48n. , 132
Alifano, E., 37
Alkmaar, 128, 130, 130t. 6.2
Allen, R.C., 7, 124t. 6.1, 126
Almagro, 62
Alps, 13
Alsace-Lorraine, 102
Älvsborg, 204t. 9.2
America, 7, 106, 175, 177, 181, 241, 242
Amiens, 88
Amsterdam, 13, 22, 123, 124t. 6.1, 128,
    129, 130, 130t. 6.2, 131, 132, 133
Anatolia, 22
Anbinder, T., 181
Andalusia, 50, 51, 51t. 3.1, 53, 54t. 3.2,
    55, 56, 62, 71
Andreev, E.M., 215
Anes, G., 55, 57, 58, 62, 69

annone.see institutions, for food
    provisioning
Antwerp, 122, 135t. 6.3, 136
Aosta Valley, 32t. 2.3
Appleby, A.B., 165
Araglen, 183n. 12
Aragon, 49, 51, 51t. 3.1, 53, 56
Aragon, Kingdom of, 49, 52
Argentina, 242
Arizcun Cela, A., 60, 61
Arles, 78t. 4.2
Armagh, 177
Arnhem, 124t. 6.1, 127
Asia, 227t. 10.1, 256, 257
Asturias, 55, 62
Athens, 254
Attlee, Clement, British prime minister,
    256, 256n. 13
Auchmann, R., 109
Augsburg, 21, 137
Australia, 241
Austria, 4, 9t. 1.1, 17, 101–17, 245, 247,
    248, 249f. 11.1, 250, 255, 256, 256n.
    11, 258
Austria-Hungary, 173
Ávila, 57, 59

Backe, Herbert, German politician, 253
Bade, K., 110
Baden, 110, 112
Badenes Martín, M.A., 55, 67
Baehrel, R., 81
Bailey, M., 123
Baku, 248
Balkans, 22
Baltic area, region or Sea, 11, 13, 14, 15,
    19, 46, 98, 160, 162, 188, 191, 220
Baltic states, 134, 193, 195, 196, 234
Banning, C., 264
Bannockburn, 151
Barcelona, 53, 55, 58
Bardet, J.-P., 88, 89f. 4.5, 91
Bari, 36, 37, 40t. 2.5, 41

Barker, D., 263
barley, 55, 69, 90, 95, 122, 150, 152, 197
Bart, Jean, French naval commander and
    privateer, 98
Basque Country, 56, 58, 59, 60, 61, 61f.
    3.2, 71
Bass, H.-H., 110, 110n. 17, 111, 112,
    112n. 18
Bassano del Grappa, 40t. 2.5
Baulant, M., 80f. 4.2
Bavaria, 107, 107n. 11, 107n. 8, 108,
    108n. 12, 110, 111, 112, 191
Bavaria, Kingdom of, 109
Beauce, 96
Béaur, G., 74, 85, 91, 98, 100
Beauvais, 74, 83, 83f. 4.3, 86
Beauvaisis, 88, 91
Beckett, F.W., 243
beggars, 69, 121, 153, 181, see also
    institutions, for assisting the poor
Behringer, W., 105
Belarus, 257
Belgium, 4, 12, 119, 135t. 6.3, 139, 241,
    242, 243, 246, 249, 252, 254, 258
Bellettini, A., 29, 31, 33
Bellinger, E.G., 225, 226
Belorussia, 263
Benedictow, O.J., 8, 35
Bengal, 172n. 6
Bengtsson, T., 207, 211
Berger, H., 22, 111
Berkeley, George, philosopher-bishop of
    Cloyne, 173, 173n. 7, 179, 179n. 11
Berkhoff, K., 254
Berlin, 247
Bern, 112
Bern, Canton of, 111
Bernáldez, A., 52
Bernat i Martí, S., 55, 67
Berthe, M., 48, 49, 51t. 3.1
Betrán, J.L., 53, 55
Bevin, Ernest, British statesman, 256
Biraben, J.-N., 79, 93
birth rate, 92, 111, 148t. 7.1, 173, 176,
    215, 223–4, 232n. 10, 260f. 11.5
Biscay, 56, 57, 59, 60, 61f. 3.2
Black Death. see plague, Black Death
black market, 268
Black Sea, 11, 19, 243
Blanco García, F., 63
Blaschke, K., 107, 117t. 5.1
Blekinge, 185
blockades, 102, 115, 198, 219, 242, 243, 245,
    247, 252, 259, see also siege famines
Blockmans, W., 121
Bohemia, 102, 107, 107n. 8, 112
Bohstedt, J., 22, 157, 177

Bohus, 204t. 9.2, 205
Bohus, County of, 204, 205
Bohuslän, 205
Boisen, M., 189
Bologna, 42
Bordelais, 93
Borders, 161
Boserup, E., 47n. 1
Boudia, Y., 136t. 6.4
Boulter, H., 167, 171, 177, 179
Bourin, M., 86
Bourke, A., 174, 184
Bouton, C.A., 62
Boutruche, R., 93
Brabant, duchy of, 137
Bradley, R.S., 17
Bräuer, H., 106, 114
Brázdil, R., 15, 102, 107
Breda, 124t. 6.1, 127
Bremen, 164
Breteuil, 88
Briffa, K.R., 187
Bristol, 143, 151
Britain, 4, 8, 9t. 1.1, 11, 141–65, 181, 244,
    246, 252, 254, 255, 257
British Isles, 143, 158, 159
Brittany, 52, 90, 95
Broadberry, S., 7
Bruce, Edward, Scottish warlord, 167
Bruegel, M., 95
Bruges, 121, 122, 135, 135t. 6.3, 136t. 6.4,
    138f. 6.1
Brumont, F., 72
Bruneel, C., 137
Brusselle, E., 138f. 6.1
Brussels, 135t. 6.3
Buat, N., 97
Buchner, T., 114n. 23
Bulgarelli Lukacs, A., 37
Bulgaria, 247, 255, 258
Bullen, R., 256
Burgos, 57, 59, 62
burials during famine, 6, 26–8, 29–33, 35,
    36, 53, 76–9, 88, 108, 128–9, 138f.
    6.1, 169, 172, 176

Cadiz, 62, 63
calories, 13, 47, 256
Cambridge, 143, 213
Cambridgeshire, 155
Campbell, B.M.S., 17, 18, 33, 34, 44, 45,
    99, 145, 146, 147, 150, 191
Campopiano, R., 123
Camuffo, D., 17, 44
Canada, 246
cannibalism, 13, 87, 166, 168, 183t.
    8.1, 218

Cantabria, 56, 57, 59, 62
Capet, Hugues, King of France, 76
Caracciolo, M., 36
Caravale, M., 36
Carbajo Isla, M.F., 59, 64, 69
Carmichael, D.J.S., 154
Carmona, J.I., 53
Carpentier, E., 121
Carr, E.H., 229
Castellón, 67
Castells, I., 58
Castenbrandt, H., 202, 203, 205, 207
Castile, 49, 50, 51, 51t. 3.1, 52, 53, 62,
    63f. 3.3, 65, 66f. 3.4, 71, see also New
    Castile; Old Castile
Castlebar, 175
Catalonia, 49, 50, 51t. 3.1, 55, 59, 60, 61f.
    3.2, 67, 71
Catania, 37, 40t. 2.5
Cattini, M., 33
cattle plague, 13, 18, 34, 45, 122, 150,
    166, 190
Caucasus, 23, 222, 226, 227t. 10.1, 230,
    232, 234, 236, 242, 252
Cavaciocchi, S., 19
Central America, 107n. 9
Cerisier, P., 97, 98
charity, private, 65, 72, 111, 115, 151, 155,
    163, 179, 217
Charles VIII, King of France, 36
Charles VIII, King of Sweden, 191
Charlieu, 91, 92f. 4.6
Chartier, François, French
    farmer, 97
Chartres, 95
Châteaudun, 83, 83f. 4.3
Chen, S., 12
Chevet, J.-M., 22, 94, 98, 99
China, 7, 256
cholera, 63, 70, 113n. 22, 223, 233n. 11
Christian II, King of Denmark, 191
Christopher of Bavaria, King of Denmark,
    Sweden and Norway, 191
Churchill, Winston, British Prime
    Minister, 243, 254
Ciudad Real, 59, 62, 67
civil war, 224, 239, 245
Clare, 175, 181
Clark, G., 7
Clark, P., 14, 165
Clarkson, L.A., 167
clearances. see evictions
Clemenceau, Georges Benjamin, French
    politician, 247
climate, 15, 17–19, 25, 44–5, 62, 71, 74,
    77, 84, 90, 93, 99, 102n. 2, 103, 105,
    107n. 9, 109, 113, 117, 137, 158,

168–9, 174, 187–8, 191, 192, 197,
    199, 210, 212–13
Little Ice Age, 14, 17–18, 44, 99, 105,
    113, 187
Clogg, R., 252
Clonmel, 177
Cloyne, 173, 179
Coevorden, 124t. 6.1, 127
Cohn, S.K., 18
Collantes de Terán, A., 50, 51t. 3.1,
    52, 53, 71
Collet, D., 104, 107n. 10, 107n. 9, 108,
    109, 114, 114n. 23, 115
Collingham, L., 254, 257n. 14, 258
Collins, L., 170n. 4
Colmenares, D. de, 53
Coniglio, G., 37
Connacht, 168, 172
Connell, K.H., 173, 182
Conquest, R., 23, 214, 215, 225, 230
Constance, lake of, 110
Copenhagen, 198, 200
Cork, 172, 177
Cork, County of, 172
Cornwall, 143
Corradi, A., 33, 34t. 2.4
Corritore, R., 42
corruption, 20, 181
Courtray, 136t. 6.4
Coventry, 151, 153
Cox, M.E., 247
Crawford, E.M., 14, 166n. 1, 167,
    173n. 8, 181
Creighton, C., 170n. 4
crime, 42, 114, 144, see also black
    markets; cannibalism; hoarding
Crimea, 218
Crimean Khanate, 218, 222
Cronin, J., 167
crop diseases, 17, 19
    potato blight, 12, 19, 111, 129, 139,
        174, 175, 182, 184
    wheat rust, 17, 19
Crotty, R., 182
Crowley, J., 174
Crowley, T.J., 18
Cuenca, 62, 63
Cullen, 172
Cullen, K., 11, 15, 106, 162, 163
Cullen, L.M., 170, 173, 174
Curran, D., 16
Curschmann, F., 104, 104n. 6, 121
Curtis, D., 123, 130
Czechoslovakia, 256, 258

D'Haenens, A., 93
Dalla Zuanna, G., 26

Dalle, D., 137
Damascus, 248
Danube area, region or river, 103, 108, 242, 243
Danzig, 164
Darskii, L.E., 215
Datta, R., 172n. 6
Daultrey, S., 170, 171
Davies, R.W., 229, 230, 230n. 9, 232
Dawson, Rev. Massye, 175
De Boer, D., 120
De La Roncière, C.M., 33, 34t. 2.4
De Maddalena, A., 42
de Meere, J.M.M., 129
De Ram, P., 119
De Visscher, M., 137
de Vries, J., 132
deaths. see famine mortality
deaths, causes of, 18, 26, 172, 176, 195, 198, 203, 205, 207, 210
Degn, O., 193, 195
Dehaeck, S., 122
Deir ez-Zor, 246, 248
Del Panta, L., 25, 25n. , 26, 27t. 2.1, 28, 29, 30, 35, 36, 37, 46, 53
Delamayne, T.H., 169, 172
Delaney, E., 174
Delft, 128
Demerson, P. de, 64
Denmark, 4, 112n. 18, 185, 187, 189, 190, 191, 192, 193, 194t. 9.1, 194t. 9.1, 194t. 9.1, 194t. 9.1, 194t. 9.1, 195, 196, 197, 198, 200, 210
Denmark, Kingdom of, 4
Desai, M., 3
Deutscher Bund, 102
Devine, T.M., 11, 168
Devroey, J.-P., 188
Deyon, P., 87, 88, 89f. 4.5
Díaz Marín, P., 70
Dickson, D., 56, 166n. , 168, 170, 171, 172, 173, 180
Diederiks, H., 130t. 6.2
diet, 22, 47, 86, 90, 95, 159, 170, 174, 184, 256
Dijkman, J., 122, 127
disease, spread of, 18, 26, 45, 56, 60, 71, 72, 79, 87, 91, 93, 107, 121, 129, 145, 158, 196, 197, 198, see also epidemics
Dobado-Muñiz, R., 48n.
Dobb, M., 213
Dols, M.J.L., 264
Dombrecht, K., 135
Domínguez Ortiz, A., 55, 56
Don district, 234
Donegal, 176

Donnelly, J.S., 174, 181, 182, 184
Dontenwill, S., 91, 92f. 4.6
Dorset, 156
Douai, 79, 93
Douglas, Sir Sholto, British Air Marshal, 257
Drake, M., 170
Dribe, M., 211
Dronin, N.M., 225, 226
drought, 17, 22, 30, 45, 46, 49, 50, 51, 71, 84, 102n. 2, 145, 154, 160, 164, 187, 190, 212, 213, 224, 225–6, 230, 231, 237, 239, 248, 260
Dry Drayton, 155
Dublin, 171, 171f. 8.2, 172, 177, 178f. 8.4
Dunning, C.S.L., 218
Dupâquier, J., 92
Dutch Republic, 11, 20, 119, 127, 128, 129, 132, 133, see also Northern Low Countries
Dvina river, 218
Dybdahl, A., 190, 191, 195, 198, 209
Dyer, C., 142, 150
Dyrvik, S., 195, 196, 209
dysentery, 18, 62, 64, 87, 113, 120, 140, 172, 173, 195, 196

East Anglia, 143
Edam, 128, 130, 130t. 6.2
Edam-Volendam, 130t. 6.2
Edinburgh, 160, 161, 162
Edvinsson, R., 187, 191, 192f. 9.2
Edward II, King of England, 151, 152
Edward III, King of England, 151
Edwards, R.D., 174
Egido López, T., 55
Egmond, 121
Egypt, 170
Eichsfeld, 102
Eiríksson, A., 22, 177
Elizabeth I, Queen of England, 164
Ellman, M., 237, 257
Emilia-Romagna, 29, 32t. 2.3
Emmison, F.G., 152
Engerman, S.L., 168
England, 1, 7, 11, 13, 14, 15, 19, 21, 34, 64, 103, 115, 116, 123, 126, 131, 141, 142–59, 148t. 7.1, 160, 161, 163, 164, 165, 166, 167, 169, 172, 174, 175, 177, 189, 191, 249, 250f. 11.2
Engler, S., 56, 168, 169, 170, 171f. 8.2, 175n. 9
Enzi, S., 17, 44
epidemics, 8, 11, 15, 21, 26, 29, 45, 46, 49, 50, 52, 53, 55, 56, 58, 62–3, 64, 70, 71–2, 81, 85, 87, 91, 94–5, 103, 104,

105, 106, 107, 112, 113, 117t. 5.1,
129, 172, 183t. 8.1, 195, 196, 197–8,
202, 203, 205, 207, 210, 222, 223,
261, see also plague; typhus; cholera
Epstein, S.R., 46
Espadas Burgos, M., 62, 69
Essex, 145
Estonia, 15, 188, 220
evictions, 168, 175
Exeter, 151
Extremadura, 51, 53, 56, 62

Faber, J.A., 123, 128, 129
Fagan, B., 17
Fagan, P., 172n. 5
Falchi, L., 42
famine foods, 158, 159, 196
famine mortality, measures of, 15, 28–33,
53–4, 61, 63f. 3.3, 67–70, 81–2, 90,
94, 99f. 4.7, 107, 128–30, 136–40,
148t. 7.1, 170–2, 173–4, 183t.
8.1, 195–8, 201–4, 205, 215–16,
223–4, 227–9, 232–3, 238, 247–51,
262f. 11.6
famine relief, 4, 20, 72, 106, 108, 114,
115–16, 133, 146, 147, 151, 156, 158,
161, 163, 165, 177, 178–81, 184, 200,
217, 219, 226, 237, 240, 243, 244,
245, 246, 254, 257
famine, causes of, 2–4, 16–23, 43–6, 70–2,
83–6, 116, 174–7, 210–11, 212–13,
224–6, 229–31
famine, definition, 2, 6, 26
Farr, W., 166
Fazio, I., 37
Fermoy, 183n. 12
Fernández Hidalgo M.C., 65
Fernando IV, King of Castile, 49
Fernihough, A., 182
Fertig, G., 103n. 3, 107n. 8
fertility. see birth rate
Filtser, D., 238
Filtser, W.Z., 236
Finland, 4, 15, 184n. 14, 185, 188, 193,
194t. 9.1, 194t. 9.1, 194t. 9.1, 196,
197, 199, 210, 220
Finzi, R., 30, 46, 47
fish and fishing, 187, 188, 198, 199,
210, 254
Fisher, H.H., 226n. 8, 243n. 3
Flanders, 52, 112n. 18, 131, 135, 137,
138, 138n. 1, 139, 140, 164
Flinn, M., 159, 160, 161, 162, 163, 165
floods, 22, 51, 70, 71, 93, 107, 110, 115,
121, 150, 160, 192
Florence, 33, 34t. 2.4, 35, 40t. 2.5, 42

Floutard, G., 91, 92f. 4.6
foetal origins hypothesis, 263–7
Fogel, R.W., 3
Foix, Odet de, Count of Lautrec, 36
food exports, prohibition of, 86, 98, 104,
110, 127, 128, 156, 180, 183t. 8.1,
195, 243, 254
food imports, 11, 12, 19, 65, 72, 112, 131,
145, 151, 156, 157, 160, 197, 241–2,
255, see also international grain trade
food reserves. see institutions, for food
provisioning
food riots, 22–3, 42–3, 55, 56, 57, 58, 62,
70, 97, 109, 110, 112, 115, 127, 128,
150, 154, 157, 163, 177
Fornasin, A., 25n.
Forsberg, H., 197
Fossier, L., 93
Fossier, R., 93, 123
Fourquin, G., 93
Fox, L., 152
France, 4, 6, 9t. 1.1, 13, 13n. 1, 14, 15,
21, 22, 49, 57, 60, 61, 62, 71, 73–100,
103, 106, 107, 115, 116, 123, 131,
134, 137, 151, 157, 158, 164, 165,
241, 244, 249, 250f. 11.2, 258
Francis I, king of France, 164
Franconia, 108n. 12
Fraser, R., 61, 69
Frêche, G., 80f. 4.2, 95, 99
Frederick I, king of Würtemberg, 110
Frederick II, king of Prussia, 107n. 10
Friis, A., 128
Frisia, 119
Frisland, 164
Friuli Venezia Giulia, 32t. 2.3
Furió Diego, A., 50, 51t. 3.1

Gadd, C.-J., 200
Gailus, M., 109
Galicia, 12, 55, 56, 246, 250
García Ruipérez, M., 65
García-Sanz Marcotegui, A., 60, 62, 64
Garnaut, A., 232
Gascon, R., 91
Gascony, 151
Gatrell, P., 246
Gauvard, C., 85
Gävleborg, 204t. 9.2, 205
Gay, G.I., 243n. 3
Geary, L., 183n. 12
Gehrmann, R., 107n. 10
Gelderland, 122
Genoa, Republic of, 46
Georgelin, J., 84
German Rhineland, 131

Germany, 4, 9t. 1.1, 12, 15, 17, 20, 101–
    17, 103n. 3, 108n. 13, 109n. 14, 129,
    146, 151, 173, 185, 241, 243, 244,
    245, 245t. 11.1, 247, 249, 249f. 11.1,
    250, 252, 253, 253t. 11.2, 254, 255,
    256, 256n. 11, 257, 258, 263
Gerritsma, B., 129
Gershchenkron, A., 213
Gestrich, A., 111
Ghazai, R., 248
Ghent, 135t. 6.3
Gibson, A.J.S., 143, 160
Gillespie, R., 165
Glaser, R., 103, 106, 117t. 5.1
Gloucester, 144
Gloucestershire, 144, 152
Göbler, W., 107n. 11
Godunov, Boris, Tsar of Russia, 219
Goering, Hermann, German Military
    Commander, 253
Goldman, D., 236
Gómez Mampaso, M.V., 50, 52
Goodspeed, T.B., 176
Goody, J., 7
Göteborg, 204, 204t. 9.2, 205
Gotthelf, Jeremias, Swiss novelist,
    112n. 19
Goubert, P., 70, 74, 82, 83, 86, 88, 91, 98,
    99f. 4.7
Gouda, 128
Goudriaan, K., 128
Goy, J., 81
Goya, Francisco, painter, 69
Grabbe, H.-J., 110
granaries. see storage, of food; institutions,
    for food provisioning
Gräslund, B., 188, 189
Gray, P., 23, 174
Great Britain, 182, 187
Great Glen, 160
Greece, 13, 22, 52, 234, 252, 254, 256,
    258, 263
Greenham, Richard, vicar of Dry
    Drayton, 155
Greenland, 186, 187
Gregorio, Leopoldo de, Marquis de
    Esquilache, Spanish diplomat and
    politician, 57
Gregory, P.R., 213, 225
Grenier, J.-Y., 74, 84
Grey, T., 153
Greyfriars kirkyard, 162
Groningen, 119, 123, 124t. 6.1, 127,
    129, 130
Grytten, O., 192f. 9.2
Guadalajara, 57, 59, 62

Guenzi, A., 22, 42, 43
Guesclin, Bertrand du, French military
    commander, 85
Guinnane, T.W., 182
Guipúzcoa, 59, 60, 61f. 3.2, 67
Gullberg, E., 205
Gunnarsson, G., 199
Gupta, B., 7
Gurría García, P.A., 53, 59, 64, 72
Gusev, A.A., 168n. 2
Gustav I, king of Sweden, 189, 191
Gutiérrez Alonso, A., 55
Gutmann, M.P., 134

Habsburg Empire, 102
Hacker, W., 108n. 12
Häger, O., 209
Hague, The 264
Häkkinen, A., 197
Hall, E., 145, 164
Halland, 185, 204t. 9.2
Halperin, C., 217
Hamburg, 164
Hamilton, E.J., 51, 52, 53, 56, 57, 58
Hammond, P.W., 145
Hamrock, I., 175
Hanover, Kingdom of, 111
Härjedalen, 185
Harrison, C.J., 142
Hart, N., 264
't Hart, P.D., 128, 130t. 6.2
Harvard, 213
Havari, E., 267
Healey, J., 157, 158
Hebrides, 161
Hecht, M., 112
Hecker, J.F.C., 113
Heckscher, E.F., 193, 195
Heerma van Voss, L., 133
Heijmans, B.T., 266
Hekla volcano, 190
Helama, S., 193, 197
Henry III, King of England, 151
Henry VIII, King of England, 153
Henry, L., 74
Herlihy, D., 33, 34t. 2.4
Hessia, 108n. 12
Highlands, 159, 160, 163, 168
Hindle, S., 144, 154
Hionidou, V., 252
Hipkin, S., 154
Hippel, W.V., 108n. 12
hoarding, 20, 22, 36, 43, 57, 84, 86, 97,
    109, 114, 116, 152, 157, 178, see also
    speculation
Hochedlinger, M., 107n. 8, 114

Hoffmann-Rehnitz, P., 114n. 23
Holland, 123, 124t. 6.1, 127, 129, 130, 131, 164
Holopainen, J., 193, 197
Holt, J.S., 143
Holy Roman Empire, 101, 115, 116
Hongerwinter, 265, 267
Hoover, H., 240, 243, 243n. 3, 244n. 4, 245, 246, 247
Horrox, R., 145
Hoskins, W.G., 142
Howard, N.P., 247
Howell, D.W., 157
Hoyle, R.W., 143, 145, 151, 158
Hruschka, R., 203
Huaynaputina volcano, 187
Hughes, William, prime minister of Australia, 247
Hugues, P.L., 164
Huhn, M., 114
Hungary, 102, 108, 108n. 12, 247, 248, 249f. 11.1, 258
Hurepoix, 91
Hybel, N., 13, 187, 189, 190, 191, 209

Ibarra Rodríguez, E., 51
Ibelings, B.J., 128
Iberian Peninsula, 13, 49, 52, 115
Iceland, 4, 18, 185, 186, 187, 194t. 9.1, 194t. 9.1, 198, 199, 210
Île-de-France, 96, 97
India, 107n. 9, 166, 223, 255n. 10
Indonesia, 18, 109, 187
institutions, 3–4, 12, 19–21, 41–3, 45–6, 104–5, 110–11, 115, 116–17, 133, 134, 140, 165
    for assisting the poor, 12, 20, 65, 69, 111, 133, 163, 180, 200
    for food provisioning, 19–20, 22, 25, 36, 41–3, 45–6, 72, 97, 104, 127, 154–6
    institutional failures, 21, 22, 46
international grain trade, 11, 19, 82, 131–2, 151, 177
Ipswich, 143
Iran, 243, 248
Iraq, 243
Ireland, 4, 9t. 1.1, 12, 14, 15, 16, 19, 22, 23, 112n. 18, 129, 141, 145, 147, 150, 161, 164, 165, 166–84, 223, 248, 258
Irish Sea, 177
Isthmus of Panama, 163
Italy, 3, 4, 6, 8, 9t. 1.1, 11, 12, 13, 13n. 1, 14, 16, 17, 20, 21, 25–47, 115, 173, 252, 254, 256
Ivan I, Grand Prince of Moscow, 217
Ivan III, Tsar of Russia, 217, 218

Ivan IV, Tsar of Russia, 218

Jabbeke, 138f. 6.1
Jacks, D.S., 135t. 6.3
Jacquart, J., 85, 91
Jäger, G., 103, 114, 117t. 5.1
Jahn, P.M., 108
Jämtland, 185, 204, 204t. 9.2, 205
Janse, A., 119
Jansen, H., 119, 129
Japan, 255, 256, 257
Jaubert, A.N., 188
Jenkins, D., 157
Jerez, 62
Jessop, T.E., 179n. 11
Johansen, H.C., 194t. 9.1, 195, 196, 197, 198, 200
Johanson, V.F., 193
Johnson, S., 168
Jönköping, 204t. 9.2, 205
Jörberg, L., 207
Jordan, W.C., 13, 35, 104, 120, 121, 122, 150, 167
Jörg, C., 103, 104, 115, 127
Juerges, H., 266
Jutikkala, E., 196, 197, 209
Jutland, 195
Jütte, R., 115, 116

Kahan, A., 213
Kaharoa volcano, 187
Kalinin, 234
Kalmar, 204t. 9.2, 205
Kamchatka peninsula, 168
Kamen, H., 56
Kampen, 124t. 6.1, 127
Kaplan, S., 43, 97, 105
Kaukiainen, Y., 197
Kazakhstan, 215n. 3, 222, 227t. 10.1, 231
Kazan, 218
Keene, D., 146, 151, 154
Kelly, J., 166, 166n., 169n. 3, 177, 180
Kelly, M., 6, 18, 176, 177
Kennedy, L., 175n. 9
Kerry, 176
Kershaw, I., 104, 150
Kesternich, I, 267
Kharkova, T.L., 215
Kiev, 216, 219, 227t. 10.2, 228, 229, 230, 232, 234
Kinealy, C., 181
Kishinev, 234
Kluge, U., 107
Knox, John, Scottish minister and theologian, 160
Kolomna, 218

318   Index

Kopparberg, 204t. 9.2, 205
Kopparberg, County of, 204, 205
Kozlov, I., 266
Krakow, 250
Krämer, D., 109, 110, 111
Kristianstad, 204t. 9.2
Kronoberg, 204t. 9.2
Krüdener, Juliane von, religious
    mystic, 111
Kuibyshev, 234
Kung, J.K.-S., 12
Kurmainz, 108n. 12
Kurmann, F., 117t. 5.1
Kursk, 222
Kuttner, E., 128
Kuwae, volcano, 187
Kuys, J., 119

La Mancha, 62
La Rioja, 59, 62
Labrousse, E., 6, 22, 70, 74, 84, 102n. 1
Lachiver, M., 14, 33, 81, 82, 87, 88, 90,
    91, 94, 106
Ladan, R., 121
Ladero Quesada, M.A., 50
Laki, volcano, 18, 187, 190, 198
Laliena Corbera, C., 49, 51t. 3.1, 71
Lamb, H.H., 15, 33
Lambrecht, T., 138
Lancashire, 143, 145, 157, 158, 159
Lancaster, 145, 157
Landsteiner, E., 113n. 21, 114
Languedoc, 13n. 1
Lappalainen, M., 15, 196
Larkin, J.F., 164
Larsson, D., 195, 196, 200, 202, 207, 209
Larsson, H.A., 209
Laslett, P., 141
Latium, 35, 36, 37
Latta, C., 91
Latvia, 188
Laurénaudie, M.-J., 13n. 1
Lázaro Ruiz, M., 53, 59, 64, 72
Le Mée, R., 74
Le Pesant, Pierre, sieur de Boisguilbert,
    law-maker and proto-economist, 88
Le Roy Ladurie, E., 15, 33, 74, 75t. 4.1,
    87, 92, 93, 94, 108n. 13
Lebanon, 248
Lee, J.S., 151, 152, 154
Lehmann, H., 105
Leiden, 21, 121, 124t. 6.1
Leijonhufvud, L., 187
Leiken, I., 232
Leinster, 172, 173
Lenihan, P., 166n. , 167

Leningrad, 13, 21, 224, 227t. 10.1, 228,
    234, 236n. 12, 239, 259, 260f. 11.5,
    263, 266
León, 56, 62, 64
Levasseur, E., 74, 75t. 4.1, 76, 93
Lewes, 156
Lewin, M., 229
Li, L., 225
Liege, 122
Liguria, 32t. 2.3, 33, 44
Lille, 97
Limerick, 172, 177
Lindkvist, T., 200
Lingren, S., 220
Lithuania, 219, 220
Little Ice Age. see climate, Little Ice Age
Livi Bacci, M., 25, 25n. , 26, 27t. 2.1,
    28, 29, 30, 36, 37, 46, 53, 58, 174,
    195, 202
living standards, 7, 100, 126, 128, 173,
    176, 184
Livonia, 15, 220
Llopis Agelán, E., 57, 58, 59n. 2, 66
Lloyd George, David, British
    politician, 247
Lo Cascio, E., 43
locusts, 52, 56, 63, 64, 71
Lombardy, 29, 31, 32, 32t. 2.3, 33, 34t.
    2.4
London, 23, 106, 143, 145, 146, 147, 151,
    154, 164, 167, 175, 255
Los Palacios, 52
Loughrea, 183n. 12
Louis XIV, king of France, 89, 90, 94,
    96, 97, 98
Louvain, 122
Løvlien, A., 198
Low Countries, 4, 9t. 1.1, 11, 12, 13,
    14, 19, 20, 21, 119–40, 147, 151,
    154, 157, 164, 165, 250f. 11.2, see
    also Netherlands; Northern Low
    Countries; Southern Low Countries
Löwe, H.-D., 115
Lower Saxony, 112n. 18
Lowery, T.S., 18
Lucas, H., 122
Luce, A.A., 179n. 11
Lumey, L.H., 265, 266, 267
Luterbacher, J., 15, 17
Luxembourg, 119, 122
Lvov, 250
Lyashchenko, P.I., 213
Lyon, 93, 97
Lyons, E., 243n. 3, 247
Lyons, M.C., 167
Lythe, S.G.E., 160

Maastricht, 124t. 6.1, 127
McCabe, D., 181
McCaffrey, H., 181
McGregor, P.P.L., 176, 180
Macroom, 172
Mac Suibhne, B., 23, 174
Madrid, 55, 57, 58, 59, 62, 63, 64, 65, 67, 69, 70f. 3.8
Mahlerwein, G., 112
Maintenon, 91
maize, 12, 47, 69, 95, 99, 180, 184
Majd, M.G., 248
Malanima, P., 25n., 37, 43, 44f. 2.3
Malawi, 184
Maldon, 154
Malmöhus, 204t. 9.2
Malthus, T.R., 1, 2, 21, 176
Malthusian theory, 1, 2, 21, 91–2, 176
Marin, B., 19, 41
market integration, 19, 20, 65, 103, 110, 111, 112, 207
marriages, reduction in, 23, 69, 70, 87, 92, 107, 140, 144, 176, 182
Massif Central, 95
Mattmüller, M., 106, 107n. 8, 108, 117t. 5.1
Mauelshagen, F., 102n. 1
Mayo, 181
Mayo, County of, 175
Mazower, M., 253
Mears, N., 154
medicine, medical practitioners, 108, 171, 267
Medick, H., 110, 115
Medina del Campo, 55
Mediterranean area, region or sea, 11, 19, 41, 49, 55, 62, 67, 98, 122, 132, 157
Meister, A., 122
Melegaro, A., 35
Menken, J., 23, 182
Menko, abbot of Wittewierum, 119
Mentink, G.J., 128, 130t. 6.2
merchants, 11, 22, 84, 87, 90, 96, 97, 127, 128, 145, 156, 157, 158, 164, 178
Métayer, M., 79, 93
Meulan, 88
Meuvret, J., 6, 70, 74, 82, 87
Midland, 144
migrations, 12, 17, 23, 66, 87, 90, 104, 106, 107–8, 110, 112, 113, 114, 117t. 5.1, 136, 137, 161, 162, 166, 175, 181, 182, 184, 216, 218
Milan, 29, 42, 45
Milan, State of, 47
Miller, J.A., 97
Minsk, 217

Mironov, B.N., 214, 225
Mitchell, B.R., 244n. 5, 249n. 8, 253t. 11.2
Mocarelli, L., 45, 47
Modena, 40t. 2.5, 41
Mokyr, J., 174, 176, 180
Moldavian Soviet Socialist Republic, 260
Moldova, 13, 22, 23, 234, 237, 238, 257, 258, 260, 261, 261t. 11.3, 262f. 11.6, 263
Molinier, A., 95
Moltmann, G., 110
Moravia, 102
Moray Forth, 161
Moreno Lázaro, J., 70
Morens, D.M., 248
Morgenthau, Henry, US Secretary of the Thresaury, 255
Moriceau, J.-M., 97
Morineau, M., 81, 83, 95, 99
mortality. see famine mortality
Moscow, 216, 218, 219, 220, 224, 224n. 6, 227t. 10.1, 227t. 10.2, 228, 234, 250
Moscow river, 218
Moscow, Grand Duchy of, 214, 216, 217, 218
Moskoff, W., 237
Mountjoy, Lord, Charles Gardiner, Irish landowner and politician, 179
Moveen, 175, 175n. 9
Moycullen, 183n. 12
Müller, G., 110
Munster, 170, 174, 177
Murcia, 51, 55
Murray, K.A.H., 244, 253t. 11.2
Mus, F., 138f. 6.1
Mussolini, Benito, Italian dictator, 234
Muster, 171
Mykland, K., 195, 196
Myrdal, J., 190, 191, 195, 196

Nadal i Oller, J., 59, 60, 61
Nairn, I.A., 187
Nally, D.P., 174
Naples, 36, 40t. 2.5, 41
Naples, Kingdom of, 35–41
Napoleon I, emperor of France, 61
Nassiet, M., 95, 99
Navarre, 49, 50, 51t. 3.1, 58, 59, 60, 61, 61f. 3.2, 67, 71
Navarre, Kingdom of, 48
Neal, F., 182
Neelsen, S., 267
Nefedov, S.A., 214, 217, 218

Netherlands, 4, 7, 12, 13, 115, 119, 120,
    121, 129, 134, 136, 139, 241, 249,
    252, 254, 258, 262, 264, 265, 266, see
    also Low Countries
Netting, R., 110n. 16
Neveux, H., 79, 81, 99
Nevskii, Alexander, Prince of
    Novgorod, 217
New Castile, 51, 52, 56, 58, 59, 62, 65, 67,
    68f. 3.7
New Zealand, 187
Newenham, T., 176
Ní Chinnéide, S., 170
Ní Úrdail, M., 169, 170
Nicholas, D., 122
Nicolai, N.M., 38f. 2.1
Niger, 184
Nijmegen, 124t. 6.1, 127, 128
Noordam, D.J., 128
Noordegraaf, L., 120, 123, 127, 128, 132
Nordic Europe, 5, 8, 9t. 1.1, 15, 185–211
Norfolk, 143, 145, 159
Normandy, 93, 164
North Sea, 120, 160
Northern Low Countries, 120,
    121, 123–33
Norway, 4, 161, 179, 185, 186, 188,
    190, 191, 192, 193, 194t. 9.1, 194t.
    9.1, 194t. 9.1, 194t. 9.1, 195, 196,
    198, 210
Notre-Dame-des-Prés, 93
Novgorod, 217, 218

Ó Gráda, C., 2, 3, 6, 12, 13, 14, 16, 17, 18,
    20, 21, 22, 23, 25n. , 26, 48n. , 56, 87,
    90, 98, 99, 145, 146, 147, 166, 167,
    168, 169, 170, 170n. 4, 171, 172, 174,
    176, 177, 178, 179, 181, 182, 197,
    241n. 1
Ó Muirithe, D., 170, 170n. 4, 179
Ó Murchadha, C., 174, 175, 181
O'Brien, H., 175
O'Connell, M., 172
O'Neill, T.P., 166, 174, 175, 180, 182, 184
O'Rourke, K.H., 181, 182
Ocaña, 65
Odenwälder, N., 101, 115
Offer, A., 244, 247
Offermans, P.H.M.G., 128
Ohlsson, R., 211
Oka, river, 218
Olaf I, king of Denmark, 189
Old Castile, 56, 58, 62, 65, 70
Olsson, M., 211
Oman, L., 18
Ore Mountains, 102
Örebro, 204t. 9.2, 205

Orkney, 161
Orlov, 222
Oslo, 200
Osnabrück, 112n. 18
Östergötland, 204t. 9.2, 205
Östergötland, County of, 204
Ostrom, E., 110n. 16
Otterness, P., 106
Ottoman Empire, 11, 19, 22, 243, 247,
    248, 250
Oudburg, 136t. 6.4
Outhwaite, R.B., 142, 153
Overijssel, 121
Overton, M., 159
Oxford, 143

Paish, George, British economist, 246, 246n. 6
Palencia, 57, 59, 62
Palermo, 36, 37
Palermo, L., 36, 42, 46
Pallach, U.-C., 103n. 5
Pamele, 136
Pamplona, 49
panzootic. see cattle plague
Papal States, 35–41
Paping, R., 12, 16, 130, 131, 174
Paris, 78t. 4.2, 79, 80, 80f. 4.2, 82, 90, 93,
    94, 95, 96, 99, 247
Parker, G., 17, 106
Parsonstown, 183n. 12
Parziale, L., 42
Pavia, 40t. 2.5
Pedersen, E.A., 188
Pelly, M.E., 256
Peña Sánchez, D., 70
Penza, 222
Peracchi, F., 267
Pérez Moreda, V., 18, 53, 54t. 3.2, 55, 56,
    57, 58, 59n. 2, 61, 62, 63, 64, 72
Pérez Serrano, J., 63
Perren, R., 247
Perrie, M., 218, 219
Perrot, J.-C., 89
Pershing, John, US military
    Commander, 246
Persson, K.G., 20, 209
Peru, 187
Pesaro, 40t. 2.5
Pestalozzi, Johann Heinrich, Swiss
    pedagogue, 108
Peter I, Tsar of Russia, 220
Petrograd, 22, 226, 227t. 10.2, 228,
    245, 250
Petty, Sir W., 167, 168
Pfister, C., 15, 102, 102n. 1, 102n. 2, 103,
    105, 105n. 7, 107, 112, 112n. 20, 113,
    117t. 5.1

Pfister, U., 103n. 3, 107n. 8
Pfrenzinger, A., 108n. 12
philanthropy. see charity, private;
    institutions, for assisting the poor
Piedmont, 31, 32, 32t. 2.3, 33
Pinto, G., 25n. , 33, 34, 34t. 2.4, 35
Piquero, S., 61
Piraeus, 254
Pistoia, 33, 34t. 2.4
Pitkänen, K.J., 197
Piuz, A.M., 103
plague, 18–19, 26, 27t. 2.1, 28, 29, 32, 33,
    44, 44f. 2.3, 45, 49, 51, 52, 53, 54–5,
    62, 72, 81, 92–3, 117t. 5.1, 117t.
    5.1, 120, 142, 150, 167–8, 170, 196,
    200, 218
    Black Death, 8, 14, 16, 18, 29, 34, 35,
    45, 49, 50, 92–4, 150
plant diseases. see crop diseases
Po Valley, 33
Póirtéir, C., 180
Poland, 13, 98, 107, 109, 219, 220,
    242, 243, 244, 247, 249, 250, 256,
    258, 263
Pollard, A.J., 150
Poltava, 220
Pomeranz, K., 7
Pontoise, 89f. 4.5
popular revolts. see food riots
Portugal, 11, 21
Pöschl, Thomas, priest, 111
Post, J.D., 15, 56, 106, 107n. 10, 108n. 13,
    109, 110, 113, 168, 179
Postel-Vinay, G., 97
Posthumus, N.W., 124t. 6.1
potato, 1, 12, 15, 19, 22, 64, 69, 87, 95,
    99, 111, 116, 117t. 5.1, 129–31, 139,
    141, 159, 163–4, 167, 168, 169–70,
    172, 173, 174–5, 177–9, 180, 181,
    182, 183t. 8.1, 184, 236, see also crop
    diseases, potato blight
potato blight. see crop diseases,
    potato blight
Poulsen, B., 13, 187, 189, 190, 191, 209
Poynder, N., 175n. 9
Poznan, 250
prayer to fight famine, 83, 95, 106, 111,
    114, 154
price controls, 37, 51, 52, 57, 65, 97
Price, N., 188, 189
Priewer, H., 107n. 11
Prims, F., 122
profiteering. see hoarding; speculation
protest. see food riots
Prussia, 107, 107n. 10, 109, 110, 110n. 17,
    111, 112, 151, 250
Pult Quaglia, A.M., 42

Queipo de Llano, José Maria, Count of
    Toreno, Spanish politician, 69

Randall, A., 157
Rankl, H., 107, 107n. 11, 107n. 8, 108,
    108n. 12
Ravn, M.O., 202
Razuvaev, V. N., 213
Reglero, C., 51t. 3.1
Reher, D., 59, 64
Reinhardt, V., 19, 37, 46
Reith, R., 102, 117t. 5.1
Revel, J., 37, 38f. 2.1
Rhine, river, 103, 110, 122
Rhineland, 107n. 10
Ribe, 192, 193, 195
rice, 139, 180
Richard of Cornwall, king of Germany,
    146, 151
Riera Melis, A., 49, 50, 51t. 3.1
Rijnsburg, 121
Rijpma, A., 20, 133
Rioja, 64
Ritzmann-Blickenstorfer, H., 110n. 15,
    112n. 20
Rizzo, M., 36
Robbins, R.G., 223
Robinson, J.A., 168
Rodrigues, T., 11
Rodríguez, L., 57
Roeck, B., 105, 115
Roermond, 124t. 6.1, 126, 127
Roessingh, H., 130
Roessner, P.R., 163
Roman Empire, 41
Romania, 247, 249, 257, 258, 260, 263
Romanov, Russian imperial house, 214
Rome, 36, 40t. 2.5, 41, 42
Rommes, R., 120, 130t. 6.2
Roosevelt, Franklin Delano, president of
    the United States, 254
Rosen, S., 174
Rosina, A., 26
Rostov, 217
Rotterdam, 128, 129, 130t. 6.2, 132
Rouen, 88
Rubio Vela, A., 49, 50
Rus, 216, 217
Russia, 4, 9t. 1.1, 14, 98, 168, 185, 197,
    203, 212–39, 241, 242, 242n. 2,
    244, 246, 247, 248, 249, 250, 252,
    263, 268
Russian Empire, 22
Russian Far East, 227t. 10.1, 231
Rutty, J., 171, 172, 172n. 5
Ruwet, J., 137
Ryazan, 222

rye, 19, 87, 95, 122, 123–6, 135t. 6.3, 139, 156, 160, 193, 195, 197, 202–4, 205, 220–1

Sackville, Thomas, Lord Buckhurst and earl of Dorset, 156
Saint-Cyr, 95
Saint-Lambert-des-Levées, 98
Salmelli, D., 31
Salzmann, M., 111, 112
Samsonova, A., 266
Sánchez Salazar, F., 66
Sánchez-Albornoz, N., 70
Sangüesa, 49
Sansepolcro, 40t. 2.5
Santa Cruz, A. de, 52
Santiago de Compostela, 56
Sarato, 227t. 10.2
Saratov, 227, 227t. 10.2, 228, 229, 250
Savy, P., 33, 34t. 2.4
Sax, P., 119
Saxony, 106, 107, 107n. 8, 108, 112
Scandinavia, 107, 115, 185, 186, 187, 191
Scania, 185, 196, 200
Schanbacher, A., 111, 112, 112n. 18
Schleswig-Holstein, 185
Schlöder, C., 107n. 10
Schmahl, H., 108n. 12
Schmidt, G., 115
Schofield, P.R., 123, 144, 145, 155
Schofield, R.S., 142, 144, 145, 147, 150
Scholliers, E., 134, 136
Schrier, A., 184n. 13
Schulte Beerbühl, M., 106
Schuppli, P., 103, 117t. 5.1
Scotland, 11, 15, 141, 143, 145, 147, 150, 154, 156, 157, 158, 159–63, 164, 165, 166, 168
Sebastián Amarilla, J.A., 57, 59n. 2
Segovia, 52, 57, 59, 62, 63, 67f. 3.5
Seine region, 131
Sellin, T., 264
Sen, A., 3, 86
Sentrie, P., 138n. 1
Serbia, 244, 250
Severn, river, 144, 154
Seville, 50, 51t. 3.1, 52, 56, 62, 71
Sharp, B., 144, 150, 151, 152, 154
Shetland, 161
Shrewsbury, 143, 151
Siberia, 223, 227t. 10.1, 231
Sicily, 37, 52
Sicily, Kingdom of, 36
siege famines, 21, 36, 45, 105, 128, 216, 239, 263, 266, see also blockades

during the Italian Wars (1494-1559), 21, 36
Leningrad (1941-44), 21, 239, 260f. 11.5, 266
Sieglerschmidt, J., 110
Siena, 21, 40t. 2.5
Simms, J.Y., 213
Skaraborg, 204, 204t. 9.2
Sköld, P., 200
Slack, P., 153
Slaveski, F., 257
Slavin, P., 150, 155, 158
Slicher van Bath, B.H., 1, 121
Smith, A., 2, 3, 20
Smith, C.A., 264
Smith, R.M., 155
Smith, Sir Ben, British Minister for Food, 256
Smout, T.C., 143, 160
Smyth, W.J., 167
Soden, J. von, 107
Söderberg, J., 187, 191, 192f. 9.2
Södermanland, 204t. 9.2, 205
Soens, T., 121, 122
Sogner, S., 198, 209
Sokoloff, K., 168
Solantie, R., 188
Solar, P.M., 6, 166n. , 175n. 9, 178
Sommarin, E., 196
Sommer, D., 111
Soria, 59
soup kitchens, 111, 112, 181, see also institutions, for assisting the poor
South Africa, 264
Southern Low Countries, 121, 122, 126, 128, 133–40, 164
Spain, 4, 8, 9t. 1.1, 11, 13, 13n. 1, 14, 15, 17, 21, 48–72, 151, 243
speculation, 20, 22, 84–5, 86, 96–7, 108, 152, 153, see also hoarding
Spenser, Edmund, English poet, 167, 168
Spoerer, M., 22, 111
Spufford, M., 155, 156
St Lambert des Levees, 99f. 4.7
St. Petersburg, 22, 220, 222, 222f. 10.2, 224, 227t. 10.1, 239
Stalhille, 138f. 6.1
Stalin, Joseph, leader of the Soviet Union, 230, 236, 237, 255
Stanner, S.A., 266
starvation, 2, 6, 13, 26, 48, 49, 52, 55, 56, 69, 76, 81–2, 87, 94, 111, 112, 120, 127, 128, 142, 150, 176, 179, 183, 198, 203, 210, 219, 236, 246, 247, 248, 252, 253, 254, 256, 257, 259, 263

Stauter-Halsted, K., 12
Steelyard, 164
Stein, A.D., 266
Stein, Z.A., 264, 265, 266
Stewart, L.A.M., 160
Stockholm, 191, 195, 200, 204t. 9.2
Stöger, G., 114n. 23
Stone, N., 246
storage, of food, 17, 19, 58, 65n. 3, 72, 97, 99, 102, 104, 107, 113, 128, 154–6
Stout, Leonard, merchant from Lancaster, 145, 157, 158
Stout, W., 145, 157, 158, 159
Strangio, D., 37, 40t. 2.5, 42, 46
Stratford, 152
Stratmann, T., 267
Strömmer, E., 103, 117t. 5.1
Struick, E., 121
Studer, R., 11, 103, 117t. 5.1
substitue foods. see famine foods
Suffolk, 145
Susser, E.S., 264
Susser, M., 265, 266
Svensson, P., 211
Swarthmore, 143
Sweden, 4, 15, 66, 112n. 18, 185, 186, 187, 188, 189, 190, 191, 192, 193, 194t. 9.1, 194t. 9.1, 194t. 9.1, 194t. 9.1, 195, 196, 197, 199, 200–9, 210, 220, 243
Swedish Empire, 219
Swift, J., 169
Swiss Plateau, 103, 106, 110n. 16
Swiss Prealps, 110n. 16
Switzerland, 4, 9t. 1.1, 17, 101–17, 173
Symeon of Durham, English chronicler, 146
Syria, 243
Syrian desert, 246
Szölloszi-Janze, M., 101

Talavera, 65
Tambora volcano, 15, 18, 109, 117t. 5.1, 187
Tambov, 222
Tanter, A., 107n. 8, 114
Tassenaar, V., 130
Taubenberger, J.K., 248
taxation, 65n. 3, 66, 83, 85, 87, 115, 120, 134, 135, 180, 192, 217
Tetivskii, 232n. 10
Teuteberg, H.J., 109n. 14
Thoen, E., 120, 122, 136
Thompson, Benjamin, Count Rumford, physicist, 64
Thompson, E.P., 22, 43, 157

Thorarinsson, S., 190
Tierra de Campos, 51
Tijms, W., 124t. 6.1, 124t. 6.1
Tilly, L.A., 3, 62, 86
Tipperary, County of, 172, 175
Tits-Dieuaide, M.-J., 99, 135t. 6.3
Tobi, E.W., 266
Tolbachik volcano, 168n. 2
Toledo, 62, 65
Tomasson, R., 190
Toomevara, 175
Toronto, 215
Toulouse, 78t. 4.2, 79, 80, 80f. 4.2
trade. see international grain trade
Transcaucasus, 227t. 10.1
transport, 98, 102, 107, 112, 114, 127, 143, 145, 158, 230, 236, 239
  of food, 65, 98, 99, 102, 107, 110, 156, 235, 237, 246, 261
Trent, 33
Trentino Alto Adige, 32t. 2.3
Trienekens, G., 264
Truman, Harry, President of the United States of America, 256, 256n. 13, 257
Tudor, English royal house, 153
Tula, 222, 234
Turchin, P., 214, 217, 218
Turgot, Anne Robet Jaquest, economist, 57
Turkey, 246
Tuscany, 29, 30, 30t. 2.2, 32t. 2.3, 33
Tvauri, A., 188
Twente, 121
typhoid, 62, 87, 139, 196, 207
typhus, 11, 13, 14, 15, 18, 26, 27t. 2.1, 46, 52, 53, 54t. 3.2, 55, 56, 60, 64, 71, 87, 94, 113, 139, 140, 195, 196, 198, 200, 203, 210, 233n. 11, 238

Udine, 25n., 40t. 2.5
Uebele, M., 107n. 8
Ugra, river, 217
Uhlig, H., 202
Ukraine, 4, 9t. 1.1, 14, 23, 98, 216, 222, 226, 227t. 10.1, 227t. 10.2, 228, 229–33, 236, 242, 252, 257, 260, 263
Ulbrich, C., 114
Ulster, 161, 162, 168, 172, 177
Umbria, 29, 30t. 2.2, 32t. 2.3
Umeå, 201, 201f. 9.3, 206, 208t. 9.4
Unger, W.S., 127, 128
United Kingdom, 19, 120, 241, 242n. 2, 245t. 11.1, 246n. 6, 248, 250, 252, 253, 253t. 11.2, 255, 256n. 11, 258, 262, 263
United States of America, 20, 110, 112n. 20, 180, 181, 236, 243, 244, 246, 255

Uppland, 193
Uppsala, 204t. 9.2
Urals Mountains, 222, 226, 227t. 10.1,
    230, 254
USSR, 4, 12, 13, 212, 214, 215, 224–39,
    241, 242, 249, 252, 253, 255, 257,
    258–63, 268
Utrecht, 121, 124t. 6.1, 128, 129, 130,
    130t. 6.2, 132
Utterström, G., 187, 190, 191, 192, 193,
    202, 205

Vågerö, D., 266
vagrancy. see beggars
Val-de-Loire, 98
Valdeón, J., 49, 50, 51t. 3.1, 71
Valencia, 49, 50, 51t. 3.1, 55, 59, 67,
    68f. 3.6, 71
Valencia, Kingdom of, 50
Valk, G., 120
Valladolid, 55, 56
Van Arcken, J.A.M., 264
Van Bavel, B., 20, 123, 131, 133
Van der Wee, H., 134
Van der Woude, A.M., 128, 130t. 6.2, 132
Van der Zee, H.A., 254
Van Leeuwen, M.H.D., 133
Van Osta, M.H., 137
Van Poppel, F.W.A., 265, 266, 267
Van Schaïk, R., 120, 127
Van Tielhof, M., 132
Van Werveke, H., 122
Van Zanden, J.L., 123, 124t. 6.1, 126,
    131
Vandenbroeke, C., 134, 138
Vanhaute, E., 12, 16, 138, 139, 174
Vanuatu, 187
Värmland, 204t. 9.2, 205
Varsenare, 138f. 6.1
Vasey, D.E., 18, 199
Vasold, M., 108n. 13
Västerbotten, 204, 204t. 9.2, 205
Västernorrland, 204t. 9.2
Västmanland, 204t. 9.2
Veneto, 31, 32, 32t. 2.3, 47
Verhaege, F., 121
Verhulst, A., 136t. 6.4, 138f. 6.1
Vienna, 109, 112, 114n. 23
Vilar, P., 52, 57
Vilius, H., 209
Villalba, J. de, 49, 50, 51, 51t. 3.1, 52, 53,
    54t. 3.2, 56, 71
Villers-Cotterêts, 77
Virlouvet, C., 19, 41
Vivier, N., 22
Voglis, P., 252, 254

Volga region, 23, 223, 226, 227t. 10.1,
    227t. 10.2, 228, 230, 232, 234, 242
Volga, river, 218, 225
Volodarskii, 232n. 10
Voronezh, 222
Voutilainen, M., 197
Voznesenskii, N., 214

wages, 86, 90, 110, 123–6, 127, 131, 133,
    147, 150
Waldorf, C., 191
Wales, 142, 143, 144, 157, 169n. 3, 249,
    250f. 11.2
Walford, C., 166
Walter, J., 19, 145, 151, 152, 154, 156
war, 5, 12–13, 15, 19, 20, 21–2, 25, 36,
    45, 55, 56, 58–61, 64, 67–70, 71–2,
    73, 74, 81, 85, 88, 90, 94, 102, 105,
    106, 109, 117t. 5.1, 133, 134, 136,
    137, 139, 141, 159, 166, 167, 180,
    183, 183t. 8.1, 196, 197, 198, 203,
    207, 211, 220, 225, 228, 233–6,
    238, 240–68
    civil war, 49, 100, 135, 153, 156, 219
Warsaw, 13, 250, 259
Washington, 256
Waterford, 177
Watkins, S.C., 23, 182
weather, role of during famine, 17, 23, 34,
    44, 45, 49, 55, 56, 64, 71, 74, 83–4,
    102, 104–5, 106, 107n. 9, 169, 180,
    183t. 8.1, 186–7, 189, 193, 210, 213,
    218, 220, 225–6, 229, 233, 234
Weber, E., 110
Weiler, P., 122
Weir, D.R., 6, 98
Wells, R., 166
West Indies, 180
wheat, 6, 14, 16, 19, 33, 35, 37–41, 42, 44,
    45, 47, 50, 51, 52, 56, 57, 58, 62, 63,
    65, 6667f. 3.4, 69, 75t. 4.1, 79–80,
    83, 84, 86, 89f. 4.5, 90, 95, 96–97,
    122, 123, 135t. 6.3, 136138t. 6.4,
    139, 155, 158, 159, 164, 167, 169,
    170, 171f. 8.2, 177, 178f. 8.4, 183t.
    8.1, 255, 256, see also crop disease,
    wheat rust
Wheatcroft, S.G., 23, 213, 213n. 1, 215,
    215n. 2, 216n. 4, 220, 221, 223, 224,
    224n. 6, 225, 226, 226n. 7, 227t. 10.2,
    229, 230, 230n. 9, 232, 233, 234, 235t.
    10.4b, 237, 238, 241n. 1, 257, 260
Widgren, M., 188
Wiegelmann, G., 109n. 14
Wilde, W., 166, 166n. 1, 167, 176
Williams, T.D., 174

Wilson, Woodrow, President of the United States of America, 243, 244n. 4, 246, 247
Wiltshire, 152
Winchester, 178f. 8.4
Winter, J., 247
Wittewierum, monastery of, 119
Wolsey, Thomas, Cardinal, 164
women, 52, 62, 91, 114, 142, 162, 172, 183t. 8.1, 245, 258, 266
Wood, G., 15
Woodham-Smith, C., 174
Woodward, D.R., 244
Worcester, 151
Worcestershire, 152
workhouses, 181, 184
Wrightson, K., 152
Wrigley, E.A., 142, 144, 145, 147, 150
Württemberg, 107n. 10, 108n. 12, 110, 111, 112

Württemberg, Kingdom of, 109
Wyffels, A., 134
Wynn, Sir John, 156

Xanten, 122

Yaroslavl, 217
York, 152
Ypres, 121
Yudkin, J.S., 266
Yugoslavia, 247, 256

Zabalza Guruchaga, M.A., 60
Zamora, 57, 59
Zealand, 195
Zima, V.F., 237
Zimmermann, C., 107n. 10, 108
Zubkova, E., 237
Zumkeller, D., 103
Zürcher, E.J., 22